6.50

D1627090

726-15-7)

# BRITAIN
# AND THE STUARTS

# BRITAIN
# AND THE STUARTS

By

D. L. FARMER

LONDON
G. BELL AND SONS LTD
1967

*First published 1965*
*Reprinted 1967*

*Printed in Great Britain by*
*The Camelot Press Ltd., London and Southampton*

# TO THE READER

ALTHOUGH planned originally to assist the young student, this book tries also to meet the needs of other readers who prefer following historical themes for a generation or so to studying in intricate detail a comprehensive narrative describing the events of a few years at a time. My arrangement of the material makes some repetition unavoidable; I hope that what was planned in the interests of clarity and completeness has not become merely tedious.

Like every author of a book of this nature, I have drawn substantially upon the researches and publications of the major modern historians who have studied the period. My debt to Miss C. V. Wedgwood, Sir George Clark, Dr. G. M. Trevelyan, Mr. D. Ogg and Mr. C. Hill is especially great, and that to many others scarcely less so.

*Sedbergh*, 1965                                                    D. L. FARMER

## NOTE TO THE SECOND IMPRESSION

The need for this book to be reprinted has given me the opportunity to extend the Bibliography with a short list of recent publications, and to make a few minor alterations in the text.

D. L. F.

# ACKNOWLEDGEMENTS

I AM grateful to the following publishers for permission to include in this volume extracts from the undermentioned works:

A. & C. Black: *The Law and Working of the Constitution*, ed. W. C. Costin and J. Steven Watson.

The Cambridge University Press: *Constitutional Documents of the Reign of James I, 1603–1625*, ed. J. R. Tanner ; *Select Documents for Queen Anne's Reign*, ed. G. M. Trevelyan.

The Clarendon Press: Clarendon's *History of the Great Rebellion*, ed. W. D. Macray: *The Early Stuarts*, by G. Davies; *Constitutional Documents of the Puritan Revolution*, ed. S. R. Gardiner; *Poems of John Dryden*, ed. J. Kinsley; *England in the Reign of Charles II*, by D. Ogg; Swift's *Conduct of the Allies*, ed. C. B. Wheeler.

J. M. Dent & Sons and E. P. Dutton & Co. (the Everyman Library): *Diary of John Evelyn*, ed. W. Bray; *Autobiography of Richard Baxter*, ed. J. M. Lloyd Thomas; Burnet's *History of My Own Times*, ed. T. Shackhouse; *Diary of Samuel Pepys*, ed. J. Warrington.

Longmans, Green & Co.: *England under Queen Anne*, by G. M. Trevelyan.

Thomas Nelson & Sons: *A Source Book of Scottish History*, ed. W. C. Dickinson and G. Donaldson.

The Oxford University Press: *The Life and Times of Anthony à Wood*, ed. A. Clark: *Milton's Selected Prose*, ed. M. W. Wallace.

Penguin Books: *Elizabethan and Jacobean Prose, 1550–1620*, ed. K. Muir.

☆          ☆          ☆

My sincere thanks are due also to some of my colleagues, for reading the manuscript; to my pupils, for arguing with me; to various librarians, for their invaluable help; and above all to my tolerant family, for their patience and encouragement.

D. L. F.

# CONTENTS

# MAPS

# GENEALOGICAL TABLES

# 1

## ELIZABETH'S LEGACY

☆

### i. *The Queen and her Councillors*

LONDON: March 1603.  The old Queen lay dying, surrounded by the few survivors of the statesmen who had made her reign so great.  For forty-five years she had fought a brilliant rear-guard action to defend the authority of the English Crown, and to protect her small Protestant country from the powerful and aggressive Counter-Reformation states of France and Spain. Her forceful personality and her determination to act in England's interests had quickly won her the loyalty of her ministers.  The qualities of her intellect had won their respect. At times she had appeared vain, and open to the flattery of a courtier like Leicester or Essex; in a crisis, though, her shrewd judgement had always saved her from the consequences of such weaknesses.  The pomp and ceremony of her Court had impressed foreign ambassadors, but she did not lack the 'common touch'; her progresses through the country had helped to make her better known and better loved than any earlier English sovereign.  The fact that she was a woman, and unmarried, made men admire her even more.  In her last years, her critics had often moderated their complaints out of respect for her age and sex.  Elizabeth had had to make some concessions, but had yielded so gracefully that they appeared to result from her goodwill, not from her defeat.  In 1601, when forced to give way in the bitter struggle over monopolies, she had calmed her last Parliament by declaring that she counted it the greatest glory of her reign that she had ruled with her people's love.  Even the victims of her policies admired her. The English Catholic clergy training at Rome had cheered the news of the defeat of the Armada.  John Stubbs, the Puritan[1]

---

[1] In this book the name Puritan is used in a very general sense. It denotes any non-Catholic dissatisfied with the tepid Protestantism of the Church established

writer, who had just had a hand cut off for publishing attacks on the bishops, had cried 'God Save the Queen', before fainting at the executioner's feet.   Now Elizabeth lay dying, and there was no one like her to follow on the throne.

Her great ministers, for the most part, were already dead. Until 1598 Elizabeth had relied on William Cecil, Lord Burghley, as the wisest and ablest of her advisers.   Burghley had controlled almost all patronage in Church and State, had supervised the management of Parliament, had presided over the Treasury, and, under the Queen, had directed foreign policy.   Despite his rivalry with Leicester, he was usually able to bend to his will the members of the Privy Council, the group of fifteen or so statesmen who controlled almost every sphere of Elizabethan government.   Burghley was almost the last of the great Elizabethans; after his death, there remained only Essex, ambitious and dangerous; Raleigh, brilliant but irresponsible; Nottingham,[1] victor over the Armada; Bacon, out of favour since he had criticized a tax the Crown requested in 1591; the two diligently persecuting prelates, Whitgift and Bancroft; and Burghley's younger son, Robert Cecil.   It was on this last, a clever little hunch-back, that Elizabeth came to depend in the years after his father's death, more than on Egerton, the Lord Keeper, or on Buckhurst, the Treasurer.

Under the Tudors, the Privy Council had invaded almost every part of English government.   It supervised all business of state, both great and trivial – from the preparation of legislation for Parliament down to ordering new clothes for a prisoner in the Tower.   It watched over the administration of the Crown's finances.   It investigated many law-suits, sometimes arbitrating between the parties, but more frequently referring the case to the appropriate law court.   It examined men accused of treason or other crimes against the state, before sending the suspect for trial elsewhere. Most Privy Councillors also held individually administrative posts with great powers and responsibilities. The Chancellor, or Lord Keeper, presided over meetings of the House of Lords, over the central secretarial

by Elizabeth, and wishing to remodel it more drastically by, for example, a stricter observance of the Sabbath, by the elimination of governmental interference, or by the abolition of the bishops and various surviving 'Popish' ceremonies.

[1] Formerly Lord Howard of Effingham.

office of the Chancery, and over Star Chamber[1] and the Court
of Chancery – together responsible for enforcing the law and
making it more equitable. The Lord High Treasurer, the
Chancellor of the Exchequer, the Master of the Wards and
Liveries, the Comptroller of the Household and the Treasurer
of the Chamber supervised the collection and expenditure of
various parts of the Crown's revenues. Then there were the
Secretaries, at times under the Tudors closer to the monarch
and more powerful in the government than any other minister.
Some Councillors – the Lord Privy Seal, the Lord High Admiral, the Lord Chamberlain, and the Master of the Horse –
held posts more honourable than onerous, but their membership of the Council gave them immense influence throughout
the country. Many of them acted as the Lord-Lieutenant of
one or more counties, working through their Deputy Lieuten-
ants to organize the militia or trained bands, to collect
forced-loans, and to track down Jesuit priests. Under the
Lord-Lieutenants were the Justices of the Peace, country
gentry whom the Tudors had burdened with extensive administrative obligations in addition to their duties as magistrates.

Complicated though this system was, in Elizabeth's reign
there was no doubt who was master. The Council advised; it
cajoled; but it obeyed. In every sphere of government the
policies it carried out were the Queen's policies. But with
Councillors more greedy and ambitious than those who served
Elizabeth, and a monarch less able to control them, the Tudor
organization would gradually crumble.

Even in Elizabeth's last years it was not easy to preserve royal
authority. The Crown's reserves of patronage had been exhausted, and Elizabeth increasingly had to reward her supporters with
monopolies which were hated by the people. The Court was
split into factions. Elizabeth's favourite, Essex, had been
provoked into treacherous rebellion against her. The cost of
fighting Spain and crushing the Irish revolt, and the rapid rise
in prices, had forced the government to turn more and more to
Parliament. Already one or two members of the commons

---

[1] This 'prerogative' Court had devolved from the fifteenth-century Council,
and still included all the Privy Councillors among its members. Its ruthless procedures made it especially effective for suppressing disorders with which the other
law courts could not deal.

had been demanding the redress of grievances before voting fresh taxes. Only Elizabeth's personality and ability had checked the decay of royal authority in the last years of her reign. A successor who lacked these qualities, who listened to incompetent advisers, whose accession irritated English national prejudices, would not be able to halt the tide in the same way.

## ii. Parliament and the Prerogative

The second half of the sixteenth century had already seen many quarrels between the Crown and Parliament. These disputes had developed around a variety of issues. Mary's House of Commons had refused to return monastic land to the Church. Elizabeth's M.P.s[1] had forced her to introduce a Prayer Book she did not like. They had frequently lectured her on the need to reform the Church, to marry, to name her successor, to adopt a more Protestant foreign policy, and to deal more severely with dangerous nuisances like Mary Stuart. Moreover, Elizabeth's ministers had never contrived to persuade Parliament to vote adequate taxes and to accept the financial responsibility for the policies the M.P.s demanded.

All these quarrels hinged on something that was vague and undefined – the extent and nature of the royal prerogative, the Crown's authority and power for governing the country. Elizabeth believed, no less than James, in the Divine Right of Kings. According to this, as her authority came directly from God, no man had the right to criticize her use of it, let alone to try to restrict it. If she had supreme God-given power over Church and State, all other institutions, such as Parliament and the Law, existed only through her favour. Privileges granted by the sovereign could always be taken away again. Elizabeth, however, never defined her prerogative. Her relations with Parliament were carried on with a rough-and-ready pragmatism: each side was usually prepared to give and take in a practical way, without bothering too much about theories. For example, Elizabeth usually allowed the Commons freedom of speech, and once the House itself sent Peter Wentworth to the Tower when he attacked the Queen's interference with debates and asserted that Parliament held its privileges by right,

[1] Throughout this book, the term M.P. denotes a member of the House of Commons.

and not by the Crown's goodwill. On the whole, though, the royal prerogative had been on the defensive throughout the reign. The leading critics might be silenced by imprisonment, but others kept on grumbling. Elizabeth's promise to her last Parliament to grant no more monopolies was in fact a promise to limit her own prerogative.

More serious and more significant than the Crown's actual concessions to Parliament was the weakening of its influence, especially in the Commons, in the last years of the reign. Burghley had directed the Privy Councillors in the management of Parliament. Through the Speaker the Councillors had controlled the course of debates, and they had dominated the Committees appointed by the House. The eagerness of the M.P.s to secure honours or pensions for themselves had kept most of them loyal to the Crown. But the situation changed during the 1590s. There was little Crown patronage left to buy support; the number of Privy Councillors in the Commons dwindled, and Robert Cecil proved less successful than his father in guiding them. There were more Committees, with more work to do, and it became impossible for Councillors to influence them in the old way.

Moreover the M.P.s themselves had changed during the century. Most of Henry VIII's M.P.s were townsmen – often reluctant – elected by their boroughs to represent them at Westminster. From the middle of the century, however, the borough seats were increasingly filled by country gentlemen. These knights and squires were eager for the social prestige enjoyed by an M.P. – and were equally anxious for the opportunity to earn government favours by supporting the Crown in Parliament. But when the favours had all been distributed, this 'invasion of the borough seats' produced a House less easily overawed by royal authority. Two other groups were also prominent in the late Elizabethan Commons: lawyers, who were soon to lead the attack on the Crown's prerogative; and merchants, outspoken against restrictions and loudly demanding aggressive foreign policies to help their trade and get them access to the markets of the Spanish empire. James, then, inherited a Parliament whose members had long been clearing their throats in preparations for an attack on royal authority, who were soon to be provoked into open opposition by the King's attempt to define his rights, and who

could not easily be controlled by the Crown.  It did not take
him long to stir up a political hornets' nest.

### iii. The Crown's Finances

Elizabeth bequeathed a debt of some £400,000 to James.
This should not have been crippling, for he also received
£300,000 voted in taxes by her last Parliament, but not
collected until after her death.  More dangerous was the fact
that she had been living partly on her capital since the outbreak
of the Spanish war in 1585.  During this period she had been
forced to sell nearly half the Crown lands. Between 1598 and
1603 alone, she had sold property worth £372,000 to help pay
for the suppression of the Irish revolt.  Such extensive sales
reduced sharply the income from what remained, and in
Elizabeth's last year the Crown lands produced only £128,000.
Most of the Crown lands were let out to tenants on long leases,
and rents could not be increased until the leases expired.

The Crown's other main income came from tunnage and
poundage, customs duties, traditionally voted for the whole
of the reign by the new monarch's first Parliament.  These,
and similar impositions, fluctuated with the volume of trade
and suffered from the activities of pirates.  Altogether, the
Treasury received about £120,000 from the profits of trade at the
end of Elizabeth's reign.  It also received the fines imposed by
the law courts, and a substantial but variable profit from the
Church – which Elizabeth exploited quite shamelessly.  The
Crown benefited little from two other financial exactions,
purveyance and wardship,[1] for over three-quarters of the profits
went directly into the pockets of courtiers.

From this income of well under £300,000 a year, the
sovereign was expected to pay all the normal costs of government and administration, defence and the royal household.
In peacetime, at least, Parliament expected the Crown to 'live
of its own', to run the country with the money received by the
monarch in his capacity as a feudal landlord.  With a thrift
she had inherited from her grandfather, Elizabeth had managed

---

[1] Purveyance was a levy (£50,000 p.a.) collected in lieu of the Crown's feudal
right to commandeer transport and buy food and fodder at low prices.  Wardship
entitled the king to profit from the custody of the young heirs of his tenants, and
was worth £40,000–£60,000 a year.

for a while to accumulate small surpluses saved in years of peace. But rising prices, and the heavy war expenditure of the last period of the reign, consumed the surplus, swallowed up income and capital, and forced her to rely on subsidies from Parliament.

The subsidy was an old-fashioned and inefficient form of direct taxation, a single subsidy bringing about £75,000 at the end of the sixteenth century. Each subsidy was collected at the rate of a fifth of a man's assessed income. But estates were scandalously under-assessed, so that even the richest men did not have to contribute more than a few pounds whenever a subsidy was levied. In the Parliament of 1601, Raleigh protested at the under-assessment of the wealthy: 'Our estates that be £30 or £40 in the Queen's books are not the hundredth part of our wealth.' By the end of Elizabeth's reign, it had become customary for Parliament to vote several subsidies at once, though the collection was always spread over several years. Because of the reluctance of her Parliaments to vote even such light taxes, and because of the delay in collecting them, Elizabeth was forced to borrow money. In 1599, for example, she borrowed £60,000 from the City of London, the Corporation negotiating the loan with the individual merchants who supplied the money.

In short, the financial situation in 1603 was not desperate – the Crown's debt was less serious than in 1558 – but the position would quickly deteriorate under a spendthrift ruler. In wartime, Elizabeth had had to come cap-in-hand to Parliament, and also create the machinery for heavy borrowing. In peacetime, and with much less excuse, James had to beg from Parliament while continuing to run more deeply into debt.

### iv. Monopolies and Trade

Lacking other forms of patronage, Elizabeth had increasingly rewarded her courtiers with patents of monopoly. These might be justifiable when used to enable an inventor to profit from his invention, or to protect an industry needed for national defence, such as gunpowder manufacture. But in most cases monopoly patents were merely royal charters empowering the lucky favourite to make as much profit as he could out of, say, the importing of sweet wines, or the manufacture of playing-cards. As there could be no competition, the monopolist was able to charge very high prices, and make a good profit despite the fees which had to be paid to the Crown. With some justification, therefore, men blamed monopolies for the sharply rising cost of living. The opposition to them was often led by men who themselves had been unsuccessful in the scramble for patents. The principal critics, though, were merchants whose activities and profits were limited by the restrictions which monopolies placed on trade. In 1601, to prevent attempts in the Commons to pass laws forbidding monopolies, Elizabeth had promised to grant no more during her reign. Such a promise, of course, was not binding on her successors. The decision in the law-suit of *D'Arcy* v. *Allen* in 1603 was a more serious challenge to the Crown. The Court of Queen's Bench declared that the playing-card monopoly was contrary to common law, and went on to define the distinction between legal and illegal monopolies: patents could lawfully be granted only to inventors, or to men who introduced new processes from abroad. The royal prerogative in granting monopolies was being threatened, not by Act of Parliament, but by a decision in the law courts.

The outcome of this crisis was a victory for the merchants over the courtiers. It was unfortunate for the Crown's relations with the merchants that both James and Charles continued to grant monopolies. The merchants were now too powerful for even the Crown to be able to cross them with impunity. The Merchant Adventurers were, as their governor boasted, 'the most famous company of merchants in Christendom'. The Merchant Adventurers, the prototype of the 'regulated' company, had three or four thousand members, a centre in London and branches in six other ports. Each member could export only a prescribed number (depending on his standing in the company) of cloths each year, but made his own bargains with the purchasers. The success of this loose organization depended on the governor and his assistants, and also on the stability of the market. A blunder such as the Cockayne project[1] of 1614 would inevitably upset trade and turn the merchants angrily against the Crown. Other trading companies were organized on the 'joint-stock' principle. In these, the members purchased shares when the company was founded, and then left the buying and selling of goods to the company's

<hr>

[1] See below, p. 34.

officers. The joint-stock companies were especially useful for trading with distant countries. By Elizabeth's death, four great joint-stock trading companies were active: the Muscovy Company was trading with Russia, the Levant Company with Turkey and Asia Minor, the Eastland Company with the Baltic, and the East India Company with the Far East. Each of these companies had a monopoly interest in one specialized area. In consequence, the fortune of each company was easily affected by changes in foreign policy. It was not long before merchants became bitterly critical of any foreign policy which did not advance their particular interests.

## v. English expansion

Though the Elizabethans had been great traders, they had not been successful colonists. The country was still too poor to rival Spain in accumulating a colonial empire. Despite the dreams of men like Raleigh, no English colony had yet taken root in American soil. Raleigh's attempts to settle a 'plantation' at Roanoke in the 1580s survived only in the name Virginia, a tribute to the Queen. The Crown could not afford to sponsor such wild speculations, and no individual could bear the cost of establishing a colony in the teeth of Spanish power, hostile natives, and a murderous climate. Until the emergence of the Chartered Companies made more capital available, plantations in the New World could not succeed. On the other hand, the successes of the Elizabethan sailors – and the publicity given to them by Archdeacon Hakluyt's *Principal Voyages of the English Nation* – had created an enthusiastic interest in the New World. The sixteenth-century voyages of exploration and discovery had at least signposted the routes which the seventeenth-century colonists were to take.

The Elizabethan speculator had not needed to go to America to invest in plantations. Ireland was much nearer. The frequent rebellions of Irish chiefs against English authority provided the excuse for large-scale confiscations of Irish land, for the law of treason declared that a traitor's possessions should be forfeited to the Crown. Moreover, by treating the chief as though he himself owned all the land of the clan,[1] it was possible

---

[1] By Irish custom, the land belonged to the members of the clan, and the clan chief was merely an elected leader. The English assumed that the chieftain was equivalent to a feudal tenant-in-chief, from whom all his vassals held their land.

to dispossess the whole clan if the chief rebelled.  During Elizabeth's reign, much of Ireland was in continual revolt against English confiscations of land, against the imposition of the English Protestant Church on the Catholic natives, and against the enforcement of English law and administration.

The last great achievement of Elizabeth's reign was the crushing of the final and most dangerous rebellion, that of the Ulster Earls of Tyrone and Tyrconnell.  Four successive Lord Deputies had failed to crush the revolt – Fitzwilliam, Russell, Brough and Essex – before Mountjoy in 1601 defeated Tyrone and his Spanish allies at Kinsale.  Fifteen months elapsed before the last pockets of resistance had been crushed; then, in March 1603, a few days after Elizabeth's death, Tyrone surrendered to Mountjoy and the rebellion was over.

But this was a Pyrrhic victory for Elizabeth.  It had cost her £1,200,000 to suppress the rebels – over four years' normal income.  From those who had contributed to the victory came a fresh clamour to be rewarded with new grants of land confiscated from the rebels.  Attempts were made to impose more strictly the English Church, the English language, and the English shire system.  The Parliament in Dublin was completely subservient to that in London.  The prerogative Court of Castle Chamber imitated the severities of the English Court of Star Chamber.  Above all, the establishment of English plantations on much of the best Irish land made a poor country even poorer, and broke up the clan system which had done much to stabilize Irish society.  A tolerant ruler – as James tried to be – might have been able to reconcile English and Irish, Protestants and Catholics, but he would have had to be ruthlessly firm in refusing to his courtiers the lands they coveted so greedily.

### vi. Foreign affairs

Elizabeth bequeathed to James a Spanish war, and a whole complex of national and religious prejudices against foreigners and Catholics.  The war had dragged on since 1585, and both England and Spain were now exhausted with their attempts to surpass each other's power at sea.  After 1588, Philip II had continued to prepare armadas for the invasion of England, but his campaigns against the rebel United Provinces and against Henry IV in France prevented the 'Empresa' succeeding.  The

1596 alliance between England, Henry and the United Provinces was weakened in 1598 when France made peace with Spain at Vervins, but Spain was not able to exploit this advantage, for she was near bankruptcy. Philip III could afford to send only 4000 troops to help the Irish revolt against England. Even so, the situation was dangerous, for England now faced the possibility of invasion from the west. But Mountjoy defeated the Spanish at Kinsale in 1601, and the survivors returned home. After this incident, the war died away, with neither side able to afford an offensive against the other. The bitterness of war, however, continued unabated. The Spanish refusal to admit English merchants to trade with the New World, stories of the barbarous treatment of captured sailors by the Spanish Inquisition, and Spain's repeated support for English traitors, all combined to breed in Englishmen a deep hatred for His Catholic Majesty and all his subjects. James never understood the extent of this national bigotry against Spain and the religion she championed.

England's relations with the United Provinces[1] were fairly good at the end of Elizabeth's reign, but the people had more enthusiasm for the Dutch than the Queen had, for she still distrusted them. Nonetheless, in the years after the assassination of William of Orange, Elizabeth needed to keep alive resistance to Spain. She loaned the Dutch money and troops, and in 1603 there were still many companies of English soldiers fighting the Spaniards in the Low Countries. But the seeds of later Anglo-Dutch rivalry had been sown. The Dutch had started to build up their commercial empire in the Far East before the English East India Company had even been founded. Dutch fisher-boats were already catching millions of herring close to the English coast, and were challenging English fishermen in more distant waters as well.

Elizabeth had got on well with Henry IV of France. The two sovereigns had much in common, for both were realists who placed the safety of their kingdoms above the niceties of theological doctrine. It was easy for Elizabeth to sympathize with a man who had abandoned his Huguenot faith to get possession of his capital; Paris was worth a Mass. Fear of Spain had kept together the two countries which had drifted

---

[1] For convenience, the United Provinces are sometimes referred to in this book as 'Holland', which was in fact only the largest of the seven provinces.

together in 1572; even the Protestant outcry at the Massacre of St. Bartholomew had not shattered the alliance. Henry's generous Edict of Nantes (1598) mollified Puritans disappointed at his apostasy and at his peace with Spain; indeed, the French Calvinist enjoyed more freedom under Catholic Henry than the English Calvinist did under Protestant Elizabeth. Trade between the two countries was increasing – France wanted English wool and cloth, England wanted French corn and wine. As yet, France had no thought of challenging England's bid for naval power. The centuries of bitter Anglo-French hostility had ended, at least for a time. For James, a Scot, it was perhaps pleasant to find that England was now a partner in the 'Auld Alliance', instead of its principal enemy!

In foreign affairs, the situation at the end of Elizabeth's reign was safer and more peaceful than that at the beginning. Had James managed to restrain the ambition of merchants and the prejudices of Protestant zealots, he might have justified in full his claim to be *Rex Pacificus*. It was unfortunate that he tried to reach the shore by swimming against the tide of public opinion.

### vii. The Church

The Anglican Church was one of the most valuable, and one of the most vulnerable, of Elizabeth's legacies. The 1559 Settlement had been under fire from both Catholics and Puritans throughout her reign, from pulpit, in Parliament and by papal Bull. By 1603, however, most of the critics had been taught to keep silent. The Court of High Commission, under Archbishop Whitgift and Bishop Bancroft, had suppressed most of the outward signs of Puritanism by means of the *ex officio* oath,[1] and the penal laws against recusancy[2] had taken the heart out of the Catholics. Hooker had published most of his *Ecclesiastical Polity*, giving a convincing philosophical and theological explanation of the Anglican position. The Prayer Book services were now a regular and familiar part of English life. Nonetheless, there were dangerous weaknesses in the Church.

Many of these weaknesses stemmed from the mediaeval law

---

[1] By which suspects could be forced to give evidence against themselves.
[2] Refusal to accept the Act of Supremacy acknowledging Elizabeth as 'Supreme Governor' of the Church.

of advowson, or patronage. In mediaeval society, the right of selecting the village priest belonged to the lord of the manor. This right was regarded as a piece of property which could be sold or given away. Over the centuries, many lords had transferred their advowsons to monasteries. Such monasteries had appointed vicars to take the services, paid them miserable salaries, and themselves kept most of the income from the parishes (chiefly the 'great' tithe on grain and livestock). At the dissolution of the monasteries by Henry VIII in 1536-40, the advowsons and 'impropriated' titles of nearly half the parishes in England had passed to the Crown. The profits from these parishes made up a large part of the Crown's income from monastic property. But the Tudors' need to raise ready money and to reward their favourites forced them to sell or give away many of these advowsons and impropriations, as well as most of the monastic land. Elizabethan patrons were usually quite unscrupulous in exploiting to the full their rights of advowson, and the Queen was equally ruthless with the patronage which remained in her hands. Parsons were forced, as a condition of their appointment, to grant away much of the income which they should have received.

Parish clergy were usually very poor by the end of the sixteenth century.[1] Their incomes were too low to attract into the Church more than a handful of men of ability, even when a parson held several parishes simultaneously – and this pluralism was strongly criticized by the Puritans. After the Reformation, the Church received very little in new charitable endowments, as almost all charitable gifts went to education or social benefits such as almshouses and hospitals. At a time when laymen were becoming more literate, an uneducated clergy – nearly half of them were not allowed to preach – could neither earn respect nor answer the challenges made by intelligent Puritans or well-trained Jesuit missionaries. Moreover, advowsons often led to disputes between the patrons and the bishops, who frequently hesitated to install the patrons' nominees.

The Crown's right to choose bishops led to further abuses. Elizabeth usually refused to appoint a bishop unless he granted

[1] In the diocese of Carlisle in 1599, according to the bishop, no vicar or curate received as much as £7 a year.

to her or to a Court favourite a large part of his income. Fletcher had to pay over £2000 and lease much of the diocese's property before he was made Bishop of London in 1595; next year, Bilson had to pay £1200 and promise £400 a year in return for the bishopric of Winchester. Moreover, a bishop had to pay annates (his first year's income) to the Crown when he received his first bishopric and whenever he moved to a new diocese; and so Elizabeth deliberately moved her bishops around frequently. Whenever a bishopric was vacant, the Crown received its revenues; Elizabeth kept the bishopric of Oxford vacant for forty-one years. In theory, the incomes of the bishops were princely; in fact, they had to resort to the most unscrupulous exploitation of their property – felling the timber, selling the lead from the roofs of the buildings – to recover their investment in obtaining their bishoprics. The bishops, too, were required to assist the government by voting loyally on Bills in the House of Lords; here, their obsequious behaviour and obscure origins angered the other peers. A bishop, often absent from his diocese, eager for promotion to a more profitable see, forced to make out of his present bishopric as much as he could, was in a poor position to lead the lower clergy in resisting the attacks on the Church. The more intelligent of the lower clergy despised their bishops; all were jealous of them. Many clergy who supported Puritan attacks on the episcopacy as an institution expected that the abolition of bishops would result in the distribution of their wealth (and that of the cathedrals) to the parish clergy.

Sixteenth-century Puritanism had flowed through a variety of courses. The main stream had undoubtedly run within the Church, through men like Dering, Greenham and Rogers, agitating for the abolition of vestments and other popish survivals in the services, sometimes attacking the bishops and secretly experimenting with Presbyterian[1] forms of organization. After his appointment as Archbishop of Canterbury in 1583, Whitgift had fairly successfully dammed this stream, but the dam was not water-tight. In the last years of the reign, thousands had obeyed William Perkins' call for stricter Sabbath

---

[1] The system of church government evolved by Calvin at Geneva. The clergy were chosen and appointed by the parish congregations. The ministers in each area composed the local presbyteries, which sent delegates to the national synod or assembly, the governing body of the Presbyterian church. It was thus essentially elective and 'democratic', and therefore hard for the secular power to control.

observance, and for regular family prayers—with which the bishops could hardly interfere. Such family piety was a major source of the subsequent Puritan revival. Moreover, a desire to make the Established Church more Puritan was still strong among the political classes. The late Elizabethan Parliaments contained many successors to the Nortons, Stricklands, Copes and Wentworths who at times had carried on a running battle against the Church Settlement. Even Burghley had occasionally used his authority to protect Puritans from the bishops. James was to learn from his first Parliament how strongly the members sympathized with the critics of the Prayer Book.

Some Puritan streams had meandered outside the Church. There were the leading Presbyterians, Cartwright and Travers; the latter was never in Anglican orders, and the former was forced out of the Church by Whitgift. These men shouted their defiance of the bishops from the safety of exile, where they were much influenced by Beza, Calvin's successor. To such strict Presbyterians, the idea of a State-controlled Church was almost blasphemous. The government was more successful in checking, almost at its source, the Separatist movement founded by Browne. The Separatists believed that each congregation should be independent and self-governing – a doctrine which seemed dangerously anarchical. The Court of High Commission, with a harshness which once made Burghley compare it to the Spanish Inquisition, had three leading Separatists – Barrow, Greenwood and Penry – hanged in 1593. Browne himself fled to Scotland, took a dislike to the reformed Church there, returned to England, and ended his life in 1633 as a conforming Anglican parson.

The end of Elizabeth's reign saw the Roman Catholics split by a fundamental disagreement. On one side were the 'secular' priests, successors of the pre-Reformation parish clergy; these had no wish to rebel against the Crown, and wanted merely to be allowed to provide the Sacraments for the existing English Catholics. On the other side were the Jesuits and their supporters, many scheming actively against Elizabeth in accordance with the papal Bull deposing her, and sworn to reconvert the Protestants. The Pope had blundered in 1598 by appointing a Jesuit sympathizer, George Blackwell, as 'Archpriest' over all the Catholic missionaries in England. The secular priests opposed him, not wanting to be forced into treasonable actions which they disapproved. The quarrel became heated when the Pope continued to support the Jesuits. While Elizabeth was dying, the government scored a minor propaganda victory by persuading a group of the seculars to acknowledge her as Queen, in defiance of the Bull. But the weakness of the leadership could not hide the fact that there were still many Catholics in the country, particularly in the north. Not many could afford the crippling fines for staying away from the Anglican services, but the number of those who owed more spiritual allegiance to Rome than to Canterbury or York amounted to tens of thousands.

The state of the Church of England was thus more precarious than it seemed to those in 1603 who saw the bishops as props of royal authority in the Lords, civil administrators in the country, active members of prerogative courts, and sources of royal revenue. The Elizabethan Church Settlement had, in fact, been undermined by its principal architect; it was fortunate that James saw in time the need to underprop the building by strengthening its economic foundations. For the moment, the building was safe from those whose gusty breath Whitgift had stifled. Some dangers, however, remained. Catholicism might return to favour at Court. Puritanism might become popular among the mass of laymen. The Millenary Petition and the opposition to the 1604 Canon Laws, like the Catholic Plots of 1603–5, soon showed that opposition to the Church had not been tamed.

## viii. Society

Elizabeth had deliberately built up a splendid Court, for she knew the value of lavish pomp in winning the admiration of her people. This she had achieved at little direct cost to herself: courtiers such as Raleigh and Essex, Leicester and Derby provided most of the glitter, as they competed with each other for the Queen's favour. Nonetheless, a successful competitor in the contest expected reward. Most men wanted the grant, lease or sale of Crown property, some office made profitable by opportunities for extracting bribes, or some monopoly which could be exploited at the expense of the public. Many courtiers, though, were more greedy for power and prestige than for wealth: an appointment to an unprofitable post as an ambassador, or President of the North, was often sufficient reward in itself, even if it brought the holder deeply into debt. In this way, much of the expense of government fell on the courtiers, not on the Queen. But this enthusiasm to serve the Crown did not outlive Elizabeth. Indeed, even in the last years of her reign, courtiers were already less anxious to press for the responsibilities which had ruined many of their friends. Leicester, for example, had died owing the Crown £70,000. James, unfortunately, could never command the romantic respect which Elizabeth had enjoyed; the courtiers of the Jacobean age were almost all greedy men on the make. The greediest of them, men like Carr and Villiers, could not be satisfied except through the impoverishment of the Crown. Like many of the difficulties of the time, the trouble stemmed from the great sixteenth-century price-rise. Incomes from land had not kept pace with the cost of living (especially at Court), and the survival of great families often depended on their success in getting favours from the sovereign. The struggle for pensions and monopolies therefore became more intense.

In his essay on 'Nobility', Francis Bacon deplored the fact that many nobles were now poor men. The 'disproportion between honour and means' did a lot to keep fluid the relationship between the different classes. It was easy to move from one class into another. The younger sons of peers were commoners, often without inherited wealth and therefore forced to make their own way in the world. The nobles had little prejudice against commerce. Many nobles married the daughters or widows of prosperous merchants, for the sake of their dowries, and themselves invested in trading ventures, voyages to America, plantations in Ireland, or the development of coal and iron mines. Many men whose grandfathers had been small squires increased their estates through Crown favour, careful management or good luck, and built up rent rolls which many nobles envied. Sometimes even lesser men, small tenant farmers and yeomen, succeeded in raising themselves into the ranks of the country gentry. On the other hand, the poorest classes had suffered under the Tudors. Landlords had often increased rents by wide margins whenever leases expired; others made their lessees tenants-at-will, liable to be turned off their holdings without notice. Enclosures in many areas had deprived the peasants of much of the common land, and the conversion of ploughland to sheep pasture had

thrown many of them out of work. Elizabeth bequeathed to
James a comprehensive system of laws forbidding enclosure and
ordering the parishes to care for the poor and aged. Unfortunately, these laws had to be enforced by the Justices of the
Peace – men from the very class which had most to gain from
ignoring them.

England was thus a country of serious social tensions at the
end of the Tudor period. The old nobles resented the power of
the 'new' men. Those unsuccessful in the scramble for Crown
patronage were likely to become embittered rivals of those
more fortunate. This was especially so when the patronage
took the form of grants of monopoly, for the lucky man gained
directly at the expense of the remainder. The Tudors had
overworked their J.P.s, who received no direct reward for their
part in the administration. James was to find it difficult to
bribe or coerce the J.P.s into carrying out their duties effectively. The poor could not easily be protected against the evils
of enclosure and rack-renting. Meanwhile, the whole machine
of Tudor administration – based on voluntary co-operation in
the work of government, supervised by the prerogative courts –
was slowly grinding to a halt.

### ix. Culture

Here, at least, one cannot doubt the value of the Elizabethan
legacy. Indeed, the renaissance in English culture survived
the Queen by thirty years or more. Spenser and Marlowe were
dead by 1603, but the greatest plays of Shakespeare and
Jonson had not yet been written. Of the prose writers,
Hooker and Hakluyt had published their main works by the
Queen's death, but Bacon and Raleigh did not produce their
most important contributions to literature until the next reign.
The poets Donne, Herbert and Herrick were also men of the
seventeenth century. The school of English miniature painting
founded by Hilliard – 'the most illuminating interpreter of late
Tudor England' – was still to produce the work of the Olivers,
the Hoskins and Cooper. Prosperous squires and gentry
continued to beggar themselves by competing with their
neighbours in the erection of splendid country mansions. The
Elizabethan madrigalists, Byrd, Gibbons and Bull, kept on
composing busily until their deaths in the 1620s.

The standard of education and literacy in the country was higher than ever before. At the end of the sixteenth century, Oxford and Cambridge each had about 3000 students. These were no longer chiefly poor scholars preparing to enter the Church, for higher education was now part of the upbringing of most gentlemen. The universities were not alone in providing this, for many young men went instead to the Inns of Court to receive education in the law. At a lower level, a host of new grammar schools had been founded during Elizabeth's reign, some by pious townsmen, some by the town authorities themselves. The universities, too, had benefited greatly from private charity. Trinity, Jesus, and St. John's at Oxford, and Emmanuel and Sidney Sussex at Cambridge, were all founded in the second half of the sixteenth century, and many other colleges had their endowments increased.

Yet there were dangers even here. Elizabeth's government needed to supervise closely what was going on in the universities, and direct intervention had often been necessary to evict Catholics such as the dons of Exeter College, Oxford, or remove Presbyterians like Cartwright from positions at Cambridge. Schoolmasters, too, could infect the minds of their pupils with dangerous ideas; Whitgift tried to force them, no less than the clergy, to conform to the Anglican service. This was a necessary task, but one which it was impossible to complete. A few years later, Oliver Cromwell imbibed much of his Puritanism from the ferocious Dr. Beard, schoolmaster at Huntingdon. The threat from the lawyers was potentially the most serious of all. It was difficult for the Crown or the Church to interfere with the teaching in the Inns of Court. Here the students soon acquired their elders' veneration for the law and dislike of the Crown's boasts about its prerogatives. Here, too, the lawyers acquired the skill in debate and argument which was to make them the most outspoken of the Stuarts' critics in Parliament.

## x. The Heir

In some ways, at least, James seemed an ideal person to tackle the problems of 1603. Elizabeth knew how successful he had been in disciplining the nobles and Presbyterian divines who had bullied him during his youth. All knew his reputation for learning. The Puritans and Catholics knew that he was a tolerant man.   The principal English ministers, led by Robert Cecil, had already successfully ingratiated themselves with James, even though Elizabeth had always refused to name him as her successor.

In fact, James cut a poor figure.   He was short, mis-shapen, with an ungainly head; he stuttered, slobbered, was often drunk, and quickly lost his temper.   His successes in Scotland made him over-confident in England, where there was no sense of loyalty to the Stuarts to help him over his difficulties.   Men who supported him in England did so because they expected to be rewarded.   His love for theory had already led him to write two works on political science, *Basilikon Doron* and *The True Law of Free Monarchies*.   The views they contained on the Divine Right of Kings did not please his Parliaments.   His dreams of toleration soon faded, and he was forced to intensify the persecution of Puritans and Catholics alike.   His failure to share English prejudices against Spain and against Rome led to an insipid foreign policy, and to the weakening of English national pride.   Perhaps the most unsatisfactory part of Elizabeth's legacy was the heir she bequeathed to her country.

## EXTRACTS

1. JAMES SECRETLY ASSURES ROBERT CECIL OF HIS FRIENDSHIP (1601):

Quhen it shall please god that 30 shall succeide to his richt, he shall no surelier succeide to the place then he shall succeide in bestowing as great and greater fauoure upon 10 as his predecessoure doth bestow upon him, and in the meane tyme ye maye rest assured of the constant loue and secreatie of

Youre most louing and assurid freinde,

30.

(In Dickenson and Donaldson, *Source Book of Scottish History*, vol. iii, p. 454.   In their correspondence James used the code-number 30, and Cecil the number 10.)

2. JAMES DESCRIBES A KING'S POWER (1598):

And it follows of necessity that the Kings were the authors and makers of the laws, and not the laws of the Kings. . . . We daily see that in the Parliament . . . the laws are but craved by his subjects, and only made him at their rogation and with their advice. . . . And as ye see it manifest that the King is overlord of the whole land, so is he master over every person that inhabiteth the same, having power over the life and death of every one of them. . . . For albeit it be true . . . that the King is above the law as both the author and giver of strength thereto, yet a good King will not only delight to rule his subjects by the law, but will even conform himself in his own actions thereunto; always keeping that ground, that the health of the commonwealth be his chief law. (From the *True Law of Free Monarchies*. In Tanner, *Constitutional Documents of James I*, pp. 9–10)

3. BACON REFLECTS ON THE NOBLES (1612):
A Numerous Nobility causeth Poverty and Inconvenience in a State: For it is a Surcharge of Expence; And besides, it being of Necessity that many of the Nobility fall in time to be weake in Fortune, it maketh a kinde of Disproportion betweene Honour and Meanes.
As for Nobility in particular Persons; It is a Reverend Thing to see an Ancient Castle or Building not in decay, Or to see a faire Timber Tree, sound and perfect: How much more, to behold an Ancient Noble Family which hath stood against the Waves and weathers of Time. For new Nobility is but the Act of Power, But Ancient Nobility is the Act of Time. . . . Nobility of Birth commonly abateth Industry; and he that is not industrious envieth him that is. Besides, Noble persons cannot goe much higher; And he that standeth at a stay, when others rise, can hardly avoid Motions [feelings] of Envy. (From the Essay *Of Nobility*)

4. BACON DISCUSSES TROUBLE-MAKERS IN THE STATE (1612):
Kings have to deale with their Neighbours, their Wives, their Children, their Prelates or Clergie, their Nobles, their Second-Nobles or Gentlemen, their Merchants, their Commons, and their Men of Warre; And from all these arise Dangers, if Care and Circumspection be not used. . . .
For their Prelates; when they are proud and great, there is also danger from them. . . . [It is also dangerous] where the Churchmen come in and are elected, not by the Collation [appointment] of the King, or particular Patrons, but by the People.[1] . . .
For their Merchants; They are *Vena porta*; And if they flourish

---

[1] As in the Presbyterian system.

not, a Kingdome may have good Limmes, but will have empty
Veines, and nourish little.    Taxes and Imposts upon them do
seldom good to the King's Revenew. . . . The particular
Rates being increased, but the totall Bulke of Trading rather
decreased.

For their Commons; There is little danger from them, except
it be, where they have Great and Potent Heads; Or where you
meddle with the Point of Religion, Or their Customs, or
Meanes of Life.    (From the Essay *Of Empire*)

5.  BACON'S THOUGHTS ABOUT COLONIES (1625):
    I like a Planatation in a Pure Soile; that is, where People are
not Displanted to the end to Plant in Others.    For else  it is
rather an Extirpation then a Plantation.    Planting of Countries
is like Planting of Woods; For you must make account to leese
[do without] almost Twenty yeeres' Profit, and expect your
Recompence in the end.    For the Principall Thing  that hath
beene the Destruction of most Plantations, hath been the Base
and Hastie drawing of Profit in the first Yeeres.    (From the
Essay *Of Plantations*)

6.  BURGHLEY CRITICIZES WHITGIFT'S SEVERITY (1584):
    But now, my good Lord, by chance I am come to the sight of
an instrument of 24 Articles of great length and curiosity, found
in a Romish style. . . .    I did recommend unto your Grace's
favour two ministers, curates of Cambridgeshire, to be favourably heard; and your Grace wrote to me that they were
contentious, seditious, and persons vagrant. . . .    But now they
coming to me and I asking them how your Grace had proceeded with them, they say they are commanded to be examined by the Register at London.    And I asked them,
Whereof?    They said, of a great number of Articles, but they
could have no copies of them. . . .    Upon this I sent for the
Register, who brought me the Articles.    Which I have read,
and find so curiously penned as I think the Inquisitors of Spain
use not so many questions to . . . trap their preys. . . .

I conclude that, according to my simple judgment, this kind
of proceeding is too much savouring of the Romish Inquisition,
and is rather a device to seek for offenders than to reform any.
(In Tanner, *Constitutional Documents*, p. 168)

# 2
# THE END OF ELIZABETHAN UNITY
## 1603–29

☆

## i. The Crown and the Court

ELIZABETH died early on March 24th, 1603. Six hours later, in a proclamation which he had approved months before, the Council declared James VI of Scotland the new King. The Council's messenger to him was, however, outpaced by two days. In a ride which has become legendary, Carey, Warden of the Marches, spurred northwards in his eagerness to profit from being the first to tell James the glad news, and reached Edinburgh in less than three days. Scores of other sycophants followed him.

James basked briefly in the unaccustomed popularity. Then, accompanied by a crowd of Scots determined to make their fortunes at the English Court, he rode south to claim his new kingdom. Ambitious men, or those with grievances, thronged to lobby him on his leisurely progress south. To all he was genial, encouraging, generous. He promised to consider the Millenary Petition, brought by Puritan-minded clergy in the Church of England; they would have had short shrift from Elizabeth. He bestowed more knighthoods in his first two months than Elizabeth in her last ten years. He met Robert Cecil, confirmed him in his office as Secretary, created him Lord Cecil, and excused him a debt of over £4000 he owed to the Crown. The Lord Keeper, Egerton, stayed in office and became Lord Ellesmere and Chancellor. Lord Buckhurst, the Treasurer, became Lord Dorset. Thomas Howard was elevated to be Earl of Suffolk; his brother Henry to be Earl of Northampton. While the plague raged within London, the new coronets were glittering beyond its gates, in the palace of Whitehall. Scotsmen, led by James Hay, crowded the Court.

Shakespeare turned from the history of mediaeval England to that of mediaeval Scotland, and wrote *Macbeth*, including in it an elaborate compliment to James (as a descendant of Banquo). Ben Jonson and Inigo Jones began to produce their spectacular masques to entertain the Court. James's expenses quickly mounted. The Court was costly, especially as all the members of the royal family had to have their own households. By nature, James was generous to the point of extravagance, and could not resist trying to build up a party of supporters by lavishing pensions on all who attracted him. By 1610, James had handed out a quarter of a million pounds, as well as annuities exceeding £30,000 a year.

During the first decade of the new reign, the administration was moderately successful, as Robert Cecil was able to captain what was in effect a junior team of Elizabethan administrators. The calm of the accession, however, was soon shattered by a series of Catholic plots. The Bye Plot[1] was of little consequence but the Main Plot was more serious. In it, Lord Cobham planned to put James's cousin Arabella Stuart[2] on the throne. Unfortunately, Raleigh, disgruntled at the success of his rival Cecil, had become indirectly involved in the plot. Coke, the Attorney-General, prosecuted him for treason, and he was sent to the Tower under sentence of death. The older Elizabethans died: Archbishop Whitgift in 1604 and his successor Bancroft in 1610, Dorset in 1608 and Robert Cecil (now Lord Salisbury) in 1612. The continuity with the past gradually came to an end. Gradually, too, the Court ceased to reflect the temper of the country. The Gunpowder Plot of 1605 increased the national hatred of popery, but Catholicism nonetheless became more powerful at Court. The Queen, Anne of Denmark, was a Catholic, and so were the members of her household. The Howards – Northampton, Suffolk and Nottingham – were Catholics, and shielded many of their co-religionists while they themselves increased their power in the administration. The arrival in 1609 of a new Spanish ambassador, Gondomar,

[1] The plotters hoped to kidnap James and force him to make concessions to ease the conditions of the Catholics.

[2] Descended, like James himself, from Henry VII's daughter Margaret. Arabella had been born in England, and her supporters argued that, as James was a foreigner, he could not legally inherit any property in England, let alone the Crown itself. Spain, and some English Catholics, favoured Arabella as they hoped to extract religious concessions from her as the price of support.

perhaps the ablest Spaniard of his time, provided a focus for the Catholic party.

The Scotsmen at Court were especially alarmed, for their influence over the King seemed to be slipping away. To check this, Hay in 1607 introduced to James an attractive and athletic young Scots rogue named Robert Carr. James immediately swallowed the bait. Within a matter of months, Carr was Gentleman of the Bedchamber; James then gave him Raleigh's manor of Sherborne (forfeited to the Crown for his 'treason'), created him Viscount Rochester, appointed him Privy Councillor, and personally instructed him in the subtleties of politics and Latin grammar. The death of Salisbury in 1612 removed the last restraint upon the King: control of policy passed almost entirely into the hands of irresponsible court gallants, puppets in the hands of Gondomar.

For the next, disastrous period of his reign, James was in the power of dangerous men. The reputation of the Court rapidly sank. The extravagance of the favourites impoverished the Crown, and forced the King to obtain money by unpopular means such as the sale of monopolies. English foreign policy seemed perverted into following the interests of Spain. Gondomar agitated for a marriage treaty between England and Spain which would undermine the recent alliance between James and the German Protestants; only the obstinate insistence of Prince Henry, that 'two religions should not lie in his bed', prevented his betrothal to the Infanta. After Henry's death in 1612, his younger brother Charles became the object of Gondomar's schemes. Carr, now running foreign policy, was tricked and fooled at every turn by the wily ambassador.

James could refuse his favourite nothing. In 1613 Carr became Earl of Somerset and Secretary of State. When Somerset wished to marry his mistress, Lady Essex, James packed the Commission appointed to consider the annulment of her existing marriage to the Earl of Essex.[1] Despite the opposition of Archbishop Abbot, the Commission granted the annulment. As the lady was the daughter of Suffolk and the great-niece of Northampton, the solidarity of the Howard faction seemed complete, for the King's favourite had now married into their family.

But Somerset's fall was even more rapid than his rise. The

[1] Son of Elizabeth's favourite.

news leaked out that Lady Essex had had a vital witness, Sir Thomas Overbury, poisoned in the Tower. A former servant of Carr, and jealous of his master's preference for the Howards, Overbury had threatened to produce evidence which would have prevented the annulment. The new Countess of Somerset confessed that she had ordered Overbury's murder, and the Lords sentenced her and her husband to death. James reprieved and pardoned them, merely banishing them from Court. The King's favourites, it seemed, could get away with murder. The scandal redoubled the country's antagonism towards the Court. Not since Elizabeth had been suspected of complicity in the death of glamorous Leicester's wife had there been a comparable scandal. Elizabeth learnt from her indiscretion; James did not from his.

Already, though, Somerset's influence was on the decline. A group opposed to the Howards – and including Archbishop Abbot among its members – in 1614 introduced another gay young man to James, in an effort to win him away from Somerset. The newcomer, George Villiers, was as charming as Carr and much more intelligent. Within a year he received a knighthood, and when Somerset was banished from Court Villiers was left without a rival in the King's affections. The Howards were now in partial eclipse. James released Raleigh from the Tower, and allowed him to visit South America in search of gold, on the condition that he did not attack the Spaniards. He failed to find gold, or to keep his promise. On his return, Gondomar demanded his death. Anxious now to placate Spain, James had him executed for his offence of fifteen years before. To the country, Raleigh now appeared to be a Protestant hero, martyred to appease Spain and the Catholics. Once again, Court intrigues had widened the gulf between James and his subjects.

Nevertheless, the power of the Howards was almost over. Northampton died soon after his dismissal in 1614 for treasonable negotiations with the papacy. Suffolk was tried by Star Chamber in 1618 and dismissed for corruption. Nottingham, too, was dismissed, for corruption, from the post of Lord High Admiral (which he had held since 1585). For the next decade Villiers had no rival. James made him Earl of Buckingham in 1617, Marquis in 1619, Duke in 1623. In 1619 Buckingham succeeded Nottingham at the Admiralty. His flatterers filled most of the offices of State: Bacon became Chancellor and the Treasury went first to Mandeville and then to Cranfield. A host of lesser men found that the only way to the King was through his favourite. Buckingham's mastery over his sentimental and doting sovereign was absolute. James remarked, somewhat blasphemously, 'Christ had His John and I have my George.' The new peer and his relations had little money of their own (until Buckingham married the heiress Lady Manners); wealth appropriate to the family's new station therefore had to be provided by the King.

At first Buckingham did not abuse his power. The outbreak of the Thirty Years War, and the defeat of James's son-in-law, the Elector Palatine in 1620, changed this. The poverty of the Crown made it impossible for the King to help the Elector without taxes from Parliament. The fickleness and the disloyalty of the favourite now became obvious to all except the King. The Commons demanded scapegoats for the earlier troubles. Buckingham provided them. Buckingham's own kinsman Mompesson was impeached[1] as a monopolist. Buckingham's obsequious follower, the Lord Chancellor Bacon, was impeached for accepting bribes – partly because of an unintentional insult to the Villiers family. James's wisest adviser was thus sacrificed. Even more reckless was the loss of prestige for the royal prerogative, implied in the abandonment of the monopolist. Moreover, the Commons had revived, with the favourite's encouragement, a weapon which could be used against any man who displeased the House. But even at this price, the Crown failed to get from Parliament either money for a war against Spain, or even approval for James's alternative scheme – a marriage between the Spanish Infanta and Prince Charles. After Parliament was dissolved, James committed himself entirely to the marriage project, by which he hoped to get a large dowry from Spain and Spanish help for the restoration of the Palatinate to the dispossessed Elector.

After some hesitation, Charles fell under the spell of his father's favourite. The Prince was shy and reserved, and saw in the charming extrovert Buckingham everything that he himself failed to be. Both became enthusiastic for the marriage, and Gondomar's schemes at last seemed to be bearing fruit.

[1] Impeachment was the legal process whereby the Lords acted as judges of a law-suit brought by the House of Commons as plaintiff.

Buckingham, though, was jealous of the Earl of Bristol, James's ambassador in Madrid, who had been put in charge of the negotiations. Buckingham persuaded Charles to join with him in a mad-cap plan which would, they hoped, speed the marriage and give no credit to Bristol. The two prevailed upon the King to allow them to go to Spain to woo the Infanta. The irresponsible escapade failed. Charles returned in October 1623, without the Infanta, but even more devoted to Buckingham. Despite James's attempts to restrain him, the favourite now proceeded to ruin his rivals. When Bristol returned to England to report to James, he was sent to the Tower on a charge of treason. The able Treasurer, Lionel Cranfield, had not allowed Buckingham what the latter considered adequate expenses for the Spanish jaunt, and was trying to persuade James to reduce the pensions he gave to his favourites. With the help of Charles, Buckingham had the Treasurer impeached, dismissed, and fined £50,000. The King remonstrated in vain. In Clarendon's words:

He said in great choler, 'By God, Stenny [Buckingham], you are a fool, and will shortly repent this folly, and will find that in this fit of popularity you are making a rod with which you will be scourged yourself.' And turning in some anger to the Prince, told him, that he would live to have his bellyful of Parliaments; and that, when he should be dead, he would have too much cause to remember how much he had contributed to the weakening of the Crown by his precedent he was now so fond of.[1]

But the King was too old and infirm to restrain his favourite, or to save from his jealous anger men like Bristol and Cranfield who had served him well. Even the King's policy of peace was sacrificed to please Buckingham, who still smarted under the insults he thought he had received in Madrid. So England rushed headlong into war against Spain.

Then in March 1625, James died, worn out with the troubles to which his weakness had exposed the country. Only twenty-two years had passed since Elizabeth's death, but the country was already being plagued by the evils which the great Queen had tried to avoid: government policy was being ruled by the

[1] Clarendon, *History of the Great Rebellion*, vol. i, p. 28.

whims and emotions of a royal favourite; spendthrift extrava-
gance was leaving the Crown exposed to the demands of
Parliament; the country was rushing hell-bent into war and
Parliament was again trying to control the administration.

The war gave Buckingham a splendid chance to show his
abilities as Lord High Admiral, and at the same time Charles's
accession increased still further his power in the State.  But
trouble came quickly.  Buckingham could not manage the
Parliament of 1625 as he had the M.P.s of 1621 and 1624.  The
Commons attacked the hasty marriage treaty Buckingham had
made with France, for the marriage of Charles to Henrietta
Maria had brought Catholicism back to Court; the Commons
granted no more than a miserable two subsidies (worth about
£140,000) for the war; led by Coke and Sandys, the Commons
ventured to criticize even Buckingham.  Nor was the favourite
successful in his post as Lord High Admiral.  The Navy had
suffered so long from the inefficiency of Nottingham that it
was in no fit state for a war.  The expedition under Viscount
Wimbledon to Cadiz was a scandalous failure.  The minister
who had seized supreme power found he could not evade
supreme responsibility.

Soon only Charles stood between Buckingham and his
enemies.  In the Parliament of 1626, Sir John Eliot, so recently
one of his flatterers, led the attack and denounced him as the
'canker in the King's treasure'.  The Commons proceeded to
impeach the favourite for corruption and neglect of his duties.
The verdict was a foregone conclusion.  When Charles tried to
intervene, he was told that it had long been Parliament's right
to bring the Crown's servants to account for their misdeeds.
The Commons offered Charles four subsidies if he would accept
the impeachment; he refused, and dissolved Parliament to save
his friend.

By now, England had blundered into war against France as
well as Spain.  In 1625 Buckingham had angered Parliament
by agreeing to lend Richelieu English ships for use against the
Protestant rebels at La Rochelle; two years later Buckingham
was trying to relieve the siege of La Rochelle by Richelieu's
troops!  But the failure of this expedition to the Ile de Ré,
guarding the entrance to La Rochelle harbour, discredited him
and his master still further.  For two years Charles had tried
desperately to raise funds by bullying men into lending money

to the Crown, but in the spring of 1628 he could no longer delay the calling of another Parliament. After much argument, Charles had to accept the Petition of Right, promising to abandon the methods by which he had collected the forced loans. Then Parliament turned once more against the favourite, in Coke's words 'the grievance of grievances'. To silence the attacks, Charles prorogued Parliament.

Two months later, Buckingham was assassinated at Portsmouth by Felton, a disgruntled survivor of the Ile de Ré campaign. Charles's steadfast loyalty to his servant had been wasted. Not everything in Buckingham's character was worthless, but the speed of his promotion had helped to ruin him. He had grown too confident and conceited to accept rebuke, even from James. Stronger or more unscrupulous monarchs, such as Henry VIII, Elizabeth and Charles II, might have profited from his administrative ability and knowledge of foreign affairs. In fact, however, no man did more to undermine the strong monarchy built up by the Tudors.

The death of Buckingham seemed to open the way for better relations between the King and Parliament. Such hopes were in vain. Within five months of the assassination, after scenes of unprecedented violence in the Commons, Charles dissolved his third Parliament and prayed fervently that he would never have to call another. Buckingham's death was not the cure for all the evils of the State. The opposition to Buckingham had overshadowed many of the other grievances against Stuart government. With the favourite removed, these other grievances stood out more clearly. With the common scapegoat dead, the critics aimed their challenge more directly at the King.

## ii. The Crown's finances

While the Crown's income was relatively fixed and inflexible, its expenses continued to soar. The country was not poor, but not until the 1680s was a monarch able to squeeze from it money sufficient for the household and the government without arousing overwhelming political hostility. The financial problems were great. The King was extravagant and the courtiers insatiably greedy. Only with difficulty could the Crown extract subsidies from Parliament or force merchants to

pay higher Customs duties. The great price-rise was continuing, and sales of Crown lands reduced still further the
King's income from his estates. James's Treasurers were never
able to accomplish the double task of raising Crown revenue
and at the same time reducing the expenditure. Salisbury
managed to increase James's income, and Cranfield to cut
his expenditure, but Dorset and Suffolk failed in both tasks.
As the King relied more and more on selling monopolies, so
prices inevitably rose and the Crown's expenditure with them.

The position in 1603 was not desperate, for Elizabeth's debt
was almost covered by the subsidies not yet collected. The
expenses of the accession and James's lavish gifts to his
friends soon upset this balance. His first Lord Treasurer, the
Earl of Dorset, floundered around unhappily and unsuccessfully
in trying to stop the slide towards disaster. Although the
Spanish and Irish wars had ended, by 1606 the Crown was over
£700,000 in debt. Trying to get a more regular and stable
income, Dorset in 1604 leased the 'Great Farm' of the customs
to a syndicate for seven years in return for £112,400 p.a. This
made it difficult for the Government to benefit from increased
peacetime trade, or from higher customs dues. It also aroused
jealousies at Court and in the City among those who had been
unsuccessful in bidding for the contract. In 1604–5 Dorset
raised over £110,000 by the unpopular method of a forced
loan. Although Parliament in 1606 voted James over
£450,000 in taxes, the Crown was slow in repaying this loan –
with the consequence that it afterwards found it much more
difficult to borrow money by any means.

Bate's Case in 1606 landed the King in further trouble. Bate
was a currant merchant who refused to pay to the Crown a levy
which had previously been paid to the Levant Company before
it surrendered its monopoly over the currant trade. The
Exchequer Court dismissed Bate's claim, the judges insisting on
the King's prerogative right to decide matters such as foreign
policy and restrictions on commerce. At the first opportunity
the merchant lobby in Parliament protested that this decision
gave the King *carte blanche* to place new impositions on trade.

Dorset died in 1608, and James appointed Robert Cecil, now
Earl of Salisbury, as Treasurer in his place. Salisbury tried
to reduce the royal debt by increasing the Crown's income,
without attempting to cut James's expenditure. In 1608,

encouraged by the favourable verdict in Bate's Case, Salisbury introduced a new Book of Rates. This placed higher customs duties on many imports, and by it the Treasurer hoped to raise another £70,000 p.a. from the merchants. In fact, it took six years before the Crown could get the rent of the 'Great Farm' increased even to £140,000, a modest rise of only 25 per cent. The Book of Rates enriched the customs farmers, not the Crown, but made Parliament more reluctant to listen to the Crown's pleas for subsidies.

Nonetheless, by 1610 Salisbury had reduced the debt to manageable proportions – about £280,000. This was possible only through the Parliamentary grant of 1606 and the sale of Crown land worth over £445,000. In fact, the extra revenue of some £900,000 reduced the debt by only about £450,000 over the four years. There was therefore still an annual deficit of over £100,000 p.a. To meet this, Salisbury put forward his most ambitious scheme, the 'Great Contract'. He proposed that the Crown should give up its feudal revenue from purveyance and wardship and certain similar rights, in return for an income of £200,000 p.a. from Parliament. After much hesitation and argument, Parliament agreed. As James had actually received very little of the money paid for purveyance and wardship, this sum would have been almost all clear profit for the Crown. At the last moment, James hung back and asked for £300,000 p.a. Parliament refused. The King's greed thus ruined the Crown's best chance for fifty years to get a regular income from Parliament.

Salisbury's last scheme was more successful. In 1611 he introduced baronetcies – hereditary knighthoods – which the King bestowed on gentlemen prepared to pay for the maintenance of thirty soldiers in Ireland for three years. Each baronet had to pay over £1000 altogether. Within three years the system raised about £90,000 towards the cost of the Irish army.

Even so, the debt was mounting again by Salisbury's death in 1612, for the Government had to borrow £100,000 from London in 1610 and collected another forced loan, of £116,000, in the following two years. Bacon's patronizing remark to James was appropriate: Salisbury was 'no fit counsellor to make your affairs better; but yet he was fit to have kept them from growing worse'. It was unfortunate that Salisbury had

concentrated on raising the Crown's income without trying to cut
expenditure.   His own ambitions were partly to blame for this.
He regarded himself as an honest administrator, by the
standards of his day, but his own total profits as a Minister
were in the region of £100,000 – mainly from money which,
directly or indirectly, should have enriched the Crown.   For
example, he leased from the Crown the farm of the customs on
imported silks for nearly £8900 p.a., but then sub-let the farm
to contractors at a profit to himself of £7000 p.a. by 1612.
When the Treasurer's new Book of Rates increased the customs
duties on silk, it was not James who benefited but Salisbury.
During his sixteen years of holding important office, Salisbury
made enough to provide for the support of one of the country's
greatest families – yet he boasted that honesty 'had ever been
the greatest study of my life'.   A Treasurer's conscience was
elastic indeed.

Suffolk, who succeeded him, was far worse.   There was now
no check on the extravagance of Carr and the rest of the
Howard gang, who were as incompetent as they were wasteful.
Expenditure on the household mounted rapidly.   The production of elaborate masques, in which the talents of Ben
Jonson and Inigo Jones were combined to stage spectacular and
expensive entertainments at Christmas and for weddings such
as that between Somerset and Lady Essex, gifts such as the
£10,000 worth of jewels given by James to Lady Essex, the
funerals of Prince Henry in 1612 and of the Queen in 1614,
the marriage of Princess Elizabeth in 1613, all contributed to
the swift deterioration of the Crown's position.   The household
consumed enormous amounts of food – every year over 2000
cattle, 13,000 sheep and 200,000 hens, as well as scores of cart-
loads of grain.   Lavish expenditure on gorgeous clothes put the
King heavily in debt to his tailors – in 1614 he owed £85,000
for 'Wardrobe and Robes' alone.

By 1614 the debt was again approaching £700,000, and the
King was finding it more and more difficult to borrow money.
The City of London refused a request for another large loan,
thinking it would be less costly to *give* him £10,000 than to
*lend* him £100,000.   James therefore had to call Parliament.
The Commons were truculent, and refused to vote any money
until their grievances had been considered.   After only two
months James dissolved the 'Addled' Parliament – so called

because it produced nothing.    Unable to get loans or subsidies, James was forced back on his own resources.

The King therefore committed himself to a rash act which did more than anything else to turn the commercial classes against him.    Alderman Cockayne of London had earlier pointed out to him that the cloth merchants of the Netherlands made at least £700,000 p.a. out of 'finishing' (bleaching and dyeing) English cloth and then exporting it to the Baltic.    Cockayne promised that if James forbade the export of unfinished cloth and gave his Company a monopoly of finishing and exporting all English cloth, the country would benefit enormously.    He agreed to pay the King £300,000 p.a. out of the profits of this monopoly.    An income of this size would have solved James's problems (at least, until the courtiers persuaded him to share it with them).    Dazzled by this tempting project, James did as Cockayne wished.

Unfortunately for James, the scheme failed.    The quality of the English-finished cloth was poor, and there was no market for it at the fairs of the Low Countries, as the Dutch banned its import.    Within two years England's cloth exports fell by more than a half, and in 1617 James had to abandon the project.    By this time the Netherlands had found new sources of unfinished cloth, and it took a generation for English merchants to recapture their old market.    Moreover, Cockayne's project had infringed the monopoly of cloth exporting which Elizabeth had sold to the Merchant Adventurers, and this great Company never recovered from its disruption through the Cockayne catastrophe.[1]    The wool and cloth industries – at the peak of their prosperity in 1613 – collapsed in a slump from which they did not recover until after the Restoration. Wages were cut, Cotswold weavers rioted and 500 clothiers were bankrupted.    As most of the spinning and weaving was still done in the homes of country people, the effects of Cockayne's gamble were felt throughout England.    The government became even more unpopular.

The administration was totally discredited.    One by one Carr and the Howards fell from office for corruption, treachery or incompetence.    Their collapse culminated in 1618 when Suffolk was dismissed.    So desperate was James for money

[1] Although James graciously allowed the Merchant Adventurers to buy back their monopoly for over £60,000.

that in the previous year he had let Raleigh out of the Tower to go to the Orinoco to search for gold. So weak was he when Raleigh returned empty-handed that he had to sacrifice the old courtier to appease Gondomar and try to cadge money from Spain.

But the Crown's economic position soon began to improve, with the rise of Lionel Cranfield in the administration. After various successful commercial ventures in northern Europe, Cranfield had invested in some of the companies which farmed the customs, and had speculated in purchases of Crown lands. In 1613 James appointed him Surveyor-General of the Customs. Within two years he had increased the yield of the customs by £33,000 p.a., and James gradually entrusted him with more responsibility. Soon Cranfield started on the unpopular work Salisbury had shirked – the reduction of expenditure. He saved £22,000 p.a. on Household expenditure by reducing corruption (mainly large-scale pilfering by high officials of State of what was bought for the Crown's use). Then, in 1618, he was appointed Master of the Great Wardrobe. Here the Crown had been spending over £40,000 a year; Cranfield undertook to manage it for £20,000 a year, provided that he could keep all the money he saved below that figure. By running the Wardrobe for £13,000 a year, he made an annual £7000 for himself. Also in 1618, he helped to expose Suffolk's corruption and inefficiency, and was the key member of the commission appointed to run the Treasury after Suffolk's fall. Reform of the Office of Ordnance [artillery] saved £20,000 a year; despite improvements in the fleet, annual expenditure on the Navy was cut by £25,000; and greater administrative efficiency in the Court of Wards increased its revenue by £8000 a year.

By 1621, Cranfield's reforms were worth over £120,000 a year to the Crown. Emboldened by the improvement in his position, and anxious to help his daughter and her husband to reconquer their territory from the Catholic princes in Germany, James summoned his third Parliament. This was a mistake. The merchants were still bitter about Cockayne's project, and the Puritans were critical about the spread of Catholicism at Court. The M.P.s joined eagerly in the impeachment of Lord Chancellor Bacon and the monopolist Mompesson. For a while, Cranfield's economic knowledge and political skill secured him attentive audiences in the Commons; then, in a foolish moment, James promoted him to the Lords as Baron Cranfield, and so lost his ablest servant in the Lower House.    Soon, James had to dissolve Parliament without getting the subsidies he wanted.    Still anxious to get money and to help the Elector Palatine, the King appealed in 1622 for a 'Benevolence' or gift from both clergy and laity.    His subjects gave him only £88,000 of the £200,000 James expected.

Without either money or a personal desire for war, James now tried to get the Palatinate restored to the Elector by arranging the often-proposed marriage alliance with Spain.    The Infanta, he hoped, would bring as her dowry £500,000 and the Palatinate, which James could then restore to the Elector as part of a general settlement of the German war.    But this was not to be.    When Buckingham and Charles returned empty-handed to England, they were determined to wage war on Spain; Buckingham, also, was determined to ruin Cranfield. The Treasurer had already persuaded James to announce that he would give no more pensions or gifts without Cranfield's approval – a grim prospect for ambitious courtiers.    More-over, he had made use of Buckingham's absence to try to persuade James to cut the pensions already granted (totalling some £74,000 a year), and – so Buckingham asserted – had not supplied enough money for the expenses of the visit to Spain.    When James's last Parliament assembled, in March 1624, Buckingham at once arranged the impeachment[1] of the Treasurer, now Earl of Middlesex.    So great was the favourite's hold over Parliament that nobles bluntly rejected James's appeals to them to support Middlesex, for their fear of 'the frowns of the Prince and the Duke'.    The merchants in the Commons, still angry about 'impositions'[2] and worried about a new Book of Rates which the Treasurer had prepared but not yet published, joined eagerly in the attack.    With Buckingham and Prince Charles directing the prosecution, the Lords found the Treasurer guilty.    For 'bribery, extortions, oppressions and other grievous misdemeanours committed by His Lordship',

[1] See footnote, p. 27.

[2] The Crown's income from customs and new impositions at the end of the reign was roughly two and a half times what it had been at the beginning.    Customs now eclipsed Crown rents as the major source of income.

Middlesex was sentenced to imprisonment in the Tower and a fine of £50,000. The King's favourite and the King's heir had succeeded in ruining the King's most competent, efficient and loyal minister, charged with the offences he had struggled most to suppress.

After this victory, and in a burst of Protestant zeal, Parliament now voted three subsidies and three-fifteenths (together worth about £300,000). To make sure that the money was spent on fighting Spain, the Commons insisted that it should be handed over to treasurers appointed by Parliament, and that it should be paid out only on the orders of the Council of War, also responsible to Parliament. This was Parliament's first attempt to establish the principle of 'appropriation of supply' – that money should be spent only on the purposes for which it had been specifically voted. It was also an attempt to increase Parliament's influence over the administration. The parliamentary grant soon proved insufficient, for the cost of help for the Elector Palatine soon absorbed all Cranfield's economies. In 1624 the debt once again mounted to a million pounds. The impeachment of Middlesex, and the entry into the Thirty Years War – both of which James had resisted – were the culminating follies of the reign, and hastened the rapid slide to disaster under Charles.

Buckingham now hurriedly tried to prepare for the war against Spain by finding continental allies and by raising an army. The army was an ill-equipped collection of ruffians commanded by Mansfeld, the most frequently defeated general of his time; it got no further than Flushing, where most of the men died of starvation and plague. Alliances were made with Denmark and the United Provinces, at the cost of paying each country for the upkeep of several thousand troops. Altogether, Buckingham rushed into war preparations that would have raised the Crown's annual expenditure to over a million pounds. It was quite beyond the resources of James or Charles to collect such a sum. Charles, indeed, received a new blow from his first Parliament: the Commons were so anxious to keep the question of impositions open for discussion that they voted tunnage and poundage for only one year, and not, as was traditional, for the whole reign.[1] Their grant of £140,000

---

[1] The Lords refused to pass the Bill in this unusual form, and so the grant of tunnage and poundage was not voted at all.

towards the cost of the war was almost an insult. Charles's
second Parliament, in 1626, was even more aggressive. It
stood defiantly on the principle of redress before supply:
Charles was offered four subsidies only if he would accept the
impeachment of Buckingham. The King once more dissolved
Parliament.

By now the situation was desperate. The royal jewels were
pawned in Amsterdam for £58,000. Only with great difficulty
could Charles borrow £60,000 in 1625 and £20,000 in 1626
from the City of London. At the beginning of July 1626 the
King ordered the Justices of the Peace to collect as a 'free gift'
the four subsidies proposed earlier in the year. At the end of
the same month he ordered the Treasury to continue to collect
tunnage and poundage, imprisoning those who refused to pay.
The 'free gift' having failed, Charles in September ordered the
subsidies to be collected as a loan. The Government collected
this forced loan with an unaccustomed ruthless determination.
Chief Justice Crew was dismissed for refusing to declare it legal,
rich men who refused to pay were put in prison, and poor men
who refused were conscripted into the army under martial
law or had troops billeted upon them. By these means the
Crown extracted about £236,000 – a large amount by earlier
standards, but quite inadequate for the needs of the time.

With the outcry against the forced loan and Buckingham's
incompetence reaching its climax, Charles had to call his third
Parliament, in March 1628. In June Parliament forced him to
accept the Petition of Right in exchange for five subsidies; it
would also have granted him tunnage and poundage for life,
had he been prepared to abandon Buckingham. Loyalty to his
evil genius made Charles prorogue Parliament again, but the
urgent need for money obliged him to continue tunnage and
poundage. When Parliament met again in January 1629, the
members were incensed at this, for they considered it a violation
of the spirit of the Petition of Right. In the Three Resolutions,
the Commons denounced as traitors those who voluntarily paid
tunnage and poundage, or advised the King to collect these
impositions, when they had not been voted by Parliament.

The position of the King could hardly have been worse. The
expected revenue was already pledged for a year and a half in
advance. The slump in trade resulting from the Cockayne
project and the Spanish and French wars had reduced the

income from customs – which many men were now refusing to pay. The revenue from Crown lands was falling as the King was again having to sell property to get ready money. In the 'Ditchfield Grant' of 1627–8, Charles had had to give the City of London £350,000 worth of Crown property to settle two earlier debts[1] before he could borrow another £120,000. Already Stuart England had gone far along the road towards civil war. The price-rise, the increased cost of government, and royal extravagance had forced the Crown to sell its capital, to make political concessions to Parliament, and to raise money by means which were offensive to the politically-active classes in the country. The economic weakness of the Crown drove Charles in 1629 to try to rule without Parliament.

### iii. The Church and its critics

Many of the weaknesses of the Church were economic in origin, stemming from its poverty and its shameless exploitation by Elizabeth, her courtiers and other lay patrons. On the one hand, the deficiencies of the Church helped make the early Stuarts more vulnerable to their critics. On the other, the attempts made by the bishops to increase the Church's power and wealth did much to provoke the political opposition to James and Charles.

As James journeyed south in the spring of 1603, a large number of Puritan-minded ministers – all of them Church of England clergy – prepared a petition to present to the new king. The Millenary Petition (so called because allegedly a thousand clergy had signed it) was moderate in tone, but nonetheless attacked many Anglican practices and challenged the Church's organization. First, the petitioners demanded that certain ceremonies surviving from pre-Reformation days should be abolished: the sign of the Cross should not be made during the service of baptism, nor the ring used in the marriage service as a symbol of union; the service of confirmation should be abolished; popish words like 'priest' and 'absolution' should be removed from the Prayer Book; the services should be shortened to allow more time for sermons, and the Sabbath Day should be kept holy. The petitioners asked that only competent preachers should be admitted to the ministry, and that others should be

---

[1] The transfer was also in part a security for the new loan.

removed, or forced to pay to maintain preachers in their
parishes.   They then demanded the abolition of pluralism and
non-residence,[1] and asked that men should not be excommunicated for trivial offences.   The Petition, despite the careful
moderation of the requests, was in fact a challenge to the
spiritual, disciplinary and economic power of the bishops.
Indirectly, it was a threat to the very existence of the bishops,
for a competent clergy could not be secured without enriching
the parish churches with money taken from bishops and
cathedrals.

As he inspected the Petition, James sensed a chance to
display his theological knowledge, and promised to preside
over a conference summoned to discuss the demands.   The
conference met at Hampton Court in January 1604.   The aged
Archbishop Whitgift and Bishop Bancroft of London led the
Church party.   The Puritans were represented by four
university dons, led by Dr. Reynolds of Oxford and Dr.
Chadderton of Cambridge.   At first, the conference proceeded
in a friendly manner, though James would accept only one of
the Puritan demands.   This was for the preparation of a
standard translation of the Bible, to be used throughout the
country: the result, the Authorized Version of 1611, was to be
the only positive achievement of the conference.

The tone of the assembly changed dramatically, however,
when Dr. Reynolds tactlessly suggested that Church discipline
should be administered by 'the bishop with his presbytery'.
Now James showed a characteristic weakness of temper.   The
hated word 'presbytery' reminded him of the humiliations
he had suffered at the hands of Melville and Buchanan in
Scotland, and he burst out vehemently in a paroxysm of
indignation.

His majesty was somewhat stirred . . . thinking that they aimed
at a Scottish presbytery, which, saith he, as well agreeth with a
monarchy as God and the Devil.   Then Jack and Tom and
Will and Dick shall meet, and at their pleasures censure me and
my Council and all our proceedings. . . .   Stay, I pray you, for
one seven years before you demand that of me, and if then you

---

[1] Where one man was allowed to receive the revenues from several livings,
paying poor curates miserable stipends to take the services in the parishes in which
he did not reside.

find me pursy and fat and my wind-pipes stuffed, I will perhaps hearken to you. . . .[1]

When the conference next met, James 'shut up all' with a speech defending the powers of the Court of High Commission, and – too late – 'a most pithy exhortation to both sides for unity'. The conference collapsed. The failure of the Puritans was hailed as a triumph for the bishops. The dying Whitgift proclaimed that James had spoken 'by the special assistance of God's Spirit'. Bancroft affirmed that his heart melted within him with joy, and James gloated that he had peppered the Puritans soundly. The King had stated his belief in the inter-dependence of Church and State, episcopacy and monarchy, summed up in the aphorism 'No Bishop, no King'. Whitgift's work in silencing the critics of the Church was fully vindicated. Now it was time for the Church to take the offensive. When Whitgift died in March 1604, his energetic colleague Bancroft succeeded him as Archbishop of Canterbury. Under Bancroft, Convocation[2] issued a set of 141 Canons (religious laws) to strengthen the disciplinary powers of the bishops. In July 1604 James ordered the clergy to accept the Canons; five months later, the Council and Bancroft ordered the bishops to expel from their parishes all those who would not conform. Over 300 clergy refused to submit, and were driven out. For the most part, these were men of high principles – men the Church could ill afford to lose. More serious, though, was the fact that the Canons weakened the Church by driving this large number of Puritan preachers into open opposition. The revival of Puritanism as an independent force dates from 1604. Moreover, for many years, the Puritans in Parliament re-peatedly protested about the sufferings of the 300 'silenced brethren'.

The Church received more support from James and Charles than any of the Tudors had given it. In 1604, to try to stop the economic exploitation of the Church, James persuaded Parliament to pass a Bill forbidding the bishops to grant away any of their lands, even to the Crown. This unselfish act made it impossible for him to reward his favourites – as Elizabeth

---

[1] From the report on the session prepared for Archbishop Whitgift, who was too ill to attend. In Tanner, *Constitutional Documents*, p. 67.

[2] The representative assembly of the clergy of each archbishopric.

had done – by forcing bishops to grant them Church property or tithes. As the Church was notoriously weak in the north, James re-founded the Deanery of Ripon, endowing it with Crown lands worth £100 a year to try to strengthen it. Such was the King's determination to protect the Church that Buckingham had to proceed very cautiously before persuading the Archbishop of York to exchange his London house for some of Buckingham's property in Yorkshire. The King was so determined to keep his royal prerogative of allowing clergymen to hold parishes 'in plurality' that he dismissed Chief Justice Coke in 1616 for his attitude in the case of *Commendams*.[1] As a direct challenge to Puritans anxious to 'keep Holy the Sabbath Day', James issued in 1618 a *Declaration of Sports* listing the games and amusements which were lawful on Sundays after morning service: archery and maypole-dancing were permitted, but bear- and bull-baiting remained banned. The *Declaration of Sports* immediately aroused the violent hostility of men convinced that Sundays should be devoted to Divine worship and Bible study, and of those who were coming to regard all pleasure as sinful.

It was unfortunate that James's support for the Church was balanced by Parliament's advocacy of Puritanism. His first Parliament warned him in 1604 that he had no power over the Church except what Parliament had given him, and in 1610 it presented him with a lengthy petition on behalf of the ministers expelled by Bancroft's Canons. The next Parliament, in 1614, insisted on receiving Holy Communion in St. Margaret's, Westminster, to avoid the 'copes and wafer-cakes' of the High Church service in Westminster Abbey. The 1621 Parliament, shocked at the blasphemy, expelled the M.P. who tried to excuse dancing by pointing out that King David had danced before the Ark of the Covenant. In the 1624 Parliament, as on four previous occasions in the reign, the Commons passed a Bill calling for the ending of pluralism; like the earlier Bills, it was defeated through the opposition of the bishops in the House of Lords.

Twenty years were to pass after James's death before Parliament was able to do away with the bishops and seize their estates, but the attack on the episcopacy was well advanced by

---

[1] Licences to hold simultaneously more than one living were known as licences to hold *in commendam*.

1625. Even in Elizabeth's reign, Puritans had tried to enlist the help of royal favourites to attack the bishops; in 1593 John Penry, one of the most eminent Puritans of his day, wrote to the Earl of Essex, promising him the plunder of the bishops' wealth if he would help to abolish episcopacy. In 1624 Dr. John Preston, equally eminent, discussed a similar proposal with Buckingham, through whose favour he had obtained a Cambridge lectureship. But not even Buckingham could risk trying to turn James or Charles against the bishops.

Bancroft's six years as Archbishop of Canterbury saw a rapid rise in the Arminian[1] movement. Its leader, Lancelot Andrewes, a famous preacher in Elizabeth's reign, had twice refused bishoprics because he would not agree to share their revenues with the Queen or her courtiers. Under James he became Bishop of Chichester in 1605, and Bishop of Ely (where he was responsible for Cambridge University) in 1609. Many of the Arminian beliefs and practices were loathsome to the Puritans; for example, Andrewes believed that Christ was truly presented in the consecrated bread and wine in the Communion Service, and in his own chapel he used incense and placed candles on the altar. By Bancroft's death in 1610, Andrewes had become almost an official spokesman for the Church, and he was widely expected to be the next Archbishop of Canterbury. James, however, in a vain attempt to conciliate the Puritans, appointed as archbishop a man who was a known opponent of Arminian ideas—George Abbot, recently promoted from Lichfield to London.

Abbot was an unfortunate choice. His position as archbishop made him distrusted by the Puritan extremists, while his resistance to High Church beliefs made him disliked by most of the other bishops. He gained a brief popularity with the Church by opposing Lady Essex's divorce in 1613, but his position was undermined in 1622 when he accidentally killed a gamekeeper. The commission of enquiry appointed to decide whether he was a 'man of blood' (and therefore unfit to hold ecclesiastical office) was evenly divided, but James and

[1] Named after Jacob Hermans or Arminius, a Dutch professor who attacked the Calvinists' belief in Predestination. In England, the name 'Arminian' was given to any opponent of the Calvinists or Puritans. The English Arminians were concerned less with Predestination and Free Will than with the restoration of dignity and ceremony to public worship and with raising the status of the Church and clergy in English society.

Charles kept him as archbishop until his death in 1633. At no time had Abbot been a strong character; isolated by his position and Puritan sympathies, and disturbed in his conscience by the shooting accident, Abbot could not give the Church a strong lead, or unite the Arminian and Puritan factions which were fast drifting apart.

The discord in the Church was demonstrated by the case of Dr. Montagu. As a contribution to the pamphlet war between Anglicans and Roman Catholics, Dr. Montagu wrote in 1624 a book entitled *A new Gag for an old Goose*, attacking the Catholic allegation that the Church of England was Calvinist.[1] In his book, Montagu expressed Arminian views which some M.P.s regarded as popery. The Commons in 1625 referred the matter to Archbishop Abbot, who told Montagu to revise the book. Instead, the unrepentant author produced *Appello Caesarem*, expressing the same opinions in a more extreme way. The Commons ordered him to appear before the Bar of the House. To protect him, Charles appointed Montagu a royal chaplain, and made the Commons release him on bail. There the matter rested until Charles's second Parliament met in 1626. Then, the Commons started to impeach him for disturbing the peace of the Church and drawing the people towards popery. The storm over Buckingham and the dissolution of the Parliament prevented Montagu's trial. In 1628, however, with a fine disregard for public opinion, Charles tactlessly appointed him Bishop of Chichester. With the Puritans thus needlessly infuriated, it was hardly surprising that Charles's third Parliament turned viciously against the Arminians. A sub-committee in February 1629 protested;

That these persons who have published and maintained such Papistical, Arminian, and superstitious opinions and practices, who are known to be unsound in religion, are countenanced, favoured, and preferred: instance, Mr. Montague made Bishop of Chichester; also the late Bishop of Carlisle, since his last Arminian sermon preached at Court, advanced to the bishopric of Norwich; a known Arminian made Bishop of Ely; the Bishop of Oxford, a long suspected Papist, advanced to the bishopric of Durham; Mr. Cosin, advanced to dignity and a great living....[2]

[1] i.e., followed Calvin in teaching that every man was from the moment of his birth predestined to either salvation or eternal damnation, and that nothing he did could alter the ultimate destination of his soul.

[2] In Gardiner, *Constitutional Documents*, p. 81.

The committee demanded that the works of Montagu and Cosin
should be burned, and exemplary punishments inflicted upon
teachers and publishers of popish opinions and on those who
practised superstitious ceremonies.    Charles naturally refused
to satisfy the Puritan choir in the Commons.    Then, with the
Speaker prevented by brute force from ending the debate, the
Three Resolutions of March 1629 coupled with the condem-
nation of tunnage and poundage the demand that: 'Whosoever shall bring in innovation of religion . . . shall be
reputed a capital enemy to this kingdom and commonwealth.'
    The violent prejudices of many members of Parliament
resulted principally from their fear of popery.    For more than
forty years before the Stuarts came to England, the Reformation
had been on the defensive.    In the second half of the sixteenth
century, the forces of the Counter-Reformation, led by Spain,
had reconverted Poland and much of Germany, France and the
Netherlands to Catholicism.    The papal Bull of 1570 had made
it a moral duty for Catholics to rebel against Elizabeth.    With
every fresh manifestation of Catholicism at Court, with every
case of leniency in enforcing the penal laws against the Catholics,
with every swing of foreign policy towards Spain, the M.P.s
felt themselves nearer and nearer to the dungeons of the
Spanish Inquisition.    It was unfortunate that individual
Catholics, by foolish acts, fanned the flames of English prejudice.
    James was genuinely tolerant, and had no wish to persecute
Catholics – or Puritans – provided there was no threat to his
political authority.    In this he was far in advance of most of his
contemporaries, who saw Church and State wedded in an
indissoluble unity and could not see how more than one Church
could be tolerated in a country without the State committing
a sort of spiritual polygamy.    Indeed, so far was James from
wishing to persecute the Catholics in 1604 that he told his first
Parliament 'I acknowledge the Roman church to be our mother
church'.    But there were very few sympathetic listeners for
James: already there had been two Catholic plots against him.
The Bye Plot (to kidnap him) had been concocted by a few
secular priests; it was revealed to the Government by the
Jesuits, jealous rivals of the seculars.    The more dangerous
Main Plot had hoped to replace James as sovereign by Lady
Arabella Stuart; Lord Cobham turned King's Evidence, and

denounced his fellow conspirators, most of whom were executed.

These plots gave Parliament the excuse to re-enact the Elizabethan penal laws, which made it high treason to practise the Catholic faith. Jesuits and secular priests in England, Englishmen who remained in foreign seminaries, those who converted men to Catholicism, and those who were so converted, were all branded as traitors. Heavy punishments awaited those who attended Mass, or stayed away from the Anglican services. The frustration of the Catholics led a handful of them to devise the Gunpowder Plot. Thirty-six barrels of gunpowder were to be exploded by Guy Fawkes when James came to Westminster to open the second session of his first Parliament, on November 5th, 1605. The slaughter of King, Lords and Commons was to be followed by a Catholic rising. But a Catholic peer betrayed the plot to the government, the gunpowder was found in the cellars beneath the Houses of Parliament, and the leading conspirators suffered the barbarous penalties for treason.

Immediately, the laws against the Catholics were made even more severe, with the penal legislation of 1606 'for the better discovering and repressing of popish recusants'. The Act required that Catholics who wanted to avoid the recusancy fines should not merely attend Anglican services, but must receive there 'the blessed Sacrament of the Lord's Supper'. It also demanded from suspected persons an oath of allegiance, renouncing the Pope's supremacy in secular matters, and expressly denying that the Pope had authority to depose a heretical ruler. Another Act, also in 1606, forbade recusants to live in London, and ordered them to remain within five miles of their permanent residence.

These laws imposed on the Catholics a burden which would have been intolerable if they had been strictly enforced. At most times, however, the penal laws were not imposed rigidly. Occasionally, to placate the fury of aggressively Protestant Parliaments, James would issue proclamations ordering the strict application of the laws; sometimes, as a gesture to gain the favour of the mob, the King would order the execution of a priest held in prison under sentence of death. The number of those imprisoned, but not executed, was high: over 4000 Catholics (a tenth of them priests) were released from prison in 1622, in James's attempt to please Spain and speed the Infanta's marriage to Charles. Only thirty or so Catholics were executed during James's reign, and in all cases the judges were careful to explain that the sentences were imposed for treason, not for the victim's beliefs.

Probably all those executed (except the plotters) could have saved their lives by taking the oath prescribed by the 1606 Act. After the Archpriest Blackwell saved himself by swearing the oath, Pope Paul V forbade Catholics to take it. James in 1607 published anonymously *An Apology for the Oath of Allegiance*, in which he argued that the oath was merely secular, and designed only to distinguish between loyal and disloyal subjects. This was answered by the great Cardinal Bellarmine, who claimed that, as the supremacy of the Pope was a matter of faith for Catholics, the oath of allegiance did in fact require them to deny their faith. James was now out of his depth, and had to leave it to Lancelot Andrewes to compose the official reply. In it, Andrewes launched a vigorous attack on the Pope's claims to secular power. Both Bellarmine and Andrewes wrote further treatises against each other, and the controversy rapidly involved theologians in most continental countries. Casaubon, an eminent French scholar, joined Andrewes's side in the argument, and was rewarded by James with a pension of £300 a year. This controversy did much to rally continental Protestants whose faiths had been weakening under the attacks of the theologians of the Counter-Reformation. 'Probably Andrewes and Casaubon contributed at least as much to the defeat of the Counter Reformation as Gustavus Adolphus.'[1]

But most Englishmen were not interested in the niceties of theological debate. To them, James was weak and inconsistent in applying the penal laws against the Catholics; they suspected, rightly, that James would promise to suspend or repeal them if it would help to marry Charles to a Catholic princess. Such a bargain was, in fact, part of the treaty by which Charles married the French princess Henrietta Maria. Soon, the Queen's household became an offensive centre of Catholicism. On one occasion the Queen and her courtiers amused themselves by running through the Chapel Royal, shouting hunting cries, while an Anglican service was in progress. Eventually, Charles had to expel the Queen's attendants, and was quite unable to keep his promise to repeal

[1] G. Davies, *The Early Stuarts*, p. 207.

the penal laws. These breaches of the marriage treaty helped
to lead England into war with France in 1627, but they gained
Charles no credit from Parliament. Memories of Parliament's
narrow escape from the Gunpowder Plot continued to embitter
the M.P.s' views of Catholicism. Not until the nineteenth
century did November 5th cease to be a public holiday; not
until the late nineteenth century were the anti-Catholic laws
completely removed.

### iv. Parliament and the royal prerogative

Parliament was the arena in which most of the struggles
between the early Stuarts and their subjects were fought out.
Financial difficulties exposed the Crown to the attacks of M.P.s
demanding 'redress before supply'. The Commons' Puritan
prejudices made their attacks more violent. Occasionally,
grievances such as monopolies or unsatisfactory foreign policies
added fuel to the fires of criticism. Their determination to
speak their minds freely, and to oppose the Crown whenever
they wished, made the Commons very jealous of what they
considered their privileges, and very resolute in resisting the
royal prerogative when it seemed to challenge their liberties.
The legal training received by many M.P.s gave them skill in
debate and a meticulous concern for what they regarded as the
'Fundamental law' of the constitution. On the other hand,
James's belief in Divine Right made him anxious to assert that,
in theory at least, Parliament enjoyed its privileges by royal
goodwill, and not by law or 'right'. For James, the principle
was more important than the practice; Charles, however, was
rather more prepared to try to drive the theories towards their
logical conclusion – the destruction of parliamentary authority.

It was not surprising that those who wrote in support of the
Crown's prerogative aroused Parliament's anger. The Commons ordered Cowell's *Interpreter* (1607) to be burned by the
public hangman, for in it Dr. Cowell, the Professor of Civil
Law at Cambridge, asserted that the King 'was above the law
by his absolute power'. Twenty years later, the Arminian
clergymen Dr. Manwaring and Dr. Sibthorpe were similarly
attacked by the Commons for claiming that Divine Right gave
Charles an absolute prerogative power.

The conflict between royal prerogative and parliamentary

privilege led eventually to the breach between Crown and Parliament in 1629, and to the Civil War, for it was at the very heart of the constitutional struggles in early Stuart England. In fact, tradition and the letter of the law were both on the side of the Crown on almost all issues. The lawyers and other parliamentarians had to search diligently among the dusty parchment records of mediaeval Parliaments and lawsuits to find the precedents they needed to excuse or justify their opposition to the King. Sir Edward Coke, for example, emphasized the importance of the almost-forgotten Magna Carta,[1] and declared that – among other things – it forbade the King to grant monopolies. But while Coke and the others, Hakewill, Eliot, Prynne and Digges, may have been poor historians and indifferent lawyers, they had an acute sense of the realities of seventeenth-century politics. Their principles were often contrary to the traditions and customs of the fifteenth and sixteenth centuries, but they were at least principles which a politically aggressive class could put into practice.

From the opening days of his first Parliament, meeting in March 1604, James quarrelled with the M.P.s over privilege and prerogative. In the writs issued to order the recent Election, James had commanded that 'bankrupts and outlaws' should not be elected, and that the Court of Chancery should judge the validity of the elections. The voters of Buckinghamshire obstinately chose an outlaw, Sir Francis Goodwin. The Court of Chancery declared the election null and void, and in a second election Sir John Fortescue was chosen. For three weeks the Commons argued the matter, claiming that they, and not the King's courts, should decide disputed elections. As one member put it, 'The case of Sir John Fortescue and Sir Francis Goodwin was become the case of the whole kingdom.' Then James gave way. He agreed that Parliament, as well as Chancery, was competent to judge election returns. No subsequent sovereign ever challenged Parliament's sole right to decide whether candidates had been lawfully elected.

In Shirley's Case, James held out longer. After the election, but before taking his seat, Sir Thomas Shirley had been imprisoned for debt on the plea of a London alderman. The Commons regarded this imprisonment as a breach of privilege.

[1] Shakespeare's play *King John* (*c.* 1597) contains no reference to Magna Carta.

After two months of angry quarrelling, James gave way and ordered Shirley's release.  Both these cases weakened the royal prerogative.  James's concessions virtually acknowledged that the Crown should not interfere with Parliament by annulling the election of unwelcome members, or by intimidating them with threats of imprisonment.  But the Commons were not content with these victories, for in June 1604 they presented the King with a document courteously entitled *A Form of Apology and Satisfaction*.  Suggesting that James had been misled by his advisers, the *Apology* claimed


First, That our privileges and liberties are our right and due inheritance, no less than our very lands and goods.

Secondly, That they cannot be withheld from us, denied, or impaired, but with apparent [obvious] wrong to the whole state of the realm.

Thirdly, And that our making of request in the entrance of Parliament to enjoy our privilege is an act only of manners. . . .


The Commons could hardly have stated more clearly their determination to resist any interference from James, and to assert their unalterable right to the privileges they were able to secure.

Soon the Commons found a way to prevent another method of Crown interference with their debates.   It was always possible for the Speaker, still under the King's control, to suspend debates or terminate sessions on the government's orders when criticism grew too heated.   On the other hand, the Speaker did not take the chair at committee meetings.  The Commons therefore devised the Committee of the Whole House – when the members wished to discuss complaints, the Commons would vote to go into committee, and would appoint one of the government's critics as chairman.  Especially as there were so few Privy Councillors in the House, the Crown could do little except wait for the petitions of grievances which the Committees of the Whole House frequently prepared.  These Committees appeared first about 1607.  Their importance quickly grew, in the session of 1610, when James was bombarded with petitions of grievances, usually prepared in the Committee and then sent to the King with the authority of the Commons behind them.

The petitions of 1610 ranged over a wide field. A petition on Religion complained of the lax enforcement of the anti-Catholic laws, the extent of pluralism and non-residence in the Church, the abuse of powers of excommunication, and the harsh treatment of the 'deprived and silenced ministers' expelled by Bancroft in 1604. A petition of Right asserted the Commons' demand for freedom of debate. A petition of Grievances criticized new customs impositions, the Court of High Commission, the use of Proclamations to alter or amend the law, and the subjection of four English Border counties to the authority of the prerogative Council of Wales. By this time James was left without a competent spokesman in the Commons; as soon as the Great Contract[1] proposals fizzled out, James therefore dissolved his first Parliament in February 1611.

When the Crown's poverty made another Parliament unavoidable, James in 1614 tried to obtain a more submissive House of Commons by influencing the elections. He persuaded persons of importance in their own areas to 'undertake' to secure the return of members favourable to the King. But the plan leaked out, and the candidates of the 'undertakers' were rejected in the election. The members of James's second Parliament, therefore, were prejudiced from the start against the King, because of his tampering with the freedom of the Commons. Most of the members of the 'Addled' Parliament were young and inexperienced, and it was easy for old hands like Hakewill to play upon the quick tempers of the new men to turn them against the Crown. With the Commons determined to secure the redress of grievances such as impositions before voting taxes, the life of this troublesome Parliament was bound to be short: James dissolved it in June 1614, after only two months. He did at least learn one lesson from it – neither in 1621 nor 1624 did he try to interfere with the elections.

The short and unproductive career of the 'Addled' Parliament forced James to gamble on the success of the greatest monopoly of them all – Alderman Cockayne's project. The failure of this scheme, and the consequent collapse of trade, made James summon another Parliament. When his third Parliament assembled, in January 1621, the King had to face a violent attack protesting at the 'decay of trade' and the widespread abuse of monopolies. Sir Edward Coke, whom James had

1 See above, p. 32.

dismissed from the post of Lord Chief Justice in 1616, was present to lead the opposition, effectively supported by Hakewill and Sandys. In March the Commons expelled one of their own members, Sir Robert Floyd, who had the monopoly for recording wills. By doing this, the House established a precedent for punishing and expelling its own members: the authority of the Commons was still expanding. The time was not far away when the majority would act violently against the minority in the House.

The Commons were eager to punish also the many monopolists who were not members, and started to attack Mitchell and Mompesson, who had held a monopoly for licensing ale-houses. Mitchell was brought before the House and sentenced without a hearing – an unprecedented and unlawful procedure. Determined that there should be no question of the legality of the treatment of Mompesson, Parliament revived the old process of impeachment – which had not been used since 1459. The Lords found Mompesson guilty and sentenced him to a fine of £10,000. Then, anxious to make full use of the rediscovered weapon, Bacon's political rivals impeached him for corruption. The Lord Chancellor admitted his offence, cringingly begged for mercy, and was fined £40,000.

The religious prejudices of the Commons led them again, in May 1621, to try to establish the right to act by themselves as both prosecutor and judge, and a quarrel with the Lords almost resulted. A rash Catholic barrister, Edward Floyd, had spoken sarcastically about the Elector Palatine, the defeated champion of German Protestantism. The Commons angrily sentenced Floyd to six hours in the pillory and a fine of £1000, but the Lords protested at this attack on their own rights of jurisdiction. After a brief argument, the Commons gave way and agreed that Floyd should be tried again, by the Lords. This was unfortunate for Floyd: the Lords were anxious to prove that their zeal for Protestantism exceeded that of the Commons, and so sentenced the wretched man to a fine of £5000 and imprisonment for life. The incident did at least reveal the latent rivalry between the two Houses, a rivalry which politically-gifted kings might have exploited. It was one of the melancholy achievements of both James and Charles to turn the Lords against them almost as much as they antagonized the Commons.

Sympathy for the Elector Palatine and his wife, James's daughter Elizabeth, led also to the other great clash of 1621. During the King's absence from London, the Commons started to discuss foreign affairs, one of the matters on which James was particularly sensitive to criticism. James forbade them:

to argue and debate publicly of the matters far above their reach and capacity, tending to our high dishonour and breach of prerogative royal.

When the Commons sent delegates to him with a petition, he remarked sarcastically on the presumption of the delegates – 'Bring stools for the ambassadors!' After various declarations by both sides, the Commons prepared a *Protestation*, aggressively stating their right to discuss any matter they chose. Such defiance was intolerable. In a full meeting of the Privy Council, James sent for the Commons' *Journal*, and then, with what dignity he could achieve in his rage, he solemnly tore out the page on which the offending *Protestation* had been written. Nonetheless, the Commons had obtained what they wanted, for there were few subsequent attempts to restrict freedom of discussion in parliament.

James called his last Parliament in February 1624, in a much happier political atmosphere. The prospect of war against Spain temporarily united the factions; even Buckingham was popular, especially when he led the attack on the Treasurer, Lionel Cranfield, Earl of Middlesex. By now, James was too old and too dispirited to worry much about the concessions he made to Parliament. He could not prevent the impeachment of Middlesex, and had to see his best servant fined £50,000 and sent to the Tower. With the country hurrying into war, James could not resist when the Commons introduced the principle of 'appropriation of supply': they voted subsidies, and tried to ensure that the subsidies were spent only on the war.[1] Having fought for twenty years to keep his right to grant monopolies, James finally surrendered tamely. The Monopolies Act of 1624 in effect forbade the King to give monopolies to individuals unless they were the inventors or introducers of new processes, and placed the control of monopolies under the Common Law Courts. Charles was later able to find a loophole in the Act,

[1] See above, p. 37.

which for a while reduced its economic significance. It remained, however, of enormous constitutional significance: it was the first limitation of the Crown's prerogative by an Act of Parliament. It was the shape of things to come.

The Parliament summoned by Charles immediately after his accession met in a spirit very different from that of 1624. Already the failure of Mansfeld's expedition warned M.P.s that the subsidies they had voted the previous year had been wasted. For a century and a half every sovereign's first Parliament had voted him tunnage and poundage for life; Charles's first Parliament did not give it to him at all, for the Commons proposed to grant it for one year only (while they discussed the whole question of impositions) and the Lords refused to pass the Bill with this unprecedented limitation. Charles, however, regarded tunnage and poundage as the Crown's inalienable right, whether voted by Parliament or not, and he continued to collect it. This remained a principal grievance between Crown and Parliament until 1641. With this *impasse* over tunnage and poundage, and the Commons' refusal to grant more than two subsidies towards the cost of the war, Charles dissolved his first Parliament in August 1625, after only two months.

The Crown's financial distress made Charles call another Parliament six months later. This time Charles tried to prevent the election of his chief critics by 'pricking' them as sheriffs; as the sheriffs had to supervise the elections, they could not themselves stand as candidates. The Parliament opened with a storm of protest over the sheriffs, and against Buckingham, now universally blamed for the failure of the recent expedition to Cadiz. The westcountry ports were filled with starving and dying men, and Cornish M.P.s like Sir John Eliot (formerly one of Buckingham's followers) turned violently against the favourite. Eliot led the demand for the impeachment of Buckingham, in a struggle which raged through the spring of 1626. With a Parliament infuriated from the start by the clumsy attempt to influence the elections, Charles could hope for no subsidies unless he yielded up his favourite to the clamour of the mob. This he refused to do, and so dismissed Parliament in June 1626.

Charles now used all the force of the law and the prerogative to collect tunnage and poundage and a forced loan, to provide some of the money he desperately needed for the war. Those who refused to contribute to the loan were imprisoned, conscripted, or had soldiers billeted on them. Many protested, but the Trial of the Five Knights (Darnel's Case) vindicated the Crown's methods. The judges declared that the royal prerogative included the right in emergencies to imprison men without giving a reason, though they also admitted that this power could lead to a military absolutism.

A new Parliament was soon necessary, for the forced loan could not provide money sufficient for the war-chests of Denmark and the United Provinces as well as England. With trepidation Charles released from prison many of those detained for refusing the forced loan; of these, twenty-seven were elected to the Parliament which assembled in March 1628. The experience gained in previous Parliaments by fiery orators like Coke, Eliot, Hakewill, Wentworth and Pym, soon proved its value. The Commons wisely delayed attacking Buckingham directly (and thereby risking immediate dissolution) until they had forced Charles to accept some of their political demands. In a series of complaints the Commons criticized the misgovernment of recent years, in particular the arbitrary taxation and arbitrary imprisonment associated with the forced loan of 1626.

Following Coke's suggestion, the Commons joined with the Lords in the Petition of Right – an example of growing co-operation between the Houses. The Petition demanded that taxes and loans should not be collected without consent of Parliament, that men should not be imprisoned without a reason being stated, that soldiers and sailors should not be billeted upon those unwilling to have them, and that martial law should not supplant the normal Common Law. Charles fought hard to keep the power to imprison men in emergencies as an essential part of his sovereign power, but the Commons refused to make any concession. There was no concession to 'sovereign power' in Magna Carta; therefore there would be none in the Petition of Right. As Coke said, 'Magna Charta is such a fellow that he will have no "sovereign".' Charles yielded, and accepted the Petition of Right as though it had been a private Bill passed by Parliament. The Commons now voted the King five subsidies, and prepared a Bill to give him tunnage and poundage for life. But before it was passed, the hot-heads once more turned against Buckingham, and soon all the Commons joined in the hunt. In mid-June the Commons sent Charles a general remonstrance on the misgovernment of the kingdom, naming Buckingham as the author of abuses. Fearful that this was the prelude to a renewed attempt at impeachment, Charles prorogued Parliament at the end of June.

In August, Felton's dagger removed Buckingham from the world he had dominated so long. With the 'grievance of grievances' dead, Charles's relations with his third Parliament might have been better when it reassembled in January 1629. But the King had continued to collect tunnage and poundage, forbidden by the spirit but not the letter of the Petition of Right, and promised to him but not voted. Now it was impossible to restrain the Commons. After angry debates on the growth of Arminianism, the M.P.s attacked the customs officers who had been collecting tunnage and poundage. On the King's orders, the Speaker, Sir John Finch, tried to suspend the meeting by leaving the Chamber. Two burly members, Holles and Valentine, held him down in his chair to prevent him. In an unprecedented uproar, with the King's guard hurrying to Westminster to quell the riot, Finch refused to put to the vote a protest prepared by Eliot. Holles thereupon shouted out the terms of Eliot's protest, and the House passed it with loud acclamation. The 'Three Resolutions' condemned as traitors all who brought in innovations of religion, or advised the King to collect – or themselves voluntarily paid – tunnage and poundage levied without consent of Parliament. With this act of defiance, Holles and Valentine released the Speaker, and the House adjourned. A week later, Charles dissolved Parliament. In a lengthy declaration, he defended his actions and criticized members who had wasted their time 'blasting the Government'.

Within five years, James's warning to his son over Cranfield's impeachment had come true: Charles had had his bellyful of Parliaments. Despite his enormous debt – perhaps because of it – the King was now determined to rule without them. However, the concessions gained by Parliament, and the procedures it had devised and revived, did not lapse during the eleven years' which followed. The 1640 Parliaments met with the same privileges, and many of the same members, as those at the beginning of Charles's reign – and with even more power.

## v. The Law

Parliament was in session for only a small fraction of the time between 1603 and 1629. In the intervals between sessions and parliaments, the constitutional struggle switched from the Houses of Parliament to the law courts. Here was another vital issue: were the judges and the law servants of the Crown, props to the royal prerogative, or were they independent of the King? Indeed, was the King himself obliged to obey the English constitution's 'Fundamental Law' (whatever that might be)?

On these matters the lawyers were divided. An increasingly large proportion, fascinated by the apparent extent of their own power, followed Sir Edward Coke in asserting the sovereignty of the law. Others, like Francis Bacon, believed that the judges should be 'Lions under the Throne', supporting the authority of the Crown. The deep personal rivalry and jealousy between Coke and Bacon intensified the conflict: Coke obtained in 1593 the post of Attorney-General which Bacon wanted, Coke married in 1598 the lady Bacon was courting, but Bacon replaced Coke as Chief Justice in 1616, and finally in 1621 Coke helped to secure Bacon's impeachment. Neither was an attractive figure. Each was vindictive and ambitious; Coke was the greater speaker and tactician, Bacon the more intelligent and wiser as a political strategist. The mutual antagonism of these two men played a significant part in embittering the struggles over the Crown's prerogative.

The first conflict was between the common law judges and the Church courts. The common law courts had been repeatedly interfering with the jurisdiction of the Church Courts by issuing writs of prohibition forbidding the latter to try a case, and thereby bringing it under their own jurisdiction. In 1605 Bancroft protested at the increasing use of these Prohibitions, and appealed to the King to confirm that the Church courts had authority equal to that of the lay courts. Coke answered these *Articuli Cleri* and further protests by Bancroft in 1607 by insisting that, as the writs had been introduced by Act of Parliament, they could not be abolished or limited except by another Act of Parliament. Moreover, he asserted that the King was beneath the law, to answer Bancroft's plea that both common law and Church courts derived their powers from the Crown.    In the face of such a sweeping judgement, James had to see the authority of the Church courts gradually wither away.

When the Commons complained in 1610 about the Crown's excessive use of Proclamations, James consulted Coke and the other judges about the validity of these non-parliamentary edicts.    The judges replied that it was lawful to issue Proclamations to remind people to keep the law, but not to create new offences, increase the penalties for existing offences, or bring common law offences under the jurisdiction of Star Chamber. They added the comment that the King had no prerogative but what the law gave him.    This decision inevitably made the Crown more dependent on Parliament for even minor changes in the laws.

By now, Coke's questioning of royal authority had irritated James, and his behaviour in Peacham's Case (1615) infuriated the King even more.    Peacham was a Somerset parson, whose notes for a sermon prophesying the King's sudden death had been accidentally discovered.    The King wanted to know whether writing these notes for a sermon which had never been delivered constituted an act of treason, and so he consulted the judges.    To avoid having Coke, as Lord Chief Justice, act as spokesman and browbeat his colleagues into agreement, James interviewed the judges individually and not as a body.    Coke protested violently against this, for it threatened to expose the judges to royal pressure to deliver verdicts favourable to the Crown.

Coke lost his position next year on account of his attitude in the case of *Commendams*.    Two men claimed in the Exchequer Court that James had given Bishop Neile, to hold in plurality, a parish of which they themselves were the patrons.    In the course of this trial over a single advowson, the men challenged the Crown's right to give clergy permission to hold more than one 'living'.    This plea seemed to James a direct attack on his prerogative, and he made Bacon warn the judges not to give a decision until the Crown's case for the prerogative had been stated.    At first Coke refused to delay the verdict.    Then James summoned the twelve judges before him, and berated them soundly.    All of them fell on their knees.    Eleven begged for pardon; Coke continued to protest. The Lord Chief Justice was thereupon deprived of his office – for reasons which were mainly political.

Ten years later, Charles made a similar attack on the independence of the judges, when Chief Justice Sir Randolph Crew was dismissed in 1626 for refusing to state that the forced loan was legal. The other judges, however, proved less obstinate. In the Trial of the Five Knights (Darnel's Case) in the same year, several distinguished men complained that they had been imprisoned (to make them pay the forced loan) by the King's writ and without the reason being stated, and that they had not been allowed bail. The judges accepted the Crown's plea that the King had the right to imprison men without stating the reason, as it would otherwise be difficult to gain time to uncover plots against the State. The decision was probably correct at law, but, following so closely upon the dismissal of Crew, it raised doubts of the independence and fairness of the courts.

On the whole, James and Charles were more successful in defending their prerogatives in the law courts than they were in Parliament. But every Stuart victory was won at a price. In the 1630s, with Parliament silent and the law suspect, men's thoughts turned more and more to the use of arms to defend their privileges and 'liberties'.

## vi. Foreign Policy

James hated war. He was a natural coward – after the discovery of Peacham's prophecy he always slept in a room padded with feather mattresses to save him from assassination – and was remarkably free from the violent anti-Catholic and anti-Spanish prejudices of men of his age. He saw immediately that Elizabeth's war against Spain was an unnecessary and expensive luxury; therefore he ended it, to help the Treasury and remove the danger of Spanish intervention in Ireland. Ignoring England's alliance with the United Provinces, still in rebellion against Spain, Robert Cecil negotiated with Philip III's ambassadors about the outstanding issues – England's demand to be allowed to trade with all Spanish possessions, and Spain's demands that England should stop trading with the United Provinces and that Englishmen should stop fighting

alongside the rebels. The Treaty of London (1604) allowed
England to trade with Spain's European territories, but not
with the New World, and to continue trading with the United
Provinces; on the other hand, it agreed that Spain as well as
the Dutch could recruit soldiers in England. The treaty was
the best England could expect, but it was very unpopular. The
claim to trade freely with Spanish America had led England
into war nearly twenty years before, so the treaty appeared as a
humiliating surrender and a betrayal of Protestant interests.
Nonetheless, England was now at peace, and the rapid expansion of trade made the fortunes of many merchants.

For various reasons, England remained on fairly good terms
with France throughout James's reign. Henry IV was a
Catholic, but he allowed the French Presbyterians (Huguenots)
more liberty than James allowed the English ones, so there was
no reason for religious prejudice against France. Henry IV's
need to keep on friendly terms with the non-Hapsburg powers
guaranteed peace between France and England while he lived.
This alliance might have led England into the Cleves-Jülich
dispute, but the assassination of Henry in 1610 prevented
French military intervention and the question was settled
peaceably by the Treaty of Xanten in 1614. The years of
peace helped to develop Anglo-French trade. Henry IV
encouraged the export of corn and wine to England, in return
for cloth and coal, and commercial treaties in 1606 and 1610
promised free trade between the two countries. Not everything went smoothly, though. As England's balance of trade
was unfavourable, gold and silver left the country each year to
make up the deficit, to the worry of the financiers. Friction
sometimes developed when English cloth did not meet French
standards of quality, as in 1614, when James had to intervene to
persuade the French to return a large quantity of sub-standard
cloth seized from English merchants. But on the whole, the
wish of each government to remain on friendly terms with the
other proved strong enough to overcome such difficulties. At
the end of James's reign a marriage alliance was arranged to
bring Henry IV's daughter, Henrietta Maria, to England as
Charles's bride.

In the marriage treaty, James and Charles had to promise to
suspend the penal laws against the Catholics, and to allow the
Queen and her household complete freedom to practise their

religion. The attitude of his early Parliaments made it impossible for Charles to keep this promise. The two countries were soon estranged, despite Buckingham's loan to France of ships to help in crushing the Huguenot revolt at La Rochelle – an act challenged hotly by the 1626 Parliament. Relations soon reached breaking point. French ships were attacked in the Channel, under suspicion of carrying Spanish cargoes; the penal laws remained in force, and many of Henrietta Maria's rowdy attendants had to be expelled from England; and Buckingham made a clumsy attempt to seduce the Queen of France. So, in 1627, England engaged in a pointless war with France. Buckingham raked together an expedition to relieve the siege of La Rochelle, and occupied the Ile de Ré outside the harbour; Richelieu closed the entrance to La Rochelle with a great breakwater or mole, and the Rochellois had to surrender in August 1628. When his break with Parliament forced him to save money by ending the war, it was a simple matter for Charles to secure the Treaty of Susa in 1629; nothing was settled, but at least the fighting stopped.

During James's reign, England's relations with the Dutch grew steadily worse. Dutch and English seamen quarrelled over the right to fish for whales off Spitzbergen, and for cod on the Newfoundland Banks. In the North Sea, and especially off the coasts of East Anglia, hundreds[1] of Dutch fishing-smacks were catching great shoals of herrings in the waters which English fishermen had long regarded as their own. In 1609 James issued a proclamation ordering foreigners to purchase licences before fishing off the English coast, but the navy was in so poor a condition that it could not enforce this order. Pamphleteers like Tobias Gentleman and John Keymer complained of the United Provinces' success at England's expense, pointing out that the British seas were the 'chiefest, principall, and only rich treasury' of the Dutch. On the other hand, the Dutch resented England's withdrawal from the war against Spain, and reacted violently when Alderman Cockayne's project endangered their cloth finishing industry. The Dutch prohibited all cloth imports from England; James in return made an unsuccessful attempt to force the trespassing fishermen to pay tolls. A treaty in 1616 ended these measures;

---

[1] According to Salisbury, two or three thousand.

in it James also agreed to take £215,000 from the Dutch in final settlement of the £800,000 owed by them to Elizabeth. But the greatest bitterness developed in the Far East, between the rival East India companies. An agreement at Batavia in 1619 for 'spheres of influence' was soon broken by the Dutch, when Governor Coen ordered the massacre of Englishmen who had set up a trading agency or 'factory' at Amboyna in the Spice Islands. The massacre of Amboyna (1623) bedevilled Anglo-Dutch relations for half a century, but there was no immediate English retaliation: by the time the news reached England, the government had already decided on war against Spain, and James had to overlook the massacre when making his alliance with the United Provinces.

The intrigues of the English ambassador at the Dutch Synod of Dort in 1618–19 had helped to victory the party dedicated to resume the war against Spain, and in June 1624 the United Provinces gladly allied themselves with James, who promised pay for 6000 Dutch soldiers. On the other hand, the Dutch were reluctant to help Mansfeld's ragged and pestiferous army when James sent it to the Continent to reconquer the Palatinate. The expedition landed at Flushing on the Island of Walcheren with no money and few rations; in the hard winter, the waterways froze over, the transport of supplies became impossible, and most of the men died. The Dutch were, however, able by themselves to defeat the Spaniards at s' Hertogenbosch in 1629, and continued their struggle for the liberation of the Spanish Netherlands after Charles's poverty had forced England to withdraw from the conflict.

Despite the wealth of the United Provinces, and the growing unity of France, Spain was still the strongest power in Europe, and so inevitably dominated foreign affairs during this period. At first, James steered clear of Spain, following a mildly Protestant foreign policy. In 1608 he became a member of the German Protestant Union, and later persuaded the United Provinces to join it. He permitted the betrothal of his daughter Elizabeth to Frederick, the Elector Palatine and leader of the Protestant Union. In these ways England's authority encouraged the weak and disheartened Protestant princes, who were fearful of a Catholic attempt to crush their religion and their independence. James hoped that this apparent strength would deter the Catholics from aggression.

England's alliance with Henry IV seemed to place her alongside France in the expected struggle with the Hapsburgs.

Then James faltered. Gondomar, the new Spanish ambassador, methodically prepared to wean James away from the continental Protestants. The Infanta's marriage dowry was a tempting lure for a hard-up King. Prince Henry was a prejudiced Protestant, and would not consider marrying a Catholic; but his death in 1612 allowed Charles to be presented as suitor for the Infanta's hand. The Spanish demands were high: the children of the marriage were to be brought up as Catholics without losing their right to succeed to the throne, the penal laws against the Catholics were to be suspended for three years before the marriage took place, and the treaty had to be ratified by Parliament. James knew that this last could never be achieved. For a while the Cockayne project offered an alternative way of paying the Crown's debts; when that failed, James let Raleigh out of the Tower and sent him to find the mythical golden city of El Dorado; when that too failed, James became convinced that nothing but the Infanta's promised dowry (of over half a million pounds) could end his financial troubles.

During James's flirtation with Spain, the Thirty Years War broke out in Germany. The Bohemian princes rebelled against their Catholic king, and the war spread rapidly when the leader of the Protestant Union, the Elector Palatine, accepted the Crown offered him by the rebels, without waiting for his father-in-law's advice. For a while James was pleased: his daughter was now a Queen, not a mere Electress. But Frederick's troops were defeated in November 1620, and soon Spanish and Bavarian forces had driven him out of Bohemia and his own Palatinate. Frederick howled to James for help. England and the 1621 Parliament echoed his cries. Parliament demanded a naval war against Spain, hoping that the capture of prizes would pay for the campaign, and that Spain would thereby be impoverished and forced to make peace. The refusal of Parliament to give constructive help (apart from inflicting a barbarous punishment on Edward Floyd for slandering the Elector) made James more resolved than ever to restore peace through a marriage settlement with Spain.

Marriage negotiations began again. James now hoped that

the Infanta would bring, not only a large sum of money, but also the Palatinate, which he could then restore to the Elector. This glossed over one difficulty: the Palatinate was in the hands of the Duke of Bavaria, not the King of Spain.   When Buckingham and Charles went off to Spain, ill-concealed as Tom and John Smith – in James's view 'two dear adventurous knights worthy to be put in a new romanzo' – their obvious anxiety to conclude a treaty led the Spaniards to raise their demands, for Olivares (the principal minister) knew how reluctant they would be to return empty-handed.   Spain now insisted that the penal laws should be suspended immediately and repealed by Parliament within three years, and that the Infanta should not leave for England until a probationary period had shown that English Catholics had been given complete freedom of worship. The behaviour of the suitors' party did not help matters: Charles offended etiquette by hiding himself in the Palace Garden to sneak a look at the Infanta, some of the attendants brawled with Catholic priests, and Lord Denbigh (Buckingham's brother-in-law) nearly set fire to the royal palace by accident. After five months of increasing humiliation, Charles and Buckingham left Madrid, without a treaty and without the Infanta.   They had been prepared to accept all the Spanish demands, but could not persuade Spain to try to get the Palatinate restored to Frederick.   To accept such terms would be to abandon hope of regaining the Palatinate, and Charles knew well that James's family feeling and loyalty to his daughter and son-in-law would never permit this.   Nor could the negotiators blind themselves to the attitude of what would undoubtedly be an outraged Parliament.

Charles's return to England, still unmarried and still Protestant, was greeted with bonfires and church bells, and with greater popular enthusiasm than anything since 1603.   Fuming at his humiliation by Olivares, Buckingham demanded war. Parliament was equally aggressive, and voted £300,000 for the defence of England and the preparation of the navy – but not for a land war to reconquer the Palatinate.   Hasty alliances bought help from Denmark and the United Provinces.   Foiled of a Spanish princess, Charles was rapidly betrothed to a French one – Henrietta Maria, a silly teenager.

A few months later, James was dead.   The words *Rex*

*Pacificus* which he had added to his title had not been unjustified, but his policy of peace had been endangered when he entered the Protestant Union without insisting on approving its actions. A less vain man might have realized that Spain would demand a high price before entrusting the Infanta to a Protestant and a Stuart. A less weak man would never have allowed Buckingham and 'Baby Charles' to conduct the vital negotiations in Madrid. But a less clear-sighted man would not have realized the military weakness of the continental Protestants in 1608 or tried to shield them from war; and a man less loyal to his family would not have sacrificed his hopes and his policies rather than accept the loss of the Palatinate. More than anything else, the war with Spain brought James some popularity at the end of his reign. It was, however, the mismanagement of this war which rapidly stirred up a violent storm at the beginning of Charles's reign.

Nothing went right. Mansfeld's troops died in shivering squalor on Walcheren. Wimbledon's attempt to capture Cadiz and intercept the Spanish treasure ships was a catastrophic failure: the ships were decayed, the provisions inedible, and the sailors too timid to fight, while the soldiers got drunk as soon as they were put ashore. Christian IV of Denmark was soon knocked out of the war, and Richelieu thwarted Buckingham's efforts to help the Huguenots of La Rochelle. Charles began peace negotiations with Spain as soon as he dissolved Parliament in 1629, but it was not until November 1630 that peace was signed. This Treaty of Madrid merely repeated the terms of the 1604 Treaty of London. Despite long argument, Charles was unable to gain any concession over the Palatinate, and his sister and her husband had to resign themselves to the loss of their lands. The early Stuarts' only experiment in an active foreign policy had proved quite disastrous. In return for the exhaustion of the Treasury and the abrupt ending of the old Tudor co-operation between Crown and Parliament, England had gained only humiliation.

### vii. Scotland

One of the most progressive of James's policies was his determination to end the long hostility between England and Scotland. His accession united the two crowns, and he styled himself 'King of Great Britain'. Henceforth English foreign policy was Scottish foreign policy. James aimed at a full political union between the two countries, so that they should 'ever acknowledge one Church and one King; and be joined in a perpetual marriage, for the peace and prosperity of both nations, and for the honour of their king'. But the English Parliament was opposed to this ideal: the merchants feared that they would be ruined if Scots were granted the commercial privileges of Englishmen, and the courtiers resented the crowd of Scottish careerists already established around the King. James begged Parliament in 1607 to remove laws hostile to Scotland, to permit 'community of commerce', and to agree that Scots should have the legal privileges of English nationality. Parliament accepted the first demand, but rejected the others. The law courts, however, made a concession, and declared in Colville's Case[1] (1608) that the *post-nati* – Scots born after James's accession to the English throne – should have the legal privileges of Englishmen, and thus be able to hold property in England. After this, except for the brief shotgun marriage of the two countries under Oliver Cromwell and some tentative proposals by Charles II, there was no significant move towards political union for nearly a century.

Meanwhile, James and Charles tried to make Scotland as similar as possible to England, especially in Church organisation. In 1592 James had had to agree to the demand of the General Assembly of the Kirk that bishops should be abolished, but he was determined to restore them again, as he had once before. In 1600, therefore, he appointed bishops with purely political functions – to represent the parish ministers in the Scottish Parliament. In the following years, he methodically weakened the General Assembly by exiling or imprisoning the leading Presbyterians, restored to the bishops the estates which Parliament had confiscated in 1587, and then appointed the bishops as perpetual Moderators (Chairmen) of the assemblies of the clergy in each region. In 1609 he restored the bishops' Consistory Courts, and in the next year set up two Courts of High Commission, with power to silence critics of 'the established order of the Kirk', and insisted that all ministers should be 'presented' to their parishes by the bishops (who could thereby veto unsuitable candidates). Then, in 1618, he

---

[1] Sometimes known as Calvin's Case, or the *Post-Nati* decision.

prevailed upon the General Assembly, meeting at Perth, to pass a series of acts ordering, among other things, that children should be confirmed by the bishops and that Holy Communion should be administered to the people 'humblie and reverentilie kneeling upon the knees'. The Five Articles of Perth were unpopular, and James therefore did not press his wish for reform of the Prayer Book. In Scotland as in England, the Church had suffered as a result the seizure of its property by the laity, and by the Crown's extensive grant of tithes to royal favourites. Between 1625 and 1633 Charles imposed a series of Acts of Revocation, whereby much of the income from tithes was made available for paying the clergy and maintaining the schools in each parish, but he did this at the cost of angering the Scottish nobles. As the Privy Council protested in 1625, 'Nothing hes at ony tyme heirtofore occurrit whilk hes so far disquyeted the myndis of your goode subjectis.'

James's reign did much to strengthen the Crown in Scotland. His control of Parliament, through the royally-nominated Lords of the Articles, became almost complete, and he was usually able to get the taxes he needed. In 1621, for example, Parliament introduced an income tax by voting that income from land rents and from bond interest should be taxed at 5 per cent; had the English Parliament been equally co-operative, the Crown's financial troubles would have been over. The authority of the King was widely extended – new burghs were established at Campbeltown, Stornoway and near the modern Fort William to help pacify the Highlands; in the Statutes of Iona (1609) Bishop Knox made the chiefs of the Western Isles and the adjacent mainland accept James's authority; two years later, Bishop Law secured the submission of Orkney and Shetland, and abolished Norse law there. The Border Commission of 1605 managed to discipline the lawless Border families, and in 1609 James appointed Justices of the Peace to prevent the 'brutall custome of deadlie feadis [feuds]'. Scotland's backward economy gradually improved, as leather tanning and soap manufacturing monopolies introduced new industries. Coal mining expanded; at Culross the mine tunnels ran a mile out to sea, and labour was so short that in 1606 an Act forbade the colliers to leave the mine where they were employed.

## viii. Ireland

After the crushing of the revolt of Tyrone and Tyrconnell, the English settlement of Ireland proceeded rapidly under Sir Arthur Chichester, Lord Deputy from 1604 to 1614. Catholic priests were ordered to leave the country, and Catholic laymen to accept the Established (that is, Anglican) Church by January 1606. This was a superb example of governmental wishful thinking. Nonetheless, Tyrone and Tyrconnell feared for their safety and fled abroad in September 1607. Their lands were seized for the Crown. Then Davies, the Attorney-General, found excuses for confiscating the lands of several other chiefs and their tenants. By 1609 the Government had seized all the counties of the modern Ulster, and was offering to lease out half a million acres to settlers. English and Scottish 'undertakers' and 'servitors' could rent estates at £5 6s. 8d. p.a. for each thousand acres, provided they took an oath acknowledging James's supremacy in temporal matters. The Catholic 'natives', who could not take this oath, had to pay twice as much. Some of the land was given to the Established Church, and some to Trinity College, Dublin, the Protestant university founded by Elizabeth. Most fortunate was the City of London, which bought for £20,000 all northern Derry, at a very low rent, but with certain responsibilities to defend and develop the area. The Plantation of Ulster did not immediately exclude all Catholic native landowners from northern Ireland, but by the time of the rising in 1641 the Protestant settlers were occupying the greater part of the area. James was encouraged by the apparent success of the Ulster Plantation, and tried to extend English influence with similar colonies in parts of Wexford, Wicklow and Leitrim. No Irishman could feel safe from English greed. Even the 'Old English' Catholic families like the Talbots and the Butlers had reason to fear the rise of men like Richard Boyle, who had arrived in Ireland penniless in 1588 and quickly built up a huge fortune from iron-smelting and linen-weaving; by the time of his death he was Earl of Cork, the richest man in Ireland, and controller of eight seats in the Irish House of Commons.

Despite the laws issued by the Lord Deputy, it was a physical and military impossibility to stamp out Catholicism in Ireland. The native Irish aristocracy might count for little in London;

it was unwise, however, for James to ignore the many peers of Anglo-Norman descent – de Burgh, Talbot, Roche, Butler, Barry and others. These were too closely intermarried with the English aristocracy to be dismissed lightly. James, at their request, reduced the number of parliamentary boroughs recently created, and agreed to introduce no new penal legislation against the Catholics. Land-greedy Protestant immigrants and the clergy of the new Church might call for the end of toleration, the first Convocation of the Protestant clergy might adopt 104 Articles of Religion markedly more Calvinist than the Anglican 39, but James was as anxious to avoid the cost of a war in Ireland as much as anywhere else. Lord Falkland, who succeeded St. John as Deputy in 1622, proved a conciliatory governor, especially when Charles had to appease the Irish during his war with Spain. In 1627 Falkland promised certain 'Graces', in return for £120,000 in taxation from the Catholics: all land tenures dating back sixty years or more were to be valid at law, and Catholics were to be allowed to practise at the Bar and hold public office. The Catholics paid the money, but the 'Graces' were not confirmed by Parliament, and were soon undermined by the attacks of land-grabbers like Loftus and Mountnorris and by Protestant bishops like Archbishop Ussher, who denounced toleration as 'a grievous sin'. By the end of Falkland's service as Lord Deputy, the Catholics were thoroughly embittered, the Old English worried about their political survival, and the new magnates like the Earl of Cork had come to dominate the administration.

## ix. Economic expansion

James and Charles tried, without much success, to extend royal control over most forms of industrial and commercial enterprise. The Crown generally had to rely upon the J.P.s to enforce its orders, and found it increasingly difficult to get them to impose regulations which conflicted with their own interests. The J.P.s seldom troubled to fix prices, and, apart from a brief period of cheap food in the 1650s, workers' wages during the seventeenth century lagged behind prices. The apprenticeship laws were widely ignored; in 1610 the apprentices of Norwich, the second largest city in the country, went on strike because of the large number of unapprenticed workmen, for the Mayor and other officials responsible for enforcing the laws were profiting from the surplus of cheap labour.   Chief Justice Coke in 1615 defended in Tolley's Case the evasion of apprenticeship laws by unskilled and semi-skilled workmen.   The Crown's attempts in the towns to revive the guild system, which it might have controlled through the Privy Council, were quite unsuccessful, as were its efforts to extend the guilds to supervise the industries developing in the suburbs and the countryside.   This lack of effective supervision of industry led to a deterioration in the quality of the products. James and Charles tried to appoint (at a price) surveyors to inspect, for example, the coal shipped from Newcastle, but the surveyors were easily evaded.   It was also easy to evade the regulations forbidding wood-fired furnaces, forges and salt-pans, issued by a government trying to conserve the country's timber.

The Crown had a long-recognized right to gold and silver ores everywhere in the country, and Elizabeth and her successors tried to assert a similar claim to ores of tin and lead containing a substantial proportion of precious metal.   In 1623, for example, James defined 'Mines Royal' of lead as those which 'yeeldeth after the rate of eight ounces of silver out of every hundred waight of oare and 60 lbs. in lead'.   Such claims naturally led to disputes between the Crown and land-lords anxious to exploit the mineral resources of their lands. The Crown never dared, however, to assert any claims over coal and iron mines, despite the great and untaxed wealth of the mine owners, who were far too powerful to be challenged in this way.

During the 1560s Elizabeth had granted the monopoly of saltpetre and gunpowder manufacture to George Evelyn, who profited from it sufficiently to bring up sixteen sons and eight daughters; in James's reign the Evelyns' monopoly came under the protection of courtiers like Worcester and Buckingham, who increased the power of their agents to inspect private property in searching for saltpetre.   No man's pigeon-house was safe from the Evelyns' investigators, and this invasion of private property caused great resentment. James's poverty prevented him from investing extensively in new industries, but he did speculate heavily in the company founded under Lord Sheffield to produce alum in Yorkshire;

between 1612 and 1617 the Crown invested nearly £70,000 in alum manufacture, and it was not until the 1630s that it got its money back. The unpopularity of the Crown's grants of monopolies has been stressed in previous pages.

At home, the government irritated men by its interference in industry; abroad, it irritated men by its failure to intervene to help English merchants. Pirates everywhere preyed upon commerce, and even attacked the collier ships between Newcastle and London; one of the charges against Buckingham in 1626 was his failure to keep the English seas free from pirates. For a century and a half England's commercial empire in India also received almost no help from the government. In 1611 the East India Company established a 'factory' or trading agency at Masulipatam on the east coast, and in the next year founded one at Surat, which was brilliantly defended in 1614 from a Portuguese attack led by the governor of Goa. Later, another factory was developed at Fort St. George (Madras), and the expulsion of the English from the Spice Islands after the massacre of Amboyna forced the Company to concentrate on the development of its commerce in India. But the English position in India was extremely weak, as it depended entirely upon the resources of the shareholders in the Company. It was not surprising that men like Thomas Mun, himself an East India merchant, pleaded with James's Standing Commission of Trade (set up in 1622) for the government to support the merchants more actively, and so prevent the waste of gold and silver through England's unfavourable balance of trade.

Only two English colonies in America managed to establish themselves during this period. The Virginia Company, given its charter in 1606, was an association of swashbuckling rogues, quarrelsome, violent, hard-living, more akin to the Spanish Conquistadores of a century earlier than to the English settlers who followed them to America in the seventeenth century. Between 1607 and 1610, over 800 settlers landed at Jamestown, attracted by the promise of cheap land. By June 1610 barely fifty survived, and the survivors were deterred from sailing back to England only by the arrival of fresh supplies and a new governor, Lord de la Warr, who had just been appointed by James to take charge. It was a minor miracle that any of the settlers had survived at all: fever and famine proved to be enemies too strong even for leaders like Captain John Smith to fight against. But the colony was saved when it was found that the soil and climate were ideal for growing tobacco, and in 1614 the first shipload of the new product was sent to England. In July 1619 the first legislative assembly of the colony of Virginia met at Jamestown, with delegates representing the ten subsidiary settlements, and it soon enacted distinctly Puritanical laws – gambling, drinking and swearing were forbidden. But the Company quarrelled with the King over tobacco duties, and the Company's patent was revoked in 1624. Virginia then became a colony under the direct administration of the Crown. Nonetheless the expansion of the colony continued; 'land-hunger' in England was sufficiently acute to force many of the poor and unemployed to try to make their fortunes in the New World.

The other colony was that founded by the Pilgrim Fathers. Independent congregations from Nottinghamshire and Lincolnshire had emigrated to Leyden in Holland to escape Bancroft's persecution. Worried by the growth of intolerant Presbyterianism there, and anxious to retain their national identity as Englishmen, some of them decided to move to America. They obtained unofficial permission from James, and a licence from the Virginia Company, to settle on part of the coast which James had originally granted to that Company. The thirty-five Pilgrims were reinforced by sixty-six adventurers from England, and they reached Cape Cod in the *Mayflower* in November 1620. Again, the settlers only just survived – only fifty were alive after the first winter, and as late as 1637, despite considerable immigration, there were fewer than 600. By 1629, the English colonies in America did little more than show that Englishmen could live there, and that one crop could be grown profitably. The great age of English expansion had not yet begun. The total number of English colonists in America would barely have filled an average-sized country town in England.

### x. Culture and Society, 1603-42

The culture of the Jacobean age was a faithful reflection of the society which it served. The tension between Catholic, Anglican and Puritan, jealousy of the *nouveau riche* and the monopolist, interest in the new worlds discovered by the sailors and the astronomers, the concern for history and the law, the sincere piety of many men, all permeate the writings of the period. The devotion to Church music of many of the composers emphasizes the religious character of the age, and the Catholics among them found at Court encouragement for their new settings of the Mass. The madrigalists continued composing for those who regarded singing as an essential social qualification. The architects used their skills to enable courtiers, merchants and country gentlemen to rival each other in the dignified exuberance of Jacobean houses. The painters pandered to the vanity of men wishing to record their faces for posterity. This was the culmination of the English Renaissance.

Most drama was for the Court. Shakespeare's great plays in this period – *Othello*, *Lear*, *Antony and Cleopatra*, *Macbeth* and *Coriolanus* – all dealt with noble themes and noble men, even if they were shamefully betrayed and overthrown. Ben Jonson's plays introduced a different tone, *Volpone* (1605) and *The Alchemist* (1610) amusing the Court with their brutal satire. *The Alchemist*, for example, pillories unmercifully the *nouveau riche* Sir Epicure Mammon and the hypocritical Puritans Tribulation Wholesome and Ananias – indeed, 'Ananias' became a popular nickname for any Puritan zealot. Later, to satisfy the tastes of Carr and Buckingham, Jonson concentrated on the preparation of splendid masques, and drama degenerated into spectacle. There were many other playwrights of ability – Dekker, Webster, Beaumont, Fletcher, Ford – but the standard of their plays gradually dropped, in keeping with the decline in the morals of the Court. They ceased to grapple with moral questions and principles, and devoted themselves to amusing sophisticated patrons with bawdy comedies sneering at moral virtues. In this they reflected the attitudes of the courtiers who patronized them, and increasingly aroused the opposition of the Puritans. Parliament's suppression of the theatres in 1642 was merely the successful conclusion of a long Puritan campaign.

The passion for exploration, investigation and discovery influenced both prose and poetry. Richard Hakluyt, James's Archdeacon of Westminster, had published his *Principall Navigations* before Elizabeth's death, but the same interest in remote and far-fetched ideas dominated the metaphysical[1] poets.   The greatest of them, John Donne, had been educated as a Catholic and a lawyer, but he persuaded himself that Anglicanism was superior, took orders in 1615, and spent the last decade of his life, 1621–31, as a Canon of St. Paul's.   No metaphor was too strange for Donne to use, in expressing the passionate imagination and 'conceits' of his genius.   His best-known poem starts:

> Go and catch a falling star,
>   Get with child a mandrake root,
> Tell me where all past years are,
>   Or who cleft the Devil's foot,
> Teach me to hear Mermaid's singing,
>   Or to keep off envy's stinging. . . .

Churchmen were among the most distinguished literary men of the age.   George Herbert, brother of the courtier Lord Herbert, retired from Cambridge to the rectory of Bemerton, where he produced in 1633 a collection of religious poems of advanced metaphysical imagery.   Another country parson poet was Robert Herrick of Dean Prior, though his poems were not published until after his expulsion by the Puritans in 1648. Robert Burton, author of the prose *Anatomy of Melancholy* (1621), was a Leicestershire rector; Jeremy Taylor, author of *Holy Living* and *Holy Dying* was rector of Uppingham.   Volumes of sermons by Donne, Lancelot Andrewes and others had a wide sale, despite their heavy and complicated style.

The most remarkable writer of the age, though, was Francis Bacon.   The first of his *Essays* were published in 1597, and he added to them in 1612 and 1625.   These were modelled on the essays of the Frenchman Montaigne, and show clearly the vast learning and wisdom of one who had 'taken all knowledge to be his province'.   His style was superbly economical and superbly balanced, as in the essay *Of Studies*:

Studies serve for delight, for ornament, and for ability. . . . Crafty men contemn studies; simple men admire them; and wise men use them. . . .   Some books are to be tasted, others to be swallowed, and some few to be chewed and digested. . . .

----

[1] Those who took their imagery from beyond the physical world.

Reading maketh a full man; conference [discussion] a ready man; and writing an exact man. . . .

Even more important than the essays were his scientific and philosophical works, the *Advancement of Learning* (1605) and the *Novum Organum* (1620), in which he proposed a comprehensive new system of philosophy, based on experiment, to replace the methods expounded by Aristotle and followed by the 'Schoolmen' of the Middle Ages. The need to base general principles on experiment had, it is true, been stressed by some earlier students, but Bacon's prestige helped to emphasize and popularize it. It was not long before the Leveller Richard Overton was wanting to test by experiment the immortality of the soul, and before the Quaker Edward Burroughs was calling for laboratory analysis to see whether the bread and wine in the Communion Service did become the Body and Blood of Christ. The simplicity and directness of Bacon's style served as guides for Newton, Boyle and other members of the Royal Society in Restoration England.

Another victim of Jacobean court intrigue, Sir Walter Raleigh, was probably the most popular prose writer of the time. His *History of the World* (1614) was widely read, especially by Puritans and others who looked forward to the winds of change. Raleigh taught men not to look back to a mythical 'Golden Age' in the past, not to wait for God to alter the course of history, nor to look upon kings as being especially favoured by the Almighty. 'From Ralegh . . . onwards the forward-looking party was calling for the use of State power to further the cause of God, profit, and national prestige.'[1] Raleigh's last work, a treatise describing parliamentary procedure and practice, was circulated secretly among his friends, two of whom – Eliot and Pym – found his advice of the utmost value in their leadership of the parliamentary opposition to Charles.

In painting, the early seventeenth century was not a time of outstanding English achievement. Only the miniaturists Nicholas Hilliard, Isaac and Peter Oliver, the two John Hoskins and (under the Protectorate) Samuel Cooper achieved any eminence in filling the role of the modern portrait photographer, but even they were dominated by the foreign masters. As Prince

[1] C. Hill, *Intellectual Origins of the English Revolution*, p. 194. These two paragraphs owe much to Mr. Hill's writings.

of Wales and as King, Charles I showed superlative taste in
collecting the works of the old Italians – Titian, Tintoretto,
Mantegna, Giorgione and Raphael – and even better judgement in commissioning works from the living Dutchmen.   Van
Dyck settled in England from 1632 until his death in 1641, and
he and Rubens were rewarded with knighthoods.

The early Stuart period saw the perfection of the Elizabethan
school of madrigalists, the best of whom were also eminent
composers of Church music.   The great Elizabethan William
Byrd was busy writing both kinds of music until his death in
1623; like the equally versatile Orlando Gibbons, he remained
a Catholic.   In the 1630s, most composers concentrated on
providing the music for the masques which so delighted the
Court that Charles I and Henrietta Maria sometimes acted in
them.   The universal popularity of the masque speeded the
decline in English music as well as in English drama.   On the
other hand, the Puritans did not follow their closing of the
theatres by banning music – though in 1644 Parliament did
order the destruction of church organs, which were associated
with popish services.

The prosperity of the country made the early seventeenth
century a great period for architecture.   Many old country
houses had been rebuilt as stately mansions during Elizabeth's
reign; the work continued after her death, and was generally
influenced by the 'classical' style introduced from Renaissance
Italy and France.   State buildings, too, adopted the new style,
with Inigo Jones as Surveyor of the King's Works from 1615
until the fall of the monarchy.   Inigo Jones's Banqueting
House in Whitehall and Queen's House at Greenwich show a
sense of proportion as delicate as any achieved by continental
'Palladian' architects.   His interiors could be equally superb,
as with the 'double-cube' room at Wilton, which Lord Pembroke further adorned with paintings by Van Dyck.   Another
outstanding work was Robert Lyminges's Hatfield House.
This was also a great age for architecture at Oxford and Cambridge.   The charitable enthusiasm for endowing education
provided the money for new buildings.   At Oxford, Laud
built a new quadrangle for St. John's, and his opponent Hakewill, brother of the colleague of Coke and Eliot, paid for the
new chapel of Exeter College.

## EXTRACTS

1. THE COMMONS PROTEST AGAINST JAMES'S ORDER FORBIDDING THEM TO DISCUSS FOREIGN POLICY (1621):

The Commons ... do make this Protestation following, That the liberties, franchises, privileges, and jurisdictions of Parliament are the ancient and undoubted birthright and inheritance of the subjects of England; and that the arduous and urgent affairs concerning the King, State, and defence of the realm and of the Church of England, and the maintenance and making of laws, and redress of mischiefs and grievances which daily happen within this realm, are proper subjects and matter of counsel and debate in Parliament; and that in the handling and proceeding of those businesses every member of the House of Parliament hath, and of right ought to have, freedom of speech to propound, treat, reason, and bring to conclusion the same. . . (In Tanner, *Constitutional Documents*, pp. 288–9)

2. THE PETITION OF RIGHT, 1628, FROM 'THE LORDS SPIRITUAL AND TEMPORAL, AND COMMONS IN THIS PRESENT PARLIAMENT ASSEMBLED':

They do therefore humbly pray your Most Excellent Majesty, that no man hereafter be compelled to make or yield any gift, loan, benevolence, tax, or such like charge, without common consent by Act of Parliament; and that none be called to make answer, or take such oath, or to give attendance, or be confined, or otherwise molested or disquieted concerning the same, or for refusal thereof; and that no freeman, in any such manner as is before-mentioned, be imprisoned or detained; and that your Majesty will be pleased to remove the . . . soldiers and mariners [forcibly billeted], and that your people may not be so burdened in time to come; and that the foresaid commissions for proceeding by martial law, may be revoked and annulled; and that hereafter no commissions of like nature may issue forth to any person or persons whatsoever, to be executed as aforesaid, lest by colour of them any of your Majesty's subjects be destroyed or put to death, contrary to the laws and franchise of the land. (In Gardiner, *Constitutional Documents*, p. 69)

3. THE COMMONS DECLARE WAR ON CHARLES'S POLICIES, MARCH 1629:

1. Whosoever shall bring in innovation of religion, or by favour or countenance seek to extend or introduce Popery or

Arminianism, or other opinion disagreeing from the true and
orthodox Church, shall be reputed a capital enemy to this
Kingdom and Commonwealth.

2. Whosoever shall counsel or advise the taking and levying of the subsidies of Tonnage and Poundage, not being
granted by Parliament, or shall be an actor or instrument
therein, shall be likewise reputed an innovator in the Government, and a capital enemy to the Kingdom and Commonwealth.

3. If any merchant or person whatsoever shall voluntarily
yield, or pay the said subsidies of Tonnage and Poundage, not
being granted by Parliament, he shall likewise be reputed a
betrayer of the liberties of England, and an enemy to the same.
(In Gardiner, *Constitutional Documents*, pp. 82–3)

4. THE FIVE ARTICLES OF PERTH DISCIPLINE THE KIRK
(1618):
An act ordaining, that everie minister sall have the commemoration of the inestimable benefites received from God by
and through our Lord and Saviour Jesus Christ his Birth,
Passion, Resurrection, Ascension, and sending doun of the
Holie Ghost, upon the days appointed for that use. . . .

An act anent [concerning] the administration of baptisme in
privat houses, when the necessitie sall require:

An act anent the catechizing of young children of eight yeers
of age, and presenting them to the bishop to lay hands upon
them, and blesse them, with prayer for increase of their
knowledge, and continuance of God's heavenlie graces with
them:

An act anent the administration and giving of the Holie
Communion in private houses to sicke and infirme persons:

An act, that the blessed sacrament of the Holie Communion
of the bodie and blood of our Lord and Saviour Jesus Christ be
celebrate to the people humblie and reverentlie kneeling upon
their knees. (In Dickinson and Donaldson, *Source Book of
Scottish History*, vol. iii, pp. 63–4)

5. BACON ADMONISHES THE JUDGES TO SUPPORT THE KING
(1617):
You that are the Judges of Circuits are as it were the planets
of the Kingdom (I do you no dishonour in giving you that
name), and no doubt you have a great stroke in the frame of
this government, as the other have in the great frame of the
world. Do therefore as they do: move always and be carried

with the motion of your first mover, which is your Sovereign...
(In Tanner, *Constitutional Documents*, p. 198)

## 6. RALEIGH POINTS OUT THAT KINGS ARE MORTAL (1614):

The Kings and Princes of the world haue alwayes laid before
them, the actions, but not the ends, of those great Ones which
preceded them. They are always transported with the
glorie of the one, but they neuer minde the miserie of the other,
till they finde the experience in themselues. They neglect the
aduice of God, while they enjoy life, or hope it. . . . (W.
Raleigh, *The History of the World*. In *Elizabethan and Jacobean
Prose*, ed. Muir, p. 250)

## 7. BACON (LORD ST. ALBANS) DEDICATES HIS ESSAYS TO BUCKINGHAM IN 1625, FOUR YEARS AFTER THE FAVOURITE RUINED HIM:

Excellent Lord,
   Salomon saies, A good Name is as a precious oyntment; And
I assure my selfe, such wil your Grace's Name bee with
Posteritie. For your Fortune and Merit both have beene
Eminent. And you have planted Things, that are like to
last. I doe now publish my Essayes; which of all my other
workes have been most Currant [popular]; For that, as it
seemes, they come home to Men's Businesse and Bosomes. . . .
And these I dedicate to your Grace; Being of the best
Fruits, that by the good Encrease, which God gives to my
Pen and Labours, I could yeeld. God leade your Grace by
the Hand.
        Your Grace's most Obliged and faithfull Servant,
                    FR. ST. ALBAN

## 8. KING JAMES DISAPPROVES OF THE PRINCIPAL EXPORT OF VIRGINIA:

And for the vanities committed in this filthie custome, is it not
both great vanitie and vncleanenesse, that at the table, a place
of respect, of cleanlinesse, or modestie, men should not be
ashamed, to sit tossing of *Tobacco pipes*, and puffing of the smoke
of *Tobacco* one to another, making the filthy smoke and stinke
thereof, to exhale athwart the dishes, and infect the aire, when
very often, men that abhorre it are at their repast? . . . But
herein is not onely a great vanitie, but a great contempt of
Gods good giftes, that the sweetenesse of mans breath, being a
good gift of God, should be willfully corrupted by this stinking

smoke. . . . A custome lothsome to the eye, hatefull to the
Nose, harmefull to the braine, dangerous to the Lungs, and in
the blacke stinking fume thereof, neerest resembling the
horrible Stigian smoke of the pit that is bottomeless. (In
*Elizabethan and Jacobean Prose*, ed. Muir, p. 89-91)

# 3

## THE ROYALIST REACTION
## AND ITS FAILURE, 1629–42

☆

### i. The Crown's finances

THE 'unseasonable, unskilful, and precipitate dissolution' of
Parliament in March 1629, wrote Clarendon sixteen years later,
was the principal source 'from whence these waters of bitterness
we now taste' flowed.   Yet there was nothing illegal, unconstitutional or unprecedented in a lengthy period without a
meeting of Parliament.   Not long previously, Parliaments had
been detested because their assembly normally implied new
taxation.   So far as the country had been concerned, if Henry
Tudor or Elizabeth could manage without Parliament, so much
the better for everyone.   But things were now different.
The five Parliaments elected between 1621 and 1628 had
clearly demonstrated that they were willing to attack the King's
policies, the King's ministers, and even the King himself.   The
House of Commons was no longer a mere assembly of countrymen eager to earn some sign of royal approval – a pension, the
lease of a Crown manor, the grant of Church tithes, a monopoly
or a knighthood.   The M.P.s who argued about the prerogative, impositions or Arminianism in the early Parliaments of
Charles I knew that they represented the classes which had
elected them.   The dissolution of Parliament appeared as a
direct attempt to silence every voice of political or religious
opposition, and as a reaction which ran contrary to the
progress of recent years.   To the muzzled Cokes and Pyms, the
Stuarts were trying to reimpose the 'Norman yoke' which
statesmen from the barons of Runnymede onwards had been
trying to remove.   The M.P.s were not, of course, democrats in
any modern sense; unlike the drafters of Magna Carta, they had
no thought of allowing to their own tenants, dependants and

servants the privileges they were claiming from the King.   But it was with this Puritan aristocracy of wealth that the only chance to restrain royal power remained.

With men forbidden even to speak about Parliaments, Charles now had to choose between two policies: either to make himself an absolute king and rule through a loyal mercenary army and paid bureaucracy – the system which Richelieu was creating in France – or to rule within the letter of the law, but exploiting every ambiguous or out-of-date statute to increase royal power.   Charles chose the latter.   The King had no talent for absolutism, nor had he the money to create a sub-servient army and administration; but his refusal to try to seize all power into his own hands also reflected the successes of the Parliamentarians and lawyers who had demanded that the King should be under the law.   For this reason, it is unfair to think of this period, from 1629 to 1640, as the 'Eleven Years Tyranny'; in comparison with Henry VIII or even Elizabeth, Charles was a very milk-and-water despot.

Nor is it more accurate to term this period the 'Eleven Years Personal Rule'.   To succeed in his aim of making old methods and statutes work, Charles needed able ministers.   With a Buckingham or a Carr at the helm, Charles's ship would soon have foundered.   In fact, no Stuart was so well served as he was between 1629 and 1641.   He persuaded Thomas Went-worth, one of the leaders of the 1628 Parliament, to change sides; 'Black Tom Tyrant' soon became one of the most efficient ministers of royal power.   Richard Weston, appointed Treas-urer in 1628, achieved such success by such methods that Parliament in 1629 was already preparing to impeach him. William Noy, the Attorney-General, was as diligent as Coke had been in searching out mediaeval laws and precedents. John Finch, the Speaker whose loyalty had been thwarted by the strong-arm methods of Holles and Valentine, later became Lord Chief Justice and as much a lion under the throne as Bacon would have wished.   Two churchmen, Laud and Juxon, revived the mediaeval tradition of great administrator-bishops. The death of Buckingham made it easier for other peers to play a more prominent part in the king's counsels: the wise Coventry served efficiently as Lord Keeper until his death in 1640, and Carlisle (the Scotsman James Hay), Holland, Dorset, Mont-gomery and Arundel were also regular members of the Privy

Council. Nonetheless, there were weaknesses. Court intrigues, such as the rivalries between Holland and Weston, and
between the Queen and Wentworth, split the king's supporters.
The Secretaries were not outstanding men – Carleton had spent
too long abroad to be familiar with the English scene, and John
Coke was a man of very few talents. Moreover, for advice on
Scottish affairs, Charles relied on the Marquis of Hamilton, a
unreliable opportunist whose counsel more than once led the
King into perilous ventures.

Charles also needed the support of the courts. He appointed
his judges *quam diu se bene gesserint*[1] and did not hesitate to
dismiss Justice Heath in 1634 as he had dismissed Crew in
1626. The Privy Council and the prerogative courts – Star
Chamber, High Commission, the Councils of the North and
Wales – made themselves hated as the agents of an intolerant
authority. But the Crown could not get the J.P.s and other
unpaid, part-time officials to support the administration as
loyally as their predecessors had done in the previous century.
The J.P.s came from the same classes as the M.P.s, angry and
frustrated at the dissolution of Parliament and outraged at the
imprisonment of their leaders Eliot, Holles, Strode and
Valentine.[2] Soon they were to be further incensed by financial
grievances such as 'distraint of knighthood' and Ship-Money.
The 'revolt of the J.P.s' was a major preliminary to the outbreak of the Civil War. The tragedy of all the Stuart kings was
their inability to rule without offending the classes on which
they most relied. The lack of a reliable body of local or
regional administrators – such as Richelieu's Intendants – was
an irreparable weakness in the system which Laud and Wentworth liked to speak of as *Thorough*.

The success of non-parliamentary government depended
entirely upon the Crown's ability to pay the costs of government out of revenue, for its credit was already stretched to the
limit. It was obviously necessary for Charles to end the wars
against France and Spain, and the treaties of Susa (1629) and
Madrid (1630) stopped the greatest drain on the Treasury. As
there was no possibility that the government could exist on the
rents of the much-reduced Crown lands, the income from

[1] So long as they shall behave well.
[2] Eliot died in the Tower in 1632 and Holles escaped, but Strode and Valentine
were not released until the eve of the Short Parliament in 1640.

customs was obviously essential.   Parliament had never voted Charles tunnage and poundage.   Still maintaining that the customs were a royal right, not dependent on Parliamentary grant, Charles collected £150,000 a year from the lessees of the Great Farm, and in 1633 leased the Petty Farm of customs on wine and currants for £60,000.   In the last years of the 1630s, with a new Book of Rates, these rents were increased to bring the Crown a total of £245,000 a year.   Merchants who refused to pay – such as Richard Chambers of London, fined £2000 and imprisoned for nearly seven years – were punished severely by the Privy Council or Star Chamber.   But most of them conformed, once they saw the King's determination – and could well afford to pay the levies when foreign trade revived after the wartime slump.

In 1630 Noy decided to impose strictly the law ordering men owning estates worth £40 a year or more to apply for knight-hoods, and thereby expose themselves to paying certain feudal dues to the Crown.   With the price-rise and the increase in the country's wealth, very many qualified men had not had them-selves knighted.   These were fined heavily for their breach of this old law: in two years £150,000 came in from this 'distraint of knighthood'.   Other out-of-date laws were also enforced, primarily for the sake of the profit from fines.   In 1634 the mediaeval forest laws were revived, and men who had felled timber, cleared waste or otherwise 'encroached' on what had once been royal forest were ordered to pay huge fines: the Earl of Salisbury paid £20,000 and the Earl of Westmorland al-most as much.   The Earl of Bedford was among the hundreds fined for building a total of over thirteen hundred new houses, mainly around fashionable Drury Lane and Clerken-well in defiance of Charles's order forbidding the building of houses in London on new foundations.   The Crown began a long series of lawsuits against the City of London for various breaches of contract (which brought the King £12,000 but apparently cost the citizens more than ten times as much). The revival of Tudor statutes forbidding enclosure and the conversion of arable to pasture helped the poor as well as the Crown, but landowners fined up to £4000 for 'depopulation' offences strongly resented such interference with their manage-ment of their property.   The Court of Wards extracted more and more money from heirs and their estates, and the Earl

Marshal's Court dealt harshly with those who had offended the laws of heraldry. By all these various means, Treasurer Weston was able to collect over £400,000 a year.

Weston also pointed out to Charles an excuse for reviving the sale of monopolies. The Act of 1624 had forbidden the granting of patents of monopoly to private individuals, but – to satisfy the City of London and the Merchant Adventurers – had allowed them to be given to companies. Monopolies established for the production of alum and soap brought the Crown a total of nearly £250,000 during the 1630s. The soap monopoly was held by a group of Weston's friends, many of whom were Catholics, and so the 'Popish Soap' patent became particularly unpopular. Charles tried, moreover, to introduce monopolies profitable to the Crown over the production of coal, salt and bricks, industries which were already too well established to need royal protection. As these monopolies were harmful to the consumer without benefiting the producer, they soon lapsed. Nonetheless, by the end of the 1630s the number of patents had so increased that the Treasury was receiving nearly £100,000 a year from them – and favoured courtiers were profiting to a similar extent, at the expense of everybody else in the country.

All the devices used by the Crown up to 1634 were legal, with the possible exception of tunnage and poundage. Charles's last method, however, was more controversial. By ancient custom, the seaports were responsible for providing ships for defence against enemies and pirates. As ships grew larger and more expensive, it became more realistic to collect 'Ship-Money' from the ports, to be spent by the Admiralty on the navy, as James had done in 1619. Charles in 1634 levied Ship-Money in this way, planning to rebuild the Navy and use it to force the interloping Dutch fishermen to pay toll. In 1635, Charles collected it again, this time demanding it from the inland counties as well as the coastal areas. He did the same in 1636, in 1637, in 1638, and in 1639. There were probably mediaeval precedents for collecting it from inland areas – but none at all for levying it afresh in several successive years. Moreover, England was now at peace, and the king could not plead convincingly that a national emergency forced him to take this action. Charles had in fact obtained from the judges (now led by the pliant Sir John Finch) an opinion that it was legal to collect Ship-Money in this way, but this did not lessen the hostility to what soon appeared to be an annual non-Parliamentary tax. The opposition was led by a wealthy Buckinghamshire squire, John Hampden, egged on by the Puritan Lord Saye and Sele. Hampden refused to pay the 20s. demanded from him for his lands at Stoke Mandeville, and was tried before the Exchequer Court in November 1637. After a brilliant speech by Oliver St. John for the defence, some of the judges reversed their earlier opinions on the legality of the levy, and it was only by a majority of seven to five that they declared against Hampden.

Hampden's Case had several consequences. Finch's speech as Lord Chief Justice re-asserted the King's claims to 'Divine Right' – 'None can share with him in his absolute power' – and seemed to point to the future trend of royal policy. Moreover, the suspicion that some judges had declared against Hampden only to please the King shook men's confidence in the independence of the law. The court's apparent refusal to protect private property (Hampden's twenty shillings) from the King's demands made men more ready in the following years to take up arms. When the judges seemingly defied the law, who else need obey it? The narrowness of the verdict encouraged other men to refuse payment. Petitions poured in to the Council from all parts of the country. Resistance was such that the sheriffs could not enforce payment. J.P.s and other administrators were among the chief defaulters. In 1636 Charles had obtained almost all he demanded, nearly £200,000; with each successive levy, the proportion collected dropped dramatically – to under 20 per cent. in 1639.

Even so, Ship-Money was a financial success. By 1638 Charles was almost out of debt, the Crown jewels had been taken out of pawn, and the government's income seemed adequate to meet normal expenditure. Weston (until his death in March 1635) and his successor Juxon proved themselves efficient Treasurers. But the political cost of financial success was immense. Charles offended every class in the country – the peers and great landowners by enclosure and forest fines, and Ship-Money, the gentry by 'distraint of knighthood', the merchants by tunnage and poundage, the common people by price-raising monopolies. By 1639 Charles was facing what was virtually an organized campaign of civil disobedience.

It was just at this time that Charles most needed the country's support. The healthy condition of the Treasury fooled the King into his most reckless action – his attempt to force the Scots to accept a church disciplined on the English pattern. With loans such as the £85,000 borrowed from Sir Peter Pindar, a leading Customs farmer, Juxon was able to assure Charles that the Treasury could afford a campaign costing £200,000. In 1639, therefore, the King moved against the Scots to force them to restore the bishops they had evicted the previous year.[1] The campaign was a disaster, and soon led to even greater calamities. The army was badly led, trained and equipped, and the King was quite unable to stir up among the people any enthusiasm for a war against the Scots. Even in the north, English Puritans found that they had more in common with Scottish Presbyterians than with Charles, Laud, and the Arminian clergy. In June 1639, with the collapse of the First Bishops' War, Charles had to make peace with the Scots on terms which left the Presbyterian leaders in control of their country. Still determined to bring the rebels to heel, Charles tried to get England to support him. The King ordered elections, in the hope that the summoning of Parliament would be a popular gesture and that the grateful Commons would vote him taxes. This was a vain hope. Parliament met in April 1640, and the M.P.s hurled such abuse at the government that Charles had to dissolve it after only three weeks.

By now, England was in passive revolt against the King's administration, but Charles was as determined as ever to restore his authority in Scotland. By desperate means, Juxon scraped together nearly £600,000 for the Second Bishops' War. This, in the summer of 1640, was another military fiasco. The Scots deliberately imposed such terms on Charles that the King had to surrender to his political opponents. By no means other than through Parliament could Charles obtain the £850 a day his representatives promised the Scottish army. Pym and his colleagues in the Long Parliament were soon able to set to work to demolish the machinery by which Charles had governed for eleven years.

[1] See below, p. 102.

## ii. The Church in England

The taxes imposed during the 1630s in the absence of Parliament were not, of course, the only reason for the crisis. They may not have been even the main reason. The first of the 'Three Resolutions' of 1629 had branded 'innovators in religion' as capital enemies of the kingdom; sixteen years later, Archbishop Laud paid with his head for his Arminian beliefs, the second of Parliament's great victims. Many historians call the Civil War period 'The Puritan Revolution'.

Charles had quickly shown where his sympathies lay, through his support for Arminian clergy like Montagu, Manwaring and Sibthorpe. The King was a man of deep piety, with a sincere belief in the importance of the Church in men's lives. Like his father at Hampton Court, Charles was convinced of the political value of the bishops to the Crown. Moreover, Charles's artistic tastes longed for the beauty and dignity of ceremonial in Church worship, and his love of order was revolted by the ranting of Puritan preachers. But it was eight years before Charles could appoint an archbishop who shared his views. The doddering Puritan George Abbot lived on at Canterbury until 1633, tormented in body by gout and in soul by having killed the gamekeeper. Archbishop Harsnett of York was too subservient, too anxious to please everybody, to lead the Church as the King wished; For similar obsequiousness to all and sundry, Charles had already dismissed from Court the *bon viveur* politician, Bishop Williams of Lincoln.

Charles found his man in William Laud, Bishop of London and Chancellor of Oxford University. The son of a Reading master tailor, Laud had already proved his efficiency as an administrator and his ability as a scholar. He was straightforward, blunt, honest and ruthless, with no talent for the pretence and hypocrisy which characterized Court life. As President of St. John's from 1611 to 1621, and as Chancellor of Oxford from 1629, Laud had enriched both College and University with money and scholarship, founding professorships in Hebrew and Arabic. He enforced tight discipline, and had a genius for attending to detail. In a schoolmasterly tone, for example, he ordered the dons of All Souls' to get their hair cut. His success in combating University Puritanism led him to fight the non-conformists in his archbishopric with similar methods. His pride in the Church and his demand for it to be respected soon turned the Puritans bitterly against him – D'Ewes called him 'a little, low, red-faced man, of mean parentage'. Many of Laud's episcopal colleagues were of similar mercantile and academic background – thirteen bishops of the time had been heads of Oxford and Cambridge Colleges. The relatively obscure origins of most of the bishops helped to prejudice the peers and the wealthier landed classes against them, particularly when the bishops claimed greater and greater spiritual and political power. In 1630, for example, there were four bishops in the Privy Council – more than at any time since the Reformation. Class-conscious snobbery eleven years later helped to make Lord Falkland, a loyal Anglican, demand that bishops should lose their seats in the House of Lords.

Laud and his Arminian friends tried to restore the dignified ritual of the Prayer Book services, somewhat tarnished during half a century of indifference, ignorance and neglect. To him, 'The external worship of God in His Church is the great witness to the world, that our heart stands right in that service of God. . . . Ceremonies are the hedge that fence the substance of religion from all the indignities which profaneness and sacrilege too commonly put upon it.' Laud was determined to have the Holy Communion celebrated with greater reverence. In a series of Visitations, in the diocese of Canterbury in 1633 and throughout the country in the succeeding years, Laud's agents carried out his policies. Clergy who refused to obey faced heavy punishment from the Court of High Commission. Priests were required to wear vestments, and not just surplices, to have candles on the altar, and to bow whenever the name of Jesus was mentioned. The Visitors ordered the altar to be at the east end of the church, and not in the middle where parishioners could leave their hats on it, and insisted that it be railed off – to protect it from the attentions of dogs wandering into the building. Some clergy placed in their churches statues of the Virgin Mary and the saints, fitted new stained-glass windows, or installed organs. To the Puritans, such decorations seemed an idolatrous breach of the Second Commandment – *Thou shalt not make unto thee any graven image*. The Puritans were not the only men to think that Laud was leading England back to Rome – even the Pope thought so, and twice offered Laud a cardinal's hat. Moreover, the activities of

Catholics at Court were highly suspect. The Queen, very influential over Charles since Buckingham's death, was a Catholic. Many fashionable ladies were converted to Rome, largely through the enthusiasm of Olivia, wife of the courtier Endymion Porter. Abroad, the continental Protestants were still struggling for survival in the Thirty Years War. What if English Protestants should find themselves betrayed into the hands of the papal enemy by their own bishops?

It was the effectiveness of Laud's actions, as much as the nature of his aims, which so incensed the Puritan opposition. Laud's objectives were little different from those of Matthew Parker, Elizabeth's first archbishop, but Parker had no efficient Court of High Commission, and much less support from his sovereign, to help him to achieve order, uniformity and discipline. In the 1630s, the Court of High Commission was more active than ever before, punishing great men for their moral lapses, licensing or censoring books, and punishing clergy who did not share Laud's enthusiasm for the 'beauty of holiness'. Where the authority of this court was not sufficient, the offender was brought before Star Chamber. In both courts, he could be made to give evidence against himself by means of the hated *ex officio* oath. Both courts acted more in accordance with what was politically desirable, rather than with what was prescribed by the law. The powers of these prerogative courts enabled Laud to deal with threats from bodies such as the 'Feoffees for Impropriations', a group of Puritans who bought up the tithe and patronage rights of parishes in towns represented in Parliament, and then appointed fervent Puritan ministers able to convert men to their beliefs. Then Laud waged war on the towns and private individuals who appointed Puritan 'lecturers', to churches such as St. Antholin's London, to supplement the preaching (if any!) of the parish priest. Likewise he quarrelled with those who contracted to 'augment' the normal income of the parish clergyman provided the patron chose someone of acceptable views. In some towns, too, the corporations had bought up the advowson – in Norwich, Ipswich, Gloucester, Plymouth, Leeds and Hull, for example – and in some of these there were lengthy struggles in the 1630s between bishops and corporations over the choice of parsons. Many of these towns were principal supporters of Parliament in the next decade.

In such conflicts, the power of Star Chamber and High Commission was the ultimate authority. Even Bishop Williams, long out of favour at Court and suspect of treason, was fined £10,000 by Star Chamber and imprisoned in the Tower. In an age already conscious of the power of propaganda, the courts naturally tried to suppress the publication of hostile books and pamphlets. Probably nothing brought the Laudian Church so much unpopularity as the brutal punishments ordered by Star Chamber for the activity of Prynne, Bastwick, Burton and Lilburne in writing or publishing attacks on the bishops. Lilburne was flogged through the streets of London, the others had their ears cut off, and all four went to the Tower. Even in the pillory, the irrepressible Lilburne continued to harangue the crowd and throw to the spectators pamphlets against the bishops.

Then, in May 1640, Laud made his most extreme attempt to enforce discipline. Despite the collapse of the Short Parliament and the general hostility towards Charles's preparations for the Second Bishops' War, Convocation produced Seventeen Canons embodying Laud's ideas. Under threat of excommunication, the clergy had to preach regularly in support of the doctrine of the Divine Right of Kings and of the established system of Church government. The railing-off of the altar at the east end of the church was made compulsory. All clergy, schoolmasters and members of other learned professions had to swear to maintain 'the government of this Church by Archbishops, Bishops, deans and archdeacons *et cetera*, as it now stands established'. What, questioned the Puritans, did this mysterious *et cetera* include? Richard Baxter, then a schoolmaster at Dudley, wrote 'The *Et cetera* oath, which was imposed on us for the unalterable subjecting of us to diocesans [bishops], was a chief means to alienate me and many others from it [episcopacy]'. The bishops could not be trusted, and the ranks of the non-conformists swelled.

Laud's attempts to improve the Church's finances were equally unpopular, and even more futile. Unless Charles was prepared and able to rule absolutely, the Church could not get back the tithes and other incomes obtained by laymen since the dissolution of the monasteries. Even Mary Tudor had failed to persuade her Catholic M.P.s to give back the monastic lands they had acquired. In Scotland, it is true, Charles had tried to restore the tithes, but his Acts of Revocation had aroused too much hostility for him to attempt the same in England. With the King afraid to help them, the bishops had little chance of getting back for the Church the revenues it had lost.

Laud and his colleagues had to move cautiously. One reason for the poverty of many parsons was that their predecessors had agreed to receive fixed sums each year instead of the tithes still remaining to them. The price-rise had made these payments relatively worthless. When the clergy tried to get the agreements (*modi*) revised, they were strongly resisted by lawyers demanding that they should keep the original contracts. In such circumstances there was little point in the Church courts protesting that canon law gave the clergy the right to receive a tenth of each man's income. The common law courts constantly enforced their supremacy through issuing writs of prohibition, thereby transferring the cases from the Church courts to themselves. Well might Fuller[1] complain that in some parishes, 'the poor Levite [priest] hath . . . not the tenth, in some not the twentieth part of the tithe.'

For a while, Laud had higher hopes of his campaign to revive and increase the payment of tithes in towns, largely evaded since the Reformation. Here, London was a test case. Henry VIII had decreed that Londoners should pay tithes at the rate of 2s. 9d. in the £ on all house rents, and in 1618 the Exchequer Court had declared that tithes should be paid at that rate on the true yearly value of all property, whether rented or not. Laud and Juxon – Bishop of London as well as Lord Treasurer – tried to get the Court decision enforced, at least to a limited extent. In 1638 the London parishes were told to assess what would be a reasonable income from tithes. Their estimates averaged £126 a year, an increase of 58 per cent. on the existing annual average. These increases were modest enough – only a tiny fraction of what the 1618 judgement ordered – but the Londoners resisted them stoutly. The decision finally rested with the King. Faced with the trouble in Scotland, Charles hesitated – and did nothing. Even with the law on his side, Charles did not dare to support the clergy against the turbulent Londoners. The opposition had succeeded. The citizens jeered at Laud in the streets, shouting 'Two and Ninepence!' at him. There was now no chance of reimposing tithes on the

---

[1] Thomas Fuller (1608-61), Anglican parson and Church historian.

towns throughout the country. The Church gained nothing but unpopularity.

The country remained sceptical about the clergy's protestations of poverty. If the Church was so poor, how could Convocation afford to vote the King large sums of money in clerical taxation? In 1628, for example, Convocation had granted five clerical subsidies, together worth £94,000; the lay subsidies voted by Parliament from the rest of the country brought in only three times as much.[1] Taxation of the clergy was attacked as a device to help Charles to escape from Parliament. The 1640 Convocation infuriated the members of the Short Parliament (which granted nothing) by voting Charles six clerical subsidies, worth about £115,000. The poorest clergy (those with livings rated at under £10[2] a year) were exempt from this taxation, and the wealthiest were assessed relatively lightly, but thousands of vicars and rectors had to pay out an enormous part of their incomes when their superiors in Convocation so decreed. Clerical taxation, in fact, helped to undermine the authority of the bishops, and there were many Anglican parsons glad to see them abolished by the Long Parliament.

By the time the Long Parliament met, therefore, the Laudian Church was under fire for the pretensions of its prelates, for the revival of 'Popish' ceremonies, for the suppression of its critics like the Feoffees and Prynne by Star Chamber and the High Commission, for church courts which challenged those of the common law, for its money demands such as the revision of the *modi* and the tithes of London, and for the political subservience of the bishops. The speed with which the 'Pope of Lambeth' was sent to the Tower demonstrated the strength of the attack. But Laud's positive achievements must not be forgotten. The Arminian movement shook the Church out of the spiritual sleepiness of the post-Reformation period. It attracted some clergy of high quality – the Laudian Church was the Church of George Herbert, Robert Herrick, Robert Burton, Jeremy Taylor and Thomas Fuller, and was able to survive the persecutions of the Civil War. Laud's drive to repair decaying

---

[1] In other words, about 25 per cent. of the direct taxation was paid by 0·2 per cent. of the population (from C. Hill's figures). It was perhaps fortunate for Charles that Hampden was not a clergyman!

[2] Lowered to £8 in 1640.

Church buildings was successful.   During the 1630s, £100,000 was given by charitable Anglicans for building or repairing churches; despite the price-rise, this figure compares well with the £2400 and the £11,000 similarly given in the decades 1581–90 and 1601–10 respectively.   The spiritual renaissance also inspired experiments such as Nicholas Ferrar's community at Little Gidding in Huntingdonshire, where some thirty of his friends lived a pious life of monastic work and prayer until the Puritans closed down the 'Arminian Nunnery' in 1646.   The most serious weakness of the church was its challenge to the finances of the gentry and to the political power of Parliament and the law courts, and its failure to win popular support. Laud had to fortify Lambeth Palace with cannon to keep off the London mob.

### iii. Wentworth and Ireland

In the summer of 1628 no Parliamentarian was more respected by his colleagues than Thomas Wentworth.   He had gained experience in four previous Parliaments – those of 1614, 1621, 1624 and 1625.   As an opponent of Buckingham, he had been pricked as a sheriff and so kept out of the 1626 Parliament. He had gone to prison for refusing to pay the forced loan. Released in time to be elected again in 1628, Wentworth quickly emerged as a leader of the Commons, and played a principal part in the negotiations between Commons and Lords. Without his work, the King might never have been compelled to accept the Petition of Right.

Then he changed sides.   Perhaps he felt that the Petition of Right was adequate as a guarantee of liberty, and that there was no need to squeeze fresh concessions from the King; perhaps a strong inducement was the peerage Charles offered him.   Whatever the reason, the Eliots, Pyms and Hampdens never forgave the 'Grand Apostate'.   Wentworth's character made him more enemies: he was arrogant, ambitious, stubborn, ruthless, prepared to betray and deceive if it suited his purposes. He was more Puritan than Arminian, but his love of order led him to support Laud's attempts to impose ritual and discipline. A curious friendship grew up between the two men, based on their common aims.   'For the State, indeed my Lord, I am for *thorough*', he wrote to the Archbishop in the summer of 1633.

There were times, indeed, when Laud was Wentworth's only
friend at Court, and the Lord Deputy of Ireland had to rely
upon the Archbishop to explain his actions to the King.   The
stubborn Yorkshireman got on badly with the other courtiers,
for he refused to give them pickings out of the revenues of
Ireland, and constantly criticized the extravagance of the circle
around the Queen.   Many who in 1642 fought for Charles had
cheered at Wentworth's execution in the previous year.

By the end of 1628, Viscount Wentworth was President of the
Council of the North, the prerogative court responsible for law
and order in the northern counties.   Within weeks he removed
two old enemies, Lord Savile and Lord Scrope, from the
Council, and soon set about reviving the decaying administration which they left behind.   Soon, too, he was a member of
the Privy Council, and one of the Poor Law Commissioners
appointed by Charles to force the J.P.s and sheriffs to impose the
Elizabethan Poor Law and to relieve social distress.   In the
north, Wentworth was determined to enforce respect for the
King and for himself as the King's representative.   This was a
most necessary task, but the Lord President went about it in a
needlessly high-handed way.   Sir Thomas Gower, Lord
Fauconberg and his son, and Sir David Foulis and his son-in-
law, Sir Thomas Leighton, were all prosecuted and heavily
punished for insolently defying Wentworth's authority or
questioning the Council of the North's power as a prerogative
court.   The Lord President, indeed, took special pleasure in
humbling the great men of the north.   Moreover, he angered
the common people by his attempts to make the weavers of
Halifax, Leeds and Wakefield obey the regulations controlling
apprenticeship and the quality of cloth.   The clothiers, as well
as embittered families like the Saviles and Fairfaxes, were
strongly for Parliament in 1640.

Wentworth's administrative gifts, though, were so outstanding that in the summer of 1631 Charles decided to appoint him
Lord Deputy of Ireland, the grave of so many reputations.
The new honour was not altogether welcome to Wentworth,
who now found himself removed even further from London, the
centre of political affairs.   It was not until July 1633 that the
new Deputy arrived in Dublin, determined to enforce the
policy of *thorough* to which he and Laud had dedicated themselves.   The problems were great.   For years Ireland had

been a regular drain on the English Exchequer. Since Falkland's recall in 1629 the administration had gone to pieces, under misnamed Lord Justices like Kilmallock and the greedy Protestant colonists Cork and Loftus as co-governors. Within a few days of his arrival, Wentworth was writing back to Weston, describing the members of his Irish Council as 'the most intent upon their own ends that ever I met with'. Lord Cork as Treasurer, Lord Loftus as Chancellor, and Lord Mountnorris as Vice-Treasurer headed factions of utterly selfish and corrupt 'new' men. Their close connexions with English courtiers meant that complaints were soon streaming back to London. Before long, Wentworth found that Queen Henrietta Maria was a jealous enemy, one who was usually able to persuade the King not to trust the Lord Deputy with the power he wanted.

Despite these handicaps, Wentworth achieved great success. He brought over his friends George Radcliffe and Christopher Wandesworth, as administrators on whom he could rely. He built up the Court of Castle Chamber as a prerogative court supreme in Ireland. He fined the Earl of Cork some £40,000 for various acts of corruption and dishonesty, had Mountnorris tried by Court-Martial and sentenced to death,[1] and in 1638 persuaded the Council to dismiss Loftus from his post of Chancellor. He prosecuted the City of London for the failure of its Companies to keep their contracts to develop Derry and Coleraine; the fine of £70,000 imposed by the English Star Chamber was later reduced to £12,000, but the Londoners lost their 'plantation'. The Irish Parliament of 1634-5 did what he wanted, expelling troublesome Catholic members, voting six subsidies, and appointing a Commission for Defective Titles to enquire into the rights by which men held their lands. The Commission was able to force many landowners and 'planters' to increase the rents they paid to the Crown, and to restore certain tithes and advowsons to the Church. The Irish army in 1633 was an ill-armed rabble of three thousand; Wentworth enlarged it, placed it under his direct control, and bought weapons for it in the Low Countries. To make Ireland more prosperous – and more profitable to England – he invested £30,000 of his own in developing the linen industry,

---

[1] Wentworth was accused of persecuting Mountnorris to discredit his bid for the customs farm. The sentence was not carried out.

improved the breeding of horses, tried to start the manufacture of glass and quarrying of marble, and repeatedly begged the English Privy Council not to raise duties on Irish imports and exports. He took swift action against pirates, knighting the first navy captain who captured a pirate ship. The revenue from customs in 1634 was 48 per cent. higher and in 1637 128 per cent. higher than in 1633. By 1637 Wentworth and George Radcliffe were themselves sole farmers of the customs, having outbid the syndicate headed by Mountnorris.[1]

He also tackled some of Ireland's religious problems. The official state religion was a Calvinist Anglicanism, headed by the Puritan Archbishop Ussher of Armagh. The established Church was poor in every sense, and under heavy fire from the Catholic majority and from the Scottish Presbyterians in Ulster. Wentworth was determined not to persecute the Catholics, but he distrusted and despised them, and refused to grant in full the 'Graces' promised by Falkland in 1627. He kept in reserve the oath of supremacy, as a useful threat for forcing troublesome Catholics to retire from political life. He did not have time, however, to carry out his plans to establish Protestant plantations in the west, in Connaught and Clare. He forced the bishops of the established Church, in the Convocation of 1635, to accept the Church of England's Thirty-Nine Articles, in place of their own more Calvinist statement of faith. Reliable and efficient friends like Bramhall and Leslie were given key bishoprics, and helped to improve the finances of the Church. Wentworth made Trinity College, Dublin, accept the strict discipline which Laud had introduced to Oxford. As in England and Scotland, such policies were likely to offend laymen who had profited at the expense of the Church: Wentworth prosecuted the Earl of Cork for the £30,000 of church property which the old rogue had seized, and forced him to remove the vast family sepulchre which he had erected in St. Patrick's Cathedral, Dublin, in place of the high altar.

Wentworth won very few friends. He did little to reduce the bitterness of the Irish natives, robbed of their lands and their religious privileges. No Irishman could approve of his efficiency in collecting taxes. In a land where cattle-stealing was almost a national industry, there was no enthusiasm for the Lord Deputy's strict justice. The new nobles like Cork and

[1] See previous note.

Mountnorris soon loathed him. Of the old Irish nobles, only Dillon and young Ormonde came to sympathize with his attempts to introduce order. His own wealth provided his enemies with ammunition – he acquired 59,000 acres in Ireland, and his income was alleged to exceed £23,000 a year. Holland, Goring and other courtiers around the Queen, and Henrietta herself, kept up their barrage of complaints against Wentworth's tyranny – partly because the Lord Deputy refused the favours they asked for their friends.

Meanwhile, Wentworth was shaken by the King's follies in Scotland. A Scottish minister appeared in Ulster, collecting signatures for the National Covenant. Wentworth's enemies in Ireland and in the north (he was still President of the Council of the North) barely concealed their sympathy and support for the Covenanters. Wentworth tried to get the Ulster Scots to swear loyalty to the King. He increased the size of the army to 9000, sending 500 of them to help garrison Carlisle. He repeatedly urged Charles to use the Irish army to seize strategic towns like Dumbarton. The jealousy of Court favourites left Wentworth's offers unanswered. It was not until Holland's army had fled at the sight of the Scots that Charles summoned his ablest servant back to England – secretly, lest the Queen find out what he had done.

The fleeting and disastrous months of 1640 were the climax of Wentworth's career, bringing the earldom he had so long coveted, and giving him the supreme power in the King's counsels he had so long desired. Despite the crisis, his achievement in Ireland was now obvious. Wandesworth and Dillon managed a completely docile Parliament, which unanimously voted the King four subsidies of £45,000 each and thanked him for the rule of the Earl of Strafford – 'for your tender care over us showed by the deputing and supporting of so good a governor'. The Short Parliament, meeting in London a month later, spoke with a different tone.

### iv. Scotland and the First Bishops' War

Charles's policies in Scotland closely imitated those in England. Taxation became annual and regular, no longer an emergency, crisis measure. The tax on income from rents and investments was collected almost every year, and in 1633

Charles raised the rate from 5 per cent. to 6¼ per cent. In 1633, too, Parliament introduced a land tax, to be paid annually for six years. The citizens of Edinburgh had additional grievances, for the King ordered them to pay for the building of a new Parliament House and new Law Courts – at a cost of £127,000 between 1633 and 1640. Moreover, when he founded a new bishopric in Edinburgh in 1633 and elevated the church of St. Giles to the status of a cathedral, many townsmen lost the shops which they had owned *inside* St. Giles's. The people of Edinburgh were less successful than those of London in the struggle over tithes, for a new assessment on house rentals enabled the stipends of the city clergy to be raised substantially.

In an attempt to increase the authority of the bishops and to help them in dealing with the General Assembly, Charles appointed several of them to the Scottish Privy Council. This angered the nobles, already annoyed at the King's seizure of tithes, especially when in 1635 Charles made Archbishop Spottiswoode the Chancellor of Scotland – a position no churchman had held since the Reformation. When, in the previous year, a number of nobles had prepared a 'Supplication' against his Church policies, Charles had one of their leaders, Lord Balmerino, condemned for high treason.

Charles, moreover, was determined to extend to the Scots the benefits of the 'beauty of holiness'. When he was crowned in Edinburgh in 1633, the citizens gaped in alarm at the sight of the copes and mitres of the Arminian service in Holyrood Chapel. Immediately afterwards he ordered that surplices should be worn in parish churches and copes in cathedrals, to the annoyance of ministers accustomed to the black 'Geneva' gown. James had abandoned his plan to impose the English Book of Common Prayer on Scotland, in view of the opposition which the Articles of Perth aroused; his son was not so cautious. The Scottish bishops protested that the introduction of the English Book would stir up national prejudices, and so tried to get Charles and Laud to agree to a Book which would make concessions to Scottish religious and national feelings. For four years the argument over the contents of the Book continued. In 1635 new Canon laws promised in advance excommunication for any who questioned the services in the prospective Book, even though their form had not yet been decided! Two years later the new Liturgy was published. It contained little that should have offended the Scots – it was not a popish or even 'High Church' Book, and was in general what the Scottish bishops wanted. Laud had little to do with it. But what was unforgivable was the way in which 'Laud's Liturgy' was introduced – by royal prerogative, not by Parliament or the General Assembly.

Without consulting the Scottish Privy Council, Charles ordered that the new Liturgy should be used throughout Scotland from July 1637; no other service book was to be tolerated. A carefully-planned tumult greeted it. The congregation rioted in St. Giles's Cathedral, despite the presence of Archbishop Spottiswoode, and most of the Privy Council. Sticks and stones showered upon Dean Hannah as he tried to read the service. An Edinburgh wench, Jenny Geddes, threw her seat at the Dean, shrieking that the Mass was come among them. The magistrates expelled the trouble makers, but the clamour from outside still drowned the Dean's words. Elsewhere, a Glasgow minister who read the service was almost lynched by women, while the Bishop of Brechin kept his congregation quiet only by pointing loaded pistols at them. This was no spontaneous outburst: great men like Rothes and Balmerino, lawyers like Johnston of Warriston, ministers like Alexander Henderson, were stirring up popular emotions and prejudices for political as well as religious purposes. Here was the opportunity for the predestined saviours of the Kirk to save themselves from Stuart interference and Stuart taxes. Dr. Baillie, a Presbyterian minister but no extremist, commented 'I think our people possessed with a bloody devill, farr above anything that ever I could have imagined, though the masse in Latine had been presented.'

It was months before Charles realized how serious things were. Three members of the Scottish Privy Council, Lord Traquair, Lord Lorne and Sir Thomas Hope, secretly supported the rebels and warned them of the King's moves. Remote from the people of Scotland even more than from those of England, Charles was completely out-manœuvred. In November 1637 the Privy Council allowed the opposition to choose commissioners, four from each 'estate' of the Parliament; these commissioners soon formed themselves into a body known as 'The Tables', and became the real rulers of Scotland. As a means to unite the nation, the crafty Johnston of Warriston brought forward the old 'Negative Confession', a declaration of Protestantism drawn up in 1580 as a test for public office. He embodied this 'Confession' in a National Covenant to assert the rights of Parliament and the General Assembly to decide the Kirk's policies. At the end of February 1638 Warriston and his friends signed the Covenant. Soon, ministers were urging their congregations, and nobles were ordering their tenants, to sign the copies of the document; within a few months, tens of thousands had 'taken the Covenant'. The Covenant was in fact a moderate document. Nothing in it attacked the bishops or the Articles of Perth. Most of those who signed the declaration, expressed in over 4000 words of heavy legal language, did not realize how moderate it was.

But it alarmed the King. For a while, in the summer of 1638, Charles considered immediate military action, but his advisers warned him that neither army nor Treasury was ready. In September the King agreed to suspend the Liturgy, the 1635 Canons, the Scottish High Commission, and even the Articles of Perth, until a General Assembly of the Kirk had considered them. Two months later, the Assembly met in Glasgow. It was carefully 'packed' and briefed by the opposition leaders, who had brought 'great bands and troops of men' to support them; the bishops were excluded, for the Covenanters threatened to put them on trial for their 'manifold crimes'. Lord Hamilton, the King's Commissioner, tried to dissolve the Assembly because of its unconstitutional nature, but it defied him. Within a month, the Assembly banned the Liturgy and Canons as containing 'many popish errours and ceremonies', deposed and excommunicated the bishops, annulled all the acts of the Assemblies between 1606 and 1618 (when James had been reviving the bishops' powers), and declared (quite dishonestly) that the 1580 Confession had condemned episcopacy. By this means the Glasgow Assembly made all who had signed the Covenant appear as opponents of the bishops. Together with the thousands of enthusiastic Presbyterians who bore arms against Charles in 1639, 1640 and 1644, there may have been many fighting because they feared the personal consequences of a royal victory.

Charles had been prepared to sacrifice the 'Liturgy'; he was not prepared to abandon the bishops. Soon, Juxon was busy

HBS

begging for Ship-Money and borrowing from courtiers and customs farmers. Charles was going to war: his Scottish subjects must be disciplined. At the Queen's request, Charles appointed Lord Holland as an independent general of cavalry – to the anger of Lord Arundel and Lord Essex, officially commanders of the army. The troops were poor, and had no heart for the coming campaign. In the north the gentry still resented Wentworth's behaviour as President of the Council, and no weapons but bows and pikes could be found for the Border levies. Moreover, the two oppositions were combining: Lord Brooke, Lord Saye and Sele, John Pym and many others were busy corresponding with the leaders of the Covenanters.

In Scotland, soldiers experienced in the German wars were training village youths in the handling of arms. The Covenanters' commander, Alexander Leslie, a veteran of Gustavus Adolphus's army, seized Edinburgh Castle in March 1639. Lord Traquair at the same time betrayed the royal arsenal at Dalkeith – and the crown jewels – to the rebels. A few days later Montrose captured Aberdeen, principal town of the royalist Gordon clan. While the Covenanters were busy in Scotland, Charles dallied on the road to York. Occasionally he reviewed a company of Court gallants, masquerading as cavalry; once, he offered the Scots pardon, but swore to execute their leaders; once in a belated bid for popularity, he cancelled a number of monopolies. The army's slender resources withered away during this leisurely progress. The fleet provided by Ship-Money reached the Forth in May 1639, under the unnautical Hamilton, but with the suppression of the Gordons by Montrose there were few men in Scotland its commander could trust.

Not until June 1st, over two months after the fall of Aberdeen, did the King's army cross the Tweed. Even at this stage, the army was disrupted by angry brawls between Holland and the other commanders. Holland's glittering cavalry, ahead of the rest of the royal army, met a body of Covenanting infantry. Without firing a shot, Leslie persuaded Holland to retreat, and the royal cavalry fled back to Berwick, pursued by the jeers of the Scots. After this disgraceful episode, the First Bishops' War soon petered out. The courtiers, with a few exceptions, grew tired of the tedious business of campaigning. Apart from the King, and men like Arundel and Essex, all welcomed the humiliating Treaty of Berwick in mid-June: Charles consented to allow the Scots to settle their own religious affairs by their Parliament and Assembly. This military fiasco was the beginning of the end for Charles. The royalist reaction of the previous ten years was failing. Rebellion was succeeding.

## v. The Short Parliament and the Second Bishops' War

The Treaty of Berwick decided nothing. With good reason, neither side trusted the other. Soon, Charles summoned a Scottish Parliament and Assembly – and proclaimed as their purpose the annulment of the acts of the 'pretended' Glasgow Assembly. He ordered Hamilton to work secretly to persuade some of the Covenanting lords to join his side, and he tried to borrow Spanish troops from the Netherlands. But he was again outwitted. The treacherous Traquair persuaded him not to summon bishops to the coming Parliament and Assembly, so that, if need be, Charles could later disown their decisions on the grounds that they were unconstitutional. In consequence, the Covenanters dominated both, reaffirmed the decisions of the Glasgow Assembly, and appointed Lords of the Articles acceptable to themselves and not to the King.

At the end of September 1639, Wentworth returned to London. His long absence from English politics gave him a mistaken view of the crisis. Ignoring the genuine economic and religious grievances of the rebels, he was determined to restore discipline and obedience in Scotland. Sternness had worked in Ireland; why should it not work also in Scotland? Remembering his influence over the 1628 House of Commons (and forgetting the hostility which his 'apostasy' had provoked), he persuaded Charles that he could dominate an English Parliament, and get it to vote taxes for a national war against the Scots to avenge the humiliation of 1639. For the moment, he was almost supreme in the King's counsels, second only to Laud. At last he received his well-deserved earldom, and it was as Strafford that he hastened back to Dublin in March 1640 to preside over the Irish Parliament. Here he was completely successful, though racked by dysentry and gout.

The illness delayed his return to London, and the English Parliament opened in mid-April without him. Before he got back, Pym had already taken command of the Commons, and was leading the cry for 'redress before supply'. Strafford managed to prevent the Lords from echoing this demand, but could not get the Crown's request for subsidies reduced to a reasonable level. Sir Harry Vane, the new Secretary, asked for twelve subsidies – worth about £840,000 – in return for the abolition of Ship-Money. The Commons voted nothing. Their leaders then started to shout their grievances over religion. Moreover, fighting had already broken out again in Edinburgh, and there was an immediate danger that the Commons might declare their support for their fellow Puritans in Scotland. The Privy Council met in emergency session – at 6 a.m. – and later that morning Charles went to Westminster and outraged the M.P.s by dissolving Parliament. After the lapse of eleven years, the King had found Parliament intolerable after only three weeks. Throughout the summer of 1640, Pym and his friends continued their vehement protests against this interference with parliamentary liberty.

In the afternoon after the dissolution, May 5th, the Council met again. The Scots were already in arms, and the treasury was empty. Strafford offered Charles the Irish army for use against the Covenanters. With unintentional ambiguity, Vane noted down Strafford's words – 'You have an army in Ireland you may employ to reduce *this* Kingdom.' The King agreed. Desperately, the Treasurer Juxon continued to borrow money wherever he could – £250,000 from the customs farmers, £40,000 from the Merchant Adventurers, £30,000 from the Duke of Lennox, £20,000 from Strafford. The Convocations normally met at the same time as Parliament; now, however, they remained in session after the dissolution and promised the King £20,000 a year from the Church. Charles began negotiating to get four million ducats from Spain for the loan of the English fleet. Even Henrietta Maria started to economize.

Then, in August 1640, the Scots crossed the Border and marched towards Newcastle. At the crucial moment the new English commander, the Earl of Northumberland, fell seriously ill. This was a heavy blow, for his prestige in the Borders was great – for centuries a Percy's word there had had more authority than the King's. With Holland discredited, and Essex and Arundel disgruntled, there was no one but Strafford to take command of the royal army. The northcountrymen might have fought for Northumberland; for Strafford, though, they certainly would not fight. Delayed by gout, Strafford had got no further north than York when Leslie's army crossed the Tyne after a skirmish at Newburn. Outflanked, the royal garrison under Lord Conway fled from Newcastle, which it had not fortified. Again, the rebels had succeeded.

This time, Strafford's presence delayed the royal collapse. He and Sir Jacob Astley drilled an army at York, numerically almost as strong as Leslie's force outside Newcastle. But they could not check the progress of pessimism and political opposition. Hamilton, in command of the fleet, repeatedly found excuses for not transporting the Irish army to Scotland. In London, the opposition peers – Brooke, Saye and Sele, Warwick – persuaded Essex, Hertford and Mandeville and six others to join them in signing a remonstrance drafted by Pym, attacking Ship-Money, monopolies and 'innovations in religion'. Nonetheless, Charles believed that most of the peers supported him, and he summoned them all to meet him in a Council of Peers at York. To gain time, he tried to conciliate his critics with concessions, even at the expense of wounding his friends, while he negotiated for help from Spain, from Denmark, and from the Prince of Orange in the United Provinces. In fact, however, time was running out. In October the Council of Peers negotiated with the Scots, and carefully drew up armistice terms which would force Charles to call another Parliament. The Treaty of Ripon agreed that Leslie's army should occupy the north of England until a final settlement was concluded with the help of the English Parliament. To encourage Charles to summon Parliament as soon as possible, the peers promised the Scots that the King would pay them £850 a day until the permanent treaty was signed.

Charles's governmental system had come to a sorry end. The nature of the so-called 'Eleven Years Tyranny' was such that the administration could no longer force its own executive officers, the sheriffs and J.P.s, to collect taxes; its military forces had twice been chased away by hastily-assembled bands of Scots; it had been powerless to deal with a defiant General Assembly; its policies had especially annoyed the citizens of London and Edinburgh, the two capital cities; its chief ministers Laud and Strafford were hated by many even of the King's supporters. Shy, remote, shielded by Court formalities and the lies of flatterers, Charles had never realized the depth and the strength of the opposition to him. His unrealistic optimism was to last eight years more, and to lead him to the scaffold.

### vi. The Long Parliament and its enemies

This was the moment for which Puritan politicians had been praying. The summer months of 1640 had allowed the opposition leaders to complete the plans they had been preparing for years in their meetings as members of the Providence Company or the Massachusetts Bay Company. As soon as Charles summoned the new Parliament, Pym set out on an election tour – the first in history – taking Hampden with him as the chief exhibit in the case against Ship-Money and arbitrary taxation. Apart from a few King's servants and courtiers, the Parliament which opened on November 3rd consisted almost entirely of opponents of the Government and its policies. In nearly thirty constituencies there were election disputes; 'packed' by the Commons' leaders, in each case the Committee of Privileges decided in favour of the opposition candidate. As Pym commented to Hyde, 'they must not only sweep the house clean below, but must pull down all the cobwebs which hung in the tops and corners'. Without delay, Parliament settled down to a threefold task – to bring Charles's arbitrary government to an end and to release its victims, to punish those responsible for it, and to make it impossible for the King ever to impose it again. On these matters, Lords and Commons worked together in remarkable agreement.

For the first week of the new Parliament, Pym let the criticism of the government gather momentum: in more than twenty petitions, the Commons listened to attacks on monopolies, Ship-Money, 'innovations in religion', and the harshness of the prerogative courts. The Speaker issued warrants for the release of Bastwick, Burton, Prynne and Lilburne, amid general rejoicing. Laud's enemy Bishop Williams came out of the Tower and back into the Lords. Then the opposition turned from the general to the particular. Dering attacked Laud as 'the centre from whence our miseries do flow', and Pym brought forward the long-prepared motion for the impeachment of Strafford, as soon as the minister got back to London from the north. Warned of what was happening, Strafford hastened to the Lords – only to find that Pym had already placed before them the impeachment for high treason. The Lords would not allow him to speak. Strafford, President of the North and Lieutenant of Ireland, was hurried off to custody amid the jeers of the crowd and the smug smiles of old enemies like the Earl of Cork.

The attack on Strafford was a great gamble for Pym. With 'Black Tom Tyrant' dead, Charles would be unable to resist Parliament's demands. But if the attack failed, Lords and Commons might well split apart, and Strafford might be able to turn the tables on his accusers; after all, it was well known that many of them had been plotting and intriguing with the Scots. With cold, calculating efficiency worthy of Strafford himself, Pym steered the Commons away from controversial topics, such as the reform of the Church, which might have divided them. To silence Strafford's friends, Pym whipped up an atmosphere of terror and panic. The Commons impeached Laud and the Bishop of Norwich. They impeached George Radcliffe. They scared Windebank, one of the Secretaries, into fleeing to France, in a rowing boat in thick fog. A fort-night later, John Finch, now the Lord Keeper, fled to the Netherlands to escape impeachment. With many bishops also threatened, Bishop Williams found it easy to persuade his colleagues not to take part in judging Strafford's impeachment.

Even so, the impeachment failed. When the trial opened, in March 1641, Strafford patiently and effectively answered the charges brought against him, replying with facts to the vague assertions of Pym, who acted as prosecutor. Soon only one main charge remained – that he had advised Charles to use the Irish army against '*this* Kingdom'. Sir Harry Vane had changed sides, and stoutly asserted that, in the Council meeting after the dissolution of the Short Parliament, Strafford had been referring to England, not Scotland. Strafford produced four other Councillors – Hamilton, Northumberland, Cottington and Juxon – to contradict Vane.

By now, the venom of Pym's attack and the dignified bearing and convincing answers of the prisoner, sick though he was, had made most of the peers decide to dismiss the charge. This would have been catastrophic for the opposition. So Pym revived the terrible mediaeval process of attainder, whereby Parliament simply passed an Act condemning the victim to death. On April 10th, as the Lords seemed about to abandon the trial, Pym's friend Haselrig introduced the attainder into the Commons. Ten days later, the Commons passed it by 204 votes to 59. Pym now prepared to bully the Lords and the King to accept it. Puritan preachers thundered for blood. London apprentices mobbed peers, crying for 'Justice!' Pym revealed the details (which he had known for a month) of a madcap Army plot to crush Parliament and release Strafford. Probably only twenty-six[1] peers voted for the attainder, but it was enough. Fear of the crowds, indecision, reluctance to offend the Commons, confidence that Charles would never accept the Bill, the death of the moderate but influential Earl of Bedford, and the absence of the bishops, prevented more than eleven peers opposing the attainder.

A few days earlier, Charles had promised Strafford that he would not let him suffer in any way; now, with characteristic courage, the prisoner wrote to Charles to release him from his promise. With the London mob milling around Whitehall, and bold spirits threatening the Queen and her Catholic ladies, Charles weakened. The crafty Bishop Williams persuaded him to accept the attainder to prevent further bloodshed. Torn in conscience, weeping, he signed the Act on May 10th. Two days later, Strafford was hurried to the scaffold on Tower Hill. With words which should have warned the master who had abandoned him, he told the crowd 'I am not the first man that hath suffered in this kind, it is a common portion that befalls men in this life.' He prayed with Archbishop Ussher, bade his friends farewell, and ordered the executioner to strike. The mob, over a hundred thousand strong, yelled in triumph. Pym and Parliament had engineered an act of arbitrary power more ruthless than anything during the 'Eleven Years Tyranny'.

The sacrifice of Strafford did incalculable harm to the King's cause. As Laud lamented, Charles 'knew not how to be or be made great'. No courtier could trust the King to save him from Parliament. In the summer of 1641 many courtiers changed sides and made their peace with Pym – Northumberland and Holland, for example. The King's original critics, not his former friends, provided most of the support for him at the end of 1641.

---

[1] Different sources disagree about the voting. The records were expunged from the Lords' *Journals*.

The King had given them Strafford, gloated Pym, and therefore would not now refuse them anything. Already Charles had accepted a Triennial Act which arranged for Parliament to meet at least once every three years, whether the King called it or not. Now Charles tamely agreed to a whole series of laws which immediately cut off most of his prerogative. On the day that he signed Strafford's attainder, he agreed to a Bill whereby the present Parliament could not be dissolved without its own consent – and so sacrificed the only legal means by which he could have stopped the headlong rush towards violence. In Clarendon's words, this 'Act for the perpetual Parliament' was 'to remove the landmarks and to destroy the foundations of the kingdom.'[1] In June 1641 Charles accepted the Tunnage and Poundage Act, forbidding all future impositions and allowing the King to collect customs duties for only two months more. Acts in July abolished the prerogative courts – Star Chamber, the High Commission, the Councils of the North and Wales – and deprived the Privy Council of its power to give judgement in law suits. In August the financial devices of the 1630s were brought to an end: Ship-Money and distraint of knighthood were made illegal, and the boundaries of the forests were declared to be those which had existed in James's reign. The lawyers had achieved their victory over the prerogative. Moreover, Charles weakened his position still further by bringing some of his opponents into the government: Oliver St. John became Solicitor-General, Warwick the Lord Admiral, Essex the Lord Chamberlain, Saye and Sele Master of the Court of Wards; even the treacherous Vane remained as Secretary until November. Bishop Williams was promoted to the vacant Archbishopric of York.

So far, the Commons had acted in remarkable unanimity. This was Pym's work, for it was he who had persuaded the Commons to refer controversial matters to its Committees. This had been the fate of the London petition of December 1640, listing twenty-eight charges against the Church, and demanding the abolition of the bishops 'root and branch'. The Commons did debate religion in the following February, however, and the division of opinion became obvious when Digby pleaded with them not to replace bishops with 'a pope in

[1] Clarendon, then sitting in the Commons as Sir Edward Hyde, does not, however, claim to have opposed it at the time.

every parish'. It was safer to leave such dangerous matters until Strafford was out of the way, and the Commons did not return to them until June and July. Some favoured moderate changes: Falkland, Hyde and Digby supported Archbishop Ussher's scheme for the reduction of the bishops' powers by forcing them to take the advice of committees of other clergy-men (in effect, Presbyteries) in running their dioceses. On the other hand, extremists like St. John, Nathaniel Fiennes (Lord Saye and Sele's son) and the younger Vane (the Secretary's son) pressed for the total abolition of bishops and cathedral chapters, and for the seizure of their lands. The Scottish commissioners, in London to discuss the peace treaty, urged on the extremists. The poet Milton entered the fray with a violent pamphlet on 'The Reformation of Church Discipline' against 'the irre-ligious pride and hateful Tyranny of Prelates'.

To get their demands accepted by the Upper House, the extremists proposed the exclusion of the bishops and Roman Catholic peers from the Lords, but the Upper House resisted such attacks on the privileges of its members. Moreover, to please the Scottish commissioners, the Commons impeached thirteen bishops, reversed the Canons of 1640, and ordered that the Sabbath should be kept holy. Annoyed at the tone of the Resolution on September 1st ('it is this day ordered by the Commons in Parliament . . .'), the Lords gave a non-committal comment, merely requesting that 'divine service be performed' according to the law. Never again did the Lords whole-heartedly support the Commons' attack on Charles. Despite Pym's attempts to keep Parliament united, the split between the supporters of modified episcopacy and the advocates of 'root and branch' suppression grew wider every week. The former were not yet royalists, however. Charles could have made them so by agreeing to a limited degree of Church reform, but he remained determined to preserve the Laudian Church as it was.

Meanwhile, Charles was trying to make new friends. Several Covenanting peers such as Rothes and Montrose swung over to his side, and in August he went to Scotland to meet them. On the way, he met General Leslie, and promised him an earldom. In Edinburgh he presided over the Parliament, and graciously accepted the acts recently passed to limit royal authority in Scotland. Several things, however, ruined Charles's chances of building up a party loyal to him.    Clan-conscious nobles were bitterly jealous of each other; in particular, Montrose had quarrelled with Lord Lorne, who had just succeeded his father as Earl of Argyle.    It proved impossible to appoint officials acceptable to everyone: Charles's nomination of Morton as Chancellor was denounced in Parliament by Argyle, Morton's son-in-law.    The King's tentative intrigues with army officers in the 'Incident' were revealed, and lost him his brief popularity in Edinburgh.    Nonetheless, he remained in Scotland.

Rebellion in Ireland shattered the autumn calm.    The very Parliament which had greeted Strafford so effusively in March 1640 turned against him as soon as it was safe to do so, and impeached his friends Radcliffe and Bramhall.    His Deputy, Christopher Wandesworth, could not control the Parliament, and his sudden death made matters worse.    Strafford from the Tower had advised Charles to replace Wandesworth with Ormonde, the ablest peer in Ireland, but only thirty years old. Instead, the King weakly appointed two Lord Justices, Borlase and Parsons, to rule Ireland.    Both were followers of the Earl of Cork: Charles thus tamely presented the government of Ireland to the Protestant land-grabbers.    In the summer of 1641 they disbanded the Irish army, with less than half the pay the soldiers should have received, and the troops went home grumbling, taking their weapons with them. With the weakening of law and order, Catholic priests flocked into the country and stirred up discontent.

At the end of October the O'Neills rose in revolt.    Other clans joined them.    Since Mountjoy's victory, forty years of English treachery, persecution and exploitation had gone unopposed; now, resentment and hatred produced a violent and almost spontaneous revolt.    To justify their actions, some of the more astute leaders claimed to be supporting Charles against his enemies and their own.    The Protestants fled from their lands, barricaded themselves in Dublin and Belfast, and cried for help to the English Parliament.

Wildly exaggerated stories of plunder and massacre reached London and startled Parliament.    An army must be raised to crush the rising; but who was to command it?    Could the Commons be sure that the King would not use it against themselves?    Indeed, was not the King already suspect of plotting with Lord Antrim, Phelim O'Neill and other rebels? Was this not perhaps a conspiracy backed by the Pope, Charles and Henrietta Maria to bring back Catholicism to Britain? With such fears the Commons assembled on November 5th, after thanking God for their deliverance from an earlier Popish Plot. Pym however, saw in the Rebellion a chance to weaken the King still further. Before Parliament voted money for an Irish army, he argued, the King must dismiss all his 'evil counsellors' and agree to rule only through men appointed or approved by Parliament. Pym followed this with the demand that Parliament should control the Militia, as an additional guarantee of safety. These were the most audacious challenges yet. Was the government the King's, or was it Parliament's?

These revolutionary demands startled the moderates in the Commons and in the Lords. The earlier proposals for Church reform had split Parliament; now this new claim threatened to make one faction royalist, supporting Charles in defence of tradition and the constitution. This was another crisis for Pym. With Charles still in Scotland, Pym decided to rush through Parliament a carefully-worded Remonstrance against the King. By this, he hoped to trick or frighten the waverers into falling in line behind him once more. In 204 main clauses, the 'Grand Remonstrance' listed the grievances of earlier years, congratulated the Parliament on what it had achieved so far, and proclaimed Parliament's future aims – establishing control over the King's ministers, expelling the bishops from the House of Lords, and subjecting the Church to the reforms of a synod of 'the most grave, pious, learned and judicious divines'. Pym thus made it impossible for the moderates to oppose the projected policies without dissociating themselves from the rest of the Grand Remonstrance.

Pym miscalculated badly. Rather than healing the breach between the groups in Parliament, the Grand Remonstrance widened it. Hyde, Falkland, Colepeper and Dering denounced it in turn, in the sixteen-hour debate on November 22nd. When the vote was taken at 1 a.m. the next morning, the Commons passed the Grand Remonstrance by only eleven votes, 159 to 148. This was a Pyrrhic victory. Nearly half the Commons now opposed Pym, defending the King and the Church against his attacks. Pym had more sense than to send the Remonstrance to the Lords, but after stormy scenes the

Commons ordered that it should be printed and circulated immediately.

While Pym looked round desperately for a means to rally the opposition, Charles returned to London. His visit to Scotland had ended amicably, for he had given absolute authority to his former opponents, Argyle's Covenanters. Slowly the tide was turning in his favour, in England as well as in Scotland. He at last plucked up enough courage to dismiss the turn-coat Sir Harry Vane from the Secretaryship. The Aldermen of London elected a royalist Lord Mayor, Sir Henry Gurney. The King's friends had loaned him more money. Only the general fear of popery and the Irish rebels remained as a barrier between Charles and most of his subjects. December 1641 was another time of crisis for the opposition.

Then Pym produced his master-stroke: he tricked Charles into making an attack on the privileges of Parliament. After the brief Christmas recess he criticized the Court even more severely, and started rumours that the Queen would be im-peached. This so infuriated the King that he decided to turn the tables and impeach the leaders of Parliament. On Jan-uary 3rd, 1642, he sent the Attorney-General to the Lords to charge Lord Mandeville, Pym, Hampden, Holles, Haselrig and Strode with high treason, that they had 'treacherously invited and encouraged a foreign enemy to invade his majesty's kingdom of England'. The Lords refused to accept the charge. Then Charles sent the Serjeant-at-Arms to the Commons to arrest the five M.P.s. The House refused to give them up. Pym continued his war of words. Next day, Charles himself marched down from Whitehall with 400 armed men to seize them – as Pym had hoped he would. Messengers warned Pym of the King's approach; he and the others escaped from Westminster by boat, and hid with friends in radical Coleman Street. Charles entered the Commons' Chamber, and found that 'the birds had flown'. Even the Speaker defied him, Lenthall protesting that he had 'neither eyes to see nor tongue to speak' except as the House directed him.

With this one rash act Charles threw away most of the good-will he had accumulated in the previous eight months. The London mob shouted hostile and warlike threats at the King's coach – 'To your tents, O Israel!' On January 10th, Charles left London for Hampton Court, just as the 'Five Members' returned to Parliament in triumph, escorted by the London trained-bands. Rumours accused the King of plotting to seize the ports and bring in foreign troops. By the end of January the King's party in the Lords was in ruins, and early in February the Upper House accepted the oft-rejected Bill to exclude the bishops.

The problem of Ireland was more acute than ever. According to rumour, 200,000 Protestant settlers (probably more than the total number!) had been massacred. Parliament had fanned the flame of the revolt by resolving the cost of its suppression should be met by fresh confiscations of Irish land, that Catholicism should be outlawed throughout the King's dominions, and that Charles should not pardon any of the rebels. The revolt exploded into a nation-wide struggle for land and religion. In February the Commons persuaded the King, now at Windsor, to agree to an Impressment Act for conscripting men to serve in Ireland under 'the King's Majesty, his heirs and successors, and both Houses of Parliament'. This did not, however, solve the problem of controlling the Militia in England. The King stoutly refused to accept the Militia Bill, by which Parliament planned to appoint its own supporters to command the trained-bands. As a last resort, Pym and D'Ewes persuaded the Lords and Commons to issue the Bill as an Ordinance, without the King's consent. This Ordinance, in effect a parliamentary proclamation, provided machinery for Pym and his allies to govern and pass laws without the King. The constitutional revolutions of the next two decades stemmed from this drastic and unprecedented measure.

Civil war was now almost certain. Already Parliament had forced its nominees upon the King as commanders of the Tower of London and the arsenal at Hull. Already it had warned Northumberland, now Admiral, to defend England against attacks from overseas, for it was believed that Spanish and Danish troops were massing to help Charles. Already it had turned against some of Charles's recent supporters, impeaching Digby and the Attorney-General, and expelling from the Commons and imprisoning Hopton and Trelawny for speaking against the attacks on the King. With war very near, Charles sent Henrietta and the Prince of Wales to the continent for safety. The struggle between King Charles and King Pym was about to move onto the battlefields.

## vii. Puritans and Catholics overseas [1]

After the noisy passing of the Grand Remonstrance, Oliver Cromwell muttered to Falkland that if it had been rejected he would have 'sold all the next morning, and never seen England more', and swore that there were 'many honest men of the same resolution'. They would have been following thousands of Englishmen who had 'sold all' – often very little – and emigrated to North America during the previous dozen years. Religion quickly overshadowed desire for land or bases for fishing fleets as the main cause for colonization.

In March 1629 the Council granted a royal charter to 'The Governor and Company of Massachusetts Bay in New England' For six years already the Rev. John White of Dorchester and his merchant friends had been sending out small groups of fishermen and 'planters' to New England, but few had survived. In the summer of 1629 three hundred new colonists joined the earlier settlers at their tiny port of Salem. Among the new arrivals was a famous Puritan preacher called Higginson. Although these colonists had not emigrated with any plan to escape from the Church of England, within a month Higginson founded at Salem a Separatist or Independent Church, on the lines of that established at New Plymouth by the Pilgrim Fathers. Two of the Governor's Council remained faithful to the English Prayer Book; they were swiftly sent home, in an early demonstration of Puritan intolerance. The Puritan sponsors of the Company, resentful of the growth of Arminianism and popery, in England, decided to move to the more godly air of Salem. Under John Winthrop as the new Governor, and with 700 more colonists, the Massachusetts Bay Company moved its headquarters in 1630 from London to Salem. The colonists swore loyalty not to King Charles, but to the government of Massachusetts. An oligarchy of members of the Separatist church monopolized political power. Within a few years the rulers created in New England a religious tyranny harsher and more efficient than Archbishop Laud's. The drunkard or blasphemer suffered in the pillory or was flogged; old women were burned as witches; later, Quakers lost their ears, were branded in the tongue, and were even executed.

[1] See map on p. 247.

One of the Salem clergy, Roger Williams, was banished for criticizing the magistrates' power and the unfair treatment of the native Indians; he fled to Rhode Island, and formed there a breakaway – and more tolerant – colony. Explorers and discontents from the other plantations also founded Connecticut and New Hampshire – like Rhode Island, without any charter from the Crown. When the Puritan Lord Brooke established a colony at New Haven, the land was granted by the Council of New England, not by the King.

One colony was not Puritan. Sir George Calvert, Secretary of State at the end of James's reign, had retired from English politics when he became a Roman Catholic. As Lord Baltimore, he moved to the New World, and tried to settle first in Newfoundland and then in Virginia. Disliking the climate of the one and the Puritanism of the other, he persuaded Charles in 1632 to grant him the northern part of Virginia, which he tactfully named Maryland in honour of Henrietta Maria. Baltimore's family developed Maryland as a tolerant colony, with a social structure based upon the English manorial system. It was a curious reflection on the English emigrants that the only colony tolerant of other Christian faiths was that run by Catholics.

England's other North American colony, Newfoundland, was of little importance at this time, consisting only of a few fishing villages. But in the Caribbean there were several English settlements successfully challenging Spanish power, on St. Kitt's, Antigua, Tobago, Barbados and Trinidad. Barbados suffered for a while through the dispute over its ownership between the courtiers Carlisle and Montgomery, but it became prosperous during the 1630s by exporting tobacco and cotton to England. The Providence Island Company, with John Pym as Secretary and the Puritan lords Warwick, Brooke, and Saye and Sele among its directors, originally planned to establish a refuge for English Puritans on the islands of Providence and Association, but it soon became involved in a private war against the Spaniards. The resources of a private company could not sustain such a war indefinitely, and in 1641, when the leaders were busy in Parliament, Spanish forces destroyed the company's last settlements.

Between the dissolution of Parliament in 1629 and the outbreak of the Civil War in 1642, nearly 60,000 people emigrated from England. Probably half of these went to the Puritan colonies. Archbishop Laud, even more than Archdeacon Hakluyt, was the cause of English colonial supremacy in North America. The colonial Companies, however, were more than a safety-valve for discontented Englishmen – they were a principal means for organizing and stimulating that discontent. The Providence Island and Massachusetts Bay Companies, together with the Feoffees for Impropriations, bound together the Puritan opposition groups in England. More than half the Feoffees were members of one or other of the companies. Three of the four M.P.s elected by the City of London in 1640 were members of the Massachusetts Bay Company, including Matthew Cradock, a former Governor of the Company. The houses of Warwick, Brooke and Pym, close together in Holborn, provided convenient meeting places for the members of the Providence Island Company. There the opposition leaders prepared Hampden's campaign against Ship-Money; there, during the spring and summer months of 1640, they planned the tactics which would outwit Charles and Strafford in Parliament. It was this unexpected cohesion of the opposition, despite eleven years without Parliament, which upset Strafford's calculations when he advised Charles to hold elections.

### viii. Foreign policy

England's relations with other countries, in the two decades after the treaties of Susa and Madrid, hardly merit the title of foreign policy. While Denmark, the United Provinces, Sweden and then France struggled against the military power of Spain and the Empire, England stood by weakly, as a spectator on the touch-line. The combat came close to her shores. Across the Channel, only the military genius of the Orange family prevented the Hapsburg troops in the Spanish Netherlands from overrunning the United Provinces, and it was tempting for Charles to try to exploit Dutch weaknesses. In 1630 he agreed to mint and to transport to Antwerp the money needed to pay Spanish troops; he collected a substantial commission for this service. His later attempts to make the Dutch buy fishing licences were generally unsuccessful and clumsy. Had it not been for the tact of the Dutch and their French allies, the 'Ship-Money' navy might well have provoked war.

IBS

When the Spanish fleet was destroyed in 1639 by Van Tromp –
in English territorial waters – Charles allowed Spanish troops
to march through Southern England from Plymouth to Dover
to evade the waiting Dutch navy in the Channel. In 1639
Charles tried to borrow Spanish soldiers for the war against the
Scots. A year later, on the day of the fateful dissolution of the
Short Parliament, the Council gave serious consideration to the
Spanish offer of four million ducats in return for a permanent
guard of thirty-five English warships to defend Spanish convoys
in the Channel. But it was certain that the navy would never
allow itself to be used in this way, and the negotiations came to
nothing.

England, therefore, was neutral only in name during the
1630s, leaning heavily towards Spain and away from France
and the United Provinces. Charles escaped war, more by
good luck than by good management, but his apparent support
for the Catholic and Hapsburg powers at the climax of the
Thirty Years War added greatly to his unpopularity at home.
It seemed so likely that England would formally enter the war
on Spain's side that the French ambassador egged on the
opposition to keep Charles weak – Pym was accused of having
received £5000 from De La Ferté Imbault who, according to
Clarendon, 'fomented those humours out of which the public
calamities were bred'. With the military decline of the Hapsburgs, however, Charles began to question the wisdom of his
pro-Spanish policy. At the end of 1640 he turned towards the
United Provinces. After secret negotiations his eldest daughter
was betrothed to William, heir of Frederick William Prince
of Orange, the most important noble in the United Provinces.
In some ways this was a degrading match, but Charles needed
the money Frederick William was willing to lend him. It was
to the United Provinces that Henrietta Maria fled in 1642 to
borrow money and buy weapons for Charles, and the Orange
family supported the royalist cause loyally throughout the Civil
War. Nonetheless, Frederick William could not persuade the
republican government of the United Provinces to give Charles
any help against his Parliament. As France and Spain were
locked together in what seemed a fight to the death, neither
country was able to intervene in English politics during
the 1640s.

In short, the inept foreign policy of the period of 'royalist reaction' angered Englishmen by its pro-Hapsburg bias and by measures such as Ship-Money designed to make it more effective. By 1642 England was of so little consequence in the foreign affairs of Europe that no country thought it worth while to interfere in the Civil War while more urgent struggles were continuing on the continent. As so often happened, Charles's policies were unsuccessful as well as unpopular. Pym and his friends in the Providence Company, indeed, had a special grievance in 1641, for the splendid 'Ship-Money' fleet did nothing to prevent Spain from wiping out the Company's colony on Providence Island.

## EXTRACTS

1. JUSTICE BERKELEY DEFENDS SHIP-MONEY (1638):

The law knows no such king-yoking policy. The law is of itself an old and trusty servant of the King's; it is his instrument or means which he useth to govern his people by. I never read nor heard that *lex* was *Rex*; but it is common and most true that *Rex* is *lex*, for he is *lex loquens*, a living, a speaking, an acting law.... The King of mere right ought to have, and the people of mere duty are bound to yield unto the King, supply for the defence of the Kingdom. (In Gardiner, *Constitutional Documents*, pp. 121–3)

2. THE GLASGOW GENERAL ASSEMBLY ATTACKS LAUD'S LITURGY AND THE BISHOPS (December 1638):

The Assembly having diligently considered the Book of Common Prayer, lately obtruded upon the reformed kirk within this realme, both in respect of the manner of the introducing thereof, and in respect of the matter which it containeth, findeth that it hath been devised and brought in by the pretended prelats, without direction from the kirk . . . to be universally received as the only forme of divine service under all highest paines, both civill and ecclesiasticall, and the book it self, beside the *popish* frame and forms in divine worship, to containe many *popish* errours and ceremonies, and the seeds of manifold and grosse superstition and idolatrie. The Assembly, therefore, all in one voice, hath rejected and condemned. . . . the said book. . . .

. . . The Assembly moved with zeal to the glorie of God, and purging of his Kirk, hath ordained the said pretended Bishops to be deposed. . . . And likewise ordaineth the said pretended Bishops to be excommunicate . . . and the sentence of excommunication to be pronounced by Mr. Alexander Henderson. . . . (In Dickinson and Donaldson, *Source Book of Scottish History*, vol. iii, pp. 107-10)

3. CLARENDON SUMMARIZES THE CHARGES AGAINST STRAFFORD (1641):

The trial lasted eighteen days; in which all the hasty or proud expressions or words he had uttered at any time since he was first made a Privy Councillor; all the acts of passion or power that he had exercised in Yorkshire, from the time that he was first President there; his engaging himself in projects in Ireland, as the sole making of flax and selling tobacco in that country; his billeting of soldiers and exercising of martial law in that kingdom; his extraordinary proceeding against the lord Mountnorris and the Lord Chancellor [Loftus]; his assuming a power of judicature at the Council-table to determine private interest and matter of inheritance; some rigorous and extra-judicial determinations in cases of plantation; some high discourses at the Council-table in Ireland, and some casual and light discourses at his own table and at public meetings; and, lastly, some words spoken in secret Council in this kingdom, after the dissolution of the last Parliament, were urged and pressed against him, to make good the general charge of an 'endeavour to overthrow the fundamental government of the kingdom, and to introduce an arbitrary power'. (Clarendon, *History of the Great Rebellion*, vol. i, p. 290)

4. BAXTER LISTS THE SHORTCOMINGS OF THE KIDDERMINSTER CLERGY (1641):

The town of Kidderminster . . . drew up a petition against their ministers. The vicar of the place they articled against as one that was utterly insufficient for the ministry, presented by a Papist, unlearned, preached but once a quarter, which was so weakly as exposed him to laughter, and persuaded them that he understood not the very substantial Articles of Christianity; that he frequented ale-houses and had sometimes been drunk; that he turned the table altar-wise, etc., with much more such as this. The vicar had a curate . . . a common tippler and a drunkard, a railing quarreller, an ignorant, insufficient man who (as I found by examining him) understood not the common points of the children's Catechism. (Richard Baxter, *Auto-biography*, pp. 23–4)

5. BAXTER LEARNS OF THE IRISH REVOLT (1641):
Two hundred thousand persons they murdered. . . . Men, women and children were most cruelly used, the women ripped up and filthily used when they killed them, and the infants used like toads or vermin. Thousands of those that escaped came stripped and almost famished to Dublin, and afterwards into England to beg their bread. (Richard Baxter, *Autobiography*, p. 32)

6. MILTON COMMENTS ON THE SAME:
The poor afflicted remnant of our martyred countrymen that sit there on the Sea-shore, counting the hours of our delay with their sighs, and the minutes with their falling tears, perhaps with the distilling of their bloody wounds . . . can best judge how speedy we are to their relief. (John Milton, *Against Prelaty*. In *Milton's Selected Prose*, ed. M. W. Wallace, p. 103)

7. MILTON CALLS FOR THE OVERTHROW OF THE BISHOPS (1641):
Though God for less than ten just persons would not spare Sodom, yet if you can find after due search but only one good thing in prelaty either to religion, or civil government, to King or Parliament, to Prince or people, to law, liberty, wealth or learning, spare her; let her live, let her spread among ye, till with her shadow, all your dignities and honours, and all the glory of the land be darkened and obscured. But on the contrary if she be found to be malignant, hostile, destructive to all these, as nothing can be surer, then let your severe and impartial doom imitate the divine vengeance; rain down your punishing force upon this godless and oppressing government; and bring such a dead Sea of subversion upon her, that she may never in this Land rise more to afflict the holy reformed Church, and the elect people of God. (John Milton, *Against Prelaty*. In *Milton's Selected Prose*, ed. M. W. Wallace, p. 144)

8. A SCOTTISH DIARIST COMMENTS UPON THE PRESBYTERIAN CHRISTMAS (1641):
Friday the 25 of December, of old called Yool-day, and wheron preachings, and praises, and thanksgiveing was [formerly] given to God in remembrance of the birth of our blessed Saviour, and therwith freinds and neighbours made mirrie with others, and had good cheir: now this day no such

preachings nor such meittings with mirrieness, walking up and
down; but contrair, this day commanded to be keeped as ane
work-day, ilk [each] burgess to keep his buith, ilk craftsman
his wark, feasting and idlesett forbidden out of pulpitts. . . .
The people wes otherwayes inclyned, but durst not dissobey;
yet little merchandise wes sold, and alse litle work wrought on
this day. . . . (In Dickinson and Donaldson, *Source Book of
Scottish History*, vol. iii, p. 395)

# 4

## THE CIVIL WARS, 1642–60

☆

### i. The end of peace

THE Militia Ordinance made the Civil War almost, but not quite, inevitable. In February Parliament persuaded a disheartened Charles to agree to the Impressment Act and the exclusion of the bishops from the House of Lords; then, for a few weeks, it tried to get him to accept the Militia Ordinance as an Act of Parliament. The King, however, steadfastly refused to give up the power of the sword – 'You have asked that of me in this was never asked of a King' – and in May he issued from York a proclamation forbidding the trained bands to act in obedience to the Ordinance. For some months a propaganda war ('paper skirmishes', as Clarendon called it) went on between King and Parliament, with each side trying to win more popular support. In June, Parliament presented its ultimatum, the Nineteen Propositions: Charles was asked to agree to the Militia Ordinance and to Parliament reforming the Church, appointing the King's ministers, and even supervising the education of his children. Charles naturally refused to be reduced to the mere 'picture of a King'; he was not willing, he declared, to change the laws of England so drastically.

The 'paper skirmishes' gave Charles and Parliament time to collect their forces. In April Charles called upon Sir John Hotham, the M.P. recently delegated by Parliament to take command of Hull, to surrender the city to him. Hotham refused. At Hull were stored the artillery and other weapons kept in reserve for defence against the Scots, and Charles thus failed to seize an invaluable arsenal. As the Tower of London was also in the hands of Parliament,[1] the King started the war very short of weapons. In June Charles issued Commissions of

[1] To placate the opposition, Charles had dismissed the royalist Thomas Lunsford only two months after appointing him Lieutenant of the Tower.

Array, to collect troops under the Earls of Huntingdon and Devonshire, but in two months barely 1000 volunteers joined him.     Meanwhile, Parliament voted in July to raise an army to be commanded by the Earl of Essex.

On August 22nd 1642, in a howling gale and torrential downpour, Charles set up his standard at Nottingham.   It was blown down the same night – a depressing omen.   With only 800 cavalry and 300 infantry, the King's position seemed desperate.   Within a month, however, Parliament's rashness gave the King a respectable army.   In early September the Houses voted that the cost of freeing Charles from his evil counsellors should be paid for out of the estates of those whom Parliament declared to be delinquents and malignants.   This in effect gave a blank cheque to Pym and his friends.   Many who would have remained neutral were frightened into joining the King's side, to defend their own possessions.   By the end of September, Charles's army exceeded 8000.   Next month his troops started to march south through the midlands, towards Oxford and London.   The campaigns had started.

It is easy to point to the reasons for the quarrels between Charles and Parliament; it is however less easy to explain why these quarrels led to war.   The economic grievances of the 1630s – monopolies, tunnage and poundage, arbitrary taxes such as Ship-Money, attempts to collect increased tithes – had been largely redressed by the summer of 1641.   The political demands of 1640 had been met: Strafford was dead, the prerogative courts abolished, and regular meetings of Parliament guaranteed by the Triennial Act.   Many of the unpopular actions of the Laudian Church would in future be impossible, for the abolition of the Court of High Commission had removed most of the bishops' effective power.   The controversies over these issues had been settled as Parliament had wished, but the bitterness which they had caused still remained, to obscure the principles over which the Civil War was fought.   There were, in fact, only two main issues between King and Parliament in 1642 – Parliament's claim to appoint and control government officials and army commanders, and its leaders' determination to reform the Church in accordance with their Puritan beliefs.

These were radical demands, but by themselves they would

hardly have led to war.   The main reason for the war was that Charles could not be trusted.   His association with the Army Plot and the 'Incident', his attempt to arrest the 'Five Members', his negotiations with Spain and (allegedly) the Irish rebels, the defiant Catholicism of Henrietta Maria and her ladies, memories of the dissolutions of 1629 and 1640 and of Charles's apparent violations of the Petition of Right, made the leaders of Parliament deeply suspicious of him.   Moreover, his sacrifice of Strafford made many of his own courtiers afraid to support him loyally.   It was Charles who had first resorted to violence, in his attempt to discipline the Scots; it was he who, by attempting to arrest the Five Members, had set the precedent for using military force for political purposes at home.   The opposition, therefore, would trust the King only if he could be surrounded and hedged in by advisers responsible to Parliament.

Charles's political mistakes increased his difficulties.   He had been too ready to appoint and too reluctant to dismiss ministers recommended by the Queen – men like Lord Holland and Sir Harry Vane.   His indisciplined Court largely betrayed him. His attempts, during the summer and autumn of 1641, to conciliate the opposition in London, Edinburgh and Dublin came too late.   His choice in November 1640 of the timid timeserver Lenthall as Speaker was a great blunder.   His greatest political mistake, though, was his unthinking acceptance of the Bill whereby the Long Parliament could not be dissolved without its own consent.   This deprived him of the normal, constitutional means for ending an unco-operative Parliament. Subsequently, Charles had no chance of controlling the situation except by violence.   Thus exposed, Charles could not meet the attacks which followed the outbreak of the Irish Rebellion.

## ii. The opposing parties

At the outset, the First Civil War was a war between the factions in Parliament.   The King, most of the Lords and over a third of the Commons opposed a few peers and the majority of the Commons.   The leaders of each side fought for what they believed was the constitution of the State and ought to be the constitution of the Church.   Gradually, though, as the war went on, the politicians on each side became of less importance.

At the start of the war, there seemed to be little difference in the composition or strength of the two parties: each contained peers, great landowners, gentry, merchants, lawyers, yeomen, townsfolk, labourers.    In general, though, the north and the west, the great landowners and the more prosperous gentry, supported the King; against him, on the whole, were the south and east, the merchants, townspeople and the less prosperous gentry. But there were thousands of exceptions – so many, in fact, that some historians doubt whether any such generalizations can safely be made.    For example, the merchants of the East India Company and most of the London aldermen were Royalist. Families were often sharply divided: in Devon, for example, there were Carews and Fortescues active on each side.    Some of Oliver Cromwell's relations supported the King.

Roman Catholics and monopolists like Bushell were solidly for Charles as they feared the consequences of his defeat. Many men supported him out of personal loyalty.    The tepid Falkland hesitated to join him and deplored the war, but nonetheless died in the King's army at Newbury.    Charles's standard-bearer, Sir Edmund Verney, fought and died for him loyally but without enthusiasm; as a small-scale monopolist, he had 'eaten the King's bread' for thirty years, and would not desert him now in the hour of his need.    Some men fought consciously in defence of the Anglican Church; others because of what they hoped to get from a victorious monarch.    Some irresponsible gallants and 'Cavaliers' joined the royal army for the thrill of battle and the chance to plunder.    Jealousies between old aristocracy and new gentry, and the ambitions of the poorer gentry, sometimes made men take up arms for one side or the other.[1]    Sir John Hotham, who had saved the Hull arsenal for Parliament, soon planned to desert to the King because he feared a radical revolution – and was executed by Parliament when his treachery was discovered.    A great many, like the 'Whitecoats' in Newcastle's regiment, fought and died for Charles because they were the tenants and dependents of a great lord who was supporting the King.

Equally diverse motives inspired men to fight for Parliament. Thousands of Puritans were determined to carry through a

---

[1] The part played by such social factors is still disputed by historians.    The arguments are dealt with conveniently in C. Hill, *Puritanism and Revolution*, pp. 3–49, 199–214

godly reform of the Church, if need be at sword point. Others saw in a Parliamentary victory a guarantee against monopolies and a safeguard against high taxation. Martyrs of earlier years, like Hampden and Lilburne, were able to get their revenge as officers in Parliament's army. The workmen of the northcountry towns remembered Strafford and fought for Parliament in the Roundhead regiments. So did the fenmen whose livelihoods had been threatened when the Dutchman Vermuyden drained the Fens to benefit Charles's courtiers. The sailors in the navy which had nearly been hired to Spain rose up against their Royalist officers, and turned the ships over to Parliament.

It was not obvious at the time, but the long-term advantages lay with the King's opponents. Charles's supporters came predominantly from the landed classes, whose wealth was almost entirely in their estates. Most of them had little ready money to loan the King, and could get only low prices for their lands if they tried to sell them to raise money. The Royalist areas were more scattered than those supporting Parliament and the King's communications between them were poor. In his nephew Prince Rupert of the Rhine (son of the deposed Elector Palatine), Charles had an experienced cavalry commander, but Rupert's tactics were more suited to German than to English conditions. Throughout the war, Charles was very short of weapons and ammunition; on at least one occasion these deficiencies stopped him winning a decisive battle. Charles's weaknesses were greatly magnified by the desertion of the navy: without it, he could not collect customs duties, or besiege successfully parliamentary sea-ports like Plymouth and Hull; with it, he could have blockaded London and brought his opponents to their knees.

London was Parliament's greatest asset, despite the Royalist sympathies of its leading citizens (who were removed by impeachment and imprisonment). Its prestige as the country's capital was as useful to Parliament as its generous loans and its relatively efficient trained-bands. The navy ensured that all foreign trade passed through London or other ports in sympathy with Parliament; not only did Parliament receive the customs duties, but its backers remained prosperous. Moreover, most of England's industrial areas lay under Parliament's control, and the wealth of merchants and manufacturers was loaned readily – at first – to Parliament. The arsenals at Hull and in the Tower of London ensured that the armies of Essex and Manchester[1] were better equipped than the King's, especially in artillery, while the navy seized all the supplies which Henrietta Maria tried to send from the continent. It was ironic that Ship-Money not only consolidated the opposition to Charles, but provided his enemies with one of their most valuable weapons!

Lack of money and munitions meant that Charles's forces would grow weaker as time went on. On the other hand, his opponents had adequate resources and would grow stronger each month as their armies improved. It was therefore essential for Charles to win a victory as quickly as possible. He had a good chance of doing so, especially as neither Essex nor Manchester, the peers tactfully appointed by the Commons as their generals, had much enthusiasm for the fight. As a precaution, Essex always took his coffin with him when he went on campaign, and Manchester was soon to moan that, even if they defeated Charles ninety-nine times, 'yet is he King still . . . but if the King beat us once we shall all be hanged'. If the Royalists had won a few quick victories, the opposition would probably have crumbled. Delay, however, would guarantee defeat.

### iii. The campaigns of the First Civil War

In October 1642 Charles felt confident enough to march towards London, with 9000 infantry under Lindsey and 4000 cavalry under Prince Rupert. Essex with a larger army had moved against the Royalists in Worcestershire; now, he had to wheel round and try to intercept Charles's army on its way to London. The two armies met at Edgehill, a few miles north-west of Banbury. Charles's army had the advantage of the ground, for his troops occupied the slopes leading to the steep escarpment of the Cotswolds, while Essex was hurrying along the road from Warwick. The Parliamentary army was not complete, for much of its artillery and the Buckinghamshire regiments under Hampden were straggling along in the rear. Essex's infantry defeated those of the King, killing General Lindsey, but Rupert's cavalry routed the Parliament horse.

[1] Formerly Lord Mandeville, one of those Charles had tried to impeach in January 1642.

Foolishly, they chased the fugitives towards Warwick for some miles, until they were stopped by Hampden's forces. Rupert made a grave mistake in pursuing so far; had his cavalry returned to the main battle it could have cut to pieces Fairfax's infantry. A more serious blunder followed: when Essex withdrew from the battle, he was allowed to place his army between the King and London – for him the main object of the encounter. Charles dallied in the Midlands for several days, capturing Banbury and occupying Oxford, before resuming his march towards London.

It was three weeks before Charles attacked his capital. By then Essex had 24,000 men under his command, largely from the London trained-bands. In mid-November Rupert broke through to Brentford, but could not use his cavalry effectively in the country of small fields and hedges which lay beyond. The Londoners sent their Sunday dinners out to the defenders; Milton wrote a jeering sonnet, sarcastically asking the Royalist officers not to harm him when they captured the city; and, after a day of minor skirmishes at Turnham Green, Charles withdrew to Hampton Court, Reading and then Oxford. It was six years before the King again got near London, and then it was as a prisoner about to be tried for his life.

The assault on London had petered out, but elsewhere the Royalists were fairly successful. Lord Newcastle captured Newark, Lichfield and Stafford, and the Cornishmen under Sir Ralph Hopton seized most of the south-west for the King. As 1643 went on, the Royalists developed a three-pronged attack on London – the most intelligent strategy of the whole campaign. Charles's armies were to march on London from the north, from the south-west, and from Wales and Oxford. Having overcome the Fairfaxes in Yorkshire, Newcastle marched southwards through Lincolnshire. At the same time, Hopton defeated his friend Waller at Lansdown and Roundway Down near Bath, and Rupert captured Bristol. The King's own army at Oxford, strengthened with the men of South Wales, checked Essex's troops at Chalgrove Field and killed John Hampden.

This seemed a desperate time for Parliament. Most of the Lords wished to surrender, and the fickle London mob was already calling for peace. Not for the first time, it was the resolute Pym who held Parliament together and persuaded it to raise new armies. But the situation was not as critical as the pessimists believed, for there were serious weaknesses in Charles's strategy. He had not expected the Cornishmen to refuse to fight far from home while Plymouth remained as a Parliamentary stronghold in their rear; similarly, the resistance of Hull and Gloucester dampened the spirits of the men from Yorkshire and Wales. The Royalists besieged these towns in vain, for they had no siege artillery, and the navy was able to ferry supplies in to the defenders.

In September 1643 Essex's army, reinforced by the London trained-bands, relieved Gloucester. Though it was not obvious at the time, this was to prove the turning-point of the campaigns. Rupert intercepted the Roundheads near Newbury on their march home. The Royalists came close to victory, but ran out of ammunition; once again, Essex was able to retreat to London, and a tactical success became a strategic defeat.

Each side now sought new allies to help it win the war of attrition. Charles had at last made Ormonde his Lord Lieutenant in Ireland, and now looked to him to raise troops to fight in England. Ormonde persuaded some of the rebels to stop rebelling, but when Charles's army in Ireland returned to England most of the men deserted to Parliament after the first skirmish at Nantwich. In London, Pym convinced Parliament of the need to hire the Scottish army at the high price demanded – £30,000 a month and the drastic reorganization of the Church in England – in the *Solemn League and Covenant*. In fact, Parliament's position was not as desperate as Pym believed. In the East Midlands the army which the 'Eastern Association' of counties had provided was improving rapidly under Manchester; in particular Oliver Cromwell was turning the Roundhead horse into a cavalry more efficient than Rupert's. Although the King held most of the country, his were the least prosperous areas. The tax assessments he was levying on the population were gradually turning the countryside against him. Even the royalist loyalty of Oxford slackened a little after Charles insisted that the Colleges give him their gold and silver plate to be melted down for his soldiers' pay. Moreover, Charles wasted his manpower by scattering small garrisons to hold down as much of the countryside as possible, in a defensive attitude which was irreconcilable with his plans for the triple attack on London.

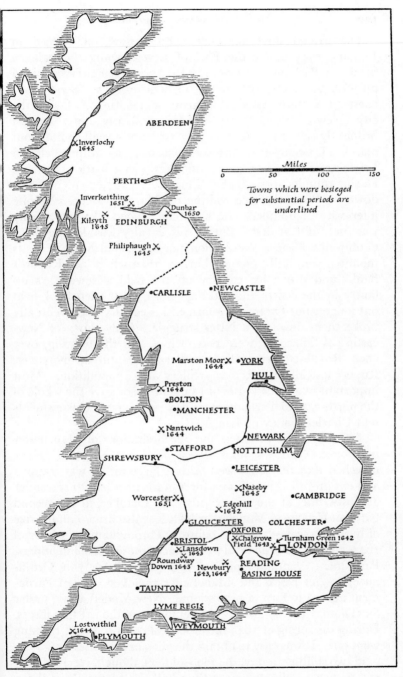

Britain during the Civil Wars

The 21,000 shivering Scots who crossed the Tweed in January 1644 under the Earl of Leven swung the balance firmly in Parliament's favour.  In April the Fairfaxes joined up with the Scots, and moved to besiege York.  Soon Manchester's Eastern Association army joined them.  Inside the city, Newcastle's infantry resisted gallantly until Rupert brilliantly raised the siege on July 1st, after a swift roundabout march of twenty-two miles.  Next day, as Rupert chased Leven's retreating besiegers, came the decisive battle of the war. During thunderstorms that evening, Leven's 27,000 men moved down on Rupert's force waiting on Marston Moor.  Despite inferiority of numbers – he had only 18,000 – Rupert's army was successful at first.  But as his cavalry was driving back Cromwell's Eastern Association horse, a small force of Scots mounted on hill ponies hurled themselves at Rupert's flanks and drove his cavalry off the field.  Newcastle's infantry in the centre and Goring's horse on the left flank held out longer, but Cromwell reformed his cavalry and eventually broke them down in a bitter struggle.  Only thirty of Newcastle's 'Whitecoats' were taken alive.  In the fighting, over 4000 Royalists were killed and 1500 captured; moreover, Rupert lost all his precious artillery and ammunition.  Most important of all, the battle of Marston Moor gave the whole of the north-east to Parliament, and a rich source of assessments sent Charles money no longer.

The ineptitude of Essex and the hesitations of Manchester postponed Charles's final defeat for another year.  Essex marched into the south-west with a large army, was trapped and cut off in Cornwall, and most of his men had to surrender at Lostwithiel at the end of July.  In October, at the second battle of Newbury, Manchester let a Royalist army half the size of his own escape back to Oxford.  Throughout the winter of 1644–5, Cromwell and Waller denounced the senior commanders. Parliament eventually found a way (the Self-Denying Ordinance) to get Essex and Manchester removed.  Then Parliament agreed to form a professional, 'New Model' army, under Sir Thomas Fairfax, out of the remnants of the existing forces. During the spring of 1645 the process of recruiting and training went on.  It was easy to obtain the 7600 cavalry and dragoons, paid two shillings a day; the foot-soldiers, though, received only eighteenpence a day, and more than half the 14,400 Roundhead infantry were unwilling conscripts.[1] This was no company of dedicated saints; the men did not share their officers' zeal for psalms and sermons, and the soldiers of one regiment mutinied when their Colonel began preaching to them. Mutinies and desertions were frequent, and it was only in battle that Fairfax's discipline proved more effective than Rupert's.

At the end of May, Rupert captured Leicester after a brief siege, and provoked the raw New Model into action. Fairfax marched northwards, his men short of food and firearms, according to one observer[2] 'an ungodly crew' and often drunk. Appointed by Fairfax to command the cavalry in defiance of the Lords' opposition, Cromwell reached the army only after it had intercepted Charles at Naseby, half way between Leicester and Northampton. Rupert, with only 9000 men against Fairfax's 14,000, wished to avoid battle until Goring's cavalry reached him from the Westcountry, but Charles's courtiers persuaded the King to overrule Rupert's wise caution. The armies met on June 14th, 1645. The Royalist cavalry advanced uphill, broke through Ireton's horse and dashed on to plunder the baggage train – the mistake Rupert had made before at Edgehill. In the centre the Royalist infantry pushed back their opponents, but Cromwell's horse swept onto their flanks and scattered them, despite Charles's own attempts to lead a counter-attack. The King's troops fled in disorder. Cromwell's cavalry cut them down as they ran, and killed or maimed most of the wives and camp-followers. Half of Charles's army, taken prisoner, was marched to London and paraded through the streets in triumph. For triumph it was. The King no longer had an army to put into the field.

The following months were a time of disaster. Goring's cavalry was routed at Langport, and Rupert had to surrender Bristol. Montrose, who had been winning spectacular successes for Charles in Scotland and leading Argyle's Covenanters a merry dance in the Highlands, ventured towards the Borders and was defeated at Philiphaugh. A military victory was now out of the question for the King: Charles must now try his skill as a politician, hoping to conquer his enemies by dividing

---

[1] In September 1645 fifty-six men were conscripted from Pevensey – and it took another fifty-six to escort them to the regimental depot.

[2] Sir Samuel Luke, Parliament's Governor of Newport Pagnell, and the organizer of an efficient spy-service which kept Fairfax informed of Charles's movements.

them. He nearly succeeded. With Oxford loyal to the last, and holding out for two months more, Charles rode north in April 1646 and gave himself up to the Scots at Newark. There he began the intrigues which led to the second Civil War.

Several reasons stand out for the King's defeat. His lack of money, munitions and artillery were serious handicaps, despite the generous loans and gifts of his friends,[1] and accounted for the inconclusiveness of the first Battle of Newbury. Unwise military tactics, and delay in following up an advantage, wasted Edgehill and lost Naseby, and Charles squandered thousands of troops in unnecessary siege and garrison duties. Charles's rowdy Court was a further handicap, for Cavalier officers who squabbled for precedence and fought duels in the Oxford meadows were not likely to work together well in battles. Moreover, indisciplined excesses such as the sacking of Bolton and Liverpool lost Charles many sympathizers, as did the heavy assessments Rupert collected at sword-point from Royalist areas. On the whole, Charles's forces were paid even more irregularly than those of Parliament. Charles, the sacrificer of Strafford and the friend of Catholics, was not a man to inspire loyalty, even when grievances like Ship-Money were becoming only memories. In 1644, in Hereford and Dorset and elsewhere, countrymen had been forming themselves into bands to fight off any army, Royalist or Roundhead, which threatened to occupy their lands; the thousands of these militantly neutral 'Clubmen' probably expressed most men's attitude towards both sides in the Civil War.

## iv. Parliament's conduct of the War

The politicians at Westminster had even less experience in running a war than their generals had in fighting one. The management of Parliament was a precarious triumph for Pym until his death in December 1643; no one else could have achieved it. His tasks were formidable – to keep Parliament strongly in support of the war, but without losing control of its extremists; to finance the campaigns; to negotiate with the King when the opportunity arose; to deal with the Scots and with foreign countries; and to carry through a puritan reform-

---

[1] Lord Worcester loaned £700,000, and Newcastle estimated that the war cost him over £900,000.

ation of the Anglican Church and all aspects of English life.

As early as December 1642, the cost of the war was frightening a large faction of the Commons into calling for peace. Pym quietened them by showing how unreasonable the King's peace terms would be. At the same time he had to silence Republican extremists like Marten, for he realized how dangerous too radical a programme would be. Pym knew that a long war lay ahead, and saw sooner than his colleagues that an alliance with the Scots was inevitable. The *Solemn League and Covenant* was negotiated in Edinburgh between Vane and Argyle, but it was Pym who in September 1643 persuaded Parliament to accept its terms. Sir Harry Vane, the son of Charles I's turncoat secretary, had agreed to pay the Scots £30,000 a month for their army and promised that the English Church should be purged of its bishops. The Treaty did not specifically promise Presbyterianism – Vane had deliberately avoided that – but the Scots and most English M.P.s could see no other alternative to episcopacy, particularly as the Treaty undertook to promote religious uniformity between England, Scotland and Ireland. The Scottish alliance was Pym's last achievement before his death. Later, in clumsier hands than his, the *Solemn League and Covenant* proved a two-edged sword which divided Parliament from its own army.

John Hampden had already been killed at Chalgrove, and after Pym died there was no Parliamentarian left of stature sufficient to hold together the factions in the Commons and to preserve the co-operation between Lords and Commons. Vane and St. John, extremists already toying with republican ideas, dominated the Commons and the Council of War, and overshadowed moderates like Denzil Holles who were pressing for a negotiated peace. Early in 1644, after the alliance with Scotland, Vane and St. John persuaded Parliament to appoint a Committee of Both Kingdoms to combine the war-efforts of the two countries. The moderates were not represented on it. Later that year, on evidence supplied by Cromwell and Waller, the Committee started attacking Essex and Manchester for their lack of zeal in carrying on the war. These attacks threatened to split Parliament, for the Lords resented criticism of their fellow peers. Morever, the Scots were already worried by the growth of the Independent sects in the army, and so supported reliable Presbyterians like Essex and Holles. By

December 1644 the moderates were considering trying to impeach Cromwell as a dangerous trouble-maker.

A remarkable compromise ended this political crisis: Parliament agreed that no member of either Lords or Commons should hold command in the army. To remove Essex and Manchester tactfully, Cromwell and Waller were prepared to give up their own commissions. At first, the Self-Denying Ordinance seemed to have thrown the baby out with the bathwater, but the military emergencies of the spring campaign of 1645 gave Fairfax, as Commander-in-Chief, an excuse to continue Cromwell in command. The Self-Denying Ordinance, despite its attempt at compromise, in fact strengthened the power of the Independents in both army and Parliament, and prepared the way for the subsequent split between Independents and Presbyterians.

The financial requirements of the campaigns produced one of Parliament's greatest worries. Loans from merchant sympathisers such as Pennington helped at first, as did the money voted for suppressing the Irish revolt. In August 1642 an Ordinance requested merchants to pay their customs duties to Parliament's agents. Later that year, another Ordinance ordered regular forced loans to be contributed by all men of property in accordance with assessments fixed locally. In March 1643 Pym persuaded Parliament to raise money by direct confiscations and sequestrations[1] from Royalist and Church property – 'licensed robbery' similar to that by which the King was collecting funds. Nonetheless, the situation grew more serious as the year went on, with interest rates on loans rising as high as 12 per cent. during the Royalist victories in the summer. To collect the money as efficiently as possible, Parliament developed a whole network of County Committees for finance – Committees for Assessments, Committees for Sequestrations, Committees for Accounts. Parliament fixed the assessment due from each county – Devon, supposedly the wealthiest, had to provide £1800 a week – but the allocation of the demands within the county was left to the scruples of the Committee members. Even this system did not suffice. To meet the cost of its army and navy in 1643 – nearly £3½ millions – Parliament introduced the Excise Ordinance, placing

---

[1] The County Committees appointed for that purpose took over the estates of the more prosperous Royalists, and paid their revenues to Parliament.

a purchase tax on goods like beer, sugar and linen.    Later in the war, the Excise was extended to the basic necessities of life. The malice of the Assessment Committees, and Excise duties bearing unjustly upon the poor, naturally made Parliament extremely unpopular, as riots in London clearly showed. Many former opponents of Ship-Money and tunnage and poundage must have considered the cure worse than the disease.    The Staffordshire man who protested 'If this be the privilege of Parliament and liberty of the subject, I pray God amend it!' was not speaking solely for his fellow Royalists.    In consequence, by the end of the First Civil War, Parliament was determined to cut expenditure and taxation as drastically as possible.    The soldiers, unpaid for many months, did not agree.

So fatal to the unity of the Long Parliament had the 1641 proposals for Church reform been, that Pym wisely left such matters alone at first.    In June 1643, however, Parliament appointed the Westminster Assembly to consider reform.    The Assembly was a large, unwieldy body of laymen and clerics, containing Independents and (at first) a few bishops as well as a large Presbyterian majority – soon to be reinforced by a vocal delegation from Scotland.    In six years the Assembly met over 1100 times, mainly to hear squabbles between its own members.    Its main achievement was the Westminster Confession of 1646, a statement of Presbyterian faith to replace the Anglican Thirty-Nine Articles.    It was not until the Independents were diverted by the Second Civil War, in June 1648, that the Presbyterians were able to get the Confession accepted by Parliament.    Meanwhile, the Puritans had their chance to plunder the Church.    Mobs of soldiers and civilians looted cathedrals like Canterbury, Rochester and Worcester, smashing stained-glass windows and destroying altars and organs.    Hundreds of parish churches suffered the same fate.    *The Solemn League and Covenant* committed Parliament to extirpate popery and prelacy (the bishops).    The Calvinist Directory of Public Worship replaced the outlawed Book of Common Prayer. Special commissioners purged the universities – first Cambridge and then, after its surrender, Royalist Oxford.    Every schoolmaster as well as every parson had to take the Covenant or suffer eviction; as with the Puritan brethren silenced in 1604, it was the men of high principles that the

Church lost. The property of bishops and cathedrals was sequestrated by Parliament to provide money for the war. Prynne took his revenge on Laud by collecting evidence for his impeachment; when the Lords dismissed the case, the Commons secured his execution by attainder. The old man, jostled by the mob, with jeering faces grinning up at him through the floorboards of the scaffold platform, declared to the last that he was a loyal Protestant.

Whereas the Westminster Assembly could agree on the destruction of the Anglican Church,[1] it could not agree on what should replace it. The Presbyterians were as convinced as Laud that the Church must be organized and disciplined, with supervision ('oversight') of the individual minister. Even the moderate *Apologetical Narration* of January 1644, in which the Independents Goodwin and Nye demanded self-governing congregations free from political ties, seemed outrageously heretical to the Presbyterians. The growth of Independency in the Army, tolerated by generals with more concern for military efficiency than for religious orthodoxy, provoked Parliament and the Assembly into attempting repressive measures. Soon Milton was protesting at the powers of the Presbyteries: 'New Presbyter is but old Priest writ large.' The multiplication of the sects in the following years prepared the way for the struggle between Parliament and the Army, with Cromwell leading the call for tolerance. But not even Cromwell would tolerate popery or prelacy – the old Anglican Church.

Almost continuously throughout the Civil War, Charles was negotiating cautiously with at least one faction among his enemies. In 1642, despite his religious scruples, he tried to win Argyle and the Scottish Covenanters to his side. He negotiated with Parliament outside London in December 1642, and received Pym's Commissioners in Oxford early in 1643. Both Charles and Pym knew the propaganda value of an appearance of 'sweet reasonableness'; moderates and neutrals in the country would be sympathetic to the side which wanted peace. Nonetheless, both Charles and Parliament made demands impossible for the other to accept. For this reason

---

[1] There was no agreement over ending tithe payments. The Presbyterian ministers in the parish churches wished to keep their tithes; less fortunate Independents wanted to abolish them.

the long negotiations at Oxford in the spring of 1643 and at Uxbridge in the autumn of 1644 both failed. The positions of King and Parliament on Church reform, control of the armed forces, and the settlement of Ireland were quite irreconcilable. Even in 1646, after his defeat in the First Civil War, Charles still refused to accept similar demands put to him in the Propositions of Newcastle. The King's notorious unreliability made Parliament's demands more extreme; as Pym had realized from the start, Parliament could not trust Charles to keep the terms of a moderate settlement. The bitterness of war – the heavy losses, the high taxation – and the conviction of each party that it was fighting the Lord's battles made compromise increasingly more difficult. God would not approve if David compromised with the Amalekites instead of slaughtering them.

The foreign policy of the Long Parliament was aimed principally at denying Charles aid from abroad. This was easily accomplished, for France, Spain, Denmark, Sweden and the United Provinces were still busy with the Thirty Years War. The English navy alone was almost a sufficient guarantee of freedom from foreign intervention. The representatives of France, Spain, Portugal, the United Provinces and Venice stayed in London, the centre of trade, instead of joining the Court at Oxford. Parliament, like Charles in earlier years, earned money by minting silver coins for paying the wages of Spanish troops in the Netherlands. The French ambassador, De La Ferté Imbault, was a close friend of Pym. The Dutch Estates were openly on the side of Parliament. Later, the brash behaviour of the English navy angered both Spaniards and Dutch, but their preoccupation with the Thirty Years War made them both swallow their resentment. The only active intervention – that of the Papal Nuncio, Rinuccini, in Ireland – was not directly concerned with the struggle of Parliament against the King. Every previous monarch had denied Parliament's competence to meddle with foreign affairs, but the Long Parliament found them the least worrying of its responsibilities.

The Long Parliament was determined that the hand of the godly should lay heavily upon England. An Ordinance of 1644 closed the theatres, long criticized for frivolity and vice. The old *Declaration of Sports* was cancelled: henceforth the

Sabbath would be kept Holy. Dancing around the maypole was banned as a pagan ceremony. No longer could the King protect Catholic priests from the brutality of the law; at Dorchester and York, as well as in London, priests were hanged and disembowelled to provide godly entertainment for the people. Elsewhere, the piety of the mob was stimulated by the execution of old women as witches: Parliament's witch-finder Matthew Hopkins sent 200 to the gallows in East Anglia alone. When satirical Royalist publications like *Mercurius Aulicus* were smuggled into London, it was natural for Parliament in 1643 to censor the press strictly – as Star Chamber had done in less happy days. Milton's *Areopagitica* (1644) protested that the licensers might 'gnaw out the choicest periods of exquisitest books'. John Lilburne[1] defied the ban and was sent to the Tower on a charge brought by Bastwick, his former fellow victim. Writing in prison in 1645, he expressed the feeling of many others in complaining that he was 'in greater bondage by my fighting for justice, liberty and freedome, then I was before'. Parliament might have won the first Civil War, but in the process many of the ideals with which M.P.s had assembled in 1640 had been forgotten. When de-eared Bastwick prosecuted pilloried Lilburne for the offence for which Star Chamber had punished them both, it appeared that Presbyterians were as keen to persecute others as they had been to escape persecution themselves. The Army did not approve.

### v. The Army and the King

It was in the period after Naseby that the unfortunate consequences of the *Solemn League and Covenant* became most obvious. The establishment of a Presbyterian State Church, more intolerant and efficient than that of Laud, and the continued collection of crippling taxes – greater than Weston and Juxon had dreamed of, but necessary to pay the armies of the two kingdoms – seemed curious victories for a Parliament which had met to end high taxation and 'innovations in religion'. Now, Parliament was torn between overtaxed merchants and underpaid soldiers, and between the rigid persecuting Presbyterianism of the Scots and the English Army's

[1] Since his release from the Tower in 1640, Lilburne had risen to hold a Colonel's commission under Manchester, and was already prominent as an Independent.

demands for toleration for soldiers of other Puritan sects.   This
was the situation which Charles tried to exploit.

In the spring of 1646 the King gave himself up to the Scots,
in the hope of winning over their army.   The price they
demanded was too high – that Charles should 'take the
Covenant' and agree to the imposition of Presbyterianism.
The King was prepared to enforce Presbyterianism for three
years, as a temporary concession; 'so as to lay', he admitted, 'a
ground for a perfect recovery of that which, to abandon, were
directly against my conscience'.   The Scots were not impressed, particularly as details kept arriving of the extravagant
promises which Charles's representatives in Ireland were
making to the Catholic rebels.   News of the King's negotiations
with the Scots and Irish made Parliament send him another
set of conditions for peace.   These Propositions of Newcastle
demanded once more that Charles should take the Covenant
and impose Presbyterianism, and insisted that he should give
Parliament complete control over the armed forces for twenty
years, and over foreign policy indefinitely, and that he should
agree to the punishment of his leading supporters.   Over
seventy Royalists were named who should 'expect no pardon'.
Clearly he could not accept such conditions.   Indeed, Charles
by now had a guilt complex over his surrender of Strafford, and
was convinced that to make any more permanent concessions
would offend God.   Nonetheless, he played for time – too
long, as it turned out.   His opponents, in disgust, made a
treaty behind his back.   The Scots agreed to sell him to
Parliament for £400,000, half the arrears of pay owed to them.
The King was brought to Holmby House, in Northamptonshire.   There, in the spring of 1647, he was able to watch his
enemies fall out among themselves.

To save money, Parliament proposed to disband about 6000
of the New Model's soldiers.   The troops refused to be disbanded until they received all the wages due to them – forty-
three weeks pay for the cavalry, eighteen weeks for the infantry.
The Army also demanded pensions for the widows and orphans
of those killed in battle, and compensation for losses suffered.
Moreover, the soldiers were afraid to disperse unless they could
be certain that Parliament would not enforce Presbyterianism
and would not suppress the sects.   Morale became so low that
only 2300 men, barely a tenth of the New Model, volunteered

for service in Ireland. For their own protection, the regiments elected 'agitators' to speak for them and represent them in what developed into the Council of the Army. Here was a direct challenge to Parliament's authority.

Parliament answered by insisting that no man who refused to take the Covenant should hold a commission, and by removing all but reliable Presbyterians from the London trainedbands. In an effort to please the Scots and win over the King, it sent the Propositions of Newcastle to him in a much-modified form. This time Charles accepted them, agreeing to establish Presbyterianism for three years and allow Parliament to control the militia for ten.

The Army was now isolated. Ordered by Parliament to volunteer for Ireland or disband immediately, all the regiments hastened to Newmarket. There the soldiers acclaimed the 'Solemn Engagement', swearing that they would not disband until the terms offered had been approved by the Council of the Army – two officers and two men from each regiment. To protect themselves from the intrigues between Charles, Parliament and the Scots, the Council sent Cornet Joyce with 500 men to kidnap the King from Holmby House and transfer him to the Army's custody at Newmarket.

The Army had involved itself deeply in politics. The Council of the Army, and agitators spurred on by John Lilburne from the Tower, prepared in mid-June the *Declaration of the Army*. In this the soldiers claimed the right to speak on behalf of the people. They demanded toleration for the sects, an Act of Oblivion to pacify the Royalists, a swift dissolution of the Long Parliament, and frequent and regular elections in future. They threatened, moreover, to purge Parliament of members who were 'corrupt' or hostile to the Army. The Council of the Army acted swiftly in support of the *Declaration*. At the end of June it called for the impeachment of eleven leading Presbyterian M.P.s, 'the old, beaten, subtile Foxes of Westminster'. Early in August, increasingly swayed by 'Leveller' agitators demanding political rights for all men, and provoked by the hostility of the Presbyterian mob, the Army occupied London. Later in the month, Cromwell, with a regiment of cavalry at hand in Hyde Park, 'persuaded' the most prominent Presbyterians to stay away from Parliament. One of them, Sir John Maynard, soon found himself in the

Tower accused of high treason, and reflecting with Lilburne on the changes of fortune since Charles had tried to arrest Pym in similar circumstances.

At the beginning of August, the Council of the Army started to negotiate with Charles, despite the objections of the Levellers. The moderate *Heads of the Proposals* drafted by Ireton suggested a constitution almost modern in character, and one which might have appealed to Charles had he realized how perilous his position was. The document proposed that Parliament should nominate the King's ministers, and control the Army for ten years, but it was to be made more representative through a redistribution of seats; elections were to be held every two years, and no Parliament might sit for more than 240 days. Moreover, all Protestant churches should be tolerated – even the bishops could come back, though without their former powers – and the Royalists could buy their pardons with light fines. Charles was unlikely to get conditions more generous than these, but once again he delayed, hoping to get his captors to raise their offers.

Meanwhile, the Leveller agitators were turning the troopers against their officers' discussions with the King. Why did the officers make such an 'idoll of the King?', asked one of them (probably John Wildman). 'Why permit they so many of his deceiptful Clergy to continue about him? Why doe themselves kneele, and kisse, and fawne upon him?' Lilburne, unable to persuade his old friend Cromwell to release him from the Tower, warned the soldiers to trust their great officers 'no farther than you can throw an Oxe!' In fact, the reasons for the officers' negotiations with Charles were clear enough: the Cromwells, Fairfaxes and Iretons were country gentry. In 1647, as in 1640 and 1642, their motives in resisting the King or checking the radicalism of their troopers were the same – to preserve the liberties and privileges of their own class. By the end of 1647, Lilburne was accusing Cromwell of 'planning to keep the poore people everlastingly . . . in bondage and slaveries, with a rotten and putrified Parliament.' The regiments chose agitators more extreme than the original ones, and these, in the autumn of 1647, produced two documents, the *Case of the Armie Truly Stated* and the *Agreement of the People*, claiming votes for all adult men, and the right for the House of Commons to pass laws without the House of Lords. They also demanded that there must be elections every two years, that constituencies must be of similar size and – perhaps of equal interest to the soldiers – that beer must be cheaper. In angry debates at Putney, the Levellers argued their case, against religious fanatics like Goffe, and conservative officers like Ireton who wanted only property-owners to have the vote. When speakers began to call for the overthrow of King, Lords and property and to denounce Charles as a 'man of blood', Cromwell brought the Putney debates to an abrupt end.

The debates worried the King, especially as he had exasperated the officers by refusing to accept the *Heads of the Proposals*. On November 11th Charles escaped from custody and fled to Carisbrooke Castle in the Isle of Wight. The governor placed him under house arrest, but did not prevent him resuming his negotiations with the Scots. By now, the strong Independency of the English army and its control of Parliament had made the Scottish commissioners doubt whether Presbyterianism would ever be established in England through parliamentary action; therefore they turned again to the King.

In December 1647 a group of Scots nobles led by Hamilton also approached Charles, now anxious for new supporters since he had broken with the Army. At Christmas they contracted the 'Engagement' with him. In return for a Scottish army, Charles promised to establish Presbyterianism for three years and to suppress strictly the Independents. The King, however, still refused to take the Covenant himself. The more astute Scots realized that Charles was again deceiving them, and that it would be very easy for him to cancel a promise which had been extracted in such circumstances. The agreement split Scotland. The Engagement, supporting an uncovenanted King, was denounced by the Kirk. Though the Scottish Estates accepted it, Leven and his army resolved to have nothing to do with a treaty which would lead them to war against their former allies in England.

The Second Civil War flared up in the spring of 1648. Royalist rebellions broke out in Kent, Essex and South Wales; nearly half the navy joined the King; Presbyterian London, and most of the M.P.s, hoped for the Army's defeat; even the counties of the old Eastern Association petitioned Parliament for the restoration of the King 'to the splendour of his ancestors'. But the 'Engagers' were delayed by Leven's refusal to fight and by the personal rivalries which made the Argyle faction oppose them. Not until July did Hamilton's raw army, composed mainly of the servants of the Scottish nobles, cross the Border to fight it out with the veterans of the New Model. By this time Fairfax had subdued the royalists in Kent and Essex. Cromwell swiftly crushed the rebels in Wales, and then hastened by forced-marches to intercept the Scots. Unpaid and bare-foot though they were, the soldiers responded devotedly. The New Model, with barely 8000 men, caught the Scottish army of 21,000 near Preston in mid-August, and cut them to pieces. The Second Civil War was over. Once again the God of battles had shown His favour to Cromwell.

The mood of the Army was now very different from that of two years earlier. The usually gentle Fairfax hanged at Colchester two Royalists who had rebelled again after com-pounding with fines for their part in the previous war. But while the generals continued in a state of godly rapture and righteous indignation against the Royalists who had sinned against divine light by rebelling again, Parliament moved to protect the King.

With the Army now so powerful, the King was more vital than ever to Parliament. In early September, Parliament repealed the earlier Vote of No Addresses (by which it had promised the Army that there should be no more negotiations with Charles), and sent delegates to him at Newport, in the Isle of Wight. Once again the King delayed, playing for time and still not realizing how perilous his position was. Meanwhile the extremists in the Army had grown stronger than ever, bitter against Charles for causing the Second Civil War. Republi-cans like Harrison snatched the lead from the Levellers, who were still more concerned with getting their new constitution than with getting rid of Charles. In the eyes of the Repub-licans, the King's delays and deceits had made it madness to trust him any further: Charles must be deposed and punished. In October and November the Army officers argued over what was to be done. By the end of November Cromwell decided that it was necessary 'to have impartial justice done upon offenders'.

But who was to try Charles? Was not the King himself the fountain of justice? How could the King be prosecuted, by the King, in the King's Courts? All depended on the attitude of

Parliament. The Presbyterian majority in Parliament would have nothing to do with the Army's demand expressed in the *Remonstrance of the Army* in late November, that Charles be 'speedily brought to justice for the treason, blood and mischief' he was 'guilty of'. The Presbyterians, needing Charles, ignored the Remonstrance – and so sealed their own fate. The Army's temper grew more inflamed, and early in December the Council of the Army sent Colonel Pride with a company of musketeers to purge Parliament. Only Independent M.P.s, known to be favourable to the Army, were admitted. One hundred and forty M.P.s were arrested by Pride, or frightened into staying away. The Commons shrank to barely fifty members. It was this tiny group, or 'Rump', which tried to give the appearance of legality to the changes of the next four years.

Having hesitated at first, Cromwell now took charge – he was even sleeping in 'one of the King's rich beds in Whitehall'. He now had no doubt that Charles deserved to die – as much as anything for heresy and blasphemy in disputing God's will as revealed in the First Civil War. For a few days he wondered whether it would not be more useful to keep the King alive, a prisoner of the Army, but at the end of December he decided to delay no longer. He hurried forward a process for bringing Charles to trial. On January 1st the Rump declared that it was high treason for the King of England to levy war against Parliament. Later that week the Commons announced that its Acts were valid without the consent of the Lords, and immediately passed an Ordinance to create a High Court of Justice to try the King – for breaking the law it had introduced only a few days earlier. The Ordinance establishing the Court named 135 judges, but stated that the Court would be valid with only 20 of them. The House of Lords and the Scottish commissioners denounced these actions.

The officers hurriedly urged on the trial, knowing how unpopular their actions were. Cromwell was determined to 'cut off the King's head with the crown upon it'. Charles was brought from Windsor; confident of what the verdict would be, the officers allowed him to have Bishop Juxon as his chaplain. Many of the judges nominated, Lord Fairfax[1] and Algernon Sidney among them, refused to have anything to do with the

---

[1] Sir Thomas Fairfax had inherited his father's title in 1648.

matter. On January 20th, the first day of the Trial, Lady Fairfax interrupted the proceedings with a loud protest. No defence witnesses were called.

The King refused to answer the charges levied against him – that 'Charles Stuart hath been, and is the occasioner, author, and continuer of the . . . unnatural, cruel and bloody wars'. He challenged the authority of the Court, and claimed to be fighting against arbitrary 'justice': 'It is not my cause alone, it is the freedom and liberty of the people of England.' After a three-day farce, Bradshaw, the President of the Court, pronounced the verdict. Sentenced to death, Charles was not now permitted to speak. Muttering 'Expect what justice other people will have!', the King was taken away.

There was now a serious hitch. Many of the judges were reluctant to sign the death warrant, despite a bloodthirsty sermon from the ranting preacher Hugh Peter, encouraging the judges from Psalm 149.[1] Cromwell himself threatened and bullied some of the hesitant. Even so, only fifty-nine judges, out of the 135 originally named, signed the warrant.

It was enough. The next day, January 30th, Charles was brought to the scaffold hastily nailed together outside his own palace of Whitehall. Dense files of soldiers kept the people back, and made it impossible for their King to address them. His dignity and courageous calm impressed everyone. The London mob which had cheered the execution of Strafford now groaned when Charles's head fell under the executioner's axe. Even the Puritan poet Andrew Marvell, writing an Ode to celebrate Cromwell's triumphant return from Ireland, had to comment on the King's behaviour on that grim January afternoon:

> He nothing common did or mean
> Upon that memorable Scene;
>
> . . .
>
> Nor called the Gods with vulgar spite
> To vindicate his helpless Right.

[1] *To bind their Kings with chains, and the nobles with fetters of iron; To execute upon them the judgement written: this honour have all his saints.*

## vi. Scotland during the Civil Wars

In the autumn of 1641, Charles had loaded with honours his hoped-for allies in Scotland. Hamilton became a Duke, Argyle a Marquis, and Alexander Leslie the Earl of Leven. But political allies in Scotland were of little value to Charles so long as the Kirk opposed him. For the Presbyterian ministers of Edinburgh, Charles's concessions in 1641 ushered in the acceptable time of the Lord. Now was the chance to build the City of God on earth, to imitate the pattern of Calvin's Geneva, to lead the peoples of England and Ireland towards the Light, to end the pagan darkness of popes and bishops, to impose a godly discipline upon the Elect of the Kirk. The Covenant obsessed them. To 'take the Covenant' was a sure sign that the Almighty had predestined one to the way of salvation; to refuse the Covenant, or to contradict the Kirk's interpretation of it, was heresy, 'sinning against the Light'. The Covenant was the price of Scottish help in England – for King or for Parliament.

Nonetheless, the history of Scotland during the Civil War was bedevilled by the clan jealousies and hostilities which so readily flared up in time of trouble. In the summer of 1643 Argyle learned that Charles was negotiating with the Irish Catholic clan of Macdonalds, hereditary enemies of Argyle's Campbells who had seized many of their Scottish lands. The Campbells and the Kirk were in danger. Argyle's friends summoned the Scottish Estates, and persuaded them to propose alliance with the English Parliament. Pym, distressed by the Royalist successes of 1643, grasped eagerly at the offer; in the *Solemn League and Covenant* Parliament agreed to pay for the raising of a Scottish Army and promised to establish in England a Church following 'the example of the best reformed churches'. Despite the efforts of Royalists like Hamilton, Montrose and Huntly, Scotland was committed to fighting against the followers of the Stuart King.

Montrose, however, was determined to carry on the struggle. Even though Huntly, head of the Royalist Gordon clan, was too envious of his successes to give him much support, Montrose scraped together a small band of highlanders, strengthened but somewhat embarrassed by a force of Irish Macdonalds led by their chieftain's son, the giant Alastair. While Leven and the Government troops helped Fairfax at Marston Moor and

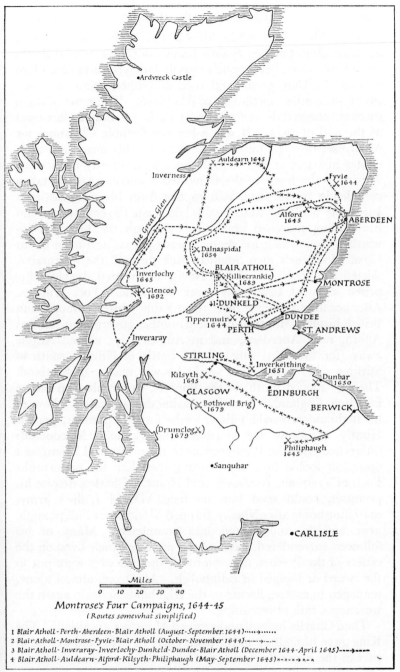

Montrose's Four Campaigns, 1644-45
(Routes somewhat simplified)

1 Blair Atholl - Perth - Aberdeen - Blair Atholl (August - September 1644)·····→········
2 Blair Atholl - Montrose - Fyvie - Blair Atholl (October - November 1644)---·→·-·-·
3 Blair Atholl - Inveraray - Inverlochy - Dunkeld - Dundee - Blair Atholl (December 1644 - April 1645)---→----
4 Blair Atholl - Auldearn - Alford - Kilsyth - Philiphaugh (May - September 1645)×-×-×→×-×

## Montrose in Scotland, and other Campaigns

Lᴮs

Naseby, Montrose[1] made himself the master of Scotland. Fighting almost always against heavy odds, he captured Perth, sacked Aberdeen, let Argyle's heavily-laden soldiers chase him around the Cairngorms and then ambushed them at Fyvie, twenty-five miles north-west of Aberdeen. The news of these successes cheered the King at Oxford as he celebrated Christmas at the end of 1644. It was a less comfortable Christmas for Montrose: through bitter weather he led his men from their winter quarters at Blair Atholl more than seventy miles westward into the heart of the Campbell country. Argyle, taken completely by surprise, had to flee from his own castle at Inveraray while the Macdonalds laid waste the country around it. Having marched northwards through the blizzards towards a trap which his enemies were preparing in the Great Glen, Montrose's men doubled back through the mountains, skirted the icy slopes of Ben Nevis, and routed Argyle's surprised army at Inverlochy, near the modern Fort William. After accomplishing the most remarkable winter campaign in British history, Montrose defeated another government army at Alford, near Aberdeen, and in August 1645 chased Argyle away (for the third time) at the battle of Kilsyth, south of Stirling. For a few brief weeks he was master of Scotland. Then he moved south, to the Borders, to recruit men before invading England. Now his weaknesses appeared. Few of his highlanders would follow, for he forbade plunder; jealous Huntly withdrew the Gordons; the Catholic Macdonalds quarrelled with the Presbyterians in the army, and Montrose's optimism fooled him into trusting men like the opportunist Earls of Traquair, Roxburgh and Home. Charles, despite his promises, could send him no help. David Leslie's army, marching home after Naseby, trapped Montrose at Philiphaugh, near Selkirk, and routed him completely. Many of his followers surrendered, having been promised their lives; on the orders of the Presbyterian ministers, the prisoners were put to the sword or hanged in Edinburgh. Montrose, almost alone, managed to escape, fleeing to the Highlands to begin again the wearisome task of recruiting.

Then Charles himself undermined Montrose's position. The King gave himself up to the Scots early in 1646, and agreed as part of the surrender terms to disown his general in Scotland.

[1] C. V. Wedgwood's brief biography of Montrose is strongly recommended.

With a heavy heart, Montrose disbanded his army and escaped
to Norway.   There was no one now to challenge the power of
the Kirk.   While Argyle and the General Assembly negotiated
with Charles, the ministers set themselves the holy task of track-
ing down the followers of the renegade Covenanter Montrose,
and the equally virtuous duty of finding and burning witches,
in an inspiring combination of sadism, piety and public
spectacle.

Their resentment at the tyranny of the Kirk, as well
as dislike of the violence of the English sects, led many Scottish
nobles to follow Hamilton in making the Engagement with
Charles in 1647.   But Argyle, the General Assembly and the
Scottish army refused to fight for an uncovenanted King, and
the 'Engagers' were consequently defeated at Preston.   Again,
the power of the Kirk had been confirmed.   While Charles was
being tried and sentenced in London, the Scottish Parliament
passed a vicious 'Act of Classes' to ban from public life and
office all who had supported Montrose or the Engagement.

Nonetheless, the execution of Charles I was even more
unpopular in Scotland than in England.   The Presbyterians
would joyfully assist to bring a King to the scaffold, but
expected to be consulted before the Independents struck his
head off.   Even Argyle, sullen, sincere bigot as he was, offered
to help the young Prince Charles – whom the Scottish Estates
hailed as Charles II as soon as news of the execution reached
Edinburgh.   Montrose, in the Netherlands, also hurried to
offer his services to the new King.   Like his father, Charles II
tried to use both Montrose and Montrose's implacable enemy,
Argyle.   He gave them both commissions to raise armies for
him in Scotland.   Montrose was trying to raise troops in
Sutherland when he was sold to Argyle by the penniless laird of
Assynt, with whom he was sheltering at Ardvreck Castle.   He
was dragged in triumph to Edinburgh, put on trial for treason
to the Covenant, and then hanged, and quartered.   The
power of Argyle and the Kirk seemed greater than ever.   With
Montrose dead and Cromwell crushing the Irish Royalists,
Charles II had to 'take the Covenant'.   When he travelled to
Scotland to lead his forces, the ministers of the Kirk forced him
to denounce the sins of his father and his idolatrous mother.
An English cartoon of the time showed the ministers holding
Charles II's nose to the grindstone while they heaped fresh

humiliations upon him! Charles got an army, however, carefully purged of three or four thousand veterans whose devotion to the Covenant was suspect; the Kirk wanted God's victories to be won by godly soldiers.

Faced with another Scottish escapade, Cromwell hurried home from Ireland in the spring of 1650. His appeals to the Scots to give up their royal puppet fell on deaf ears. 'I beseech you', he pleaded with them, 'in the bowels of Christ, think it possible you may be mistaken.' The God of battles would have to decide. The New Model crossed the Border late in the summer of 1650, in pursuit of the Scottish army commanded by the skilful David Leslie. For once Cromwell was outmanœuvred, and was trapped in a narrow coastal strip between the coast at Dunbar and the Lammermuir hills, some thirty miles east of Edinburgh. Leslie's men occupied the high ground, in an unassailable position. Impatient for the slaughter of their foes, on September 3rd the ministers per-suaded Leslie to move his men down from the hills to prevent any English escaping by the flanks. With the Scots dispersed, Cromwell attacked. For the loss of only thirty men he routed an army of over 20,000. The God of battles had decided; and His verdict was not favourable to the Kirk. In the following months the confidence of the Elect was undermined, and a more tolerant wind blew across Scotland. Charles was crowned at Scone – by Argyle himself; the Estates repealed the Act of Classes; and the political influence of the Kirk faded rapidly.

Through the winter of 1650–1 Cromwell held Edinburgh and Southern Scotland, while Leslie at Stirling blocked his path north to the Highlands which Charles was now ruling from Perth. In July 1651, however, Lambert crossed the Forth and defeated the defenders of Fife at Inverkeithing. The road to the north was now open, and Cromwell soon occupied Perth. But Leslie, with Cromwell north of him, now had a road open to England. The Royalists fell into the trap. Cromwell had realized the impossibility of crushing the Royalists in the Highlands, and had deliberately lured them into England. As Charles's army marched past Carlisle and down through Lancashire, General Lambert and General Harrison moved across behind them, blocking their retreat. Disliking the Scots and fearing Crom-well, few Englishmen joined Charles. On September 3rd,

1651, exactly a year after Dunbar, Cromwell closed the trap and crushed the invaders at Worcester. God had shown him His 'crowning mercy'. The young King escaped the battle, evaded the soldiers scouring the country for him, and eventually found a small boat to carry him to France.

Cromwell could now leave Scotland to his capable deputy, General Monck. Within a few months the occupation was complete. The only Royalist insurrection, under Glencairne and Middleton, was suppressed in 1654 in a single battle at Dalnaspidal, in a lonely pass half way between Perth and Inverness. For nine years Scotland received the unfamiliar benefits of fair, efficient and honest government. There was no interference with Presbyterian worship. The Council in London, at first inclined to treat Scotland as a conquered province, was later persuaded to prepare a scheme to admit Scots to the English Parliament; in the *Instrument of Government* of December 1653, Cromwell agreed that Scotland should send thirty M.P.s to Westminster. Commissioners (mainly Englishmen) dealt out impartial justice and helped to tame the Highland clans. Scots were admitted to all the trading privileges possessed by Englishmen. Cromwellian Ordinances granted full union with England, and the 'Commonwealth of England, Scotland and Ireland' was proclaimed.

But the Scots did not enjoy the Cromwellian occupation. The cost of Monck's army was enormous. At first, £10,000 a month was demanded in assessments upon property, and large sums were also collected from excise and customs duties. The country's poverty was such that the assessments had to be reduced to £6000 a month. By the last year of the Protectorate, more than half the cost of governing Scotland, £307,000 in that year, was coming from England. The Kirk could worship freely, but it lost its wide disciplinary powers and the General Assembly (now strongly Royalist) was suppressed. Scottish merchants, ruined by the wars against Holland and Spain and by Royalist pirate ships, could not benefit from the new freedom of trade. Presbyterians did not welcome union with the heretical sectaries in power in England. The Restoration of Charles II, already King of Scotland for eleven years, ended the unpopular union. But the Presbyterians who cheered in 1660 changed their tone in 1662, when Charles II set about restoring the powers of a persecuting Episcopal Church.

## vii. Ireland during the Civil Wars

Even more than in England and Scotland, the King's supporters in Ireland failed because of their disunity. As an Irish poet wrote at the time, the clans were overthrown because

> It was God's justice not to free them,
> They went not together hand in hand.

In 1641, the Irish Revolt embarrassed Charles not least because some of its leaders claimed to be acting in his name. By the summer of 1642, however, he was looking more favourably upon the rebels, whom Parliament had infuriated by the 'Adventurers' Act.[1] There were soon several armies in the field. The rebel army was under Owen Roe O'Neill, nephew of the great Tyrone who had fought against Elizabeth's viceroys. The 'Old English' settlers, for the most part Catholics, had an army under Preston, lately a successful commander of Irish troops in Spanish pay. Ormonde, belatedly made Lord Lieutenant by Charles, commanded a small force of English settlers loyal to the Crown. Most of the 'New English' fought on the other side, in the various regiments raised by the Irish Parliament under commanders like Inchiquin and Broghill. Ormonde realized that the attitude of the 'Old English' confederates was of critical importance, and so tried to win them to support the King, first by promises and then by force. At first he had little success with them, though he did sign a truce – the 'Cessation' – with O'Neill's rebels in September 1643, agreeing to end hostilities.

Charles's own attempts to gain friends in Ireland were failures, and lost him friends in England and Scotland. His offers to Lord Antrim, chief of the Irish Macdonalds, fell into Argyle's hands and helped to provoke the *Solemn League and Covenant*. The promises made in 1645 by his envoy, the Catholic Lord Glamorgan, became known in England; when Charles renounced the 'Glamorgan Treaty', Irish as well as English grew yet more suspicious of his motives and doubtful of his honesty. In the autumn of 1645, more trouble arrived, in the shape of the Papal Nuncio Rinuccini bringing money from Rome and France. Although Ormonde still tried to win over

[1] Promising lands in Ireland to those who paid for its conquest.

both the 'Old English' and the Irish rebels, Rinuccini soon persuaded the Catholics to fight for their religion, not their King. 'Old English' Catholics who hesitated to accept the leadership of O'Neill were excommunicated, and the Nuncio's opposition repulsed the generous peace offer made by Ormonde in 1646 on Charles's instructions. Jealousies between O'Neill and Preston lost them the chance to crush the Parliament troops after the former's victory at Benburb in 1646. Next year it was too late. Colonel Jones and 8000 men of the New Model wiped out Preston's army at Dangan Hill. Ormonde then surrendered Dublin to Jones, preferring 'English rebels to Irish rebels'. Lord Inchiquin reconquered Munster and routed the Macdonalds. By the end of 1647 Ireland was almost subdued.

The rise to power in England of the Independents changed the situation. Inchiquin, and many others Presbyterian peers, decided to join Ormonde. So did the survivors of the 'Old English', especially after they had persuaded Rinuccini to go home. But O'Neill's army remained loyal to the Nuncio, and refused to support Ormonde even after Charles I's execution. Consequently, Jones was able to defeat Ormonde at Rathmines (near Dublin) early in August 1649. A few days later Cromwell arrived.

The military problem facing Cromwell was only one of his worries. Large but isolated garrisons were holding huge areas against him, and poor communications still further complicated his task. Even if his opponents were divided, there were still 40–50,000 men in arms against him. Moreover, Cromwell had to carry out the decisions of the Long Parliament to suppress Catholicism and seize the lands of the rebels. The poverty of Ireland and the high cost of the English army there meant that there was no hope of paying the costs of occupation by assessments and excise and customs duties. A military victory, though, was the first requirement. Convinced that the Irish were subhuman idolaters, and determined to avenge the massacres of 1641, Cromwell put the defenders of Drogheda to the sword when he captured the town in September. Typically, he gave the credit to the Almighty: 'I am persuaded that this is a righteous judgement of God upon these barbarous wretches, who have imbrued their hands in so much innocent blood.' A month later he treated the town of Wexford in a similar way. Hundreds of fugitives were drowned

The following labels appear on the map:

- Londonderry 1689
- Carrickfergus
- Belfast
- ULSTER
- Benburb 1646
- Enniskillen 1689
- Newton Butler 1689
- Dundalk
- CONNAUGHT
- Battle of the Boyne 1690
- Drogheda 1649
- R. Boyne
- Galway
- R. Shannon
- Dangan Hill 1647
- Dublin
- Aughrim 1691
- Rathmines 1649
- CLARE
- LEINSTER
- Limerick 1691
- Clonmel 1650
- Wexford 1649
- Waterford
- MUNSTER
- Cork 1690
- Kinsale 1601, 1690
- Bantry Bay 1689

*Area shaded lightly is that reserved for the 'transplanted' Irish 'beyond the Shannon'.*

Miles
0 10 20 30 40

The Conquests of Ireland

when their boats capsized; again, it was God's 'righteous justice'. Cromwell hoped, of course, that the slaughter of those who had resisted him at Drogheda and Wexford[1] would save his soldiers' lives by frightening other Irish garrisons into surrendering more tamely. By May 1650 Cromwell had captured almost all the ports and most of the south, despite a defeat at Clonmel in which he lost 2000 men – the heaviest reverse of his career. In that month he returned to England, leaving his son-in-law Ireton to supervise the savage campaigns which culminated in the conquest of Galway two years later.

The pacification of Ireland could now proceed. To get rid of the rebel troops, Ireton allowed 30,000 of them to leave for service in the armies of France and Spain. Thousands more were transported to the West Indies, to labour more or less as plantation slaves. A new High Court at Dublin sentenced the leading rebel and royalist officers to death. In August 1652 the Rump passed an Act of Settlement under which its enemies were punished. Protestant royalists like Ormonde and Inchiquin, as well as 'Old English' and rebel leaders, forfeited their lands. As the 'Adventurers' Act' had promised ten years before, the Irish had to pay for their own conquest. The Commonwealth discharged its debts and even paid its soldiers with grants of Irish land. So rapacious was the demand that in 1653 Cromwell agreed that the Irish gentry should be 'transplanted' to the far west, to the barren lands of Clare and Connaught, while the rest of Ireland was occupied by English soldiers, lording it as squires over the native labourers remaining behind. Cromwell, indeed, tried to found a new feudal occupation, with the English soldier-squires keeping their tenantry in order. The soldiers, however, disobeyed Cromwell's order that they should not marry Catholic girls – there were few alternatives available in Ireland – and some, at least, of the new settlers were gradually absorbed into native society.

In some respects Cromwellian rule was relatively enlightened. Justice was fair and honest. Ireland, like Scotland, received the privilege of sending M.P.s to the Parliaments at Westminster. Cromwell also allowed her to trade freely with England. These concessions, however, benefited only the English settlers.

---

[1] Even in England, Cromwell had allowed his soldiers to sack Basing House and slaughter its resolute defenders to encourage other Royalist garrisons to yield more peacefully (October, 1645).

For the others, deprived of their lands, their religion persecuted more vigorously than ever, the 'curse of Cromwell' lay heavy on them.   In 1649 Cromwell had warned the governor of Ross not to expect toleration: 'If by liberty of conscience you mean a liberty to exercise the mass . . . where the Parliament of England have power, that will not be allowed of.'   While the government did not try to drive the Catholics to Protestant services, it toiled to prevent them attending their own.   Rinuccini's activities had incensed Puritan bigotry, and Cromwell's agents drove most of the priests into exile on peril of their lives. Nevertheless, the temper of the administration gradually grew more moderate under new Deputies.   Ireton had died in 1651, and was succeeded in turn by Lambert, Fleetwood and Henry Cromwell.   The moderation of the last, the ablest of Oliver's sons, kept Ireland sullenly quiet until the Restoration.

### viii.  The Commonwealth

For eleven years England tried to escape from the consequences of Charles's execution.   In a way which has become familiar in the twentieth century, the Army seized power in the name of the people.   Moreover, it claimed this by Divine Right, through the special inspiration of the Almighty.   So swift and radical was the overthrow of the constitution that nothing stable could replace it until the old form was restored in 1660. In December 1648 Pride's Purge subjected the Commons to the Army; in the next month, the Army and the Rump ignored the Lords in bringing Charles to trial; in March the Rump voted to abolish both the Lords and the Monarchy.   Henceforth, England was to be ruled by a Council of State, working through various sub-committees.   In effect, a group of regicides, army officers and extremist M.P.s now held legislative power, in place of government by a Parliament of King, Lords and Commons.

From the start, the new system was unpopular, attacked by extremists and Presbyterians as well as by Royalists.   During the King's trial the Levellers had presented their demands to the Rump in the *Agreement of the People*.   The Rump ignored them.   Lilburne dashed into print again, with *England's New Chaines Discovered*, printed within a month of Charles's death. In March the Council of State sent him back to the Tower,

Cromwell thumping the table with his fist and calling for the
punishment of the Levellers – 'If you do not break them, they
will break you'. In April there were Leveller mutinies in the
Army, and several regiments refused to leave for Ireland unless
the Rump approved the *Agreement*. Cromwell used the loyal
regiments to suppress the mutinies, and executed the ring-
leaders.

Meanwhile, a wave of royalist emotion swept the country,
stimulated by the secret publication of *Eikon Basilike* [The
Image of a King]. This appeared to be Charles's own memoirs, written as he lay in close confinement in Carisbrooke
Castle.[1] The King blamed himself for the sacrifice of Strafford,
explained his reluctant participation in the war, and prophesied
the troubles which lay ahead – 'I know the sharpe and necessary
tyranny of my Destroyers will sufficiently confute the calumnies
to tyranny against me'. 'The Pourtraicture of his Sacred
Maiestie in solitudes and sufferings' was a best-seller, despite
the Government's attempts to suppress it. In its first year
over thirty editions were printed. Three editions satisfied the
public demand for the official reply, *Eikonoklastes* [The Image-
breaker], which Milton was ordered to write. The picture of a
pious King suffering for his faith long remained. In 1662
prayers commemorating King Charles the Martyr were added
to the Prayer Book, and remained in it for two centuries.

In May 1649 the Rump declared England to be a Commonwealth, governed by 'the supreme authority of this nation, the
representatives of the people in Parliament'. In practice,
though, the supreme authority was the Army, without which
the Rump could not have existed. Fairfax, as Commander-in-
Chief, had so little liking for the events of January that he
increasingly allowed his deputy, Cromwell, to take charge. It
was Cromwell who suppressed the Leveller mutinies; it was
Cromwell who went to Ireland in 1649 and Scotland in 1650 to
crush the Royalists. Even before he became Protector, the
reins of power were firmly in his hand. Each new victory –
Marston Moor, Naseby, Preston, Drogheda, Dunbar and
Worcester – strengthened his conviction that he was the chosen
of God, predestined to deliver England, a Messiah riding, not
on a peaceful ass, but at the head of the New Model's cavalry.

[1] In fact, *Eikon Basilike* was probably written by Dr. John Gauden, later made
Bishop of Exeter by Charles II.

It was not long before he quarrelled with the Rump and the Council of State, both of which became more Presbyterian in reaction against the extreme sects.  A practical man despite his confidence in his destiny, he realized that the Commonwealth could only be permanent if it were made more popular, and if the Royalists were reconciled by fair treatment.

He saw the need for the Commonwealth to win more support by reducing taxation, by granting an amnesty to the Royalists, by allowing religious toleration (within limits), and by a degree of political and legal reform.  On all these points he fell out with the politicians.  The Council of State rushed into a war with the Protestant, republican United Provinces – the Commonwealth's natural ally – and the cost of the war demanded higher taxation.  The Rump passed an Ordinance of General Pardon and Oblivion, but with so many exceptions that the Royalists greeted it with derision.  Moreover, at the same time the Rump passed an Ordinance ordering the sale of Royalists' estates forfeited for treason.  This was not the path to reconciliation.  The Rump did abolish the penalties for not attending Church on Sundays; but neither could it agree on any form of Church government to replace the Bishops, nor would it accept the Independents' demands for freedom from authority.  The legal reforms were violently reactionary.  One new law, in the spirit of the Old Testament, made adultery punishable by death. Fearing the Levellers, the Rump made it treason to incite the Army to mutiny, and a new prerogative High Court of Justice was created to try without jury all cases of treason.  The licensing of books became more strict, with penalties for the purchasers as well as the authors, printers and publishers of unauthorized books.  Those who refused to swear loyalty to the Commonwealth lost their rights at law.  Political reform seemed impossible.  The mood of the country was such that a free election like that of 1640 would have returned an overwhelming majority of Royalists and Presbyterians.  The members of the Rump were determined to hang on to power as long as possible, but only by turning a blind eye to strong public opinion could the Commonwealth avoid a lawful counter-revolution which would have cost many their heads.

Nevertheless, the Army leaders pressed for the Rump to dissolve itself and risk a new election – under Army supervision. At length, early in 1653 the Army persuaded the Rump to dissolve itself by the end of the following year. In April the M.P.s tried to rush through a Bill to enable the existing members to keep their own seats, and to judge the fitness of the men elected from the other constituencies. This would have given the Rump perpetual control of the membership of Parliament and, so Cromwell feared, would guarantee the election of a Presbyterian majority sworn to suppress the Independent sects.

Disgusted, Cromwell intervened. Having hastened to the House with a file of musketeers as the Commons were about to vote on the 'Perpetual Bill', he listened briefly, and then rose to speak. He denounced the members individually and collectively for their corruption and dishonesty. Then, speaking on behalf of the Almighty, he cried to the Rump 'In the name of God – Go!'. Less resolute than he had been in 1642, Speaker Lenthall went. The mace remained. 'Take away this bauble', Cromwell shouted to the soldiers. 'May God deliver us from Sir Harry Vane', he roared as his former friend protested. That evening, Cromwell suspended the Council of State and ordered the officers to support him.

This act ended the first constitution of the Interregnum. The execution of the King had lost the Army the support of all but the republicans; the suppression of the Rump lost the Army the support of even these. Vane and Bradshaw, regicides in 1649, were now among Cromwell's most bitter opponents. Some of the members of the Rump, at least, had been elected legally in 1640; the constitutions and parliaments of the period 1653–60, however, were merely creations and creatures of the Army.

The fate of the first experiment was typical. For a few months in the summer of 1653 Cromwell ruled with a council of ten, seven officers and three civilians, while the theorists argued about constitutional reform. A few extremists like General Harrison, a Fifth Monarchy man who believed that Christ was about to come in person to rule the world, wanted a nominated council of saints to purge the land in preparation for the Messiah. Most, however, were unwilling to abandon the appearance of a Parliament. With taxes urgently needed, Cromwell chose the compromise which produced the Nominated Parliament. The Independent congregations nominated candidates, and from the names put forward Cromwell and the officers chose 140 of the most suitable. This system should have produced a Parliament of reliable saints loyal to the Army. It did not.

The members of the Parliament of Saints, or 'Barebones' Parliament,[1] met in July 1653. The writs for assembly had been sent out by Cromwell in his own name, and it was again Cromwell who gave the saints their instructions. Such a body of godly amateurs was unlikely to achieve much. Though there was not a lawyer in the House, the 'Barebones' Parliament decided to reform the law completely. It abolished the Court of Chancery, notorious for its delays and costliness – without devising anything to replace it. Extremists called for the Common Law to be replaced by the law of Moses. Others demanded the abolition of tithes, to the anger of gentry still receiving them and to the dismay of Presbyterian ministers installed in parish churches. Others interpreted Cromwell's desire for toleration as a licence for every lunatic-fringe sect to preach against the established order in Church, State and Society. Others prepared to attack the universities and all professional clergy – 'hireling shepherds'. A series of Royalist intrigues underlined the country's dissatisfaction: in August three Army colonels were sent to the Tower for plotting, and a rebellion was expected in Warwickshire the next month.

By December it was obvious that the godly could not govern. The irresponsibility of the fanatics, 'artificers of the meanest trades, known only by their gifts in praying and preaching' (Clarendon), ensured the downfall of the 'Barebones' Parliament. In December 1653 the more moderate Saints, led by General Lambert, met at Westminster early one morning. They persuaded themselves of the need to dissolve, secured the necessary majority, and resigned their powers into Cromwell's hands. Lambert immediately persuaded Cromwell to accept the position of Lord Protector in a new Constitution which the Army officers had sketched out. Cromwell agreed. With the republicans and extremists howling their protests at the new interference with Parliament, the Commonwealth ended and the Protectorate began. The fate of the 'Barebones' Parliament emphasized how unstable the country was in the years after the King's execution, how strong the jealousies were

---

[1] Named after 'Praise-God' Barebones, a leather-seller and preacher, who was a prominent member.

between Presbyterian and Sectary, and how little the soldiers could trust anyone but themselves.

### ix. The First Protectorate

The *Instrument of Government*, pressed on Cromwell after the suicide of the 'Barebones' Parliament, was a remarkable document. It tried to create a balanced constitution like those of mediaeval Italian city-states. Cromwell was to be Lord Protector, but his powers were to be limited by the Council of State. The members of the Council were to hold office for life, and thus be free from any attempt by the Protector to intimidate them. Parliament was to meet every three years, for at least five months. The *Instrument* redistributed Parliamentary representation: three-quarters of the members of the Long Parliament had come from the boroughs, but the *Instrument* allotted two-thirds of the seats to the counties and only one-third to the boroughs. Even so, many new manufacturing towns – Manchester, Leeds, Halifax – were represented for the first time. Moreover, in the counties the franchise was greatly reduced: the man with freehold land worth 40 shillings or more a year lost the vote unless the total value of his property was at least £200. Thirty seats each went to Scotland and Ireland, to be distributed as the Protector and Council of State thought fit. The effect of these changes was clear – to put Parliament firmly under the control of the gentry and reliably Puritan[1] towns. Such a system, Lambert and Cromwell hoped, would produce a reliable, co-operative and effective Parliament, especially as the sixty seats for Scotland and Ireland could produce a loyal phalanx of Government supporters. It was the most radical attempt to alter Parliamentary representation before the nineteenth century.

The problems facing the Protectorate were the old familiar ones. The *Instrument* promised taxation sufficient for the normal costs of government, the navy and, an army of 30,000. In fact, the Army was nearly twice this size. The soldiers had little desire to return to their humble civilian trades, and feared to disband unless they were guaranteed toleration for their sects. The *Instrument* offered toleration for all but popery,

---

[1] The Independents were more likely to be influential in the new towns where the parish system – usually now in Presbyterian hands – was less developed.

prelacy and extreme sects which 'under the profession of Christ, hold forth and practise licentiousness'. Would Parliament agree? In any case, would Parliament accept the Protector as an independent Single Person, high above the storms of political struggles? Would Parliament approve of taxation continuing at more than four times the level during Charles's rule? How far could the Army and Parliament trust each other?

The *Instrument* stated that the first 'Triennial Parliament' must meet by September 3rd, 1654; in the meantime, Cromwell and the Council of State were to govern by themselves. This period proved the most useful and constructive part of the Interregnum. A new High Court of Justice was created to try treason cases, and the barbarous practice of disembowelling the victim ceased. Cromwell restored the Court of Chancery (suppressed, but not replaced, by the Parliament of Saints) but reduced its fees and its powers. To reform the country's behaviour, Ordinances banned cock-fighting and limited horse-racing, outlawed duels and forbade drunkenness and swearing. Previous Parliaments had squabbled over abolishing tithe payments; Cromwell by-passed the problem by trying to ensure that only worthy ministers received tithes. Therefore he created a Commission of 'Triers' to examine and approve or reject all candidates for parish ministries, and followed it by appointing local Commissions of 'Ejectors' to remove existing clergy suspect of crimes such as drunkenness, blasphemy, immorality or using the old Book of Common Prayer. The universities and schools were purged again in the same way. Other Ordinances of this busy period provided for the improvement of roads and the postal services, tried to help debtors, and ordered the licensing of hackney-coachmen, the taxi-drivers of the time, whose vehicles were choking the narrow streets of London. This was Cromwell's version of the *thorough* government of Strafford and Laud. There were more than a few echoes of Hampden's trial in Cony's Case (1654), when the Council sent the merchant Cony and his lawyers to prison for protesting against a customs duty on silk.

The First Triennial Parliament met on the last permissible date. Immediately, its members attacked the *Instrument*. As the constitution had not been introduced by Parliament, it was, they declared, quite illegal. At first Cromwell tried to reason with Parliament. He was prepared to allow the Triennial to modify the *Instrument*, provided it did not tamper with four 'fundamentals' – government by a Single Person and Parliament, regular elections, liberty of conscience, and the sharing between Protector and Parliament in the control of the armed forces. He insisted, however, that the M.P.s should swear a 'Recognition' of loyalty to the Protectorate. Ninety republicans refused. The Army therefore kept them out of Parliament. The remainder demanded that the Council of State should be elected afresh by each new Parliament, that the army should be reduced in size, and that the 'damnable heresies' of the sects should be suppressed. With tempers rising high, Cromwell resolved to get rid of the First Triennial Parliament at the earliest possible moment. The *Instrument* guaranteed its survival for five months: on January 22nd, 1655, after five *lunar* (not calendar) months, Cromwell dissolved it.

In words which Strafford would hardly have dared use, Cromwell had told Parliament that the need for strong, effective government overrode democratic theories: 'The people will prefer their safety to their passions, and their real security to forms, when necessity calls for supplies.' From the Republicans, and fanatics like the Fifth Monarchy men, came more than wailing and gnashing of teeth: a wave of insurrections and assassination plots threatened the country's stability. Royalists saw their chance, and Penruddock's rising in the west-country achieved a brief success before the Army crushed it. The Royalist reaction in the 1630s had failed partly because of the 'revolt of the J.P.s'; to guard himself against a similar collapse of the administration, Cromwell introduced in June 1655 a new system of authoritarian rule. He divided the country into eleven districts, placing each under a Major-General at the head of 500 picked cavalrymen. The original purpose of the Major-Generals was to make sure that the local magistrates did their duties, and to nip in the bud any threatening revolts. Soon, however, power-drunk zealots like Desborough, Fleetwood and Goffe were using their powers to carry through in their areas their own ideas of puritan reform. England groaned under the tyranny of a military police snooping into all aspects of private life. More than any other innovation, the Major-Generals made the Interregnum hated. But the Protector did not enjoy governing in this authoritarian way.   If his victories in battle had not convinced him that God supported him, he might well have abandoned his struggle against ambitious politicians and intolerant Presbyterians.   Even though his obligation to the Army over-shadowed his obligation to the 'constitution', he was reluctant to rule openly as a dictator.   When his expensive foreign policy forced him to seek new taxes, it would have been easy for him to use the Major-Generals to collect them, whether a Parliament had approved or not.   Instead, he summoned the Second Triennial Parliament to meet in September 1656, more than a year before it was due under the *Instrument*.   This time he used all the power and influence at his disposal to secure a favourable House.   The Major-Generals carefully altered borough char-ters, and used both influence and threats, to try to get Indepen-dents elected.   A hundred of those elected were prevented by the Council from taking their seats in Parliament, and fifty or sixty more refused to take their seats unless the others were admitted.

Even when purged in this way, the Second Triennial Parlia-ment refused to approve the Militia Bill to continue the powers of the hated Major-Generals, and Cromwell had to withdraw them.   Parliament did at last confirm the constitution created by the *Instrument*, but suggested the introduction of a Second Chamber to interpret the *Instrument*'s articles.   Which were the sects, for example, which 'held forth and practised licentious-ness'? Cromwell had already had to intervene to stop Parliament punishing savagely the mad Quaker prophet James Nayler, who claimed to be Christ and had staged a Messianic entry into Bristol riding on a white donkey.   A Second Chamber would reduce the need for Cromwell's interference with Parliamentary business.   The Protector, and the more responsible M.P.s, welcomed the proposal.

The discovery in January 1657 of Sindercombe's Plot to assassinate the Protector emphasized another dangerous problem: who would succeed Cromwell?   Would his death prove the signal for civil war between ambitious generals? Sindercombe's Plot brought home the precariousness of the situation: England's peace depended on the life of a tired and sick man.   Would it not be safer to establish by law a form of hereditary monarchy and empower Cromwell to nominate his successor?   Moreover, there was another reason for offering

Cromwell the name and position of King: if – as seemed possible – the Stuarts were eventually restored, would not Henry VII's *De Facto* Act[1] protect Cromwell's supporters from the law of treason?

Consequently, in March 1657 Bulstrode Whitelocke and other moderates persuaded Parliament to offer Cromwell the title of King. The *Humble Petition and Advice* also offered him the right to name his successor and to nominate the members of a Second Chamber – in effect a House of Lords. Cromwell hesitated. How would the Army react? General Monck in Scotland sent his approval, but a small group of officers in London prepared a petition against it. Cromwell's friends, Desborough and Fleetwood, and leading Independent ministers like Nye and Owen, warned him that if he took the title he would split the Army, and play into the hands of jeering Royalists. Unwilling to face the sneers of those charging him with ambition, Cromwell accepted his friends' advice. After two months of wrangling, Parliament agreed to offer him the *Humble Petition* in a revised form, giving him the same powers as before, but without the dangerous title of King. This time Cromwell accepted immediately, and the Second Triennial Parliament adjourned. In June 1657 Cromwell was formally installed, wearing robes of purple and ermine, and carrying a golden sceptre. Only the Crown was missing.

His troubles were still not over. One of the terms of the *Humble Petition* was that the hundred excluded republicans should be re-admitted. Moreover, Cromwell moved up into the Second Chamber his most loyal supporters – the generals and the members of his own family. When the Second Triennial reassembled in January 1658 the extremists and their sympathizers dominated the Lower House. Haselrig, Scot, Vane and their republican friends launched such an attack on the constitution established by the *Humble Petition*, in particular upon the Second Chamber, that Cromwell had to dissolve the Parliament in little more than a fortnight. Disappointed, weary, impatient, his plans frustrated by the extremists yelping around him, he thundered at them: 'Let God be Judge between you and me!'

[1] This stated, in effect, that one could not subsequently be charged with treason if one had supported the King actually on the throne – whether he occupied it legally or not.

The Second Triennial Parliament had ended, but the costs of
the war against Spain were still an urgent problem. The
*Humble Petition* had promised the government £1,300,000 a year.
In fact, it needed £2,500,000 – ten times the revenue Elizabeth
had found sufficient. Attempts to raise over a million pounds
by monthly assessments and a new tax on buildings around
London were unpopular failures; the new Book of Rates throt-
tled trade and reduced revenue; the 'farming' of the excise
proved unprofitable. By the summer of 1658, when the
military reputation of England was higher abroad than ever
before, the Protectorate was racing towards bankruptcy. The
sailors were owed more than £500,000, and the soldiers more
than £300,000, in arrears of pay. The generals advising
Cromwell were demanding that he should collect new taxes by
military force, but the Protector decided to gamble on the outcome of another Parliament. Then, on September 3rd, the
anniversary of Dunbar and Worcester, worn out by his long
struggles to win the wars and keep the peace, Oliver Cromwell
died.

His achievement, by any standards, was remarkable. For
eight years, since Fairfax's retirement from politics in 1650,
Cromwell had kept England from civil war in a period of
constitutional chaos following Revolution. By means which
were never quite those of naked military power, Cromwell had
imposed violently unpopular forms of government upon a
rebellious country. Some of his earlier objectives – conciliation
of the Royalists, reduction of taxation, a more representative
Parliament – had proved impossible to achieve in the bitterness
and hostility which followed Charles's execution. Cromwell's
toleration of all but the most extreme Independent sects had
protected from Presbyterian bigotry many of the most original
thinkers of their day. On many occasions – in 1647, 1648,
twice in 1653, 1654, 1655, 1656 and 1658 – he had ordered or
approved the suppression or purging of an unco-operative
Parliament; yet he was quite sincere in claiming 'That
which you have by force I look upon as nothing.' In an
emergency – to win a war, to protect the Independents, to
preserve peace at home – the use of force was the lesser evil.
Strafford and Laud would have agreed on this, even though
they would not have shared Cromwell's views on what constituted such an emergency. All three of them were deeply

convinced that they were fighting God's battles. Cromwell, however, could claim evidence that God Himself was fighting alongside as an ally.

Perhaps the most eloquent witness to Oliver Cromwell's greatness was the speed with which the Protectorate crumbled after his death. The power which had preserved peace, even if it was based upon the Army and cemented by family marriages to the leading generals, could not be passed on to another. Certainly a peace-loving country squire like Richard Cromwell, Oliver's eldest son and designated successor, could not arrest the decay. The Protectorate was a unique institution, created for and by a unique man. Despite the *Humble Petition*, it could not be bequeathed or inherited.

### x. Foreign affairs, 1649–60

The execution of King Charles shocked every country in Europe. Governments which had with satisfaction watched England weaken herself by civil war were reminded sharply of the horror of rebellion – but there was little they could do to weaken the revolutionary régime in London or to help the young Prince Charles. France and Spain were still at war, and the treacherous Condé was besieging Paris in the bitter wars of the Fronde. In the north, Sweden was still licking the wounds she had received during the Thirty Years War, and was hemmed in by neighbours jealous of her success. In the republican United Provinces, the great Orange family, led by William II, husband of Charles I's eldest daughter, was not yet ready to challenge the cautious burghers of Amsterdam for power, though the States-General felt outraged by the rejection of the pleas for mercy it had sent to London in the hectic weeks before the King's death. The Commonwealth's special envoy to Holland, Isaac Dorislaus – a Dutch lawyer who had helped prepare the trial of Charles I – was murdered at The Hague by followers of the exiled Montrose; the populace helped the assassins to escape. The sudden death of William II of Orange soon afterwards prevented a *coup d'état* which might have led the United Provinces to war in support of Charles II.

To get itself recognized by foreign powers, and to prevent them from aiding Charles II were the most urgent foreign problems facing the new republic. The hurried construction of some forty large warships between 1649 and 1651 helped to guard against continental intervention, as well as to enable Blake to destroy Rupert's pirate fleet of Royalists.[1] As the Commonwealth grew more secure, with the crushing of revolts in Ireland and Scotland, so the Council of State, the Rump and the Army began to consider more forceful and aggressive aims in foreign policy. Many pressure groups were active. The merchants demanded Government help in challenging Dutch competition and in opening up the New World to English commerce. With the ashes of the Thirty Years War not yet cold, many Puritans called for a godly crusade to save German Protestants from popery, and to help French Huguenots betrayed by Buckingham's blunders in 1627–8. Moreover, the Commonwealth was sensitive about its prestige, and determined to insist that foreign vessels in the 'British Seas' should dip their flags in salute, and that they should allow themselves to be searched to prove that they were not carrying Royalist goods or supporters. Cromwell and some others hoped to persuade the United Provinces to join with Britain in a full political union, as a preliminary to a great Protestant crusade in Europe. Ambitious and unrealistic though some of these aims were, England now had, for the first time in twenty years, a recognizable foreign policy. Even more significant, for the first time for centuries she had the means to carry it out. On the other hand, the political cost of foreign ventures – as the Lancastrians and the early Stuarts had found out – soon overshadowed the achievements of the commanders.

At first, however, the Council had to tread warily. The murder of Dorislaus in Holland was followed by the state funeral of the victim in England, not by the punishment of his assassins. England and Holland merely withdrew their embassies from each other, without proceeding to war. But in November 1650 William II died, the rise of the Orange family was halted, and the way seemed open for better relations between the two countries. In March 1651 St. John and Strickland went to The Hague, amid jeers of 'Cromwell's bastards!' shouted by the mob. Three months of abortive negotiations followed, the English demanding a full political confederation, and the Dutch insisting on free commerce and unlicensed fishing, without political ties. When the Dutch

---

[1] Part of the navy had joined the King in the Second Civil War.

seized one of the Scilly Isles (as a base for defending Dutch ships against Rupert's pirates), and made an advantageous trading treaty with Denmark, the failure of the negotiations was certain. St. John and Strickland returned home at the end of June 1651, angry and humiliated.

In early August, the Council of State adopted, and the Rump Parliament soon passed, the Navigation Act which was proposed by St. John, eager for revenge on the Dutch. The Act insisted that goods brought into England, Ireland or the 'plantations' should be carried in English ships or in ships of the country which produced them, that English ships trading with the colonies must be manned by predominantly English crews, that no salted fish could be imported into England unless caught and processed by Englishmen, and that no foreigner should be whole- or part-owner of a ship engaged in the English coastal trade. The Council of State hoped thus to ruin the Dutch carrying trade and their fisheries, not only off the English coast, but also off Greenland and Spitzbergen where the great whales were found. The Levant, Eastland and Russia Companies were delighted with the Act, for they had long been clamouring for protection against Dutch competition. The Merchant Adventurers opposed it, as they feared reprisals against their exports of English cloth, but they were already so much in decline that the Council of State ignored their protests. The Council paid no greater attention to the anxious complaints of a Dutch embassy late in 1651. The Navigation Act had, however, one great defect – it could not be enforced. So great was the Dutch command of the carrying trade that there were far too few English vessels available for transporting the commerce from which the Dutch were now excluded – and so merchants were forced to evade the Act for which they had pleaded.

Disputes over the Navigation Act inevitably made worse the already tense situation. To encourage anti-Dutch feeling, the Government re-printed pamphlets describing the atrocities of the 1623 massacre of Amboyna; there were skirmishes at sea over the English claim to search Dutch ships for 'contraband', and the Dutch decision to make ready an additional 150 warships increased the tension. By May 1652 the English were demanding not only recognition of the Navigation Act and the 'right of search', but also that the Dutch should pay for the right to fish, and should salute the Union Flag in the 'British Seas'. At the end of May, the fleets of Blake and Van Tromp met off Dover, and in nervous excitement blundered into a minor battle. Despite sincere Dutch attempts at conciliation, the Council of State remained adamant. Early in July 1652 Britain entered her first mercantilist war.

The Dutch started the war with more warships – Van Tromp had 112, Blake only 85 – but the English ships were larger and carried heavier guns. Moreover, most of the Dutch ships had to be used to defend the great lumbering convoys of merchantmen ploughing their way up Channel, or trying to evade English patrols by following the northern route past the Shetlands and around Scotland and Ireland. Van Tromp and De Ruyter disliked this passive policy, dictated by the Dutch merchant oligarchy, but their attempts to force Blake to fight decisive pitched battles off the Shetlands and the Kentish Knock sandbank were frustrated by foul weather and the inadequate equipment of their fleets. Early in 1653, in a three days' battle off Portland and Beachy Head, Blake drove Van Tromp back to Gravelines with heavy losses, and so closed the Channel to Dutch shipping. The Dutch counter-stroke against the collier ships plying between Newcastle and London was a failure even though Denmark entered the war on Holland's side. In June Blake again defeated Van Tromp near The Gabbard shoal, fifty miles east of Harwich. The English were now masters of the seas. The Dutch ports were choked with merchant ships not daring to run the English blockade, and the great convoys due from India and Spain lingered in foreign ports awaiting escort. In a desperate attempt to break the English blockade, Van Tromp lost many ships, and his own life, in the battle of the Texel in August 1653.

Facing economic disaster, the United Provinces could fight no longer. Already De Witt, the Grand Pensionary, had sent an embassy to Cromwell, who had just driven out the Rump – and with it the most enthusiastic supporters of the war. The fanatics in the 'Barebones' Parliament wanted the war continued so that 'the seas should be secured . . . in order to prepare for the coming of Christ', but after December 1653 Cromwell, as Lord Protector, was able to accelerate the discussions. Although the Dutch obstinately refused Cromwell's proposal for political union, the war was ended in April 1654 by the lenient Treaty of

Westminster. With Cromwell still hoping to conciliate the Dutch by kindness, the Treaty did not demand payment for the right to fish, and was vague about the right of search. The Dutch had to promise to salute the British flag in the Channel, to pay compensation for Amboyna, and to refuse help to Charles II – but these concessions were humiliating, rather than harmful. In a parallel treaty, Denmark granted England the trading privileges in the Baltic she allowed Holland.

Superficially, these seem small gains from a successful war. Yet England has often gained less from treaties which promised her more. The capture of hundreds of Dutch vessels increased the merchant marine so much that the enforcement of the 1651 Navigation Act became practicable. Moreover, English merchant trade had increased considerably during the twelve months or so when few foreign ships could get through the blockade to Holland. In the next decade English merchants expected Charles II to carry on the Commonwealth's policy of expanding trade through war – and Dutch resentment was to provoke De Ruyter's revenge in the Medway in 1667.

In 1649 Spain was still locked in combat with France. When the Commonwealth seemed to be moving to war against France, the Catholic King of Spain accordingly swallowed his pride and became the first ruler to recognise the Protestant republic. In consequence, Portugal, struggling for independence from Spain, helped Charles II and sheltered Rupert's pirate fleet. Blake made the Portuguese pay dearly for this. The English fleet blockaded Lisbon, and captured half the treasure fleet returning from Brazil. In the treaty Portugal was forced to accept in 1652, she promised to pay compensation to the English merchants who had suffered through Rupert's activities, and also to pay England for the cost of Blake's naval operations. Two years later, a submissive Portugal promised to allow Englishmen the right to trade freely with her colonies, as well as granting them religious toleration on Portuguese territory. Blake's fleet, moreover, re-opened the Mediterranean to English shipping, and in 1655 consolidated this success by subduing the pirates of Tunis.

The Commonwealth's relations with Baltic countries were dominated by the need for naval supplies, especially the 'tall timber' essential for ships' masts. The Council of State hoped to secure an alliance with Sweden, particularly after Sweden's

old enemy Denmark had joined Holland in opposing England.
A generation earlier, Gustavus Adolphus had led the Swedes
into Germany to save Protestantism, but his daughter, Queen
Christina, had no such zeal;[1] the courtiers were concerned
principally with preserving Sweden's territorial conquests; and
her merchants were already worried by England's claim to the
sovereignty of the seas. Consequently, the English envoy
Whitelocke returned from his mission in 1653 with little more
than a promise that Sweden would not help Charles II. Nonetheless, Swedish ships brought across the timber which the
English dockyards needed, and the treaties with Holland and
Denmark allowed Cromwell to boast to the first Protectorate
Parliament in September 1654 that the Sound had been opened
and English merchants admitted to full trading privileges in the
Baltic.

The peace of the Baltic was rudely shattered when Charles X
became King of Sweden, for he was a Protestant champion in
the mould of Gustavus. But he was determined to get control
of the mouth of the Vistula before attacking the Catholic
Empire, and his siege of Danzig in 1656 worried English
merchants and forced the Dutch to send a fleet to restore peace.
Attacked in 1657 by Denmark and the new Emperor, Leopold,
Charles appealed to Cromwell for help. Anxious to secure a
base from which he could help the Protestants of North Germany, Cromwell demanded the port of Bremen, acquired by
Sweden in the Thirty Years War. Charles refused. Cromwell
would therefore do no more than persuade the Dutch not to
join actively against Sweden. The Treaty of Roskilde between
Sweden and Denmark restored peace for a few months in the
spring of 1658; then Sweden again declared war. Alarmed,
England and Holland agreed to send fleets to pacify the Baltic.
Then Cromwell's death precipitated a year and a half of
political turmoil at home. Although an English fleet under
Montagu visited the Baltic, it was Dutch statesmen who
negotiated, and the Dutch fleet which enforced, the settlement
which followed Charles X's death in February 1660.

France took hard the execution of Charles I, and for several
years Mazarin and the Council of State allowed French and
English ships to carry on an unofficial war at sea. But at home
France was in chaos, produced by the continuation of the war

[1] In 1654 she became a Catholic and abdicated.

against Spain and by the revolts of the Parlement and the nobles in the Wars of the Fronde. The time seemed opportune for the New Model Army to intervene to aid the Huguenots, and perhaps to regain that foothold on the continent which England had lacked since the loss of Calais in 1558. Until 1654, war with France was very near, averted only by the troubles in Ireland and Scotland and by the Dutch War. After the Treaty of Westminster, Cromwell and John Thurloe, who acted as foreign minister throughout the Protectorate, proposed an alliance with Spain for joint military action against France. In return, they demanded concessions like those already wrung from Portugal – toleration for Englishmen on Spanish soil, and freedom to trade with the Spanish colonies. But fearing heresy at home and interlopers in the Empire, Spain refused.

Angry at this rebuff, Cromwell made one of the rashest moves of his career. He ordered an attack on the Spanish West Indies, trying to get a base in the area from which the Providence Island Company had been rudely evicted in 1641. Part of the English fleet sailed for the Caribbean at the end of 1654 under Admiral Penn, carrying 2500 of the scum of the New Model under General Venables. Weakened by dysentry, cowardly and ill-led (Venables was caught in an ambush twice in the same place), the expedition failed to capture Hispaniola and San Domingo. The survivors re-embarked, landed on Jamaica, and drove the few Spanish settlers into the hills. When the news reached Europe, Spain withdrew her ambassador from London. The Protectorate was again at war.

The time was ripe for a *rapprochement* with France. Cardinal Mazarin responded readily to Cromwell's advances. At Cromwell's request, the Cardinal forced the Duchy of Savoy to halt the massacre of the Vaudois Protestants – a persecution which inspired one of Milton's noblest sonnets:

> Avenge O Lord thy slaughter'd Saints, whose bones
> Lie scatter'd on the Alpine mountains cold,
> Ev'n them who kept thy truth so pure of old
> When all our Fathers worship't Stocks and Stones. . . .

A treaty of alliance quickly followed, and the English fleets put to sea. Stayner captured most of a Spanish treasure fleet off Cadiz. Blake remained on patrol off the Spanish coast throughout the winter of 1656–7, thus accomplishing the old Elizabethan dream of Hawkins and his friends. His patience was rewarded, for in April 1657 he destroyed the Spanish treasure fleet in the Canaries. The government in Madrid was soon tottering towards bankruptcy. One Spanish army, gathered to crush the Portuguese revolt, deserted for lack of pay. Another unpaid army was on the verge of mutiny in Flanders as it awaited the combined land forces of England and France. By a treaty in March 1657 Cromwell had committed 6000 veterans of the New Model to fighting under Turenne, in return for Dunkirk and Mardyke when they had been captured from the Spanish. In the first year only Mardyke was taken, but in June 1658 the French and Protectorate troops defeated an army of Spaniards and English royalists in the Battle of the Dunes, and Dunkirk immediately surrendered. Then political chaos at home deprived England of any effective share in the negotiations leading to the Treaty of the Pyrenees which ended the war between France and Spain in 1659.

Three months after the Battle of the Dunes, England's greatest feat of arms on the continent for more than two centuries, Cromwell was dead. As Clarendon – who fell from power largely because he failed to continue the successes of the Commonwealth's foreign policy – said of him, 'His greatness at home was but a shadow of the glory he had abroad.' Some of Cromwell's original aims had been secured. He had forced hostile countries to recognize the republic, and had made them abandon Charles II; he had greatly assisted English trade with the Baltic, the Mediterranean and the New World; but his ultimate aim, the advancement of Protestantism, had proved impracticable in a mercantilist age. Indeed, the original aims of the Commonwealth were mutually incompatible. To launch a Protestant crusade against France and Spain would have given Charles II powerful supporters. To extend England's trade inevitably involved a clash with Holland, the other Protestant republic. The true success of Cromwell's foreign policy is seen more in the unprecedented military and naval prestige of England in 1658 than in the degree to which he and Thurloe achieved their early objectives. The New Model Army, largely Cromwell's own creation, had overcome the most celebrated of continental armies, led by the most famous of continental commanders. Under Cromwell and Blake, the

Navy – equally a New Model – had achieved far more than under Elizabeth and Hawkins. England had become a world power.

## xi. The New World colonies

The military and naval might of the Commonwealth was as significant in the history of the British Empire as in the diplomacy of Europe. The Navy brought back the American colonies under economic subjection to England, halting the rapid move towards independence and preparing for the imperialist mercantilism of the following century. But for Cromwell, Britain might have had to accept the fact of American independence in 1660, not 1783.

For twenty years before the execution of Charles I, England's control over her American colonies had been waning. Only a few months after getting its charter in 1629, the Massachusetts Bay Company moved its headquarters from London to Salem. Quite unjustly, it claimed that, by granting the charter, the Crown had surrendered all authority over the colony. The rigid Puritanism of the settlers was safer, the founders believed, in independence of the Crown. Lacking a fleet to enforce obedience, Charles I had to tolerate this defiance. During the 1630s, three other settlements were founded by emigrants from Massachusetts – Rhode Island by those who disliked the religious intolerance of the parent colony, and New Haven and Connecticut by settlers seeking better farming land. All three professed allegiance to the Crown, but governed themselves in almost complete independence of England. Even in Virginia, a royal colony since the original company had forfeited its charter in 1624, Charles had to accept by 1639 the powers of the representative assembly, which had already been meeting unofficially for a decade. The Baltimores ruled the new proprietary colony of Maryland with more-than-royal authority, with 'full, free and absolute power to ordain, make and enact laws of what kind soever'. Like Virginia, it was still administered from England, but Lord Baltimore had total authority over it as proprietor and feudal sovereign. An absolute though benevolent ruler, there was no legal appeal from his judgements, and at times he even minted his own coins. By 1642 Charles had lost control of his own capital city of London; certainly he could not control colonists three thousand miles and six weeks' sailing away.

Moreover, the colonies had become restless under English economic domination. In the embryonic 'Old Colonial System', England had protected colonial products such as tobacco,[1] and did not tax the plantations directly, though promising to defend them from enemies. In return, she required the colonies to trade directly with her, imposed light duties upon goods imported from them, and discouraged the development of colonial industries which might compete with those at home. In the earliest days of the plantations, these arrangements had benefited the colonies; by the 1640s they seemed burdensome restrictions blocking progress.

During the Civil Wars, the plantations remained neutral or supported the King. With the energies and the riches of the colonising classes committed to the struggle in England, no new colonies were founded, and trade between England and America slumped. England's troubles seemed to provide a splendid opportunity for the colonies to escape still further from political and economic dependence on the home country. In Massachusetts, Boston and Salem became important ship-building and commercial ports; Virginia, too, tried to develop new industries in addition to her staple product of tobacco. Interloping Dutch merchantmen captured much of the external and inter-colonial trade of the American settlements, particularly in tobacco, by charging lower shipping rates. English merchants and manufacturers alike were distressed at the decline of their markets in the New World.

As no military help could be expected from England during the Civil War, in 1643 Massachusetts, Connecticut, New Haven and Plymouth formed themselves into a loose federal association. This New England Confederation was principally for defence against Indian, Dutch and French attacks, and survived until 1684 despite the reluctance of Massachusetts to submit to majority decisions. This early experiment in federal union was a precedent which greatly influenced the founders of the American Constitution in the next century.

Once the revolts in Ireland and Scotland had been broken, the Council of State could turn its attention to the colonies in revolt against English authority. A Navigation Act of

[1] To help Virginia, the growing of tobacco in England was prohibited.

October 1650 asserted that the colonies should be 'subordinate to and dependent upon England', that the Parliament at Westminster had legislative authority over the colonial assemblies, and that foreigners should be banned from trading with any of the plantations. Oliver St. John's great Navigation Act, passed a year later, defined precisely the nature of colonial dependence upon the mother country. The plantations, it made clear, existed mainly if not entirely for the benefit of England.

In 1651 the Council sent a fleet under Ayscue to bring the colonies to heel. Nowhere was there significant resistance; the colonies were not yet ready to challenge the military power of England. Barbados, Virginia and Maryland soon submitted, and Parliamentary delegates quickly persuaded the New England Confederation to accept the authority of the Commonwealth. In tolerant Maryland the Puritans seized control, but a later revolt, to transfer the Baltimores' feudal powers to a representative assembly, was easily crushed. Now tamed, the colonies agreed to support England's foreign policy. In 1654 the Confederation promised to attack the Dutch settlement of New Netherland (though peace was signed before the settlers were ready to advance). Next year colonial volunteers helped Venables's troops to capture Jamaica.

After the eviction of the Rump – too sensitive to pressure from English commercial interests – Cromwell relaxed the enforcement of the Navigation Acts. Like Walpole in the next century, he saw the need to pacify the colonists by conciliation. Unlike Walpole, he saw how British naval power could be used to expand the colonial empire and how essential it was for the navy to be strong if the empire was to be kept together. To his credit, Charles II also realized these principles of imperial policy, and struggled to maintain them with a navy sadly depleted by parliamentary parsimony. Cromwell added to the empire only Jamaica, but he managed to shepherd the older plantations back into the British fold and, above all, pointed the way to future imperial greatness.

### xii. Political and religious thought

The middle of the seventeenth century was an age of fervent investigation in most aspects of philosophy. In part this was the result, in part the cause, of the conflicts between King,

Parliament and Army. On one hand there were lawyers insisting that the Crown should be '*sub Deo et lege*', Levellers pleading for universal suffrage, and radicals demanding that England should be freed from the 'Norman yoke' of the King, the law, and social institutions. On the other were Presbyterians, Independents and other sectaries with widely divergent convictions about church authority. Together they produced a fever heat of philosophical and theological speculation without equal in English or European history except perhaps during the Reformation.

Most active Puritans believed that Christ's second coming was imminent. The victories over Papists and Arminians seemed to be ushering in 'the acceptable time of the Lord'. As Charles I's head was struck off, the Rev. Hugh Peter was shouting 'Mine eyes have seen Thy salvation, which Thou hast prepared before the face of all people'. Nevertheless, long before 1649, Puritanism was disintegrating into sects. If Christ came, He would have found His saints fighting among themselves. The Presbyterians, easily the most powerful at the beginning of the Civil War, became increasingly conservative, and by 1660 were willing to agree that the authority of bishops was better than no authority at all. Leaders like Prynne and Baxter, parliamentary stalwarts in earlier days, lived to welcome the Restoration.

The Independents, in the Army and elsewhere, broke from the Presbyterians by denying any spiritual authority above that of the independent congregation. Hugh Peter, coarse but persuasive, and his disciple John Goodwin, guided the consciences and actions of many Army leaders. These men remained loyal to the principles of the Commonwealth, Peter being hanged in 1660 as a regicide. The weakness of the Independents, though, was the number and variety of the sects they fathered. Nonconformity bred Nonconformity.

The least extreme of the new groups was the Baptist sect, differing from the parent stock chiefly through the belief that baptism should be delayed until the person reached the age of responsibility. Unfortunately, most people confused these men with the radical Anabaptists of Germany who preached anarchy and communism, and Cromwell came to fear their influence in the Army – especially when some of the Baptists began to preach pacifism.

Other groups to emerge from the Independents were the

Seekers, the Ranters, the Quakers and the Fifth Monarchy men. The first were so troubled by the world they saw around them that they believed that every institution was so imperfect that they had to 'seek' afresh for the truth. The Ranters objected to all authority which clashed with the dictates of the individual's conscience, and were accused of 'a cursed doctrine of libertinism, which brought them to all abominable filthiness of life'. The Quakers – so Baxter thought – 'were but the Ranters turned from horrid profaneness and blasphemy to a life of extreme austerity on the other side'. In their early days the Quakers were not famed as men of peace. The diarist Evelyn, meeting some in Ipswich in 1656, thought them 'a new fanatic sect, of dangerous principles, who show no respect to any man, magistrate or other, and seem a melancholy, proud sort of people, and exceedingly ignorant'. Feared as trouble makers, the Quakers were persecuted vigorously at first. But George Fox and Isaac Pennington soon formulated new doctrines, and secured toleration from the Protector. The Quakers' 'Light from Within' led them to look forward to the second coming of Christ, and to the 'Society of Friends' in which there would be no barriers of class or wealth.

The Fifth Monarchy men bordered on the lunatic fringe of independency. They held that there had been four great monarchies in the past – those of Assyria, Persia, Greece and Rome – and that the overthrow of popery and prelacy had prepared the way for the fifth, foretold in the Book of Daniel, when Christ would come to rule in person. As this was expected in 1666 (a figure arrived at by adding up the ages of the Old Testament patriarchs), they, the 'Lamb's Military Officers', hoped to seize power and destroy existing institutions which might make it more difficult for the Messiah to establish His kingdom. With Major-General Harrison as their leader, the Fifth Monarchy men were influential in the 'Barebones' Parliament – and never forgave Cromwell for becoming Protector and ending the rule of the Saints. Writers like Aspinwall and John Rogers demanded that Sabbath-breaking should be punished with death, and denounced as hirelings all professional lawyers and clergy. Thomas Venner, a London cooper, led Fifth Monarchy risings in London in 1657 and 1661, proclaiming 'The Lord Jesus' as King, and getting hanged for his pains by those who preferred Charles II.

In addition to these sects were small groups gathered around certain interesting zealots. James Nayler, a Quaker, scandalized the Protectorate Parliament by riding into Bristol on a white ass, in the belief that he was the reincarnate Christ. Another volunteer Messiah, John Robins, proposed to lead a crusade of 144,000 men to reconquer the Holy Land, but was drowned while crossing to Holland to raise recruits. Ludovick Muggleton denied the doctrine of the Trinity, condemned prayer and preaching, and believed that Reason was the creation of the devil; rather surprisingly, there are still some Muggletonians in the twentieth century! Another group, the Adamites, tried to return to the primitive innocence of the Garden of Eden by practising nudity, despite the unsuitability of the English climate. The closing of the theatres, the destruction of maypoles, the punishment of blasphemers and Sabbath-breakers clearly failed to preserve morality. By 1660, the outraged conventions of respectability seemed to demand a Restoration.

Two groups did not share in the toleration provided by the Commonwealth. One was the old Church of England. In 1644 the Long Parliament banned the Prayer Book and deprived the bishops of their authority. Ordinances of 1646 and 1649 ordered the sale of the bishops' and the cathedrals' property. Clergy who refused to accept the *Solemn League and Covenant*, or who were in other ways suspect of scandalous behaviour, were evicted by Commissioners under Parliament or by Cromwell's 'Ejectors'. Other Commissions purged the Universities of those obstinately loyal to prelacy. Some of those evicted were imprisoned, usually briefly, if they were considered politically dangerous, but there was no general persecution of individuals. The sacrifice of Archbishop Laud, executed in January 1645 by Act of Attainder after four years' imprisonment, seemed a sufficient atonement for the indignities Prynne and others had suffered from the High Commission. Even the evicted clergy were allowed to receive one-fifth of their successors' incomes. Nevertheless the Commonwealth tried hard to suppress Anglican worship. A few parsons continued to hold secret services for the faithful, but in most parts of the country it was very difficult for the loyal Anglican to get married, buried, or have his children baptized, in what he thought a decent way. Some Anglican clergy went into exile, serving congregations as far away as Constantinople. Others became tutors and private chaplains in familes opposed to the Commonwealth – despite Cromwell's 1655 edict forbidding it – and helped to educate a new generation of prejudiced Cavaliers. In England Bishop Duppa and some of his colleagues tried to keep the extruded clergy together, and secretly ordained new priests. Other leading Anglicans were at the court of Charles II, trying hard to preserve the young king from the wiles of the Covenant, the lures of Rome and the reputed atheism of his tutor, Thomas Hobbes. The mild persecutions of 1644–60 helped to purge the Church of much of its dross, and to prepare for the restoration of its spiritual power when Charles II returned. Many Englishmen appreciated the Church more when it was banned than when it was in power.

The Roman Catholics in England suffered little more than the Anglicans did. Cromwell's attitude to both groups was normally that a man's private opinions need not be interfered with, but public acts such as attending Mass or Prayer Book services challenged the authority and therefore the safety of the State. Priests were sometimes executed – twenty between 1641 and 1649, but only two under the Commonwealth and Protectorate – but for treason rather than for their faith. To people so long accustomed to persecution, the experiences of these two decades were not especially harsh. The Long Parliament had ordered all Catholics to forfeit two-thirds of their property if they refused to swear an oath denouncing papal supremacy and transubstantiation, but then an Ordinance of 1650 made worship at the parish church no longer compulsory and so they ceased to pay recusancy fines.

For economic as well as spiritual reasons Cromwell allowed the Jews to return to England, for the first time since Edward I expelled them in 1290. The study of the Hebrew scriptures made many people more sympathetic to this long-persecuted race, and mercantilist England soon learnt their importance in the commerce of Portugal and the Levant. When Manasseh ben Israel, an Amsterdam rabbi, begged Cromwell in 1655 to allow Jews to settle in England, the Protector overrode the prejudices of the Council of State and granted the request. Unlike Anglicans and Catholics, they were allowed to worship freely, and to build synagogues.

While the Council of State and the Protector were prepared

to tolerate most of the religious innovators thrown up by the Civil Wars, the political innovators were less fortunate. The revolutionaries of 1642 and 1649 had to become conservatives to protect what they had gained. The parliamentary rebels were conservatives by 1647. The military usurpers of 1649 became progressively more reactionary as the *Instrument of Government*, the Major-Generals and the *Humble Petition* paved the way for the return of royal authority. At no time was republicanism widely popular. When the war against the King had already been in progress for a year, the Commons sent to the Tower the first member who voiced republican opinions in the House. As late as 1647, Ireton and Cromwell were hoping to preserve a constitution with King, Lords and Commons.

Even when the republic had been accepted, there was still no thought of encouraging 'democracy'. Despite the popularity of Leveller ideas in the army, the officers rejected every plea for the extension of the franchise. Repeated spells of imprisonment without trial failed to silence Lilburne and the other Leveller leaders – Walwyn the silk merchant, the brains behind the movement; Wildman, the orator at the Putney debates in 1647; Overton, the critic of enclosures. With his 'appetite for martyrdom' (Clarendon), Lilburne was imprisoned in succession by the bishops, the Lords, the Commons and the Council of State. A fortnight before Charles's death, the Levellers re-issued the *Agreement of the People*, demanding the vote for all adult men and also the drastic re-distribution of parliamentary seats. The Council of State was unimpressed. In March 1649 Lilburne published the bitter *England's New Chaines Discovered*, and, undaunted by repeated spells in prison, continued to attack the army leaders who had betrayed the soldiers by refusing them the vote. So long as the army was commanded by gentlemen like Fairfax and Cromwell, the tyranny of the mob was not going to replace the tyranny of the King. When the *Instrument of Government* changed the basis of parliamentary representation, it narrowed the franchise, instead of widening it, and placed political power even more firmly in the hands of the country gentry. In the seventeenth century – as for much of the nineteenth – a political society not based on property was almost unthinkable. Leveller ideas quickly faded as the heady emotion of a successful war died away. The most advanced democratic movement yet to emerge, the Levellers were two centuries ahead of their time.

Violent controversies over temporal authority reflected the Presbyterian struggles with the Independents on ecclesiatical authority. Thomas Hobbes, the most profound English philosopher of the century, published *Leviathan* in 1651 to prove that a government ought to have unlimited powers. He argued that, to escape from the state of nature when life was nasty, brutish and short, men had combined to create a sovereign authority, supreme over them all. Nothing the sovereign did could break this original contract. On the other hand, if the sovereign failed to protect the citizens from each other, the *person* or *nature* of the sovereign could be changed even though the *institution* of sovereignty must remain intact. This justification for absolutism caused a furore among the Royalist exiles in Holland, where Hobbes was working as mathematics tutor to young Charles II, for it permitted a parliament as well as a King to be supreme. Hobbes seemed an atheist because he believed that the state was a human, not a divine, creation. Moreover, his arguments implied that the deposition of Charles I and the establishment of the Commonwealth were justifiable. Driven out of Holland, Hobbes made his peace with the Commonwealth. Back in England, he applauded the strong rule of Cromwell – and welcomed the Restoration,[1] for it ended the anarchy which followed Oliver's death. Hobbes had no body of personal followers, for everyone professed to abhor his atheism. Nonetheless, the benevolent despotism he preached was very close to that which Cromwell practised. There might be violent disputes within the government, but no responsible man challenged the government's right to be obeyed.

But a challenge did come from the Fifth Monarchy men. The authority of Protectors and magistrates, laws and landlords, clearly obstructed the coming of Christ's Kingdom, and so must be swept away. The 'Barebones' Parliament made a brave start by sweeping away the Court of Chancery and attacking tithes, before its more responsible members brought its own life to an end. To Cromwell and his friends, the lesson of the 'Barebones' Parliament was clear. England's liberties depended on the preservation of authority. Charles I

[1] Charles II gave him a pension of £100 p.a.

had said much the same as he mounted the scaffold in 1649.

Very few of the theorists of the age were concerned directly with social and economic equality. Even the Levellers paid little attention to it, though some of them criticized old grievances like enclosures. The economic troubles of the seventeenth century produced many agitators complaining about the extortions of landlords, but such men can be found at almost every period of English history, and certainly do not deserve to be regarded as political scientists, any more than the Muggletonians and Adamites merit serious consideration as theologians. But one small group of social reformers was of rather greater importance. Probably inspired by some of the ideas of the Leveller Walwyn, Gerrard Winstanley and twenty or so friends decided to found a Christian community, 'having all things in common'. In April 1649 they built huts upon the common land on St. George's Hill in Surrey, and planted vegetables. Fairfax visited the 'Diggers' and thought them harmless, but they began to send out appeals to men in other counties to join them in asserting their rights. Worried by this venture at a time of noisy Leveller agitation, the Council of State sent soldiers to knock down their huts. Despite this suppression, Winstanley persistently tried to persuade Cromwell to support his attempt to establish Christian communism. On the whole, the very radicalism of the Diggers made them comparatively harmless. More insidious and more dangerous to the revolutionary 'Establishment' was the extent to which uneducated tradesmen and labourers had grown into the habit of criticizing and denouncing their social superiors for moral, religious or political shortcomings. For a few brief years, the subservience of centuries melted away. The winds of change blew coldly on the propertied classes, and sent them scurrying into the haven of the Restoration and the social structure which went with the monarchy.

A curious amalgam of political and economic ideas is found in James Harrington's *Oceana*, published in 1656 as the model for a constitution. Harrington, an aristocrat, had realized that the old society based on the feudal hierarchy had been replaced by one based on wealth. *Oceana* proposed a republican constitution which would guard the propertied classes from governmental absolutism and from the power of the mob. No man should be excessively rich – £2000 p.a. was to be the limit – but the lower gentry with under £100 p.a. were to be less well represented in Parliament than those with more than that income, and the poor were to have no vote at all. The social ideas of *Oceana* cannot have been unwelcome to Cromwell, though of course he could tolerate no plan which would have weakened the Army's position. The book created immense interest. The Rota Club formed in 1659 to discuss its proposals was probably the first public debating society – and a precedent for the political clubs of the 1670s and later. *Oceana* influenced not only Englishmen like Halifax, Locke and the Chartists, but also many eighteenth century revolutionaries in France and America in their searches for constitutions.

Harrington and Hobbes were secular in their attitudes, but in this they were quite exceptional. Most of the philosophers were sincere Puritans, and most of them were seeking for the form of political society which would be most pleasing to the Almighty and which would prepare for the Christian millennium. When the reformers had shaken off the shackles of Churches which tried to intervene between sinful man and an all-powerful God, the individual became responsible for the state of his own soul. By his actions, a man demonstrated to the world what state of Grace his soul was in. To fight for and to preach what he believed was not – as for believers in Free Will and Salvation by Works – an attempt to buy his way to Heaven; it was an outward and visible sign that he was already one of the Elect, predestined for Paradise. Such convictions produced the Puritan philosopher, proud and melancholy like Evelyn's Quakers. This quality of unshakable self-assurance developed successful generals and admirals from farmers and merchants, political scientists from schoolmasters, and theologians from tradesmen. For generals playing at politics, for Parliamentarians torn between opposing factions and for preachers divided between squabbling sects, it was essential to find philosophical principles to guide their actions, and equally important for them to express them publicly and emphatically.

### xiii. Science and the arts

The intellectual turmoil of the Civil Wars encouraged speculation in science. This was not, however, a new subject. In earlier years the Elizabethans had realized how important the study of mathematics and astronomy was to seafarers.   In 1588 the Privy Council endowed a mathematics lectureship in London.   By the end of the reign, the seven professors at Gresham's College, founded by the great economist, were lecturing to the citizens of London on subjects which included physics, astronomy and geometry, and Francis Bacon was busy explaining the merits of the experimental method.   Under the early Stuarts, the interest in science – 'experimental philosophy' – grew wider.   Even at conservative Oxford and Cambridge there were professorships of geometry and astronomy, founded by Sir Henry Savile.   William Harvey discovered how the blood circulated – even though he had no microscope – and received the post of Royal Physician from Charles I.   A Scots laird named John Napier invented logarithms.   Mathematical textbooks were published, the most influential being that written by an obscure country parson, William Oughtred.

Gresham's College attracted scientists from all over the country.   In the early years of the Civil War, a group of men interested in the new philosophy began to meet weekly at Gresham's to discuss a wide variety of scientific subjects. Among them was a young parson, John Wilkins, who had written, at the age of twenty-four, a book to prove that men could live on the moon.   In 1648, when Parliament purged Oxford of Royalists, the Visitors installed Wilkins as Warden of Wadham. He attracted to Oxford many of his friends from Gresham's. His equipment fascinated the diarist Evelyn, who visited him at Oxford in 1654:

He had, above in his lodgings and gallery, variety of shadows, dials, perspectives, and many other artificial, mathematical and magical curiosities, a way-wiser, a thermometer, a monstrous magnet, conic and other sections. . . .[1]

Wilkins was the centre of a brilliant circle of dons and students like Seth Ward, Christopher Wren and Robert Boyle.   He married Oliver Cromwell's sister, became a founder-member of the Royal Society, and was appointed Bishop of Chester in 1668.   According to Evelyn, Wilkins used his privileged position as the Protector's brother-in-law to save the universities from too much interference.   The great achievements of

[1] J. Evelyn, *Diary*, vol. i, p. 295.

Restoration scientists would have been difficult without the inspiration derived from the discussions at Gresham's College and in Wilkins's rooms in Oxford.

In literature also, this was a vigorous period. When the activities of the Long Parliament made it impossible for the bishops to maintain their censorship of the press, a blizzard of pamphlets swirled across England. Few pamphlets were of literary merit, for most were stuffed full of Old Testament history and language, but the exceptions were superb. Milton's pamphlets were not always free from clumsiness, but his passionate prose rhetoric in attacking the bishops, and defending the execution of Charles I in *Eikonoklastes* and *Pro Populo Anglicano Defensio*,[1] would have won for him an eminent place in literature even if he had never written a single poem. But his finest prose work was *Areopagitica*, written in 1644 to defend the freedom of the press against the decision of the Long Parliament to reimpose censorship. A sincere Independent, Milton served the Commonwealth as Latin secretary until he lost his sight. After 1660 he could never bring himself to accept the Restoration (although Charles II gave him a pension), and wrote his three great epic poems as a sort of political testament. The theme of *Paradise Lost, Paradise Regained* and *Samson Agonistes* (published between 1668 and 1671) was that England had slumped into moral, religious and political decadence, preferring comfort to 'strenuous liberty'; however the devout could still turn the tables on the ungodly, and by action such as Samson's could bring back an upright Puritan commonwealth. By this time, though, Milton's was a lone voice crying in a Restoration wilderness. The experiences of the Civil Wars had warned men against seeking godliness and morality through political action.

Although the most zealous, Milton was not the only writer to serve the Commonwealth. The economic troubles of families which had previously patronised writers and artists became so acute after 1642 that literary men without private means had to earn their livings by other occupations, since profits from sales were insignificant. Andrew Marvell, the author of that *Ode to Cromwell* which praised the martyred King more deeply

---

[1] Written in 1653 to refute the criticisms of Salmasius, a continental scholar hired by Royalist exiles to attack the regicide government in England. Milton's intensive work on this was largely responsible for his blindness.

than his conqueror, assisted Milton in the Latin secretaryship. Dryden, the outstanding Restoration poet and dramatist, served in Cromwell's household.  Young Samuel Pepys, as a humble but well-connected clerk, was getting experience in Navy and Exchequer administration as the republic crumbled.

Of the writers not directly involved in the struggles of the Civil Wars, the most distinguished was probably Sir Thomas Browne.  His *Religio Medici*, written about 1635 and published in 1642, was the work of a man hesitating on the frontiers of the new scientific studies, for it tried to combine a critical, sceptical approach with an implicit belief in divine revelation. He claimed to follow 'the dictates of my own reason' while accepting traditional doctrines—'where the Scripture is silent, the church is my text'.  His next major work was *Pseudodoxia Epidemica*, an attempt to expose popular fallacies and super-stitions—even though Browne himself believed in witches and alchemy.  In 1658 he followed it with *Hydriotaphia or Urn-Burial*, an account of the funeral customs practised in various lands and societies.  Browne's works were written in prose as well-balanced as Bacon's had been, but in an ornate and latin-ized style owing more to the florid characteristics of continental 'baroque' than to English models.  In 1671 Charles II rewarded this versatile Norwich doctor with a knighthood.

Other arts fared less well.  The theatres were closed by order of Parliament from 1642 until the Restoration, which brought a return of the cynical and immoral drama which had earlier provoked Prynne to denounce the stage in *Histrio-Mastix* (1633).

For economic reasons, the Commonwealth decreed in 1649 that Charles I's magnificent art-collection should be sold.  For several years its brokers haggled with the agents of Mazarin, Philip IV of Spain, and Archduke Leopold William, Governor of the Spanish Netherlands, and many lesser men.  When the Restoration came, few of the pictures remained in England. In reaction against Mytens's and Van Dyck's tactful flatteries of Royalist courtiers, the paintings of the republican period were nothing if not honest.  Samuel Cooper's superb miniature of Oliver Cromwell did not shrink from portraying the warts. The Dutchman Peter Lely, altering his style after the over-throw of the Cavaliers, was equally frank – on Cromwell's express orders – and showed the Protector as a puzzled and

worried man.   Earlier, for a few brief years before his death in
1646, William Dobson had been painting portraits of a distinctly English nature, free from courtly flattery and from
excessive Puritan sobriety.   Probably the greatest English
painter up to that time, Dobson helped to weaken temporarily
the fashionable preference for foreign artists, who had dominated painting in England since the time of Holbein.

During the Civil Wars, most of the foreign architects and
landscape gardeners returned home.   Their departure allowed
national characteristics to develop more freely.   The economic
troubles of the time, abetted by a desire for functional simplicity, had a profound influence on English architecture.
Large country houses, in the balanced dignity of the Palladian
and derivative styles, capacious enough to accommodate a visit
from the Court, were needed no longer.   Those who could
afford the cost built solid rectangular houses, standing four-
square in the midst of their estates.   The finest of these was
Coleshill in Berkshire, designed by William Pratt; for more than
half a century it influenced most of the builders of the smaller
country houses.   But there were not many of these built
during the Interregnum; in disordered times men do not build
houses.

Many Puritans were deeply suspicious of music.   Church
organs were associated with popery, fiddles and wind instru-
ments with dancing, and gentle madrigal tunes with the
lascivious words of many of the songs.   Nonetheless, republican England was not a land without music.   Cromwell had
his own official organist, and a large orchestra played at the
marriage of his daughter Frances.   Singing, perhaps encouraged by Puritan fondness for metrical versions of the
psalms, remained popular with all classes.   The first full-time
music publisher in England, John Playford, achieved great
success with *The English Dancing Master* (1650) – despite a title
hardly pleasing to strict Puritans!   The suppression of plays
indirectly assisted the birth of English opera as a public
entertainment: Davenant's *Siege of Rhodes* (1656) helped to
prepare the way for Purcell's *Dido and Aeneas* some thirty years
later.   There may have been little great music in England
between the time of Byrd and that of Purcell, but Englishmen
did not lose either their ear or their love for it.

*xiv. Changes in industry, commerce and society*

The Civil Wars acted as a powerful catalyst in speeding up industrial developments. The enormous contracts placed by the Long Parliament and the Commonwealth for military and naval equipment encouraged the growth of larger units of industry. In 1644, for example, a single ironmonger was employing over a hundred men on the manufacture of stirrups and other cavalry gear. The wars benefited clothiers under contract to provide uniforms, ironmasters and others producing weapons, and dockyards labouring to build and equip the new ships for Blake's Navy. With the exhaustion of native timber supplies, coal became increasingly important for warming homes and as fuel for salt-pans, lime-kilns, soap-boilers, brick works and breweries. By 1660 coal production probably exceeded two million tons a year; certainly over half a million tons were being shipped to London alone by the hostmen, of Newcastle. The Scots' occupation of the Newcastle area in 1640 and 1644 powerfully influenced the policies of the City, for the Londoners could not manage without their fuel. London's dependence on 'sea-coals' was emphasized when the Dutch threat to the coal ships in 1653 raised the price of coal in London from £2 to £5 a chaudron. If successful, the mine owners could make huge profits, but there were many men like William Beaumont who, according to a writer in 1649, invested £30,000 in a mine and lost the lot. The small-scale coalmaster, with limited capital, was unlikely to succeed in what had become by 1660 England's second industry.

The dominance of the woollen industries, however, remained. As a result of the wars, they were rather less prosperous – during the 1650s the average price of English wool was only three-quarters of what it had been in the two previous decades – but the gradual introduction of new techniques and marketing arrangements was making them more efficient. The 'New Draperies' – worsteds and serges – were replacing the old broadcloths, and sold in Mediterranean countries more readily than the heavier materials. The manufacture of linen and cotton cloths also increased, but the 1651 Navigation Act raised the cost of imported raw materials and so hampered these new industries. William Lee's invention in 1589 of a mechanical frame for knitting stockings gave England a great technical advantage, and by 1660 over 600 of the frames were working, mainly in London.   Stocking-frame factories and speculations in the new materials all required heavy investments of capital. Usually only those who were already prosperous had the chance to become more wealthy.   The marketing as well as the manufacture of cloth tended to become concentrated in relatively few hands, in those of the factors at Blackwell Hall in London, at Norwich, Wakefield and Exeter.   Most of the old local markets decayed into insignificance.

Sometimes the merchant oligarchy tried to consolidate its power by reviving the guild system.   In 1650 the Rump created a corporation of fifty-four master weavers to control the worsted industry in Norwich and Norfolk.   Seven years later the stocking frame masters were similarly incorporated. These revivals of mediaeval protection, on the whole, had little success.   Even the apprenticeship laws had to be waived after the Restoration to allow the thousands of disbanded soldiers and sailors to enter industrial trades.

In external trade, the great merchant companies were not uniformly successful.   The Civil Wars discouraged trade, particularly as the London merchants were under strong compulsion to invest their capital in Parliament's campaign.   To reduce the loss of silver (£100,000 a year) from England the Long Parliament banned the importation of currants from 1642 to 1645, to the acute distress of the Levant Company. Later, however, the Levant Company benefited more than any of its rivals from the achievements of Blake's fleet.   The Tsar's disgust at the execution of the King made him ban the Russia Company from his dominions, and the fortunes of the Eastland Company fluctuated with the strength of English naval power in the Baltic.   The Merchant Adventurers, already in decline, suffered from the Dutch War and moved their Staple from Rotterdam to Dordrecht in a desperate attempt to get better trading privileges.   The East India Company, however, after several poor years began to prosper when it turned itself into a permanent joint stock company in 1657, and it was soon earning an average of 18 per cent. on its share capital of about £370,000.   This Company was unlike its rivals in that it was owned by a large number of shareholders – over 900 at the Restoration.   Nevertheless, the general pattern of industrial and commercial developments was that property and power were both becoming concentrated in fewer hands; the rich were becoming richer and fewer.

The changes in the countryside were more strongly marked, especially in the lower levels of society.    The Long Parliament was at first keen to retain the goodwill of the poorer classes, but the need to placate the gentry changed this.    By an Ordinance passed by the Second Triennial Parliament in 1656, landlords were freed from feudal obligations to the Crown; the tenants' duties to their landlords, however, remained in force. The old laws restricting enclosures were forgotten.    At times Parliament used the army to prevent peasants breaking down new enclosures robbing them of their common lands. Moreover, the high taxation of the period forced landlords to inflate their rents and to try to farm more efficiently – always at the expense of the small tenant or agricultural labourer. Especially where the estate had passed into new hands, the owners exploited their property and their tenants to the full. In 1656 Parliament gave the Forest of Dean to Cromwell, and the Protector immediately tried to improve his possession by driving away nearly four hundred poor families of 'squatters'. With the Excise duties raising the cost of even the basic necessities of life, and with a succession of bad harvests adding to their difficulties, the Civil Wars nearly wiped out the old copyholders and cottagers in many parts of the country.    The poor had no cause to love the republic.

Even if few of the writers were directly concerned with social justice, the Wars could not avoid challenging social, as well as political and spiritual, authority.    When gentry, merchants and lawyers confronted the King, the bishops and the Court, and used as their tools the yeomen, the London mob and the common sailors, the conflict inevitably shook the foundations of society.    Thus, even if the Leveller programme did not demand economic and social equality, the fact that the representatives of the common soldiers could meet together and discuss political reforms in orderly debate threw out a challenge to the established classes.    The frequency with which ill-educated and educated and unprofessional preachers tried to harangue the Protector and the Army grandees was a similar threat.    Cromwell might tolerate the preacher, but the Leveller went to the Tower.    The Restoration Parliament was equally severe with both.

The Civil Wars produced the greatest change in English landownership between the dissolution of the monasteries and the introduction of death duties.   Royalists like Newcastle and Worcester had loaned heavily to Charles I, selling their estates to raise ready money.   The confiscations of their remaining estates by the victors further reduced the economic strength of royalist families.   The Long Parliament and the Commonwealth sold these confiscated estates (or, more frequently, used them as inducements to persuade their creditors to increase their loans to the government) to those with the money to buy them – merchants rich from overseas trade, thrifty members of the gentry, and the more prosperous tenants of the former owners.   This redistribution of land did much to enrich members of the classes which had supported Parliament.   Not only did it consolidate the gentry class at the expense of the Crown and the old nobility; it also strengthened them against their own tenantry, towards whom the new owners seldom felt any seigniorial obligations.   The land transfers also created the most explosive of the problems which faced Charles II in 1660: should the old Royalists get their lands back, or should those who had bought them be allowed to keep them?

## xv. *The Republic crumbles*

Oliver Cromwell's death swiftly led to the downfall of the Protectorate.   For five years he had stood alone striving to preserve a balance between Army and Parliament, between naked military force and the semblance of popular representation.   For five years he had struggled to get from Parliament the taxes needed to sustain England's foreign responsibilities.   For five years he had tried to moderate the extremism of the sects and the intolerance of the Presbyterians.   For five years his reputation as a soldier and his ability as a statesman had delayed the anarchy implicit in the events of 1649.

For a short while after his death on September 3rd, 1658, he ruled England from his splendid tomb in Westminster Abbey: his reputation alone kept the country quiet.   The funeral emphasized the true nature of the *Humble Petition*'s constitution: on the hearse lay Cromwell's effigy, wrapped in royal robes, wearing a crown (at last!) and holding orb and sceptre.

His eldest son Richard (nominated in accordance with the

*Humble Petition*) succeeded him.   At first an uneasy calm prevailed, though at Oxford undergraduates pelted the mayor with
carrots and turnips as he proclaimed the new Protector.
According to Baxter, 'all men wondered to see all so quiet in so
dangerous a time'.   Unfortunately, the Army leaders – on
whose shoulders Oliver had leaned so heavily – had no respect
for his son.   Richard was no soldier; a peace-loving country
squire, he preferred hunting foxes to chasing Royalists or papists.
Soon ambitious generals like Fleetwood and Desborough,
were planning to use him as a puppet controlled by themselves.
Moreover, by tactless remarks Richard quickly annoyed the
more devout of the army leaders.   By the end of October
1658 the officers began once more to hold prayer meetings – an
ominous sign.   Soon their grievances crystallized in the demand
that the posts of Protector and Commander-in-Chief should be
separated – in other words, that Richard should give up the
power of the sword.   Charles I's refusal to do this had precipitated the First Civil War; Richard Cromwell's refusal
ensured the downfall of the Protectorate.

In Parliament, too, Richard had many enemies, despite his
attempt to revise the constitution in his favour.   The *Instrument of Government* had transferred the majority of the English
constituencies from the boroughs to the counties, and it was
from the counties that the strongest opposition to Oliver had
latterly come.   Now Richard returned to the earlier system of
English representation while still keeping the members from
Scotland and Ireland – most of whom were blindly obedient to
the government.   Nonetheless, Haselrig, Vane and the other
republicans kept up their bitter attacks on the powers of the
Protector and the existence of the Upper House.

The Parliament of the Second Protectorate met in January
1659, and quickly angered the Army in the way all its predecessors had done.   The officers complained that most of the
members were too eager to suppress the extreme sects, too
friendly with known Royalists, too reluctant to vote the taxes
needed to meet the arrears of pay owed to the soldiers.   In
April Parliament resolved that Army officers must promise not
to disturb the meetings of the Parliament and not to hold any
council of officers during parliamentary sessions.   After a trial
of strength, Richard realized that the soldiers would follow their
officers rather than himself.   Knowing how impossible it was

to try to govern without the support of the Army, Richard dissolved his Parliament on April 22nd. To all effects he had abdicated. A year of anarchy followed.

In early May, the Rump of the Long Parliament re-assembled, and the republicans resumed the squabbles Oliver had interrupted six years before. Soon they proclaimed the restoration of the Commonwealth, the constitution of 1649. By accepting it, Richard Cromwell resigned his own power. As Evelyn wrote, 'the nation was now in extreme confusion and unsettled, between the Armies and the Sectaries . . . so sad a face of things had overspread us'. As the summer and autumn went by, the crisis became less political and more a struggle for power by ambitious individuals. Each of the Army leaders thought himself fit to wear the mantle of the dead Protector, and Fleetwood, Desborough and Lambert grew increasingly jealous and suspicious of each other. At the same time their hold over their men lessened, for the unpaid soldiers resented their officers' speculations in the arrears of pay.[1] The Rump made things worse by trying to purge the Army of officers who had been prominent supporters of Oliver, and by nominating a Council of State on which two-thirds of the seats were filled by the Rump's own members.

The climax came in mid-October. The Rump voted that Lambert and Desborough should be sacked from the Army. For the time being, most of the soldiers stood by their officers, and surrounded the Parliament building. The members of the Rump were prevented from entering; once again the Army used force against Parliament.

But there was one general who disapproved. George Monck, the commander in Scotland, had earlier assured the Speaker of his loyalty to Parliament, and he took hard his colleagues' interference with it. Moreover, he convinced himself that Richard Cromwell's abdication had absolved him from his oath to maintain the Protectorate. Carefully he strengthened his own position. The Scottish Estates voted him an assessment which would keep his troops paid until the following spring. He purged his army of elements disloyal to him, removing over a hundred officers. His agents spread propaganda

---

[1] Some officers bought up, at much less than face value, the I.O.U.s given to the men in place of pay; or paid their men their wages only in return for a proportion of the money for themselves.

throughout England on his behalf, making him appear the champion of constitutional liberties against the ambitions of the other generals and the disorders stemming from unpaid soldiers living off the land.

Alarmed, the other officers persuaded Lambert to move north to restrain him. But Lambert's army began to melt away, for the men had no stomach for fighting for generals spurred on merely by personal ambition. The officers now faced the imminent collapse of their authority. In December they again restored the Rump, but the members once more refused to co-operate with either the Army or old Parliamentarians like Prynne, who had been excluded since 1648. This made the Rump as unpopular as the Army. In every quarter men began to demand elections for a free Parliament. They were soon to have their wish.

On January 2nd, 1660, Monck marched southwards from his base at Coldstream on the Scottish border. Already he had enlisted the help of Lord Fairfax – who had lived since 1650 in retirement from public life, and had kept a reputation in the north and with the soldiers which was untarnished by recent events. Fairfax seized York, trapping Lambert between Monck and himself, and holding open the road for the march south.

From dozens of petitioners Monck heard the cry for a free Parliament, to be preceded by the return of the members excluded since Pride's Purge. At first he kept his thoughts to himself – and consequently was received hesitatingly by the Londoners when he occupied the City early in February. But on the 11th he took the action expected of him: he summoned back the survivors of the old Long Parliament (save for the old Royalists), having made them promise to dissolve themselves immediately. Thus the law Charles I had foolishly signed in 1641 was obeyed: the Long Parliament consented to its own dissolution. The Presbyterians – now the majority in Parliament – joyfully agreed that elections should be held immediately and that the new Parliament should assemble on April 25th.

Meanwhile, Monck kept order in the City. He purged Fleetwood's army of its troublesome officers, and divided it up into small detachments quartered well away from London and each other. Lambert was shut up in the Tower; he escaped, could find only a few squadrons to follow him, and was swiftly brought back to the Tower when his men refused to fight. Convinced at last that the restoration of the monarchy was essential to avert perpetual chaos, Monck began to communicate with Charles II. He urged the exile to offer a free pardon, the payment of wages owed to the soldiers and sailors, liberty of conscience and the recognition of all sales of land made since 1642.

These requests Charles largely granted in the Declaration of Breda, which he sent to Monck for him to publish when the time was ripe. Hyde craftily persuaded Charles to add a note to Monck's four points, in which he promised to accept whatever Parliament decided on the controversial matters. By this Charles appeared to be a constitutional King, entrusting the Restoration Settlement to Parliament. In fact he had neatly transferred to Parliament the responsibility for any unpopular decisions, and gave himself an excuse for not carrying out his promises.

The new Convention[1] Parliament met at the end of April, and listened to sermons from Richard Baxter and Dr. Gauden, the probable author of *Eikon Basilike*. At first the Presbyterians tried to exclude peers and M.P.s who had been proscribed as Royalists, hoping to retain the majority and force Charles to sign a treaty guaranteeing their religion. Monck dissuaded them. Then he sent to crowded Houses the Declaration of Breda which Charles had given him. Both Houses immediately agreed that, according to the 'ancient and fundamental laws of this kingdom, the government is, and ought to be, by king, lords, and commons'. The Convention chose delegates to announce the glad tidings to Charles, and to invite him to return to his kingdom.

The return was very different from his last departure, hunted through England with a price on his head after Worcester. Montagu and the fleet escorted the King across the Channel; Monck was waiting for him at Dover, to be embraced and addressed as 'Father' by his grateful sovereign. Throughout England the church bells pealed and bonfires blazed their welcome; the rabble jigged around maypoles to taunt the Puritans, and cautious men like Colonel Morley, Governor of the Tower, cursed their own slowness in changing sides. On

---

[1] Known as a 'Convention' because, like that of 1689, it was not summoned in the correct legal manner for a Parliament – by writs issued by the King.

May 29th Charles entered London, on his thirtieth birthday. Twenty thousand troops escorted him, in a procession which took seven hours to wind through the City.    The fountains ran with wine, flowers covered the streets, and the windows and balconies were crammed with people eager to see their King come home.

### xvi. Why the Restoration succeeded

The swiftness of the Restoration was quite unexpected. Only two years before, Dr. Hewer, 'that excellent preacher and holy man', had been beheaded on Tower Hill for intriguing with Charles II.    Premature royalist risings in 1659, led by Booth and Middleton in North Wales and Cheshire, had been crushed easily by Lambert's army.    After the Restoration, Dryden lamented that

> *Booth's* forward Valour only serv'd to show
> He durst that duty pay we all did owe.

In 1659 there were very few men willing to take up arms on Charles's behalf.    Certainly few would have prophesied that the Stuarts would be back within a year, and back without concessions more precise than the promises in the Declaration of Breda.    In the summer of 1659, it seemed much more likely that one of the generals would seize power as a dictator, after crushing his rivals in another civil war.

Many factors combined to bring about the downfall of the second Commonwealth and the speedy recall of the monarchy. Perhaps the most fundamental was economic – the generals' inability to pay their troops, resulting from the size of the Army and Parliament's reluctance to vote adequate taxes.[1]    This weakness was at the root of the Army's quarrels with all the Parliaments it had created since 1649.    It was also a major reason for the Army's unpopularity in 1660, for discipline was breaking down and the troops were foraging for themselves. The years of high and often unconstitutional taxation had turned the country against the greedy and power-drunk instrument Parliament had long ago called into being.    The soldiers,

---

[1] Monthly assessments – previously the main means of paying the Army – ended when the *Humble Petition* forbade the collection of a land tax.

moreover, were being demoralized by the hostility shown to them everywhere. Monck and Charles knew well how effective their promise to pay off the soldiers would be.

The pretensions of the Army had foiled every attempt to create a new constitutional system. Even the 'Barebones' Parliament of 1653, with its members chosen by the Army, had proved incompetent and unreliable. The Rump and Protectorate Parliaments had been too tight-fisted over pay, too keen to purge religious fanatics, for the Army ever to trust them with complete power. The long series of political crises from 1649 to 1660 resulted directly from the execution of Charles and the abolition of the House of Lords; not until monarch and peers were restored could these crises be ended. In the last years of exile, Hyde had persuaded Charles to pose as the champion of the law; in 1660, therefore, the monarchy appeared to be the best way of guarding the constitution and preventing disorder. Charles's promises from Breda showed that he was prepared to accept the decisions of Parliament – something the Army had failed to do.

The religious developments of the 1650s were also favourable to the return of the King, though not necessarily to the revival of the political power of the Church of England. Most Presbyterians had become Royalists – after all, Charles II had 'taken the Covenant' in Scotland – in reaction against the blasphemies of the Sectaries. Even the Sectaries had become less militant, with the growth of reformed Quakerism. Meanwhile, the Church of England had benefited from her ordeal. Many priests had remained completely loyal: they had given up their parishes and travelled around the country secretly visiting Anglican congregations, holding Prayer Book services and administering the sacraments. Others had conformed outwardly, but still used the Prayer Book for private services. Others had gone into exile at Charles's court, or had become missionaries for the Anglican Church in distant cities. Nonetheless, the Anglicans were not a political force in England in 1660, and the Restoration would have been impossible but for the co-operation between Monck and the Presbyterians of the old Long Parliament. With the Declaration of Breda offering 'liberty to tender consciences', and Charles's promise to accept whatever Parliament wanted, the Presbyterians felt safe.

By 1660 England was weary of Puritan morality, often inconsistent, sometimes hypocritical, always repressive.  The Rump had ordered that adultery be punished with death, and Cromwell's Major-Generals had made themselves loathed by enforcing ordinances against Sabbath-breaking, swearing, drunkenness and dancing round the maypole.  Even the new generation which had grown up since 1642 had no enthusiasm for Puritanism or the English society it tried to create.  Unpaid soldiers, copyholders and cottagers thrust off their land by new 'improving' landlords, and poor men hard-hit by the Excise duties were not going to fight to save a system which denied them even Milton's 'strenuous liberty'.

Opposition to the Restoration might, however, have come from those who had bought the confiscated estates of royalists. The Declaration of Breda allayed their fears, to some extent, by promising that the 'Land Problem' should be settled by Parliament.

Finally, Charles's offer of a general amnesty and pardon (to all except those Parliament should exclude) helped to win over the waverers.  The Restoration was accomplished 'without one bloody nose' (Baxter), because the republic was bankrupt economically and politically – and nearly so in religion; because Monck's army and the Presbyterians created a favourable opportunity; and because the statesmanship of Monck and Hyde enabled Charles to seize his chance.

### xvii. The legacy of the Civil Wars

The chaos of the final eighteen months, however, did not destroy all the positive achievements of the Civil War period. Thanks to the skilful Declaration of Breda, Charles II came back 'without conditions', without formal recognition of restrictions on his power.  But the Restoration left untouched the legislation which Charles I had accepted up to the beginning of 1642.  Consequently, the apparatus of absolute monarchy was seriously weakened.  Charles II did not try to revive the prerogative courts; the Privy Council did not regain its former judicial powers in emergencies; the King made no attempt to collect taxes without Parliament's approval.  Moreover, the philosophy of absolutism – the 'Divine Right of Kings' – had suffered during the eighteen years defiance of the

Crown. The monarchy was restored in 1660, but it was not the monarchy of the royalist reaction in the 1630s.

Nor could Charles II completely turn his back on the achievements of the Cromwellian army and navy. By force of arms, and then by parliamentary representation, Scotland and Ireland had been brought under closer control. The Navigation Acts had tried to consolidate England's commerce. Penn and Venables had added Jamaica to the empire. Blake's fleet had re-opened the Mediterranean, and had shaken the sea-power of Holland and Spain. The New Model had helped to defeat the Spaniards in Flanders, and had won Dunkirk for England. But during the disorders of 1659-60 France and Spain had ignored England's interests in making the Treaty of the Pyrenees, and the Dutch fleet had dictated a settlement in the Baltic. These were developments it was perilous for Charles to overlook. The republic had made England a world power; would Charles be able to maintain her prestige?

The period left its mark, too, on English society. At the top were dozens of men who had obtained wide experience in the responsibilities of government. Thousands more had learned something of leadership and the arts of war in the army and navy. Before the century was out, the Stuarts were to regret the political and military experience of the English middle class. The reverse side of the coin, though, was that Englishmen had developed a powerful hatred for standing armies and ambitious generals, as the great Duke of Marlborough was to find. The period accelerated the disappearance of the small tenant from the countryside, for the gentry were quick to force through Parliament in 1660 an Act confirming the republic's agrarian legislation, which helped them at the expense of their tenants.

Before long there was a revival of stricter morality, in reaction against the excesses of the Court; the characteristic prejudices of the 'Nonconformist conscience' preserved the Puritan tradition. In architecture and to some extent in painting the period developed a more national style and prepared the way for a golden age, to which the writers and musicians also contributed. Finally, the arguments of the philosophers, scientists and theologians helped to nurture Boyle, Newton, Locke and the Cambridge Platonists.

## EXTRACTS

1. PARLIAMENT AND THE SCOTS AGREE TO ENFORCE PRESBYTERIANISM IN ENGLAND:

We shall . . . endeavour the extirpation of Popery, prelacy (that is, Church government by Archbishops, Bishops, their Chancellors and Commissaries, . . . Deans and Chapters . . .), superstition, heresy, schism, profaneness, and whatsoever shall be found to be contrary to sound doctrine and the power of godliness. . . . (*The Solemn League and Covenant* (1643). In Gardiner, *Constitutional Documents*, pp. 268–9)

2. MILTON PROTESTS ABOUT PARLIAMENT'S CENSORSHIP OF THE PRESS (1644):

Who kills a Man kills a reasonable creature, God's Image; but he who destroys a good Book, kills reason itself, kills the Image of God, as it were in the eye. Many a man lives a burden to the Earth; but a good Book is the precious life-blood of a master-spirit, embalmed and treasured up on purpose to a life beyond life. . . . We should be wary therefore what persecution we raise against the living labours of public men, how we spill that seasoned life of man preserved and stored up in Books; since we see a kind of homicide may be thus committed, sometimes a martyrdom, and if it extend to the whole impression, a kind of massacre . . . whereof the execution . . . strikes at . . . the breath of reason itself. (From *Areopagitica*. In *Milton's Selected Prose*, ed. Wallace, p. 280)

3. RICHARD BAXTER, A PRESBYTERIAN ARMY CHAPLAIN, MEETS THE SECTARIES (in 1645):

Abundance of common troopers and many of the officers I found to be honest, sober, orthodox, men, and others tractable, ready to hear the truth and of upright intentions. But a few proud, self-conceited, hot-headed sectaries had got into the highest places and were Cromwell's chief favourites, and by their very heat and activity bore down the rest or carried them along with them, and were the soul of the army, though much fewer in number than the rest. . . . (Richard Baxter, *Autobiography*, p. 49)

4. MONTROSE REPORTS TO CHARLES I (FEBRUARY, 1645):

I departed out of Argyleshire, and marched through Lorne, Glencoe and Lochaber, till I came to Loch Ness, my design being to fall upon Argyle before Seaforth and the Frasers could join him.   My march was through inaccessible mountains, where I could have no guides but cow-herds, and they scarce acquainted with a place but six miles from their own habitations.   If I had been attacked but with one hundred men in some of these passes, I must have certainly returned back, for it would have been impossible to force my way, most of the passes being so streight that three men could not march abreast. . . . (In Dickinson and Donaldson, *Source Book of Scottish History*, vol. iii, p. 132)

5.   THE SENTENCE OF THE 'HIGH COURT OF JUSTICE' UPON THE KING:

. . . this Court is fully satisfied in their judgments and consciences, that he has been and is guilty of the wicked design and endeavours in the said charge set forth; and that the said war hath been levied, maintained, and continued by him as aforesaid . . .; and that he hath been and is the occasioner, author, and continuer of the said unnatural, cruel, and bloody wars, and therein guilty of high treason. . . .   For all which treasons and crimes this Court doth adjudge that he, the said Charles Stuart, as a tyrant, traitor, murderer, and public enemy to the good people of this nation, shall be put to death by the severing of his head from his body.   (In Gardiner, *Constitutional Documents*, pp. 379–80)

6.   THE 'INSTRUMENT OF GOVERNMENT' PROCLAIMS THE PROTECTORATE AND OFFERS TOLERATION (TO SOME) (1653):

I.   That the supreme legislative authority of the Commonwealth of England, Scotland, and Ireland, and the dominions thereunto belonging, shall be and reside in one person, and the people assembled in Parliament: the style of which person shall be the Lord Protector of the Commonwealth of England, Scotland, and Ireland.

. . . .

XXXVII.   That such as profess faith in God by Jesus Christ (though differing in judgment from the doctrine, worship or discipline publicly held forth) shall not be restrained from, but shall be protected in, the profession of the faith and the exercise of their religion; so as they abuse not this liberty to the civil injury of others and to the actual disturbance of the public peace on their parts: provided this liberty be not extended to Popery or Prelacy, nor to such as, under the profession of Christ, hold forth and practise licentiousness.   (In Gardiner, *Constitutional Documents*, pp. 405 and 416)

7. THE ARMY'S ATTITUDE TOWARDS RICHARD CROMWELL:

The army set up Richard Cromwell, it seemeth, upon trial, resolving to use him as he behaved himself; and though they swore fidelity to him, they meant to keep it no longer than he pleased them. And when they saw that he began to favour the sober people of the land, to honour parliaments, and to respect the ministers whom they called Presbyterians, they presently resolved to make him know his masters, and that it was *they*, and not *he*, that were called by God to be the chief protectors of the interest of the nation. (Richard Baxter, *Autobiography*, p. 89)

8. TROOPS DISTURB A SECRET ANGLICAN SERVICE:

I went to London . . . to celebrate Christmas-day . . . Sermon ended, as he was giving us the Holy Sacrament, the chapel was surrounded by soldiers, and all the communicants and assembly surprised and kept prisoners by them. . . . In the afternoon, came Colonel Whalley, Goffe, and others, from Whitehall, to examine us one by one; some they committed to the Marshal, some to prison. When I came before them, they took my name and abode, examined me why, contrary to the ordinance made, that none should any longer observe the superstitious time of the Nativity (so esteemed by them), I durst offend, and particularly be at Common Prayers, which they told me was but the mass in English, and particularly pray for Charles Stuart. . . . (John Evelyn, *Diary*, vol. i, p. 327)

9. THE PURITANS ARE ACCUSED OF HYPOCRISY:

They would not goe to ale-houses or taverns, but send for their liquors to their respective chambers and tiple it there. Some would in publick; but then, if overtaken, they were so cunning as to dissemble it in their way home by a lame leg, or that some suddaine paine there had taken them. (Anthony à Wood, *Life and Times*, p. 93)

10. DISORDERS IN OXFORD OVER MAYPOLES (MAY 1ST, 1660):

A May-pole against the Beare in Allhallows parish, set up on purpose to vex the Presbyterians and Independents. Dr. John Conant, then vice-chancellor, came with his beadles and servants to have it sawed downe, but before he had entred an inch into it, he and his party were forced to leave that place. . . . (Anthony à Wood, *Life and Times*, p. 96)

11. CHARLES II ENTERS LONDON (MAY 29TH, 1660):

And he no sooner came to Whitehall but the two Houses of Parliament solemnly cast themselves at his feet, with all the vows of affection and fidelity to the world's end.   In a word, the joy was so unexpressible and so universal, that his majesty said smilingly to some about him, that he doubted it had been his own fault that he had been absent so long, for he saw nobody that did not protest he had ever wished for his return.   In this wonderful manner, and with this miraculous expedition, did God put an end in one month . . . to a rebellion that had raged near twenty years. . . . (Clarendon, *History of the Great Rebellion*, vol. vi, p. 234)

12. A POET CHANGES HIS SONG:

His *Grandeur* he deriv'd from Heav'n alone;
For he was great e're Fortune made him so. . . .
His Ashes in a peacefull Urne shall rest,
His Name a great example stands to show
How strangely high endeavours may be blest,
Where *Piety* and *Valour* joyntly goe.
(From John Dryden, *Heroic Stanzas to the Memory
of Cromwell* (1659))

And welcome now (*Great Monarch*) to your own. . . .
The Land returns, and in the white it wears
The marks of penitence and sorrow bears.
(From John Dryden, *Astræa Redux* (1660))

# 5

# THE TRIUMPH OF THE CROWN
## 1660−85

☆

### i. Problems unsolved: the Age of Clarendon

THE new occupant of the throne had little in common with his predecessors, theologian James and Arminian Charles. He was pleasure-loving, sensual (he had his first mistress when he was eighteen), without any spark of religious enthusiasm, often lazy, and cynically unscrupulous. He admired and envied the absolute power which Mazarin had created for Louis XIV; was interested in the pageantry of the Roman Catholic Church; and had no firm principles except a vague belief in hereditary right and a strong determination not to go on his travels again. These characteristics accorded well with the exuberant joy of Restoration England, but they were a poor foundation for a lasting settlement. It was a foreign rather than an English monarch who reoccupied the Stuart throne in 1660.

As in Henry VIII's reign, the laziness of the King thrust great responsibilities upon his chief minister. Sir Edward Hyde had opposed Strafford and helped to prepare the reforming legislation of 1641; subsequently, however, he had loyally supported Charles I and had become his son's political adviser and, in 1658, his Chancellor. It had been on Hyde's advice that Charles had issued the Declaration of Breda in a way which promised a lawful, Parliamentary settlement and so avoided a humiliating treaty such as William III later had to accept. In the share-out of honours which followed the Restoration, Charles made him Earl of Clarendon. At the same time, he gave the Chancellor so much authority over the other ministers that Clarendon was generally accused of being the 'principal Minister or Favourite'. Other members of the administration were jealous of his power with the royal family –

his daughter Anne had married the King's brother James – and there soon developed a faction determined to oust him from power.

The problems facing Clarendon were enormous, despite the popularity of the Restoration. The old Royalists had to be satisfied, without losing the support of those former Parliamentarians who had summoned Charles back. The Crown must heed the demands of those who wanted it to continue the mercantilist policies of the interregnum. The Crown must be given an adequate income. Above all, it must reach a satisfactory working arrangement with Parliament. Notwithstanding his own ability and the enthusiastic goodwill of 1660, Clarendon succeeded in none of these tasks.

The Convention Parliament continued until the end of 1660. It passed an Act of Indemnity and Oblivion pardoning all except about fifty named persons. Of these, only ten were executed in 1660, all regicides, 'in sight of the place where they put to death their natural prince, and in the presence of the King his son, whom they also sought to kill'. Two years later, the unpleasant republican Sir Harry Vane (the younger) suffered a like fate. In general, though, Charles was as lenient as he had promised to be, and he refused to listen to some courtiers and Anglican clergy who tried to urge him to take a bloodier revenge on his enemies. Even though 'the carcases of those arch-rebels Cromwell, Bradshaw and Ireton' were dragged out of Westminster Abbey, hanged at Tyburn and then buried beneath the gallows, there was no sharp break with the past. The Parliamentarians who had turned Royalist were amply rewarded: General Monck became Duke of Albemarle, Admiral Montagu the Earl of Sandwich, and Ashley Cooper received a barony. Such generosity was wise, though it angered the extreme Royalists.

The land problem, unavoidably, generated most bitterness. Those who had purchased Crown and Church property[1] had to surrender it, but other land transactions were left to the jurisdiction of the law courts. Royalists deprived of their estates by illegal force (that of the Long Parliament or the Republic) had a good chance of getting them back, but those who had sold their lands to pay fines or raise money had little hope of success. The expenses of the law suits added to the

[1] Amounting together to nearly three-quarters of the total confiscations of land.

misfortunes of the unlucky, and made them determined to get revenge on the Puritans they blamed for their troubles. Soon the cynical were calling the Act of Indemnity and Oblivion indemnity for the King's enemies and oblivion for his friends! The Royalists' resentment at this treatment bedevilled the political history of the whole reign. There were few sounds at Charles's Court louder than their cries for 'compensation'.

The Convention Parliament postponed the settlement of religion, though most priests began again to use the Prayer Book openly and some read the Thirty-Nine Articles to their congregations. New bishops were consecrated and new priests ordained even before the Church was officially reinstated in power.

There was no delay, however, in re-enacting two of the most significant Ordinances of the interregnum. The Act of 1660 abolishing feudal tenures confirmed the privileges the landowners had gained from the Ordinance of 1656. The 1660 Navigation Act asserted even more vigorously the principles of the Rump's Acts of 1650 and 1651.

Clarendon blundered badly over government finance. Despite high taxation, the republic had been nearly bankrupt. Clearly, Charles must try to remain solvent and at the same time collect lower taxes. To pay off the arrears owed to the soldiers, the Convention collected eleven monthly assessments and a Poll Tax. These impositions were so unpopular that it became impossible for Clarendon to get an adequate regular revenue for the King. Moreover, the Act abolishing feudal tenures had ended the Crown's right to purveyance, wardship and feudal aids. Clarendon estimated that Charles would need about £1,200,000 p.a. for personal and governmental expenditure in peacetime. To provide this, the Convention allocated only customs and excise duties expected to yield £800,000 p.a., in addition to the King's £100,000 p.a. from Crown lands and a number of small revenues from sources such as the Post Office. Together, these should have amounted to well under a million pounds a year. In fact, until the 1670s the customs and excise duties yielded less than had been expected of them. Despite the efforts of Lord Southampton, an efficient and honest Treasurer, the Crown was short by some £400,000 p.a. of what had been promised. Even in peacetime, Charles's annual expenditure was usually well over £1,200,000 p.a. Soon the

Crown was speeding into debt. Royalist pleas for 'compensation' went unanswered. The inadequacy of the financial
settlement not only increased Charles's dependence on Parliament: it also weakened English foreign and commercial policy
and made it unpopular, and provoked the vindictive acts of the
disappointed Royalists in the Cavalier Parliament.

The Convention was dissolved in December 1660. The
Royalists won overwhelmingly in the elections held next spring.
The Cavalier Parliament which met in May 1661 contained
almost no opponents of the King and only about sixty Presbyterians and Independents. There were no Scottish or Irish
representatives; the Cromwellian union was over. The
Anglican bishops were back in the House of Lords. The
Cavaliers first set themselves to make it impossible for the
Puritans ever to threaten Church and State again. They
attempted this through the Corporation Act (1661). In many
of the towns represented in Parliament, the franchise was
largely controlled by the mayor and aldermen. By excluding
Puritans from the town corporations, the Cavaliers hoped to
make sure that the boroughs always elected Anglicans and
Royalists. Therefore the Corporation Act imposed certain
tests upon members of town corporations: they must take 'the
Sacrament of the Lord's Supper according to the Rites of the
Church of England', they must renounce the *Solemn League
and Covenant*, and must swear never to support armed rebellion
against the King.

Meanwhile, representatives of the Anglicans and Presbyterians were meeting at the Savoy Conference to try to reach a
compromise church settlement. After three months of fruitless
argument, the Conference broke up in July 1661. The
Convocations appointed a Committee to revise the Prayer
Book, accepted its recommendations, and submitted them to
Parliament. In May 1662 the Act of Uniformity enforced the
use of the revised Book. Moreover, all clergy and schoolmasters had to repudiate the Covenant, denounce the use of
arms against the King, and swear to use the new Anglican
liturgy. Furthermore, the Act ordered all beneficed clergy
who had not been ordained by a bishop to get themselves so
ordained or leave their parishes by St. Bartholomew's Day.
The date, with its memories of the massacre of French Protestants in 1572, was unhappily chosen. Nearly 2000 refused to

conform, and surrendered their benefices. Such was Parliament's interpretation of Charles's promise of 'liberty to tender consciences'.

Charles's dislike of this measure led to his first argument with Parliament. In December 1662 he issued a Declaration of Indulgence, promising to ask Parliament to allow him to suspend the operation of the Act. Clarendon opposed the request, partly because he feared the Declaration's effect on Parliament, partly because Charles had been advised to issue it by Sir Henry Bennet, one of the Secretaries of State and a rival of the Chancellor. Whatever his reasons, the Nonconformists never forgave Clarendon, for Parliament rejected the King's request and forced him to cancel the Declaration.

The Cavalier Parliament soon added other injuries. A Licensing Act (1662) tried to prevent the publication of 'heretical schismatical blasphemous seditious and treasonable Books Pamphlets and Papers' by insisting that books on theology and law should be approved by the Church and legal authorities respectively, and that all other controversial publications should be examined by appropriate officials. The Quaker Act (1662) resulted from the unjustified belief that Quakers had supported the Fifth Monarchy rising in 1661; over a thousand were imprisoned as a result. The Conventicle Act (1664) imposed heavy penalties for attendance at 'conventicles', services other than those of the Church of England. The Five Mile Act (1665) forbade Nonconformist clergy to come within five miles of any corporate town or any place where they had previously acted as ministers. This not only tried to deprive congregations of their ministers, and ministers of any influence in important towns; it also sought to ruin these clergy by making it impossible for them to earn money as schoolmasters. The Nonconformists angrily called these Acts the 'Clarendon Code'.

Of this later legislation Clarendon did not approve, but he did not dare to try to check the prejudices of the bishops and Parliament. While the King was so short of money, the Chancellor could not stop the Cavaliers from entrenching themselves securely against their rivals. The King had used Venner's Fifth Monarchy rising as an excuse for keeping Monck's Coldstreamers on as a small standing army, but the power of the sword was really in the hands of the more prosperous landowners. Charles's poverty gave Parliament indirect control of the standing army, and the Militia Act of 1662 gave the landowners the power of the sword in their own counties – against the lower classes, if not against the Crown. The Militia Act ordered the Lord-Lieutenants to recruit for their militias only the well-to-do: volunteer infantrymen had to possess at least £50 p.a., while at least £500 p.a. was necessary to qualify for the militia's cavalry. The class-selfishness of the Cavalier Parliament also appeared in the taxes it imposed; when it had to increase Charles's income in 1663, it invented the hated Hearth Tax which fell, like the Excise, unfairly upon the lower classes.[1]

In two ways, however, the Cavalier Parliament altered the law in favour of the Crown. Formerly no one could be convicted of treason unless he had committed an *open* act of rebellion or treachery. The 1661 Treason Act ordered that anyone daring to 'imagine, invent, devise or intend . . . to levy war against His Majestie' should suffer the penalties for high treason. It was therefore treasonable merely to plot rebellion; no open act was now required. In 1664 Parliament revoked the 1641 Triennial Act, which had specified arrangements for summoning a Parliament every three years even if the King refused to issue writs of summons; the new Triennial Act of 1664 declared that Parliament should meet at least every three years, but left the arrangements entirely in the King's hands.

Finance was at the root of most of the troubles which toppled Clarendon from power in 1667. The courtiers blamed him for accepting a settlement which kept the Crown so poor that Charles could not compensate them for the losses they had suffered. More particularly, the country blamed him for various failures in foreign policy, all of which resulted from the Crown's poverty. In 1662 England sold Dunkirk – most spectacular of Cromwell's gains – to the French for £400,000. As the maintenance of the garrison at Dunkirk had been costing over £100,000 p.a., the sale was probably justified, but it was nevertheless a sad blow to English prestige. In the same year, Charles II married the Infanta of Portugal, Catherine of Braganza. Her face was less attractive than her dowry – she was olive-skinned and rabbit-toothed – but the marriage brought

---

[1] The very poor, about one-third of the total population, were exempt from the Hearth Tax.

£330,000 and the ports of Tangiers and Bombay. In return, England promised to help Portugal in her rebellion against Spain. The marriage had been urged by Louis XIV, for France was always ready to help the enemies of Spain. In consequence, England was dragged into an inactive but protracted war with Philip IV. Clarendon had no enthusiasm for the alliance, but could not suggest a more profitable match. The cost of the marriage festivities and the new Queen's household increased Charles's difficulties. Soon the Catholic priests attending Catherine swelled the number of those in the household of the Queen-Mother, Henrietta Maria; popery was becoming fashionable again. As first minister and long-established adviser to the King, Clarendon could not escape censure for binding Charles to a Catholic foreigner, apparently under French influence.

Moreover, enthusiastic mercantilists like George Downing and Henry Bennet were persuading Charles to permit acts of provocation and aggression against the Dutch – with whom Clarendon had negotiated a sensible and fair settlement in 1662. Incidents in the Channel and off Africa led to the Second Dutch War in 1664. Parliament voted £2,500,000 (to be collected over two and a half years) for waging war – little enough, for the fleet was in poor condition.

Then a series of tragedies undermined England's ability to fight at all. In June 1665, while the English fleet was defeating the Dutch off Lowestoft, the plague was spreading rapidly in London. Three months later nearly a thousand a day were dying in London alone. The Court fled to Oxford and Salisbury, but soon the red crosses of infection were being painted on doors throughout the kingdom. A year after the Battle of Lowestoft, the Dutch had their revenge in the Four Days Battle off the Downs; after a frenzy of dockyard activity, the English fleet sailed out again and routed the Dutch off the North Foreland. Then, early in September 1666, while the plague was still raging, the Great Fire burned down much of the City. Spreading quickly among narrow, crowded streets, the fire destroyed some 13,000 houses. Many of the richest merchants were ruined. No longer could the goldsmiths and others afford to lend Charles money for the war against Holland.

The expense of refitting the fleet in the summer of 1666 had drained the treasury, and in 1667 Charles could not afford to send the battle fleet to sea.   This gave the Dutch their chance. With great skill and bravery, De Ruyter sailed his fleet into the Medway, burst through to Chatham, sank six English ships, and towed two others back to Holland.   One of these prizes was the *Royal Charles*, flagship of the fleet, the great vessel which seven years before had brought Charles back to England (having been tactfully renamed – previously it was the *Naseby*).

The triumph of the Dutch and the humiliation of the English knew no bounds when the Treaty of Breda ended the war in July 1667.   The triple disasters of the Plague, the Fire and the Dutch seemed, to Bible-trained Nonconformists, undoubtedly God's punishment for the Sodom and Gomorrah created at the Restoration.   Charles hastily denied responsibility, but a scapegoat had to be found.   The mob chose its victim, and rioted outside Clarendon's Piccadilly residence, sarcastically nicknamed 'Dunkirk House'.

Clarendon had become a dangerous liability for the King. The Chancellor had almost no supporters.   The mob hated him for the sale of Dunkirk, the Catholic marriage and the Medway disaster.   The Nonconformists hated him for the Clarendon Code, and the Church despised him for his reluctance to persecute the Dissenters.   Parliament feared him, for he had warned it that there must be limits to its authority.   The courtiers were jealous of his long-privileged position, strengthened as his daughter became, first mistress (to her father's fury), and then wife of James, the heir-presumptive.   Charles himself had grown tired of him, for the Chancellor was too fond of lecturing him on the extravagance and laxity of the Court. Moreover, since 1661 the influence of Sir Henry Bennet (now Lord Arlington) had been increasing; it was he, rather than Clarendon, who deserved the blame for the Dutch War. Anxious to make Clarendon the scapegoat, Arlington now persuaded the King's mistress (Lady Castlemaine) to get Charles to dismiss him.

In August 1667 Clarendon surrendered his seals of office as Lord Chancellor.   But he remained deaf to hints that he should go into exile, so Parliament concocted a process of impeachment against him.   Remembering too vividly the fate of Strafford, Clarendon scurried across to France.   Parliament then passed an Act sentencing him to perpetual banishment.

He had failed partly through bad luck, but also because he did not realize how narrow was the basis of his power.　Charles had entrusted the work of government to him, but too frequently had taken the advice of less able rivals like Arlington.　Clarendon should not be blamed too harshly for failing to carry out policies of which he disapproved.

He lived until 1674, a lonely half-forgotten figure, ill-rewarded for his years of devoted service.　These last years, however, gave him time to finish his *History of the Great Rebellion*. At times it rambles, but its value to the historian is immense, for Clarendon had an unrivalled personal knowledge of the political history of the Civil Wars.　It was not published until 1702, but then the work proved so popular that it helped to establish the prosperity of its publisher, the Oxford University Press.

## ii. The Dutch Wars and the Cabal

French influence at Court developed steadily during the 1660s, after the appointment in 1662 of Sir Henry Bennet as Secretary for the South – the minister chiefly responsible for English foreign policy.　At the same time the government grew more hostile towards Holland.　It was to France that England sold Dunkirk in 1662; it was with Louis XIV's goodwill (and a gift of £50,000) that Charles decided to marry the Portuguese princess Catherine.　The mercantilist group led by George Downing and John Shaw had many friends at Court, among them James, Duke of York and High Admiral. The Commonwealth had waged a successful war against the Dutch; why should not the monarchy do the same?　Bennet shared this view, and encouraged the printing of Mun's *England's Treasure by Fforraign Trade*, the outstanding English mercantilist treatise of the century.　In 1663 Bennet, the Duke of York, the Queen, the Queen-Mother and the Duke of Buckingham – son of Charles I's favourite – were among the sponsors of the new Royal African Company.　Its main aim was to snatch from the Dutch the profitable slave trade from West Africa to the West Indian plantations.　In 1663 the African Company's fleet captured some of the Dutch trading forts on the African coast.　Next year, however, De Ruyter drove off the English and recaptured most of the forts.

Meanwhile, England's attempts to enforce the Navigation Act of 1660 were causing further trouble with the Dutch. This Act was more specific than its predecessors, and was less concerned with capturing the Dutch coastal trade than with keeping them out of the American plantations and depriving them of their oceanic commerce. Over a thousand Dutchmen had settled on Long Island off the Hudson River, and were helping the neighbouring New England colonies to break the Navigation Acts. In 1664, therefore, Charles allowed a small expedition to sail from Portsmouth to capture Long Island and discipline the New Englanders. It was successful. At the same time, England was protesting vehemently about Holland's refusal to give her the Spice Island of Pulo Run, as had been promised in Clarendon's Anglo-Dutch treaty in 1662; the courtiers were forming the Royal Fishery Company (1664) to drive the Dutch herring-busses from the English coast; and the Duke of York was further irritating the Dutch by insisting on the 'salute to the flag' in the British seas.

At first Charles restrained the war party. He knew how weak the fleet was, and feared the cost of war. But the peace party led by Clarendon and Coventry fell silent when news arrived of De Ruyter's successes off Africa, and of the Dutch seizure of a Swedish ship carrying ships' masts to England. It was not until March 1665, however, that England formally declared war. By then the £2,500,000 granted by Parliament the previous autumn was beginning to trickle into the Treasury, but the fleet was still in poor shape, despite the attempts of York, Sandwich and Coventry to get it ready.

England fought the Second Dutch War under the handicaps Holland had experienced in the previous encounter – long trade routes, merchant ships expecting to be convoyed, an ageing fleet and shaky finances. Moreover, there were too many Court gallants in the Navy, and too few Cromwellian veterans. However, the first battle went well for the English, for the Duke of York defeated Opdam's fleet off Lowestoft in June 1665. Later in the summer, however, Sandwich failed to capture the Dutch East India fleet in Bergen,[1] and Denmark consequently allied with Holland. Early

---

[1] The King of Denmark had permitted the attack on this theoretically-neutral port, in return for the promise of a share in the spoils. When the attack failed he was obliged to side with Holland.

in 1666 France also declared war on England, in accordance with her defensive treaty with Holland, but tactfully took little part in the fighting. Charles was still supporting the Portuguese in their revolt against Spain, so the combination of hostile powers looked very serious for England.

The prospects for 1666 were grim indeed. By February the Navy faced a debt of £800,000, even though Parliament the previous autumn had voted an additional £1,250,000. At sea the war went badly. Sandwich had been dismissed after the Bergen fiasco and replaced by old Albemarle (Monck). The English fleet was foolishly divided, one part under Prince Rupert attacking the French fortress of Belle Isle, and it was with little more than half his fleet that Albemarle faced De Ruyter at the outset of the Four Days' Battle off the Downs. The Dutch drove the English back to port with the loss of twenty ships, but could not exploit their success. Desperately the dockyards toiled to repair the surviving ships. The press-gangs relentlessly combed the streets and taverns to find enough men for the crews, while the Navy Board pledged the Government's credit to the uttermost to raise more money for stores and victuals. The miracle was accomplished. Six weeks after they had limped home, the fleet sailed out again to challenge De Ruyter and prevent the French navy from Toulon joining with him. At the end of July Albemarle was able to defeat the main Dutch fleet off the North Foreland, and Holmes burned over a hundred Dutch merchantmen sheltering off the island of Vlieland.

Nonetheless, the Dutch also recovered quickly and had a fleet at sea again within two months. England was losing the war of attrition, particularly as the truculence of a dissatisfied Parliament and the catastrophe of the Fire of London made it impossible to get enough money. The Dutch were able to blockade London and stop the Newcastle colliers. At a time of 'great frosts, snow and winds' (Evelyn), the price of coal rose to £5 10s. a chauldron. The miseries of the unpaid seamen, thousands of them badly injured, revived memories of Buckingham's expeditions forty years before. Not surprisingly, Charles and Clarendon decided to start negotiations for peace. The discussions began, with Sweden acting as mediator, and dragged on through the spring of 1667. To Coventry, the Secretary of the Navy, it seemed extravagant to maintain the battle fleet at sea while the negotiations went on. De Ruyter, on the other hand, planned a final blow which would strengthen the Dutch position in the treaty discussions. In June De Ruyter landed men at Sheerness and sailed up the Medway to Chatham Harbour. Without serious loss he sank six English ships and, as we have seen, towed two others, including the flagship, away with him. Evelyn travelled down to see the Dutch ships riding at anchor after their victory:

How triumphantly their whole fleet lay within at the very mouth of the Thames, all from the North Fore-land, Margate, even to the buoy of the Nore – a dreadful spectacle as ever Englishmen saw, and a dishonour never to be wiped off.[1]

Near-panic spread through the country. The Dutch were rumoured to have landed at Dover, at Portsmouth, at Plymouth.

In these conditions peace could be delayed no longer. The Treaty of Breda, signed in July 1667, was not as unsatisfactory as it might have been, for the Dutch were worried by the growth of French power and were anxious to end the war. England modified the Navigation Acts to allow Dutch ships to carry to England the produce of Germany and the Spanish Netherlands; agreed to demand the 'salute to the flag' only in the Channel; and gave up her claim to Pulo Run. In return, she kept New Netherland, conquered by the 1664 expedition, and renamed its capital (New Amsterdam) in honour of the High Lord Admiral: New York. It was not obvious at the time, but England's single gain at Breda was to prove more valuable than all her concessions, for it closed the gap in the English settlements along the north-east American coast. Nevertheless, England had burnt her fingers badly in her second adventure in aggressive mercantilism, and it was not until nearly a century later that she consciously attempted such a policy again.[2] At the same time as the treaty with Holland, England made peace with Denmark and France by returning to the *status quo ante bellum*.

As Clarendon's star fell, so that of Arlington and his friends rose into the ascendant. With his old tutor out of the way,

---

[1] J. Evelyn, *Diary*, vol. ii, p. 27.
[2] Though the Tories demanded that the French wars of 1689–1713 should be fought for mercantilist objectives.

Charles decided to govern with a small committee of men he liked, the group which became known as the Cabal, from the first letters of their names. At their head was Sir Thomas Clifford, one of the Treasury Commissioners, an enthusiastic advocate of the recent Dutch War, and a suspected Roman Catholic. Arlington, Secretary for the South, was similarly associated with the war and with Roman Catholicism (despite his protests of denial). Buckingham was a silly rich man playing at politics, the 'Zimri' whom Dryden caricatured as

> Stiff in Opinions, always in the wrong;
> Was every thing by starts, and nothing long:
> But, in the course of one revolving Moon,
> Was Chymist, Fidler, States-Man, and Buffoon.

Ashley Cooper was the ablest member of the Cabal, and knew it. A wealthy landowner, he had already betrayed Charles I, and was soon to do the same to his son. Lauderdale completed the Cabal, but in fact had little to do with English affairs as he attended almost exclusively to Scotland. Lauderdale and Ashley Cooper had Presbyterian sympathies, and Buckingham connexions with the Independents. With two crypto-Catholics, there was not a single reliable Anglican in the Cabal. This was a source of great weakness in the Cabal's relations with the Cavalier Parliament.

Louis had helped Holland in the recent war, in the hope of getting the use of her fleet in his projected attacks on the Spanish empire. In April 1667 France invaded the Spanish Netherlands in the War of Devolution. The Dutch, however, refused to assist the growth of French power. As England had no wish to see more of the Channel coast-line pass into French hands, it was in the interests of both Holland and England to bring the war to a speedy end. Arlington consequently sent Sir William Temple to get Holland to join with England in persuading or forcing Louis to end the war. Holland agreed, Sweden offered to help, and the Triple Alliance was signed in January 1668. Its immediate success was spectacular. Louis made peace. He kept his conquests in Flanders, but returned Franche-Comté. Spain agreed to recognise the independence of France's ally Portugal. This permitted better relations between England and Spain. No one was more relieved than Charles II. He knew how dangerous it would have been if Louis had called his bluff, for Parliament had refused to give him more than £300,000 for refitting the navy.

The next five years saw a disastrous change in the relations of Crown and Parliament. The Commons were so angry at the waste of money during the Dutch War that they forced the King to accept a Committee to investigate the Government's revenue and expenditure. The members of the Committee had a hard task before they were able to present their report in 1669. Their report was confused, and showed how much the country's accounting system needed overhauling. The report also seemed to show that more than half a million pounds voted by Parliament had not been spent on the war. Believing that had been embezzled by officials, pocketed by courtiers or wasted by the King on his extravagant pleasures, Parliament forced the King to purge the Navy Board; of the men who had supervised the navy's administration in the recent war only Samuel Pepys kept his place. Parliament's attempts to remove inefficient or dishonest ministers, a significant episode in establishing that officials were responsible to it and not the King, naturally annoyed Charles greatly. For the moment his poverty made him tolerate Parliament's aggressive behaviour, but other developments soon made him decide to look elsewhere for money. The two Houses were quarrelling between themselves, locked in a dispute over the case of *Skinner* v. *The East India Company*, with the Lower House claiming that every commoner had the right to petition it directly for the redress of grievances. At the same time Parliament angered the King by proposing to impeach the Earl of Orrery for his fraudulent administration in Munster. By now the Cabal had little influence left among the Cavaliers, and Charles thought it wise to prorogue Parliament in December 1669.

The King, his brother, Arlington and Clifford were now considering another way to get money. The government could collect no taxes in England without Parliament's consent; Parliament refused to vote money, and the goldsmiths and other London bankers pleaded that they were unable to lend any. But across the Channel was a rich monarch, already patiently planning to isolate the Dutch – so recently England's enemies. Moreover, Louis XIV was a pious and zealous Catholic. The Duke of York had just been converted to Rome, and the King was strongly tempted to follow him. 'Minette', Charles's

favourite sister Henrietta, was married to the brother of the
French King, and so the personal correspondence of Charles
and his sister provided an admirable opportunity for secret
negotiations.   In December 1669, in the greatest secrecy, the
discussions began.   Charles was offering to hire out English
forces to serve against Holland, and to impose Catholicism on
England, in return for French subsidies and troops (if Parliament proved recalcitrant).   Louis was interested, but not
generous in the value he placed on England's assistance.   In
the spring, however, Charles was in a better position to
negotiate, for in February the Cavalier Parliament had voted
him[1] additional duties on wine and vinegar, estimated to be
worth £400,000 p.a.   It was in a more confident spirit that
Charles went to Dover at the end of May to meet 'Minette'.
Louis was prepared to raise his bid, and within a week the two
allegedly Catholic members of the Cabal, Clifford and Arlington,
completed a secret treaty with the French ambassador, Colbert
de Croissy.

By the treaty, England promised to join France in an attack
upon Holland.   In return, France would pay Charles £250,000
p.a. during the war, and would also pay for 6000 English troops
fighting with the French army.   England would supply a
fleet of sixty warships, under the Duke of York, to join with a
smaller French fleet in landing on the coast of Holland while
Louis's army invaded by land.   England would receive from
the war the island of Walcheren and the ports of Sluys and
Cadzand at the mouth of the Scheldt.   In addition, however,
Charles was to declare himself a Catholic – for which Louis
agreed to give him £167,000 and promised to lend him 6000
troops to deal with any Englishmen reluctant to follow their
sovereign to Rome.   During the negotiations Charles had
shown considerable ability as an intriguer and diplomat, and
had managed to tie Louis down to accepting conditions more
precise and specific than those binding himself.   In subsequent
months Charles and the whole Cabal openly negotiated another
Treaty, designed to bamboozle Parliament and the country.
In December the open Treaty was signed; there was no mention
in it of the arrangements for converting England to Catholicism.
Otherwise its conditions were much the same.

[1] Largely because he had agreed to an even more severe Conventicle Act against
Nonconformists.

It was a pity that Charles had not used for some nobler purpose the abilities he had displayed in the discussions with France. His motives in making the two Treaties, however, are by no means clear. Was he serious in hoping to lead England to Rome? Was he anxious to help England by ruining the Dutch? Had he counted the cost? Undoubtedly courtiers like York, Arlington and Clifford were anxious to avenge the failures in the Second Dutch War, and the chance to get French help *and* subsidies in crushing Holland seemed very attractive to them, for they seemed to make Holland's downfall certain. But Charles should have realized that £250,000 p.a. was quite inadequate to keep a battle fleet at sea, and that Catholicism could not be imposed on England with £167,000 and a few thousand troops. It has been argued that Charles never intended to try to convert England, and that he was merely deceiving Louis in order to get more money. It is true that even before the end of 1670 he was irritating Louis by shifty delays in announcing his conversion – he wanted to negotiate with Rome through an English prelate, he would wait until the old Pope died, and so on. On the other hand, Louis would probably have been glad to purchase Charles's support even without the 'conversion' agreement, for France needed the help of the English fleet. The probability is that a burst of rash enthusiasm, and the Catholic faction at Court, led Charles into a policy which he was later too scared to put into effect. In any case, the cost of warfare made both treaties dangerous gambles, especially as Parliament's grant of the additional £400,000 p.a. made French subsidies unnecessary.

It was more than a decade before Charles surmounted the political crises resulting from the Treaties of Dover. At first, though, the preparations for war went forward smoothly. Parliament was fooled splendidly by the open Treaty, and voted Charles another £800,000 (more than the total he received from Louis between 1670 and 1678). But the government's credit was shaken when, in January 1672, Charles ordered the Stop of the Exchequer. This suspended the payment of government debts for a year, and made sure that the new revenues would not be swallowed up in settling old debts. This was another gamble, for it naturally made bankers much more reluctant to lend any additional money to the Crown. Two months later, in March 1672, England stumbled into the Third Dutch War.

Nobody wanted it, except the Catholic courtiers and a few hard-bitten mercantilists. The government tried the old trick of reprinting tales of Dutch atrocities at Amboyna and elsewhere, but the people remained doggedly indifferent to the war. In effect, England entered the Third Dutch War as a mercenary in French pay. The immediate pretexts for war were trifling – the Dutch had refused to lower their flags in salute when the tiny yacht *Merlin* sailed through the Dutch fleet, and had fought back against Admiral Holmes when he had attacked the Dutch convoy from Smyrna. Two days before the declaration of war, Charles alarmed England by a rash gesture. In 1662 Parliament had refused to allow him to suspend the early Acts of the Clarendon Code. Now, on the eve of war, the King again challenged the legislative supremacy of Parliament:

We do . . . declare our will and pleasure to be, That the execution of all and all manner of penal laws in matters ecclesiastical, against whatever sort of non-conformists, or recusants, be immediately suspended.

This Second Declaration of Indulgence was as near to helping Catholicism as Charles dared sail. Even the Nonconformists disliked toleration if they had to share it with the Catholics. It was not long before Charles's critics began to connect the Declaration with the Treaty of Dover and with the military alliance with Louis XIV, whose zeal for persecuting Protestants was notorious. The Third Dutch War was not a popular one; there were not many Englishmen praying for French victory over the Protestants of Holland.

It was essential for Charles that the Dutch should be defeated very quickly. The first encounter was unpromising. De Ruyter caught York's Anglo-French fleet on a lee shore in Southwold Bay, and in a long and ferocious battle scattered the raw French navy and damaged the English fleet too much for it to dominate the North Sea as had been hoped. Consequently, the English forces could not land on the Dutch coast in an attack concerted with Turenne's great advance in May and June. The Anglo-French fleet was ready again by July, but a storm dispersed it off Texel. Meanwhile, the desperate Dutch had removed the Grand Pensionary John de

Witt, and appointed William III of Orange, Charles II's nephew, as their Stadtholder. For thirty years William was to remain the relentless enemy of France. Now he called upon his countrymen for supreme sacrifices. As his great-grandfather had done a century before to check the Spanish advance, William persuaded the Dutch to breach their dykes. The water and mud slowed and then halted Louis's army. The war dragged on, to the dismay of Charles and his courtiers. In actions off Schonveld in June and July 1673 De Ruyter again prevented the Anglo-French fleet landing troops. In August De Ruyter once more fought them off, in the great battle of Texel which ended English attempts at a sea-borne invasion.

By that time the political situation in England had changed for the worse. At the start of the war, Charles had increased the individual powers of the members of the Cabal. Clifford had received a peerage and became Lord Treasurer, and Ashley Cooper became Earl of Shaftesbury and Lord Chancellor. In the winter of 1672–3, the Chancellor issued writs on his own authority for the elections of over thirty members to fill seats which had fallen vacant since Parliament had last met almost two years previously. When the Cavalier Parliament reassembled in February 1673, its first act was to unseat the new members and issue writs for fresh elections, in defiance of the Chancellor.

An opposition group swiftly developed, known as the 'Country' party, to challenge the influence of the 'Court' faction. It was strong enough to dictate to the King. Before Parliament would grant Charles any money, it extracted from him what has been called[1] the most important royal surrender of the century – it forced him to cancel his Declaration of Indulgence. For the King to over-ride laws which Parliament had passed seemed more outrageous than even the implied threat to the Cavaliers' Church. Then Parliament forced Charles to accept the Test Act, which debarred Catholics from office in the state. Every person holding 'any Office or offices Civill or Military or . . . any Pay, Salary, Fee or Wages . . . from his Majestie' had to receive the sacraments of the Church of England and denounce the doctrine of Transubstantiation. 'Liberty to tender consciences' was dead and buried. With the King shackled in these ways, Parliament voted him

[1] D. Ogg, *Charles II*, vol. i, p. 368.

£1,240,000 from monthly assessments to clear off the debts and bring the war to an end.

The Test Act, as its sponsors had intended, broke up the Cabal. The Duke of York, the Cabal's most enthusiastic supporter, had to resign the command of the Navy. Clifford, now a professed Catholic, had to give up the Treasurer's white staff of office. Moreover, Shaftesbury had defied Charles by supporting the Act. The Chancellor had done this partly because his ambitions made him jealous of the Catholic member of the Cabal, and partly because he was angry that he had not been told about the secret Treaty of Dover. When Shaftesbury permitted attacks on the Duke of York's marriage to the Catholic Mary of Modena[1] after his first wife's death, Charles dismissed him. In the winter of 1673-4, Parliament turned against Arlington and Buckingham. The former was known as a Catholic sympathiser – his coach once overturned in London, and Arlington stepped from the wreckage accompanied by a Catholic priest in full vestments – and Buckingham had had a hand in most of the recent troubles. The Commons began to murmur about impeachment. Arlington and Buckingham immediately tried to excuse themselves by blaming each other for England's misfortunes. Buckingham resigned before Charles had time to sack him. Arlington remained Secretary until September 1674, but by then his policies had been superseded.

The truculent attitude of Parliament and the collapse of the Cabal brought a speedy end to the Dutch War. At the end of 1673 Louis had sent £500,000 to try to stop Charles making a separate peace. It was wasted. In February 1674 England made the Treaty of Westminster with Holland. The Dutch agreed to pay an indemnity of £180,000 and to salute the British flag from Cape Finisterre northwards to Norway; otherwise the countries returned to the *status quo*. The Third Dutch War achieved none of the ends Charles had hoped to secure. So far from reimposing Catholicism on England, the King had been forced to withdraw his Declaration of Indulgence and accept the Test Act banning Catholics from public office. So

---

[1] Sister of the Duke of Modena, an Italian princeling under French domination. Louis XIV provided her dowry (£100,000). Evelyn's *Diary* (vol. ii, p. 92) for November 5th, 1673, records, 'This night the youths of the City burnt the Pope in effigy, after they had made procession with it in great triumph, they being displeased at the Duke for altering his religion, and marrying an Italian lady.'

far from helping the Crown out of its financial difficulties, the war had cost England over £6,000,000. Charles had hoped to emulate Louis's absolutism; instead, he had failed even to establish his power to suspend particular laws.

Each of the Dutch Wars brought about the collapse of a system of government. The Rump oligarchy tumbled in 1653. In 1667 the great minister Clarendon fell. Now, government by royal favourites, heedless of public opinion, also collapsed.

### iii. Danby, Shaftesbury and the Exclusion Struggle

The break-up of the Cabal widened the divisions in Parliament between the supporters of different ministers. By the end of 1674 Clifford was dead, Shaftesbury an outspoken leader of the opposition to Charles, Buckingham nearly disgraced, and Arlington a vindictive enemy of those who had ended his power; Lauderdale alone remained in office. A new man was in charge of the administration – Sir Thomas Osborne, who had become Treasurer in February 1673 when the Test Act forced Clifford to resign. Osborne owed his promotion to Buckingham's influence, but it was not long before he eclipsed his former patron and placed himself at the head of 'Zimri's' followers – Edward Seymour, Henry Coventry and Heneage Finch. Osborne – soon made Earl of Danby – was above all a Parliament man, and saw how essential it was to improve relations between King and Parliament. This could only be done by increasing the King's popularity. To achieve this, Danby had to make Charles appear as the protector of the Anglican Church, and to make England's foreign policy more popular, by friendship with Holland rather than France. In return, he hoped to get more taxes from Parliament. These would make the Crown solvent at last, provided Danby could also eliminate extravagance and limit corruption in the royal expenditure.

These were no easy tasks. The Commons no longer consisted of a chorus of Cavaliers singing in unison. In the parliamentary sessions under the Cabal there had developed recognizable factions in both Lords and Commons, but these were 'interests' rather than parties, and there was little consistency in the way members voted. The two most obvious

'interests' had been those of the 'Court' party – the followers of
the Cabal – and their critics in the 'Country' party, led by
William Coventry, Richard Temple and William Garroway.
The collapse of the Cabal upset whatever allegiances had been
created, for it threw first Shaftesbury and then Arlington into
opposition.   Even loyal Court men like 'Iron' Strangways of
Dorset were demanding to know more about the Treaty of
Dover: 'The public articles are ill enough; what are then the
private articles?'

The problems facing Danby were complicated by two
major constitutional issues.   The Commons challenged the
King's right to create new constituencies, as he tried to do with
Newark in 1673; Charles won, but the row deterred him from
ever trying again.   Moreover, the two Houses were at logger-
heads in the case of *Shirley* v. *Fagg*, over whether a member of
the Commons could be obliged to appear as a defendant in a
trial before the House of Lords; again the Commons lost.   With
great patience and skill Danby was able to create a bare parliamentary majority for the Crown out of this hotch-potch of
public and private 'interests'.   It was almost as difficult for him
to manage the Court as to manage Parliament, for Charles
disliked the intolerant Anglicanism and pro-Dutch foreign
policies which Danby fostered.   The Treasurer's influence was
repeatedly undermined by intriguers like the Duchess of
Portsmouth (the King's current mistress) and professional
back-stairs politicians like Chiffinch.   The organization of the
opposition Green Ribbon Club by Shaftesbury and Sacheverell
added to Danby's difficulties after 1675.

In the circumstances, therefore, Danby's achievement was
remarkable.   By economies in administration and by the more
efficient exploitation of the Excise and Hearth Taxes, and through
the rise in customs revenue produced by the trade boom, the
Treasurer was able to pay off old debts and make the Crown
solvent.   The Crown's position in Parliament became slightly
more stable.   Danby built up a party of King's supporters with
bribes from the Exchequer and gifts from William of Orange,
anxious to foster pro-Dutch sentiment in England.   Many
by-elections occurred as old members of Parliament died or
retired from politics; Danby was ruthlessly efficient in using
every scrap of personal and Crown influence to persuade the
constituencies to elect men who would support him.   The

Cavalier Parliament quickly became the Pension Parliament, with a high proportion of its members receiving money or honours in return for supporting Danby. He gained the goodwill of the Anglicans by putting the Clarendon Code into operation. In 1677 Danby completed the reversal of English foreign policy by persuading the King to agree to the marriage of William of Orange to Mary, the Protestant elder daughter of the Duke of York by his first marriage. This Protestant–Dutch alliance was of the utmost significance, for Mary was second in line of succession to the throne. If Charles died without legitimate children, and if James died without a son by his second marriage, Mary would inherit the Crown.

Shaftesbury tried to counter Danby's power in Parliament by calling for fresh elections and a Place Bill. The former would, he expected, weaken the representation of the 'Court' party, while the latter would make it difficult for Danby to buy support for the King, by excluding from the Commons those holding offices of profit under the Crown. Both campaigns failed. In 1677, moreover, Shaftesbury, Buckingham and Wharton were sent to the Tower for insolently arguing that the Parliament had become illegal and that its acts were invalid.[1]

Shaftesbury's party seemed on the brink of collapse, when help suddenly arrived from an unexpected quarter – France. Parliament had been demanding that England should intervene on the continent to prevent Louis XIV crushing the Dutch, and Danby had to urge Charles to take this course, though it conflicted with the King's instinct and inclination. The navy was prepared, and a large army collected. Previously Louis had been helping Charles with substantial subsidies, on condition that the English Parliament was repeatedly prorogued (so that it could not demand war) without being dissolved (for an election would have produced a House of Commons even more hostile to France). But now that Danby's supporters were so set on war, Louis could not risk relying on Charles to keep England from helping Holland. The surest way to keep England neutral was for France to subsidize Danby's opponents. For this reason in 1678 Louis became the paymaster of Shaftesbury's supporters. At the same time Holland and Spain were

[1] Parliament had recently been prorogued for fifteen months. Shaftesbury appealed to a Statute of Edward III's reign, ordering that Parliament should meet every year. There had, of course, been many much longer periods without meetings of Parliament. Shaftesbury's argument was a poor one.

also trying to protect their own 'interests'; in the sessions of 1678 there were few members who were not in the pay of at least one foreign power.

Ironically, it was on the charge of negotiating secretly with Louis that Shaftesbury eventually brought about Danby's downfall. In the spring of 1678 Danby had sent Montagu to Paris to beg secretly for fresh subsidies, and had obtained a promise of £500,000 annually for three years, provided England remained neutral. The money was never paid, for the war ended almost immediately. Later in the year Danby offended Montagu, an ambitious careerist, by refusing him a government post. With a bribe from the French ambassador, Barrillon, to loosen his tongue, Montagu revealed to Parliament the terms of the agreement with Louis. Memories of the 1670 negotiations, and the panic caused by the news of the 'Popish Plot', combined to disrupt Danby's followers. By 179 votes to 161, the Commons agreed to impeach him. The Lords refused to do so. There was only one way out of the constitutional crisis – Charles had to dissolve the Parliament (January 1679).

After eighteen years the Cavalier Parliament had come to an end. Less than half of those elected in 1661 survived as members until 1679, and despite Danby's skill in manipulating elections many of the new members were hostile to the Court and lukewarm about the Church of England. The last sessions of the Parliament had seen the development of organized factions. As Shaftesbury's followers became increasingly associated with Nonconformity in the following years, the Royalists nicknamed them after the 'Whiggamores', the Presbyterian rebels in Scotland. With even less justice, the Court's supporters were soon nicknamed 'Tories' after Irish Catholic rebels.

Since James's conversion and marriage to Mary of Modena, the Court had grown rather more Catholic. As Catherine of Braganza failed to produce an heir for Charles, many prudent courtiers thought it wise to please James, the heir-apparent. At the same time, the Cabal's foreign policy had increased the country's fear of popery. Louis of France heightened the tension by aggressive Catholicism at home and abroad. Andrew Marvell's *Account of the growth of popery and arbitrary government in England* (published anonymously) was one of the best-sellers of 1677. The next year started in a frightening manner, with eclipses of the sun and moon, followed by a reputed appearance of the Devil in Scotland. It was a credulous age, when rumours and heavenly portents were trusted uncritically. The country was already near to panic when news reached the King in August of a Catholic plot to murder him (by three separate and different methods), burn London again, and establish popery. The scare came as a godsend to Shaftesbury and his faction.

The plot was concocted by a third-rate scientist and a fourth-rate parson. The former, Dr. Israel Tonge, had lectured on biology to the Royal Society, and had developed a fanatical fear of Jesuits. The latter, Titus Oates, had been sacked from a naval chaplaincy and a parish in Kent, had joined the Jesuits, received a doctorate of divinity from Salamanca University, and learned enough gossip at the Jesuit College of St. Omer to be able to tell a convincing tale when he decided to team up with Tonge. In August 1678 Tonge told his story to Danby: the Catholics had arranged, at a great meeting that April, for the King to be poisoned by the Queen's doctor, shot by Jesuits, and stabbed by Irishmen for good measure; the French were to invade Ireland, while Catholics in England murdered obstinate Protestants and made the Duke of York King. The story was fantastic, but the conspirators were lucky. Enough coincidental evidence appeared to make most men believe them, and Parliament and Shaftesbury rewarded them richly for their information. Oates and Tonge left a sworn deposition of the evidence with Sir Edmund Berry Godfrey, a popular London magistrate; a month later Godfrey was found dead.[1] The correspondence of Coleman, James's tactless secretary, was searched; letters more foolish than treacherous sent him to the scaffold. More informers scurried forward. Anyone who had supported Danby was liable to be accused. The shop of a French fireworks-maker was repeatedly searched for gunpowder; so were the cellars of the Houses of Parliament. Five Catholic peers were hurried off to the Tower. Another Test Act (November 1678) banned Catholics from sitting in either House of Parliament, though the Commons agreed by two votes to let the Duke of York remain. Oates and Bedloe (another renegade Catholic) appeared before the Commons;

[1] It is at least possible that, as was generally believed, he was killed by Catholics; but more likely that he was murdered by robbers.

they convinced the members to a man of the truth of their stories.   Even the Queen was accused of being in the plot to kill the King.   Innocent Jesuits charged with complicity were dragged to grisly deaths at Tyburn.   It was in this explosive atmosphere that Montagu revealed Danby's correspondence with Louis, forcing Charles to dissolve Parliament to save his minister.   It was in the same atmosphere that three elections followed in less than two years.

Charles   could   not   manage   without   Parliament.   The expense of preparing the forces required for the emergency of 1678, and the high cost of the garrison at Tangiers, threw too heavy a burden upon his regular revenues.   Subsidies from Parliament or from Louis were still necessary.   Louis, however, was less than lukewarm.   Charles had deceived him too frequently, and Louis thought that he could purchase the Duke of York more cheaply and more certainly than he could buy the King.   Moreover, Louis was still subsidizing Shaftesbury's men to keep England too divided to be able to interfere with his European policy.   Shaftesbury gave good value, for he and Sacheverell had built up an efficient party organization.   The three  Parliamentary  elections  of  1679–81  proved  how  well Louis's subsidies had been spent.

Originally Shaftesbury's policies were concerned only with unseating Danby and weakening the influence of the Crown. Danby's fall allowed the opposition to develop a more positive programme.   Their main interest was on the succession.   At first Shaftesbury wanted Charles to divorce Queen Catherine and marry a Protestant, but he soon became committed to Exclusion, to making it impossible for James or any Catholic to rule.   Some proposed that there should be a regency after Charles II's death, with an acceptable Protestant such as the Duke of Monmouth ruling in James's name; others demanded that the Crown should pass directly to James's daughter Mary. The more moderate 'Whigs'[1] like Lord Halifax preferred to allow James to succeed his brother (for they feared taking a step so revolutionary as interfering with the succession), but wanted to hedge him in with such tight restrictions that he would be unable to strengthen royal power or aid the Catholics.

[1] For the sake of convenience this nickname is used here to denote the opposition faction during the Exclusion struggle, though it would be more accurate not to use the term until later.

It was fortunate for the Crown that the Whigs were divided on this issue. They were more united, however, in their opposition to royal interference with Parliament at election time, or in the choice of Speaker, or in bribing members or in fixing the times at which the Houses should assemble and disperse. They repeated earlier demands that Parliament should meet regularly, whether the King summoned it or not,[1] and that elections should be frequent (to prevent the King gradually building up a party of adherents). They were bitterly opposed to a standing army (partly because it threatened the authority of the militia) and to any extension of royal power. The Whigs were sympathetic towards the Nonconformists, but could not agree whether the Clarendon Code should be abolished altogether, or merely have its teeth drawn by remitting the penalties with which Dissenters were threatened. When courts began to question the evidence of Oates and other informers, the Whigs started to demand that judges should hold office only so long as they behaved themselves. Towards the Catholics the Whigs were unrelentingly hostile.

The Court party had a less specific policy. Danby's alliance of Church and Crown still held, and the Anglicans opposed any move to lighten the load on Nonconformists. The votes of the bishops, usually about a quarter of all the peers taking part in the Lords' debates, more than once enabled Charles to survive the storms which lay ahead. The Church was loyal to the principle of hereditary succession, and pressed for laws to enforce oaths of 'non-resistance' to the Crown.

The election for the Parliament was fought on party lines, with the Whigs demanding the punishment of papist conspirators and those who had held royal pensions in the previous Parliament. The Court party lost heavily; there were barely thirty members on whom Charles could rely. There was trouble at the start over the choice of Speaker; it was Charles who gave way. The new assembly – the First Whig Parliament – proceeded to impeach Danby, and was infuriated when Charles gave him a free pardon. To forestall a constitutional crisis (and a possible Bill of Attainder), Danby surrendered to the Lords and spent the next five years in protective custody

---

[1] The Triennial Act of 1664 had amended the 1641 Triennial Act by removing the machinery whereby Parliament would assemble every three years whether the King summoned it or not.

in the Tower.   The Whigs then induced Charles to accept a
new governmental system proposed by Temple – a Privy
Council of thirty, composed of fifteen members of the administration, ten peers and five members of the Commons.   It was
too unwieldy to be effective, and Charles gradually dismissed
the members who would not co-operate with him.

In May 1679 the Whigs introduced the first of the Bills to
prevent James succeeding his brother.   Shaftesbury by now
had an alternative candidate to put forward as heir – the Duke
of Monmouth, the eldest of Charles's bastard sons.   Monmouth was a witless youth, popular with the Nonconformists
and easily dominated by Shaftesbury.   The Whigs claimed that
Charles had in fact married Monmouth's mother Lucy Walters,
and that the proofs of the marriage had been stolen by Catholics
and were now kept in a little black box so that no one should
stand between James and the Succession.   Even in that
age of rumours the story seemed a little unconvincing.   Nevertheless, Shaftesbury was able to mount a double offensive, that
Monmouth was the rightful heir, and that James should be
excluded from the Succession.   The Commons passed the first
Exclusion Bill in May 1679, but paused before passing it on to
the Lords.   Perhaps unwisely, Shaftesbury diverted Parliament's attention into passing the *Habeas Corpus* Act, to prevent
prisoners being detained indefinitely before trial (a favourite
weapon of absolutism), and encouraged the Commons to
investigate charges of corruption in the Pension Parliament.
While the members were arguing, Charles suddenly swooped
and dissolved Parliament.

So far, Charles had avoided making major political concessions, but only by consenting to the judicial murder of harmless Catholics.   It was not until July 1679 that the Chief
Justice dared to question the testimony of Oates and Bedloe;
as a result of Scroggs's brave action, the jury acquitted the
Queen's doctor – to the mob's disgust.   August brought a fresh
danger, for Charles fell seriously ill.   James hurried back from
Brussels (where Charles had sent him out of the way).   For an
anxious fortnight there was danger of civil war between the
supporters of James and Monmouth if Charles died.   Fortunately Charles recovered, and banished both brother and son.
He summoned a new Parliament in October 1679, disliked the
look of the members, and immediately prorogued it while he

pleaded with Louis for new subsidies. The King's position gradually improved, even though Louis was obstinate, for wiser heads remembered the outcome of the crises of 1641–2. Even the fiasco of the Meal Tub plot, thought up by Crown supporters in an attempt to discredit the Presbyterians, did not weaken the anti-exclusion party seriously.

During the winter of 1679–80, Charles weeded out many Whig members of the Privy Council, and ruled instead with a few friends – Sunderland, Godolphin and Lawrence Hyde (Clarendon's son). To these young men – the 'Chits' – Charles wisely added Halifax. 'Trimmer' Halifax was probably the ablest statesman of his time, and was always prepared to compromise. Now he joined Charles, in return for a promise that James's powers as King should be tightly restricted by Act of Parliament. By this, Charles split the opposition. Shaftesbury unsuccessfully tried to extend the crisis to Ireland: the Irish ruffians he hired to testify against the Catholics were bribed by the Crown into changing their minds and giving evidence against Shaftesbury instead. Perjury, indeed, was now a very profitable profession: Israel Tonge's son was bribed into swearing that he knew his father and Oates had invented the plot, and Oates's brother Samuel was soon to join the paid informers giving evidence against Shaftesbury and the Whigs. In this atmosphere of perjury and cross-perjury the trials went on, but the acquittals grew more frequent.

For a year Charles kept the members of the Second Whig Parliament kicking their heels before he allowed them to meet. The repeated prorogations did not cool them off as much as he had hoped. Parliament met in October 1680, and the Commons immediately passed a Bill to exclude James from the succession. This time the Bill reached the Lords. Halifax defeated Shaftesbury in debate, and the peers rejected the Bill by 63 votes to 30. The majority was largely accounted for by the votes of the twenty-six bishops. The Commons angrily attacked their enemies, threatening impeachment against Halifax, Edward Seymour, Justice Scroggs and Justice North. The Lords would have nothing to do with this vindictive violence, but tried to appease public opinion by sending to the block old Lord Stafford, one of the Catholic peers accused by Oates. Encouraged by the London mob, the Commons continued their noisy defiance of the Lords and the King. In

January 1681 Charles again silenced them by dissolution. This, however, offended Halifax, for it frustrated his plan to place restrictions on James, and he retired from the ministry. From Whig politicians and from corporations like the City of London there poured in a flood of petitions against the dissolution. The King's friends opposed this organized petitioning, and for a while the two groups were consequently known as 'Petitioners' and 'Abhorrers'. Already Sunderland had gone, sacked for supporting the Second Exclusion Bill, and Godolphin could not be depended upon. Charles was now very much alone. Once more he appealed to Louis.

The *dénouement* came in March 1681. Charles summoned another Parliament, this time ordering it to assemble at Oxford. By now, Royalist morale was improving. Filmer's *Patriarcha*, written many years before, had just been published; its emphasis on the Divine Right of Kings helped to cement the alliance between Crown and Church. Even a few extreme Whigs like Sacheverell had moderated their views, and were prepared to accept something less than Exclusion. Moreover, the University of Oxford was Royalist, and with Guards regiments from Windsor controlling the mob Charles was certain of a favourable atmosphere (even though Shaftesbury took some of the London rowdies with him to Oxford). For a week rival bands of partisans disturbed the town while Parliament debated Exclusion. Should James be shut out altogether, leaving the succession open either for his daughter Mary, or for Monmouth? Should James be bound in with tight restrictions, or should there be a regency ruling in his name? While the Whigs argued openly in the Commons at Christ Church, or haggled privately at their lodgings in Balliol, Charles held his hand. Then once again the Whigs lost the scent. The Commons began pressing for the impeachment of Fitzharris (one of the Irish informers persuaded to turn against Shaftesbury), and demanded that details of how M.P.s voted should be published, so that the electors would know if they were controlled by the Crown. While these red herrings were being dragged through the Chapter House of Christ Church, where the Commons were sitting, Charles at last decided to act. He hurried there, with his robes and royal insignia carried secretly in a closed sedan chair. The members expected him to submit, and accept the principle of Exclusion. Instead, he dissolved

Parliament once more, for Louis XIV had promised £400,000, and Charles was safe. Shaftesbury had over-played his hand, and the moderates who remembered the events of forty years before had swung over to the King. The Oxford Parliament was a tremendous gamble for Charles – in many ways an unnecessary gamble, for Louis's promise of money arrived before Parliament met – but the consequences justified the risk the King took.

The Exclusion struggle was over. Charles had fought a successful action to defend the principle of hereditary right, on behalf of a brother he disliked. Many reasons contributed to the King's success. He had won because of his own courage and political skill; because the Whigs were too easily diverted from Exclusion to other matters; because the bishops and the Church supported James, and hampered close co-operation between the two Houses of Parliament; because the Lords hesitated to provoke the disorders of another 1642; because the mob was placated by the sacrifice of Catholic victims; but most of all because Louis realized at last that without a subsidy for Charles there would be little chance of a Catholic coming to the English throne. For the arguments and bitterness of a dozen years there was little to show. The Crown had not been deprived of any major privilege or prerogative, though the Church had been given the protection of the Test Acts, and the individual the nominal safeguard of *Habeas Corpus*. Nonetheless, the party struggles between Whig and Tory set a precedent for two centuries of rivalry and provided the labels for generations of family alliances. Amazing though it would have seemed a few years after the collapse of the Whig party in the Oxford Parliament, most of the Whig aims were secured within twenty years – many of them being passed by Tory parliaments.

### iv. The Crown triumphant

By his swift and unexpected dismissal of the Oxford Parliament, Charles caught the Whigs on the wrong foot. In such confusion, they had no chance to organize opposition. This was fortunate for the country, for tempers were hot and swords ready to flash out in civil war. The King and the Tories used their opportunity to move over to the offensive. A fortnight after the dissolution, Charles sacked Chief Justice Scroggs – too fair and honest to be useful – and replaced him with Francis Pemberton.  The law courts swung into action against men dangerous to the King.  Fitzharris was hanged as the author of a seditious libel – probably to prevent him revealing information harmful to the Crown.  A London carpenter, Stephen College, was executed for possessing a sword and pistols and distributing ribbons embroidered 'No popery: no slavery' in Oxford during the late Parliament.

Then Charles directed his attack against a more dangerous opponent: Shaftesbury was put on trial for planning to wage war on the King.  The case, however, was heard in the Old Bailey, before a jury chosen by Whig sheriffs; the jurymen refused to be bullied by Pemberton, and acquitted the Whig leader.  This was a short-lived success for Shaftesbury, for Dryden's satire *Absalom and Achitophel* was published at the same time.  The poem's theme was how 'false Achitophel' (Shaftesbury)

> In Friendship False, Implacable in Hate:
> Resolv'd to Ruine or to Rule the State . . .

by persuading Absalom (the Duke of Monmouth) to stand as 'Champion of the publique Good' and oppose King David (Charles II).  The piercing wit of this superb satire pricked the balloon of Whiggery more effectively than did the charges of high treason.

Nonetheless, Shaftesbury's acquittal by a jury packed by Whig sheriffs was the signal for Charles to start a long-considered attack on the privileges of the towns and their officials.  In this the King was joined by local magnates who wanted to assert their own authority over neighbouring towns. The Duke of Beaufort in the westcountry, Lord Yarmouth in Norfolk, Lords Peterborough, Abingdon and Ferrers in the midlands, helped the Crown by making complaints about the towns in their districts.  As a result of their complaints, the Court issued writs of *Quo Warranto*, to enquire by what charters the towns claimed their rights.  Few towns could withstand such close scrutiny.  As more and more towns forfeited their charters, so many others yielded up theirs voluntarily, hoping to appease the King and begging for new charters.  The Crown carefully re-modelled the town constitutions, nominating the first office holders and reserving the right to approve or reject the corporations' suggestions for their successors.  The greatest corporation of all, London, had to submit in 1683 and accept a new charter.  Henceforth every Lord Mayor and every sheriff had to be approved by the King.  If the corporation would not propose someone acceptable to him, he would himself appoint the official directly.  Charles intended to have no more Whig sheriffs in London.

At the same time the Clarendon Code was enforced more strictly.  The association between Whiggery and Nonconformity during the three Whig Parliaments had been clear; the King's friends had taunted all their opponents with being Presbyterians.  Now that Tories and Anglicans were once more in command, they again tried to weaken the political power of their opponents by suppressing their religious meetings and arresting the more persistent Nonconformists.  During the winter of 1683–4, in weather so cold that the Thames at London was frozen for over six weeks, there were more than 1300 Quakers shivering in prison.  Thousands of Dissenters emigrated to America, among them many Quakers travelling to the new settlement which Charles II had granted to William Penn early in 1681.

After his trial, Shaftesbury left the Tower a broken man.  He still kept up his connexion with Monmouth, and sent him into the northcountry in the autumn of 1682 to add to his popularity there by displaying his handsome face and skill at running and riding.  Then Shaftesbury involved himself in rash discussions with desperate Covenanters and men like Wildman, a leading Leveller thirty years before.  In the midst of these subversive activities he lost his nerve.  With warrants out for his arrest, he slipped away to Holland in November 1682 and died there two months later.  There was now no man capable of keeping the remaining Whigs together.

But the Whigs had not yet drained their cup of sorrows.  Their 'Council of Six' – Monmouth, Russell, Sidney, Essex, Howard and Hampden[1] – had foolishly joined in a plot with some old Cromwellian soldiers and other malcontents, though not all of them were fully committed.  The King was to be murdered at Rye House (near Hoddesdon) as he rode back

[1] Grandson of the opponent of Ship-Money.

to London from Newmarket races in April 1683, and Anne (James's younger daughter) was to be placed on the throne. These plans were disrupted when Charles returned from Newmarket a week earlier than had been expected. The conspirators could not keep silent. One of the minor accomplices 'informed'; Howard turned 'King's evidence'; Essex cut his throat while awaiting trial; Sidney and Russell went to the scaffold; Hampden was fined £40,000, and Monmouth was pardoned. The Rye House Plot completed the dismemberment of the first Whig party, and Charles humbled some of the greatest families in the country.

The work of retribution went steadily on. The old Whig sheriffs of London were fined for criticizing the Duke of York and for disorders at the sheriff-elections of 1682, one of them (Pilkington) having to pay over £100,000. The former Lord Mayor had to flee to Holland to escape trial for perjury after testifying on Pilkington's behalf. Chief Justice Pemberton was too slow to satisfy the King, and Charles replaced him with the ruthless George Jeffreys. The judicial bench became the pliant and obedient instrument of royal absolutism. The tradition of Coke and Crew seemed to have had fallen asleep.

By changes in the administration, too, Charles seemed to be preparing for absolutism. James came back from exile, and soon resumed control of the Navy. Sunderland became Secretary of State. Lawrence Hyde received an earldom, and as Lord Rochester served as Treasury Commissioner and then as Lord Privy Seal. Judge Jeffreys became a Privy Councillor. These men, together with his mistress, the Duchess of Portsmouth, and the French ambassador Barrillon, dominated Charles's last government.

Strangely enough, this assertion of royal power was popular, especially after the Rye House Plot had reminded the country of the perils of anarchy. In April 1683 the 'smart lads' of Oxford had been shouting 'A Monmouth!' outside All Souls'. By September, the 'smart lads' were

crying for the King and the Duke of York, and all people had York in their mouths, and his health was drank publickly in most halls at dinner.[1]

For the last four years of his reign, Charles managed without

[1] A. à Wood, *Life and Times*, p. 267.

Parliament. By the time of his death a meeting was nearly eleven months overdue, but there was now no means of enforcing the original Triennial Act. The King feared that to revive Parliament would be to revive Whiggery, or at least to give the opposition in Parliament a chance to re-form. Fortunately for Charles, Louis still wanted to keep England out of continental affairs while he absorbed Strasbourg and Luxemburg, and was prepared to help Charles yet again. Moreover, in the interests of monarchy he felt obliged on principle to help a fellow-monarch, and he particularly wanted to ensure the succession of Catholic James. Subsidies from France and the unexpectedly high yield of the customs kept the Crown solvent. Even the standing army was brought to a high pitch of efficiency. As they reviewed their troops on Putney Heath in October 1684 Charles and James could congratulate themselves on possessing one of the essentials of absolute monarchy. Of the other – a devoted bureaucracy – there was perhaps more doubt. The judges were loyal, and for the time being it suited the country magnates and squires to serve the Crown (and themselves) as J.P.s and militia officers and to watch over the town corporations. The Tory alliance of bishop and peer, parson and squire was a reliable social foundation for the monarchy. But the events of 1685–8 were to show that without this support the throne would quickly topple.

Charles's end came suddenly. He had an apoplectic fit on February 2nd, 1685. For four days the surgeons bled him, cupped him, purged him and made him vomit. All was in vain. As he was nearing the end, he gave his keys to his brother, asked him to look after his mistresses and his children, and, as Evelyn records, 'entreated the Queen to pardon him (not without cause)'. A little while before he died, he sent away the Anglican bishops waiting to give him Holy Communion, and was received into the Roman Catholic Church by Father Huddleston, whom James had smuggled in by the back-stairs.

Charles was probably the most popular and least worthy of the Stuart kings of England, but the monarchy was nevertheless stronger than it had been since the reign of Henry VII nearly two centuries earlier. The Treasury had an adequate income, there were no foreign enemies, the country was united, the Church powerful, the merchants prosperous, and the King apparently master of the constitution. To men like Evelyn who could remember the 'villany of the rebels' on that grim January day thirty-six years earlier, the events of Charles's reign seemed a bewildering kaleidoscope of changes. 'The history of his reign', he wrote, 'will certainly be the most wonderful for the variety of matter and accidents, above any extant in former ages: the sad tragical death of his father, his banishment and hardships, his miraculous restoration, conspiracies against him, parliaments, wars, plagues, fires, comets, revolutions abroad happening in his time, with a thousand other particulars.'[1]

## v. *Trade and the Colonies, 1660–89*

The reign of Charles II was at least as important as the Interregnum in the history of trade and colonial development. More cosmopolitan than his ancestors, Charles was personally interested in overseas matters, and his exile in Holland had shown him how a tiny country could grow rich through commerce. The King's enthusiasm was shared by his Court, who invested eagerly in the new trading companies founded in the reign. The Duke of York was the first Governor of the Royal African Company, which received its charter in 1663, and Charles, the Queen and Prince Rupert were among the shareholders. James was also Governor of the Royal Fishery Company, founded in 1664; it did little fishing, but ran a profitable lottery. The Hudson's Bay Company was presided over first by Rupert and then by James. Significantly, it received its charter in the year of the Treaties of Dover, although it infringed French claims to North America: Louis might pull the strings of English diplomacy in Europe, but the strings could not reach across the Atlantic. Early in his reign, Charles's interest in colonial development led him to appoint a committee of the Privy Council to advise him on the plantations. This committee was the forerunner of the Board of Trade established by William III, and also in some ways the ancestor of the Cabinet system.

In general, Charles merely continued and developed the colonial and commercial policies of the Commonwealth and Protectorate. Many of the old advisers stayed on after 1660:

[1] J. Evelyn, *Diary*, vol. ii, p. 211.

Ashley Cooper, Downing, Povy, Modyford. The Navigation Act of 1660 demonstrated this continuity. It insisted that all trade between England and the colonies, as well as the coastal trade of England and Ireland, should be carried in English ships, with crews at least three-quarters of whom were Englishmen; that only English subjects could be merchants and agents in the colonies; that foreign goods brought into England must be shipped directly from their countries of origin; and that 'enumerated' commodities – sugar, tobacco, raw cotton and dyestuffs – produced in the colonies must not be exported except to England, Ireland, or other English colonies. Other clauses specified how these instructions were to be enforced. The purpose of the Act was obviously to exclude interlopers such as the Dutch from profiting from the English plantations, either as traders or ship owners. The 1660 Act did not ban direct trade between the colonies and foreign countries in goods other than the 'enumerated' commodities – but an Act of 1663 'for the Encouragement of Trade' filled this gap and tried to reserve for England alone all her colonial trade. The Treaty of Breda (1667) moderated the Navigation system slightly by allowing the Dutch to export to England goods from Germany and the Spanish Netherlands, but across the Atlantic the laws were made even more burdensome. An Act of 1673 forbade the colonies to trade in the 'enumerated' articles even between themselves, and the government also tried to prevent ships with colonial produce docking in Ireland. There was, however, one Act which broke away from Commonwealth policy: a law passed in 1663 expressly legalized the export of bullion. For half a century the East India Company had been criticized for depleting the country's bullion reserves by sending out gold and silver for the purchase of goods in the East, where there was no demand for English woollens and coal. Sir Joshua Child now persuaded the King and Parliament to legalize what had always been the Company's practice, on the grounds that the re-export of Indian calicoes and other goods would bring in more bullion than was exported originally to purchase them.

It was of course extremely difficult to enforce unpopular laws on settlements three thousand miles away. The colonists welcomed Dutch traders, as they were usually willing to charge less than English merchants. Nonetheless, despite highly-organized piracy and smuggling, the Navigation system benefited English trade. Tobacco imports from Virginia and Maryland almost doubled between the Restoration and the end of the century, most of the increase coming in Charles's reign. In London the tobacco sold for about a shilling a pound, though the planter was lucky to get more than a penny; the Crown collected two pence from customs and impositions, but the remainder, three-quarters of the sale price, enriched the merchant, the ship-owner and the shopkeeper. By the end of the century the tobacco trade alone was worth a quarter of a million pounds a year. The sugar trader (though not always the grower) was just as prosperous: by 1700 over forty million pounds a year were imported, with a value of £630,000, and the housewife could buy it for less than half the 1660 price. In the same period the import of calicoes and linens increased enormously, to a value of £1¼ millions a year. By the end of the century, the imports of manufactured goods like linen, the imports of commodities like tobacco and wine, and the imports of raw materials like silk, flax and timber, each averaged about £2 millions a year. The total value of exports was even higher, and England had a favourable trade balance of nearly half a million pounds a year. This great commercial expansion made the fortunes of the luckier merchants: Joshua Child rose from being a merchant's apprentice to dominate the East India Company, to build a huge house in Epping Forest, and to marry his daughter to the Duke of Beaufort's heir – with a £50,000 dowry.

The Treaty of Breda ending the Second Dutch War confirmed England's acquisition of New Netherland. Charles granted the territory to his brother, as a proprietary colony modelled on Maryland. James's administration was a good one, and New York prospered with the development of trade and communications. His governors kept on good terms with the neighbouring Indians, and eventually fortified it strongly against attack (after the Dutch had captured it in 1673 and restored it in the Treaty of Westminster). James granted the southern part of his territory to Berkeley and Carteret, and there they founded New Jersey. The early history of this colony was not a happy one: there were bitter arguments over religion (for it admitted Nonconformists, including Quakers), and the colonists also suffered from squabbles between James and the lessees. Similar troubles affected Carolina, founded in

1663 as a proprietary colony granted to a group of eight courtiers including Clarendon and Ashley Cooper. This enormous area was peopled only very thinly with settlers, for the land was infertile and the climate unattractive, and for many years the colony had to endure a variety of radical constitutions. During the 1680s, however, its policy of religious toleration attracted more settlers. The last of the new colonies was Pennsylvania, granted to William Penn in 1681. Penn was the son of Cromwell's admiral, and was a close friend of James, although a Quaker. Partly because Charles had borrowed heavily from Penn, James was able to persuade the King to grant Penn a charter for the area west of New York, and it was there that he established Philadelphia as his capital. The new settlement was tolerant in matters of religion, and attracted many Quakers. The founder's high ideals were shown by the kindness with which the Indians were treated.

Things were rather different in the New England Confederation. Here the brutality of the settlers provoked expensive wars with the Indians, and narrow Puritan intolerance led to the torture and execution of Quakers. After the Restoration Massachusetts resisted royal authority by sheltering fugitive regicides and by hostility towards Anglicans. England was too concerned at first with getting the Navigation Acts observed to act swiftly to deal with this political challenge. Before long, Massachusetts had grown too powerful to be brought easily to heel: she was dominating her partners in the Confederation – Plymouth, Connecticut and New Haven – and her port of Boston was very prosperous, with industries concerned with shipbuilding, iron founding and manufacturing prefabricated wooden houses for export to the West Indies. In 1676, however, Danby appointed, to investigate the colony's affairs, a Commissioner who soon produced a scathing indictment showing that she was already acting as though independent of England. In 1683 a writ of *Quo Warranto* challenged the settlers' rights; next year the Court of Chancery declared that Massachusetts's charter was forfeit. At the same time Charles cancelled the charters of Connecticut and Rhode Island, and then prepared a grandiose scheme for combining Massachusetts, Rhode Island, Connecticut, New York and New Jersey in a great crown colony of New England. But the first two Governors, Colonel Kirke and

Edmund Andros, failed to weld the settlements together; the men of Boston rebelled as soon as they heard of the Revolution of 1688, and New England promptly fell apart.

Maryland, the original proprietary colony, had a difficult time after the Restoration.   There were too many small farms, and the colony was too dependent on tobacco.   In years of good harvest the planters produced far more than they could sell, and prices were ruinously low.   The colonists opposed the Navigation Acts, and nearly forfeited their charter in 1684 after the Deputy Governor had murdered a customs officer. Virginia was more prosperous than Maryland, although also largely reliant upon tobacco, but had her troubles as well.   Her Governor, Berkeley, was a doddering old man who did little to protect the colony against enemies, European or Indian.   In 1676 a young settler named Bacon organized a protest demanding adequate defence; the protest quickly exploded into rebellion.   Berkeley suppressed the revolt, but Commissioners went out from England to investigate, with the result that the Governor was dismissed in disgrace.

The West Indian colonies, with one exception, were only moderately successful after the Restoration.   The English fleet defended the Leeward Islands from the French and Dutch, but could not make the islanders pay the costs of administration and defence.   The Windward Islands were prosperous at first, and bought hundreds of slaves from the Royal African Company at £16 a head, but suffered when the price of sugar in England dropped.   The sugar refiners of Barbados, in particular, complained bitterly about the duties on sugar imports into England, heavier on refined than on unrefined sugar (to protect English refiners).   In Jamaica, however, the Restoration period was one of uninterrupted prosperity, based on sugar, indigo, cocoa – and piracy!   The notorious buccaneer Captain Morgan was lieutenant-governor of the island in the 1670s.   By then, Jamaica's population was about 15,000, having expanded quickly when the government from 1663 to 1668 allowed her exports to enter England free of duty.

In the East, Catherine of Braganza's dowry involved England in more trouble than had been anticipated.   Tangiers proved too isolated to prosper as a commercial centre, though it was useful as a harbour from which the navy could dominate the Straits of Gibraltar.   The maintenance of Tangiers cost about

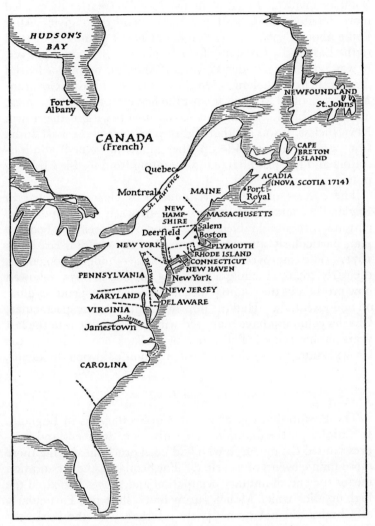

English Colonies in North America

£70,000 p.a., and Charles was probably wise to evacuate it in 1683 – having failed to find a purchaser for it. Even Bombay involved England in trouble, for Charles demanded more territory than Portugal had intended to give! After losing about £5000 p.a. on Bombay, Charles granted it in 1668 to the East India Company for £10 p.a. rent. Soon, however, it was prospering under Governor Aungier, despite a fearful death rate from cholera. On the east coast of India, Governor Masters fortified Madras against the fierce Mahratta tribesmen, and established an efficient government within the town. Nevertheless, it was another eighty years before the East India Company directors made up their minds to be civil administrators and not just merchants operating from fortified trading posts.

The success of these developments is clearly reflected in England's commercial expansion. Between 1660 and 1680 customs revenues doubled, from £300,000 to nearly £600,000 p.a., particularly after the 'farming' of the customs ceased in 1671. The improved yield of the excise – under £300,000 in the early 1660s, reaching a peak of £700,000 in 1675 – showed how prosperous the country was, for people were spending more on non-essentials. Had the improvement been less spectacular, Charles could not have managed without Parliament in the last years of his reign. Politically as well as economically, the Crown's interest in trade and colonization paid rich dividends.

### vi. Scotland

The Restoration was as popular in Scotland as in England. In Edinburgh the fountains ran with wine, and bells and bonfires saluted the monarch who had been proclaimed King there more than eleven years earlier. For Scotland, the Restoration meant the end of military occupation and, it was hoped, of the high taxation which Monck's army had collected. Particularly as Charles did not immediately interfere with the Kirk, the Scots were glad to see a Stuart back on the throne. With this encouraging welcome the Crown quickly resumed its former powers over the Privy Council and the Lords of the Articles. It thus re-established control over the Scottish Parliament. In this work, Charles relied for twenty years on the crafty and efficient Earl of Lauderdale. As Secretary of the Scottish

Privy Council, Lauderdale forwarded to Edinburgh the instructions of Clarendon (and later the Cabal). His fellow-Councillors were usually able to make Parliament accept them.

Parliament assembled in Edinburgh in January 1661, and immediately turned its back on the recent past. In return for Charles's promise 'not to retaine any remembrance . . . of the failings of his Subjects dureing those unhappie tymes', the Act Rescissory cancelled all the Acts passed since 1633. An oath of supremacy forced all those in public employment to acknowledge Charles as 'supreme governor of this kingdom over all persons and in all causes'. Another Act temporarily permitted Presbyterian worship and organization to continue until the King decided what to do with the Church, but meanwhile several leading ministers were persuaded to accept consecration as bishops. Among those who travelled to London for ordination was James Sharp, a former Covenanter who now showed such zeal for episcopacy that he was made Archbishop of St. Andrews. Altogether, the Scottish Restoration Parliament hurried through 393 Acts in the first six months. By the summer of 1661 it had granted Charles the sole right to summon and dismiss Parliaments, and to make war and peace, as well as promising him an annual income of £40,000 in English money.[1] In the following year, within a few weeks of the passing in England of the Act of Uniformity, the Scottish Parliament restored the bishops to their spiritual, disciplinary and parliamentary duties, outlawed the *Solemn League and Covenant*, banned conventicles, and ordered all preachers and schoolmasters to seek licences from their bishops.

Another Act of 1662 ordered all clergy who had not been nominated by lay patrons[2] and 'collated' by bishops or presbytery to secure patronal presentation and episcopal consecration within a month. As a matter of principle, nearly 300 ministers refused to do this, and were deprived of their parishes. Next year, further Acts forbade the deprived ministers to live within twenty miles of their former parishes, and ordered that laymen refusing to attend divine service should forfeit a quarter of their incomes. In 1669 an Act of Supremacy laid down in uncompromising terms the powers of the King: the government and policy of the Church 'doth propperlie belong to his Majestie'

[1] A Scottish pound was worth only one-twelfth of an English pound.
[2] Lay patronage had been abolished in 1649.

as an inherent right of the Crown.    Although at first there was only slight opposition, the deprived ministers were not as ready to surrender unto Caesar as the Act hoped.

At first the settlement seemed moderate.    It was even less bloody than in England, claiming only two victims: Argyle suffered in May 1661 the fate to which he had sent Montrose, and bigoted old Warriston followed him in 1663.    With these two veteran Covenanters out of the way, there was no obvious leader for a revival of Presbyterianism.    Moreover, Charles did not attempt to impose 'Laud's Liturgy', and public worship continued much as before.    With the connivance of moderate bishops, the kirk sessions, presbyteries and synods still operated effectively in many areas, though the General Assembly ceased to meet.

However, this tolerant arrangement was ended by the enthusiasm of the new Archbishop of St. Andrews.    Sharp was an unfortunate appointment, for the moderate and scholarly Bishop Leighton of Dunblane would have been a Primate more in keeping with the needs of the time.    Knowledge that many of the deprived ministers were still preaching to their congregations secretly in houses or on the wind-swept moors made Sharp angry, and in 1664 he persuaded the Council to revive a Court of High Commission to end such obstinacy.    But in many areas – the south-western counties and Fife – where the landlords remained Presbyterian at heart, the Council and the new Court had no means of enforcing their orders except by sending soldiers.    Officers like Tom Dalziel, trained in the Russian army, did not use gentle methods when they led their troopers to collect fines and taxes and to impose the Church laws upon stubborn Covenanters.    Soon the men going to the 'field conventicles' stopped relying on secrecy alone, and to protect their families took weapons with them on their Sabbath pilgrimages. Moreover, the stubborn Covenanters – or 'Whiggamores' – were so much in sympathy with the Dutch during the War of 1665–7 that England feared a major rebellion, in concert with a Dutch invasion.    It was, however, the repressive policies of Sharp and Rothes, the High Commissioner, rather than pro-Dutch sentiment, which provoked the only revolt of this period.    In a desperate little rising in November 1666, nearly a thousand rebels dashed towards Edinburgh, but were routed by Dalziel in the Pentland Hills south of the capital.

This period of persecution did not last long. It was checked by the fall of Clarendon, who had been Sharp's principal supporter in England. Soon afterwards Charles removed Rothes to the less influential post of Chancellor. In 1669 the King issued a moderate Letter of Indulgence, promising to restore deprived ministers to their former parishes if they would accept episcopacy and the royal supremacy. When Archbishop Burnet of Glasgow protested at such tolerance, the Council dismissed him and replaced him by promoting the mild Bishop Leighton. This attempt to gain goodwill came too late, for very few of the deprived ministers were prepared to submit to these terms. The time for conciliation had gone, and the situation was made even more critical by the failure of proposals for union between England and Scotland. For some four years the discussions had ranged through familiar problems, once again bedevilled by the jealous fears of merchants and by past centuries of prejudice. Lauderdale himself was opposed to union, for by it he would have lost his uniquely-privileged position. He realized too that after union it would be much harder for Charles to use the Scottish army against England in time of emergency. After intrigues which degenerated into 'a drunken scuffle in the dark' (Archbishop Leighton), Charles brought the negotiations to an end in March 1671.

This was the signal for Lauderdale to begin another period of repression. New Acts in 1674 and 1677 forced employers and landlords to give sureties or 'Bonds' that their tenants and employees would not 'be present at any conventicles, either in houses or in the fields'. Then, partly as a punishment, and partly to provoke them into a rebellion which would provide an excuse for a standing army, Lauderdale called out the 'Highland Host'. Six thousand clansmen followed their chiefs down to the Covenanting areas of the south-west. For six weeks they were quartered on Whiggamore families like the Hamiltons, and terrorized the lands of Ayr, Renfrew and Lanarkshire before returning home with their plunder. The visit of the 'Highland Host' did not provoke the widespread rebellion Lauderdale half-expected, but it added greatly to the bitterness of the Presbyterians, now experiencing the persecution they had enjoyed inflicting a generation before.

There was no general revolt, but some Scots were angry enough to act by themselves. In May 1679 Archbishop Sharp was pulled from his coach and murdered by a gang near St. Andrews. A few weeks later a band of Whiggamores defeated Claverhouse's government troopers at Drumclog. To deal with this threat of disorder, the Duke of Monmouth was appointed Captain-General in Scotland, and he quickly gathered an army large enough to crush the opposition. At first Monmouth offered generous terms to the Whiggamore bands – peace and pardon if they would lay down their arms – but their ministers persuaded them to fight, since the Lord would surely help them. As at Dunbar, the Presbyterian clergy were proved mistaken. The rebels were swiftly defeated in the battle of Bothwell Brig in June 1679. Monmouth tried to be merciful, but the Council was determined to make an example of the prisoners. Two hundred and ten Whiggamore prisoners refused to submit to the Council, and were sentenced to transportation to Barbados as slaves. Their boat was shipwrecked off the Orkneys, and almost all were drowned. Nevertheless, his attempt at leniency stood Monmouth in good stead with the Whigs in England.

The victory at of Bothwell Brig placed the government in a very strong position. Not only did it have a powerful army; it also had the justification for keeping it in existence. The army in Scotland was as disturbing to English Whigs as Strafford's army in Ireland had been to the Long Parliament. As the Exclusion crisis in England reached boiling-point, Charles was careful to make sure of his position in the north. At the end of 1679 he sent his brother James to Scotland as Commissioner to Parliament. Next year, the resignation of Lauderdale through ill-health gave James almost unlimited power in Scotland.

After Bothwell Brig very few of the 'field preachers' remained active. Those who did showed a courage which matched well with their extremism. Chief among them were Cameron and Cargill, leaders of a small group which became known as the Cameronians. In June 1680 they nailed to the town-cross of Sanquhar a declaration in which they renounced their allegiance to Charles and declared 'a war with such a tyrant and usurper and the men of his practices, as enemies to our Lord Jesus Christ'. These wandering prophets did not long survive. Cameron was killed in a skirmish, and Cargill was captured and taken to Edinburgh for execution. Despite attempts by other men, such as James Renwick, to keep the

Covenanting spirit alive, the government's repressive measures had to all appearances succeeded. The Royalist troops led by Dalziel and by John Graham of Claverhouse, had shown how a loyal army could crush opposition. At the same time, the Lord Advocate, Sir George Mackenzie, demonstrated how the judges might bend the law to suit the King – some years before Judge Jeffreys achieved the same in England. The 'bluidy Mackenzie', indeed, boasted that he never lost a case for the Crown. The development of royal autocracy in Scotland was not the least of the worries exciting the Whigs during the Exclusion Struggle. Their fears were well grounded. Four months after the collapse of the Oxford Parliament, the Parliament in Scotland obediently declared that the right of succession to the Crown could not be altered by any law or religious discrimination. Also in 1681, it passed a clumsily-worded Test Act to exclude Presbyterians from public office. For hesitating to accept it, Argyle (son of the victim of 1661) was sentenced to death on trumped-up evidence. He temporarily cheated the hangman by escaping and fleeing to Holland.

By the time of Charles's death in 1685, Scotland was cowed and conformist. It was also mildly prosperous. One of the first Acts of 1661 had created a Council of Trade, and it was quickly followed by a succession of laws to prohibit the export of raw materials, to restrict the import of manufactured articles, and to encourage the introduction of new industries by freeing them of export duties. During the Interregnum Scottish merchants had been permitted to build up an extensive trade with the American colonies. This trade continued after the Restoration, despite the prohibitions of the English Navigation Act, especially when the two Dutch Wars interrupted Scotland's trade with her principal European market. Glasgow, in particular, grew rapidly. For many years economic development was hampered by the lack of capital for investment, but by the end of the reign this was a less serious handicap. In 1681 Parliament extended earlier legislation by ordering a complete system of protection for home manufactures, particularly cloth. The Merchant Company of Edinburgh, chartered in the same year, was followed by some fifty other companies also formed to take advantage of the 1681 Act. Further encouragement came in Acts such as that of 1686, ordering that every corpse should be buried in linen cloth, spun and woven in Scotland.   At the same time, ambitious men were looking overseas, planning to start Scottish colonies in New Jersey and South Carolina – projects which were soon to lead to the disastrous Darien scheme.   With the mines of Fife and elsewhere sending some 50,000 tons of coal a year to England, the country's economy was in fairly good shape.   The Navigation Act and high taxation[1] were still substantial grievances, but at least the money was now paying Scottish, not English, soldiers, and was probably helping to stimulate the economy. Certainly, Scotland seemed very far from general revolution when James VII was hailed as King in February 1685.

## vii. Ireland

In Ireland the Restoration aroused feelings which were more mixed than those in England and Scotland.   The Catholic natives were glad to be freed from 'the curse of Cromwell', but the thousands of Protectorate soldiers given Irish land in lieu of wages were less enthusiastic.   The land problem in Ireland was far more dangerous even than in England.   The Commonwealth's troops had driven the Irish back beyond the Shannon, and by 1660 the Protestant settlers occupied over two-thirds of the 'profitable' land.   Charles's first governor, the Duke of Ormonde, had to try to satisfy the grievances of the dispossessed Irish without angering the Cromwellian soldiers – an impossible task.   The Act of Settlement of 1661 agreed to let the new settlers keep their estates, but promised to compensate evicted Catholics (provided they had supported the Crown during the 1641–6 wars) out of land confiscated but not yet distributed.   There was not enough spare land available, so Ormonde introduced the Act of Explanation in 1663 to force the Cromwellian settlers to surrender one-third of their pre-1660 estates to help compensate the 'innocent' Catholics. These decisions unloosed a flood of law-suits which swamped the Court of Claims, and in desperation that Court had to cease functioning in 1667.   Over 3000 Catholics thereby failed to get restitution.   The land settlement left nearly three-quarters of the population (the Catholics) holding barely one-quarter

---

[1] About £80,000 (English money) a year – £50,000 from customs and excise, and £30,000 from the 'cess' (monthly assessments like those levied by Monck).

of the good land.   The Restoration had done little more than confirm the social and territorial power of the immigrant Protestant settlers.   The land problem so perplexing to nineteenth-century Liberals derived largely from the settlement of the 1660s.

The political weakness of Ireland was another enduring legacy.   Ireland stopped sending M.P.s to Westminster, and her own Parliament was completely under the control of the Cavalier Parliament in England.   During Charles's reign it met only from 1661 to 1666.   The oath of supremacy[1] excluded Catholics from membership, and the Protestants – once assured that they could keep their lands – voted generous taxes. With a revenue from customs, excise, hearth tax and other subsidies, Charles's government in Ireland was usually securely solvent, for income rose during the reign from about £150,000 to £300,000.   As Governor from 1661 to 1668, and again from 1677 to 1685, Ormonde repeated many of Strafford's successes, without arousing the hostility provoked by 'Black Tom Tyrant'. For most of the time, at least, Charles II supported Ormonde loyally, and leaned on him as much as he did on Lauderdale.

Much of Ormonde's success was due to his enlightened religious policy.   Early in the reign a large group of Catholic laymen and a few priests had welcomed the 'Remonstrance' compiled by Bellings and Father Walsh.   The Remonstrance asserted that no 'foreign power' could release Charles's subjects from their allegiance to him, thereby denying the papacy's claims to be able to depose heretical rulers.   But the Catholic bishops and the Papal Nuncio denounced the Remonstrance in 1665, and so ended the Remonstrants' hopes of winning full legal toleration.   In the period 1670 to 1677, when Lord Berkeley and Lord Essex served as Viceroys, the Catholics' hopes rose again, for the governors permitted them to purchase town houses without taking the prescribed oath of supremacy. At the same time Charles sent Prince Rupert to investigate the claims of dispossessed Catholic landlords.   Unfortunately, the Cavalier Parliament in 1673 forced Charles to recall Rupert's Commission, as part of the anti-Catholic measures which were exacted in return for aid against the Dutch.   But the government never enforced the penal laws against the Catholics, and

---

[1] Acknowledging the King as Head of the Church, the oath became a shibboleth to exclude Catholics from public or political office.

in general prevented the Titus Oates scare from disturbing Ireland. The Plot claimed only one notable Irish victim, Oliver Plunkett, the aged Catholic Archbishop of Armagh. His execution at Tyburn in July 1681 was inexcusable, for by that time the Whigs were in disorder. The Catholics were not actively persecuted in Ireland, but the Anglicans had all the advantages. The Anglican Church had been re-established there in 1661, with two archbishops and ten bishops consecrated together in Dublin Cathedral. It served the needs of the ruling class, but collected tithes indiscriminately from Catholic and Protestant alike. Most of the former Presbyterians and Independents soon came to accept Anglicanism; in Ireland, Protestant Dissent ceased to be a serious problem, except among the Scottish settlers in Ulster.

Ireland was fairly prosperous in the post-Restoration years, despite the selfish policies of England. Ormonde followed Strafford's example in trying to develop industries for producing linen and woollen cloth at Carrick, Clonmel and Dublin. These attempts were stifled by English laws restricting the import of Irish textiles, and by the Navigation Acts banning the Irish from participation in colonial trade. Despite Ormonde's protests, the Cavalier Parliament decided to protect English farming from Irish competition: in 1663 an Act forbade the importation of Irish cattle during the summer and autumn, and in 1666 this prohibition was extended throughout the whole year. As the Irish tried to develop sheep rearing and dairy farming, so England increased the number of prohibited imports. By 1681 the protectionists at Westminster had banned the import of Irish cattle, sheep, lamb, butter and cheese. Moreover, the Navigation laws prevented Ireland from trading directly with the American plantations, and other laws excluded her from fishing for whales off Greenland, or for 'stockfish' off Newfoundland. In these circumstances of oppression and restriction – in which Ireland suffered all the handicaps of the Old Colonial System with very few of the advantages – it is surprising that the country managed to be relatively prosperous. The victualling of America-bound ships at Cork and other ports provided a useful outlet for farm produce, and there was also a ready market in England for coarse Irish wool. But the restoration of law and order was probably the principal reason for the country's economic recovery during the reign of Charles II.

## viii. The Church militant

For several months after the Restoration it was uncertain what form the religious settlement would take. The Presbyterians in the resurrected Long Parliament and in the Convention had played the major part in restoring Charles. In less happy days the King himself had 'taken the Covenant'. At Breda he had promised 'liberty to tender consciences', and in October 1660 he issued a further Declaration allowing wide toleration until a future national synod settled the controversies. Even when it became clear that the old episcopal Church of England would be restored in some form or other, it remained uncertain whether it would be the uncompromising, intolerant Church of Laud, or one which would make concessions sufficient to entice the Presbyterians to return to it. Charles favoured the latter, but the Cavaliers who swarmed into the Commons in 1661 demanded the former.

There were many obstacles to a peaceful settlement. Most of the existing parish clergy had accepted the *Solemn League and Covenant*, often to avoid eviction. Those who had refused to conform to Presbyterianism had been ejected, and were now demanding the return of their benefices. The newer clergy had not been ordained by bishops. Enthusiastic Puritans had wrecked organs, smashed stained-glass windows, burnt vestments and Prayer Books, knocked down altar-rails and seized Communion vessels, candlesticks and altar crosses. Many churches had fallen into disrepair. Death had emptied many of the bishoprics, and episcopal authority itself had been outlawed for sixteen years. While many Presbyterians were prepared to accept the return of the bishops (to help suppress the Independents), they were as opposed as ever to ceremonial and to the Romish survivals in the Book of Common Prayer – which their own Directory of Public Worship had replaced since 1644.

Charles's spirit of compromise was soon out of date. In the month after the Restoration, young Samuel Pepys was already gaping at the organ, the surpliced choir and the 'overdone' ceremonies in the King's Chapel at Whitehall. Old bishops like Juxon of London and Duppa of Salisbury had the King's ear: Juxon was elevated to Canterbury and other Laudian clergy were quickly nominated to the other vacant sees. They attempted with some success to win over Presbyterian leaders like Baxter, Calamy and Reynolds, in the hope that the 'rank and file' would follow them in accepting the return of episcopal authority.    It was as Bishop of Norwich that Reynolds attended the promised national synod.

This met in April 1661 at the Savoy, the palace of Sheldon, the Bishop of London.    Twelve episcopal and twelve Presbyterian representatives attended it.    Sheldon, who presided as Juxon was ill, took it for granted that bishops and Prayer Book would be restored, and put the Presbyterians on the defensive by asking them to state their objections.    Baxter as their principal (and very tedious) spokesman was prepared to accept a 'limited' episcopacy such as that proposed by Archbishop Ussher twenty years before, but he was still doggedly against the Prayer Book.    Although Bishops Reynolds and Gauden tried to be conciliatory, the certainty that the King was now on their side made the episcopalians impatient with Baxter's pedantic obstinacy over trifles.    Baxter had met his match: even he had to bow to the knowledge of Cosin and Gunning about the practices of the early Church.    When the bishops took their seats in the new House of Lords, and the Cavalier Parliament ordered the *Solemn League and Covenant* to be burnt, the episcopalians knew there was no need for them to compromise.    So the Savoy Conference ended in failure.

Nevertheless, when the Convocations subsequently revised the Prayer Book they offered some minor concessions to the Puritans.[1]    The main one was a comment, after the service of Holy Communion, that kneeling to receive Communion did not imply 'Adoration . . . either unto the Sacramental Bread and Wine . . . or unto any Corporal Presence of Christ's natural Flesh and Blood'.    They added a new service for the baptism of adults (for baptizing 'Natives in our Plantations' and those who had not been christened as children during the Interregnum), and provided additional prayers for those at sea – a reflection of England's new maritime interests.    There were also new prayers to commemorate King Charles the Martyr. In April 1662 Parliament passed the Act of Uniformity imposing the use of the new Prayer Book, and ordering all clergy and

[1] The Preface printed at the beginning of Anglican Prayer Books explains the motives behind the revision of 1662.

schoolmasters to swear that they accepted it, to repudiate the *Solemn League and Covenant*, and deny that it could ever be right to take up arms against the King. Moreover, all parish clergy who had not been ordained by a bishop had to obtain episcopal ordination by St. Bartholomew's Day or give up their parishes. In all, nearly 2000 clergy surrendered their parishes, in addition to some hundreds evicted earlier when 'extruded' Anglicans secured the return of their benefices. The prejudices of the Cavalier Parliament and the unrealistic attitude of the Presbyterians at the Savoy Conference had wasted a splendid chance to unite England's two largest religious groups.

The Cavaliers' vindictiveness did not stop with the Act of Uniformity. The Corporation Act of 1661 had already excluded Dissenters from membership of town corporations, in an attempt to weaken the political power of Puritanism. The Act of Uniformity turned them out of the churches and the schools; the Conventicle Act of 1664 prevented them meeting for worship, and the Five Mile Act of 1665 forbade former ministers to approach within five miles of any corporate town or place where they had previously preached. After the abortive attempt of the first Declaration of Indulgence in 1662, Charles had to accept this bitter 'Clarendon Code' as the price of getting taxes from his Parliament.

The Anglican Church created by the Clarendon Code was intolerant towards all other sects, closely tied to the Cavalier majority in Parliament, and deeply loyal to the Crown and the principle of hereditary monarchy. The old doctrine of the Divine Right of Kings lost some ground in favour of the more sophisticated belief in the duty of Passive Obedience, but for nearly thirty years after the Restoration the Church (and in particular the bishops in the House of Lords) appeared the most dependable of the Crown's supporters. Archbishop Juxon did not long survive, and in 1663 he and his old master Laud[1] were buried side-by-side in the Chapel of St. John's College, Oxford.

For the next fourteen years Gilbert Sheldon was Archbishop of Canterbury. Sheldon was prepared to criticize the King's immorality, but was otherwise a devoted advocate of Divine Right – even though he fell from favour in 1670 and afterwards took little part in political affairs. Imprisonment and eviction

---

[1] His corpse was moved from Barking, where it had been buried after his execution in 1645.

from his Oxford fellowship in 1648 had made him hostile to the Dissenters, at the Savoy Conference and in subsequent years, and many of the other bishops took their cue from him. Like his two predecessors, he was deeply loyal to Oxford, and as the university's Chancellor gave £25,000 for a building more suitable for the bawdy Degree ceremonies than was St. Mary's Church. Wren's Sheldonian Theatre is still used for this purpose, even though the ceremonies are now more dignified! After Sheldon's death, William Sancroft succeeded him at Canterbury. The new archbishop was by repute a timid man, and served the Crown obediently during the Exclusion Struggle; the events of 1688–9, however, were to show that Sancroft was made of sterner stuff than James II and William III suspected.

Charles did not revive the political powers of the old Laudian bishops. No Churchman held high office in the state. The Church Courts declined, under the continual assault of writs of prohibition transferring cases to the secular courts. The King did not try to restore in England the old Court of High Commission. Meetings of Convocation became less important as the clergy were no longer taxed separately. With the creation of new peers the proportion of bishops in the House of Lords became smaller. On the other hand, the Church did retain its authority over publication: by the Licensing Acts of 1662 and 1685 the Archbishop of Canterbury and the Bishop of London were ordered to inspect all books except those written on law, history or heraldry. This power did much to stifle intellectual thought, after the relative freedom of the Commonwealth.

Yet the Church itself enjoyed a remarkable spiritual renaissance. Enforced idleness during the Commonwealth had given many clergymen time for travel and study. The researches of Bishops Cosin and Gunning on the Early Fathers, and the publications of Canon Thorndike on the Eucharist, and Bishops Pearson and Bull on the Creeds, were particularly celebrated. For his treatise on the Nicene Creed George Bull won the respect of Bossuet and a formal vote of congratulation from the French Catholic clergy. Bishops Wilkins and Sprat were enthusiastic members of the Royal Society. In his 1667 *History of the Royal Society* Sprat insisted that the Church must accept the new scientific discoveries if it was to be 'fit for the present genius of this nation'. His successors in the nineteenth century were much less progressive.

Attempts to reconcile religion and science also inspired the Cambridge Platonists, mostly fellows of Emmanuel College, who followed Henry More, Benjamin Whichcote and Ralph Cudworth in claiming that man must use his reason in judging religious truths. They were influenced by Plato, and by their near-contemporary, the Frenchman Descartes. Their beliefs made them advocate a tolerant church, for they could not deny that Dissenters too might be guided by 'the spirit in man [which] is the candle of the Lord'. The nickname originally given them – Latitudinarians – was later applied to their intellectual successors, Stillingfleet, Tillotson and Tenison. These were distinguished, broad-minded and moderate men, who deplored enthusiasm and urged the need for common sense. Their apparent lack of zeal and their scientific interests earned them sneers as 'Socinians' who. . . .

. . . nature's King through nature's optics [telescopes] view'd.
Revers'd they view'd him lessen'd to their eye,
Nor in an Infant could a God descry. . . .

The philosophical ideas of intellectual bishops may have been above the heads of most worshippers, but the Latitudinarians' zeal for down-to-earth preaching came to have a profound effect. By the end of the century the Anglican Church was a preaching Church, not a sacramental Church as Laud had planned. This was reflected in the design of Wren's churches built in London after the Fire: their design emphasized the pulpit, not the altar. The works of Jeremy Taylor, *Holy Living* and *Holy Dying*, became increasingly popular and influential, and Taylor was rewarded with bishoprics in the Anglican Church in Ireland. Another widely-read devotional book was the anonymous *Whole Duty of Man*, almost a textbook of Non-Resistance, teaching the poor to look for 'pie in the sky', for a heavenly reward for patient sufferings on earth.

The best of the bishops were as active in their pastoral as in their intellectual work. After the Restoration, largely through the keenness of the bishops, the traditional parish services were quickly brought back, and the missing Church and altar furnishings replaced. Less commendable, though, was the action of the bishops who enriched themselves rather than the Church by pocketing the 'entry fines' paid for renewing the many Church leases which had expired during the interregnum. Indeed, the return of the bishops meant that the parish clergy were generally worse off than before the Restoration.

But the worst side of the Restoration Church was its attitude to the Nonconformists. Even though most dispossessed Anglican clergy had been fairly well treated under the Commonwealth, the Church was determined to get revenge. Many of the clergy evicted in 1662 were soon imprisoned on trumped-up charges under the Conventicle Act, libellously attacked to discredit them (the Licensing Act prevented reply), and generally hounded around the countryside. Baxter complained 'What a joy would it have been to them that reproached us as Presbyterian seditious schismatics to have found but such an occasion as *praying with a dying woman* to have laid us up in prison!' The Quakers suffered most harshly, for they refused to obey the Conventicle Act at all. Baxter noticed that 'many turned Quakers, because the Quakers kept their meetings openly and went to prison for it cheerfully'. In 1670 the Cavalier Parliament made the law even stricter with a new Conventicle Act imposing fines on people who permitting their homes to be used for religious meetings, and allowing constables to break into houses in search of conventicles. The tyranny of snoopers and professional informers, seeking rewards for denouncing nonconformists, was scarcely more tolerable than the tyranny of Cromwell's Major-Generals had been.

So far from wiping out the Dissenters, the persecutions moulded English Nonconformity, for the first time quite outside the administration and direct authority of the Anglican Church. It was not long before their sufferings made the Nonconformists more popular, especially when dozens of Dissenting clergy crept back to their London congregations after the Plague had frightened away many of the Anglican parsons. The growth of Shaftesbury's Whig party helped to make their grievances heard. Books such as John Bunyan's great allegory, *Pilgrim's Progress*, comforted them as they struggled through the Slough of Despond and past the Restoration's Vanity Fair. Bunyan's own sufferings (he was imprisoned in Bedford Gaol for twelve years) inspired others to follow him. Even the troubles of Restoration England – the Plague, the Fire, the Dutch – could give them some melancholy satisfaction, in seeing the hand of God heavy upon an idolatrous and immoral nation. The themes of Milton's two greatest poems reflect the emotions of Puritans in the later seventeenth century – Man's fall from Grace through taking bad advice (in *Paradise Lost*) and *Samson Agonistes*, God's chosen champion, suffering patiently humiliation and persecution worse even than that of the Clarendon Code, and finally triumphing over those who mocked him.

The law nominally placed on the Roman Catholics burdens even heavier than those on the Dissenters. The old recusancy fines were not revived, but much of the Clarendon Code applied to popery as well as to Nonconformity. The King's attempts to secure toleration for all politically-obedient sects, in the Declarations of Indulgence of 1662 and 1672, conflicted with the Cavaliers' fear of Rome as well as their hatred of Puritanism. Consequently the Test Acts of 1673 and 1678 excluded Catholics from public office and from membership of Parliament. Nevertheless, popery grew at Court, around the households of Queen Catherine, Henrietta Maria the Queen-Mother, and the Duke and Duchess of York. The revival of Catholicism ignited England's Protestant prejudices in the Titus Oates scare, when Charles was forced to sacrifice innocent Catholics to appease the mob and save his brother's right to the throne, but at other times Catholicism was fashionable and therefore safe to practise. In contrast, Nonconformity was too closely associated with Whiggery, political rebellion and lower-class 'enthusiasm' ever to commend itself to courtiers and thereby become 'respectable'.

## ix. Restoration Society

The Clarendon Code and the Militia Act placed political and military power firmly in the hands of the embittered Royalist gentry, and throughout the reign the landowning classes were able to use these powers to increase their economic and social privileges. New laws helped the producer, not the consumer. An Act of 1663 waived the mediaeval prohibitions on regrating and engrossing, thus permitting speculators to corner the market by buying up all available produce and then selling it at scarcity prices. To stimulate the textile industry and help sheep farmers, a law of 1666 ordered that all corpses should be

buried in English woollen shrouds.    To encourage agriculture,
the government paid bounties on corn exports.    Harsh Game
Laws in 1671 forbade the freeholder worth less than £100 a
year to shoot game – even on his own land.    Aided by such
measures, the Royalist landowners planned to make good their
losses in the Civil War.

Many of them were successful, though the less provident had
to sell out to more fortunate merchants.    These gains were
made at the expense of the poorer classes.    The improving
landlord was an enthusiastic encloser, an unscrupulous rack-
renter; in this age of competitive mercantilism, the industrial
employer also was forced to exploit his workers to the uttermost.
The paternal care of monarchs like Elizabeth and Charles I
had been prompted partly by a fear of social disorders if the
poor were not assisted.    Now, with the gentry in control of the
militia, there was little danger from such troubles.    There
were a few outbursts, quickly suppressed – dockyard strikes in
the 1660s, weavers' riots in London, Essex and Wiltshire in the
mid-1670s, and various attempts by carpenters and journeymen
cloth-weavers to form trade unions to keep up wages.    The
wretched conditions of the unemployed helped the authorities
to frighten these movements into submission, and enabled all
employers to keep wages low.

Despite the assistance sometimes provided from the poor rates,
there were so many paupers needing help that most of
them lived below starvation level.    To discourage beggary,
the overseers of the poor made the workhouses as harsh and
brutal as possible.    The J.P.s joined in the work of repression, for an Act of 1662 – in the spirit of the Tudor statutes
against sturdy beggars – allowed them to send back to their
parishes of origin all newcomers to the district who might
become charges upon the poor rates.    The problem of long-
term unemployment and chronic destitution was probably more
serious now than ever before. Restoration England saw
the development of the poor as a distinct social class.

Government action, then, helped to prepare the way for a
competitive capitalist economy.    Except in agriculture, the
Elizabethan Statute of Labour was a dead letter.    There was
no further attempt to breathe life into the dead carcase of the
guild system: three-quarters of the boroughs in England now
had no guilds.    In London the exclusive Masons' Company

lost its monopoly when it could not provide all the labour required for rebuilding after the Fire; even earlier, Parliament threw the linen industry open to all. Great commercial systems like the Merchant Adventurers and the Eastland Company gradually lost their protected trading markets.

In these circumstances little mattered except the acquisition of money. With money successful merchants like Child could buy estates for themselves and noble husbands for their daughters – to the disgust of older families not able to offer such rich dowries. On the other hand, the progressive landowner was often as likely as the merchant to get great wealth. New crops increased the value of land: in some of the more advanced counties turnips and clover were already enabling a few progressive farmers to rear more and better cattle. The landowner with coal seams under his property was especially fortunate, though many men were ruined by unwise colliery ventures. Although it often cost £1000 or more to sink a single shaft, coal was mined in nearly half the counties of Restoration England. The nature of colliery finance, and the inhuman conditions of mining underground, combined to make the mine owner more remote from his workers than was usual in industry; in much of the country this helped to widen the gulf between the divisions of society.

Most, but by no means all, of the profits of industry and trade went on the purchase of land, for ownership of property secured social prestige in a way that possession of full money chests did not. Freehold property gave a man the vote – at least in the counties. Without it, he could not qualify to enter county society by serving with the gentry in the militia, and would be unlikely to get into Parliament. But it was often necessary for the successful man to wait before buying an estate he coveted, and many men deposited their cash with goldsmiths for safe keeping. Increasingly, however, men were prepared to lend money to the Crown, despite discouragements such as the Stop of the Exchequer in 1672. In general the Crown's credit was fairly good, for the repayment of loans was usually guaranteed by promises of specific customs and excise revenue due to be collected. Goldsmiths like Viner loaned large sums of money to Charles, and became widely used as bankers. Even at the height of the Exclusion crisis the Treasury was able to borrow at 8 per cent. interest, partly because it had been established since 1662 that repayments of debts should be made 'in course', that is, in strict rotation. Much of the money borrowed by the Crown still came from the companies farming the taxes, usually as advances upon expected revenues, but individual short-term loans to the government became more and more important. The Exchequer came to spend a large part of its time in administering these loans. During the reign there were many proposals for establishing government-sponsored banks, but it required the war emergency of 1694 to bring these schemes to fruition.

The economic and social rift was widening, between the Crown, the nobles, the financial grandees, the merchants, capitalists and landowners on the one hand, and the weavers, the miners and the farm labourers on the other. This was also true of fashions in manners and morals, though here the division was between the Court and the rest of the country. It was not easy for the ex-Presbyterian or sectary to lay aside Puritan standards at the Restoration, to forget that he had recently been purging the land of evil in preparation for Christ's Second Coming. The Court did not share these inhibitions. The example set by the King was imitated by the courtiers around him. Soon Milton was thundering out in *Samson Agonistes* against spiritual wickedness in high places, and even the lecherous Pepys was complaining of the lewdness of the Court. The theatres, entertaining their fashionable patrons with the cynical and cheerful immoralities of Restoration drama, encouraged the collapse of moral standards, and shocked the more straight-laced Royalists like Evelyn, who recorded in 1666 that

foul and undecent women now (and never till now) [were] permitted to appear and act, who inflaming several young noble men and gallants, became their misses [mistresses], and to some, their wives. Witness the Earl of Oxford, Sir R. Howard, Prince Rupert, the Earl of Dorset, and another greater person than any of them [the King]. . . .

The ugliness of his barren Queen drove Charles to sample the charms of a large number of pretty mistresses, whose bastard children were acknowledged by the King and honoured with peerages. At times the more aristocratic of the mistresses –

Lady Castlemaine and Lady Portsmouth – exercised great influence over him, but Charles seems to have been fondest of the actress Nell Gwynn. When Nelly's coach was attacked by rioters thinking she was the Catholic Lady Portsmouth, she won the mob's support by shouting 'I am the *Protestant whore!*'

Despite the Catholicism of the Court, centring around the Queen-Mother Henrietta Maria, around Catharine of Braganza, and later around the Duke of York, the country at large remained stubbornly hostile to the claims of Rome. Louis XIV emerged as a popish bogy more fearsome than even Philip of Spain had been. Long before the Revocation of Henry IV's tolerant Edict of Nantes in 1685, hundreds of Huguenot families had fled from France to England. Huguenots such as Papillon and Dubois were among the most prosperous merchants in the country. Many of their business rivals – Penn, Child, Kiffen – also were prominent Nonconformists. It was an unfortunate development for the Crown that financiers on whom it relied were men strongly opposed to Louis XIV, to Rome, and to the behaviour of the Court. It was no less significant that the emotions of the common people, once the exuberance of the Restoration had worn off, had nothing in common with the extravagance and the Frenchified manners and morals of the Court.

The popularity of coffee was another social change with unexpected political consequences. Evelyn had not heard of the drink until he met at Oxford in 1640 a student from Greece, but within twenty years it had been introduced and coffee-houses had opened in London. Soon Anthony à Wood was complaining that (then as now) coffee-houses were keeping Oxford undergraduates from their studies. Well before the end of Charles II's reign the coffee-house had become important in political society. The opposition leaders of the 1630s had met privately in the guise of discussing commerce; those of the early 1670s met openly in some favoured coffee-house. Each house attracted different patrons: Whigs, Tories, the clergy, poets, Nonconformists and Quakers could all be sure of meeting their fellows in one or other of them. By the end of the reign, despite the Crown's attempt in 1675 to suppress them, the coffee-house served a gentleman as his political association and as his social club, where he might discuss matters of State or gamble away his property. Altogether, the coffee-house played an important if indirect part in raising the standards of society, and in weaning the man-about-town away from his preoccupation with amorous conquests.

This was also true of two sports which Charles II helped to make popular. One was yachting for pleasure, a Dutch past-time which the King brought back with him. The other was horse-racing. Charles and his courtiers frequently patronized the races at Newmarket, where the King kept a house. Evelyn visited it in 1670, and afterwards rode over Newmarket Heath 'the way being mostly a sweet turf and down, like Salisbury Plain, the jockeys breaking their fine barbs and racers, and giving them their heats'. The 'barbs' were the Barbary stallions which Charles and others were importing to improve the breed. Even horse-racing was coming under foreign influence!

### x. The Arts

Restoration drama and literature faithfully reflect the social divisions of the country. The 'Court Wits' — the Duke of Buckingham ('Zimri'), the Earls of Rochester and Mulgrave, Lord Buckhurst, Etherege and Wycherley – were themselves poets and playwrights; as the patrons of many others, they fostered a peculiarly aristocratic culture. For nearly two decades the theatres had been closed; now there was a splendid chance for the Cavaliers to fill the stage with plays sparkling with French wit and gallantry, with the refined bawdiness suitable for a sophisticated audience. The Restoration comedies were full of amoral attacks on the conventions of marriage. All the bourgeois virtues were satirized. The country squire, the London citizen, the jealous husband were all ridiculed for the amusement of the nobles and ladies of the Court. Etherege's *She Would If She Could* (1668) and *The Man Of Mode* helped to set the fashion, and were joined by Wycherley's *The Country Wife* and *The Plain Dealer*. Wycherley's satire, however, was more brutal and cynical than the carefree cheerfulness of Etherege, and suggests that he was not wholly in sympathy with the spirit of the time. In *Marriage à la Mode* (1672) Dryden captivated the Restoration rakes who were now his patrons, but his heroic dramas were even more successful.

His bombastic and spectacular tragedies like *The Conquest of Granada* and *Aureng-Zebe*, imitating French models, attracted the same audiences as the comedies – courtiers who wished to identify their own performances in love, statecraft and war with those of the characters portrayed.

Technically, at least, the Restoration theatre made notable advances. The general adoption of the proscenium arch gave the stage the 'picture-frame' appearance it retained almost universally until the twentieth century. Actresses were now recognized if not respected, though their talent was often little greater than their virtue. The high cost of producing these plays, as well as their content, limited their audience to the wealthy and witty. There was no place in the Restoration theatre for the Elizabethan groundlings who had cheered the buffoonery of Falstaff. While the comedies were not too far removed from the traditions of Jonson, and Beaumont and Fletcher, the heroic dramas were cast in the alien mould of the contemporary French theatre.

French standards also had a direct influence upon English poetry. For years the arbiter of good taste was M. de Saint-Évremond (whom Charles appointed Keeper of the Ducks in St. James's Park). The formal ceremonies of their court had encouraged French poets to concentrate on the niceties of style and good form, and Boileau's *L'Art Poétique* eclipsed even Dryden's *Essay of Dramatic Poesie* in establishing the fashionable conventions of taste and style. Dryden's own poetry had few rivals, for by now Marvell was concentrating on political pamphleteering and Milton – though publishing his greatest works *Paradise Lost, Paradise Regained* and *Samson Agonistes* in this period – was so much against the current that he must be regarded as a Commonwealth poet. The old Cavalier Sir John Denham, the Surveyor-General of Works, was experimenting with poems which combined scenic descriptions with 'recollections in tranquillity'. Samuel Butler's *Hudibras*, a superb attack on fanaticism and prejudice, set the fashion for verse satire, condemning

> Such as do build their Faith upon
> The holy text of Pike and Gun,
> Decide all Controversies by
> Infallible Artillery. . . .

The part played by Dryden's *Absalom and Achitophel* in the over-throw of Shaftesbury and the Whigs has already been described. It says much for Charles II's frank admission of his own sensual nature that the Poet Laureate dared write

> Then Israel's monarch after Heaven's own heart
> His vigorous warmth did variously impart
> To wives and slaves, and, wide as his command,
> Scattered his Maker's image through the land. . . .

Subsequently Dryden abandoned politics for religion, attacking in *Religio Laici* the claim that faith could be based on reason. Then, after his conversion to Catholicism in James's reign, his *The Hind and the Panther* (1687) expressed the hopes and fears of the moderate Catholics under the reckless King, in a curious zoological allegory about the Panther (the Church of England), the Hind (the Catholic Church), and a whole menagerie of Nonconformist animals.

As a poet Dryden was less profound than Milton, but he was probably superior to him as a prose writer. During some thirty years, from *The Essay of Dramatic Poesie* onwards, Dryden wrote in smooth and elegant sentences a series of commentaries upon stylistic and aesthetic principles. These often appeared as prefaces to his plays or his translations from Homer, Virgil and Ovid. His verse and prose had a circulation wider than that of his plays, but still did not touch the literates among the lower classes. It was left to John Bunyan, a Puritan tinker from Bedford, to provide in *The Pilgrim's Progress* (1678) a prose work which inspired the poor with a homely allegory of 'Christian's' pilgrimage to the Heavenly City. Four years later, Bunyan's *The Holy War* provided an equally stirring allegory of the struggle between good and evil. For the Nonconformist, perhaps suffering – as Bunyan did – imprisonment for defying the Clarendon Code, these works provided spiritual food more nourishing than the biblical and classical obscurities of Milton.

This was also a great age of autobiography. The Diary kept in shorthand by that busy and ambitious Navy clerk, Samuel Pepys, is crammed with intimate detail on the Restoration years 1660–9. The diary of John Evelyn is even more valuable to the historian, as it spans the period 1640 to 1706, and records the reactions of a moderate but sincere Anglican and Royalist to the Revolutionary age in England. The autobiography of Richard Baxter, the Presbyterian divine, and even the Oxford gossip collected by Anthony à Wood, also provide valuable material for the student of English society in the mid-seventeenth century. The merit of these works as pure literature may be limited, but they demonstrate an important development: men were writing prose, just as the 'Court Wits' were dabbling in poetry, for their own personal gratification and satisfaction, with no thought of publication.

In complete contrast were the newspapers, produced for political purposes. Three had appeared in the last years of the Commonwealth, but their circulation was restricted in 1662 by the Licensing Act. Roger L'Estrange served Charles both as Government spy and as editor of the semi-official *The Intelligencer*, supplanted after the Fire of 1666 by the *London Gazette*. The function and even the name of this paper copied the *Gazette* founded by Richelieu as an organ of French Government propaganda. The closing years of the reign saw L'Estrange publishing in support of the Crown other papers – *Heraclitus Ridens* and *The Observator*. Even before this a specialized paper – *The City Mercury* – was being printed for the particular needs of merchants.

The interest in history which lawyers and M.P.s had fostered at the beginning of the century, in decline during the Commonwealth, revived after the Restoration. Within seven years of its foundation, Bishop Sprat was writing the history of the Royal Society. At the time of the Exclusion Struggle, Bishop Burnet was publishing the first part of his *History of the Reformation in England* – which won him a formal compliment from Parliament. A few years later, John Aubrey completed his *Brief Lives*, describing the careers of English worthies of the previous 150 years. Soon, too, the activities of the pamphleteers and philosophers like Locke were to bring English history once more into the forefront of political controversy.

No great native painter was produced by Restoration England. Samuel Cooper and Flatman continued to dominate miniature painting, but the fashionable Court painters were the Dutchman Lely, the German Kneller and the Swede Dahl. In architecture, however, things were very different. The styles favoured were based upon the symmetrical proportions of the Palladian model, tempered by the traditional English hankering after the Gothic, by the Dutch fondness for bricks, and even by the luxuriance of contemporary French and Italian baroque. These conflicting elements might have produced buildings which were nothing but a hotch-potch of irreconcilable characteristics, but the English architects were great enough to avoid such traps. The most eminent of them was Christopher Wren, Professor of Astronomy at Oxford and a founder-member of the Royal Society. His earliest designs were the Chapel of Pembroke College, Cambridge, and the Sheldonian Theatre in Oxford, both based on Roman models. On a visit to France in 1665 he met the great Bernini and was impressed by the vastness of Louis XIV's schemes. Immediately after the Great Fire, he offered Charles a comprehensive plan for the rebuilding of London, but the scheme was too costly to be accepted. His earliest ideas for the new St. Paul's failed for the same reason, but eventually the great cathedral began to rise again, to Wren's designs, and financed by a levy on London's coal imports. His particular genius, for combining simple cubic buildings with ambitious steeples and spires, appeared best in parish churches like St. Stephen's, Walbrook and St. Mary-le-Bow. Wren's secular works included the Library of Trinity College, Cambridge, and the government Hospitals at Chelsea and Greenwich.

The buildings of the time were complemented by the skill of sculptors like Pierce and woodcarvers such as the Dutchman Grinling Gibbons. In some places continental styles were imported with little or no modification. Verrio, a favourite of the King, redecorated part of Windsor Castle in the extravagant baroque of his native Italy. The new royal fortress above Plymouth (built – with memories of the siege of 1643 – with guns pointing towards the town as well as out to sea) imitated the superb fortifications perfected by Vauban, and was appropriately guarded with the gateway in the more restrained style of French baroque.

The age saw an eager search for comfort and elegance indoors. The furniture makers had to try to satisfy a variety of imported fashions culled from continental courts. Catherine of Braganza's Portuguese household started a craze for oriental objects, and soon the lacquered cabinets and screens imported from the Far East were being copied by craftsmen in England.

The high-backed chairs which can be seen in the Dutch 'interior' paintings came into vogue, and were adorned by the furniture makers with elaborate carving and scroll work. 'Day-beds', on which ladies could recline while receiving their admirers, and 'love-seats', small settees just wide enough for two people to sit close together, reflect the preoccupations of Restoration society – no less than the plump cupids favoured as ornaments. Rich fabrics upholstered the chairs and settees, and concealed the wooden framework of the wide and lofty beds of the time. The tables of the middle class as well as the wealthy carried vessels of foreign-inspired Lambeth majolica and Bristol Delft pottery, and the more native flint-glass which Ravenscroft perfected in 1676, the slip-ware produced at Wrotham or by the Toft brothers in Staffordshire, and the stoneware patented by Dwight in 1671. Only the prosperous, though, could afford the magnificent long-case ('grandfather') and table clocks of Tompion, Quare and Jones. The pocket-watches were less successful mechanically, and were more decorative than accurate. Even so, both watches and clocks benefited from the discoveries of Huygens of Holland, and the Dutch Fromandeel family who worked in London through the middle of the seventeenth century.

The Restoration started a boom in the silversmiths' craft. Much of their work was ceremonial, such as the silver-gilt wine fountain which the town of Plymouth presented to Charles II on his coronation, but much of it was made necessary by the new fashions and tastes of the time. Silver coffee-pots and tea-pots were required for the new drinks; and sugar casters and pepper-boxes also reflected England's expanding commerce. The refinement of manners kept the silversmiths busy making forks, previously little used. Charles's spendthrift habits made him commission lavish gifts such as a £900 silver bed for Nelly, and for another mistress a wine-cooling cistern weighing 1000 oz. Royalist families and Oxford colleges gave the smiths more work, replacing the silver plate they had melted down to help Charles I. The English craftsmen were joined by dozens of Dutchmen and, before the end of the reign, by Hugue-not refugees from France. For two generations English silver was much affected by the characteristics of Dutch style – heavily-embossed acanthus leaves and curious jungle scenes of birds and animals against floral backgrounds. By the time of

Anne's accession, though, simpler designs in more restrained taste were supplanting the baroque extravagance of much Restoration silver.

Despite the prejudices of many Puritans, music had long been the most vigorous of the English arts. The Restoration immediately subjected it to foreign influence. Charles sent promising musicians to study under Lully, the Italian who dominated the music of Louis XIV's Court. Banister, the master of the King's orchestra, had to surrender his post because he preferred English to French violinists. Many English composers concentrated on writing the ornate concert arias which Charles especially admired. Even Purcell, probably the greatest composer of his age, deliberately imitated French and Italian models. Nevertheless, something of the native traditional interest in music survived, and was stimulated by the first series of public concerts. After his dismissal by Charles, Banister organized at his house in 1672 the first regular daily concerts ever given. These were supplemented in 1678 by weekly concerts sponsored by Britton, a Clerkenwell coal-merchant, performed in a loft over his warehouse, and patronized by distinguished members of society. Samuel Pepys and his middle-class friends were keen musicians, playing at home on lute and flute, and on the new spinet, and joining together to sing madrigals. Playford continued to publish music for this wide public, while others printed satirical songs and ballads for the common people. In general, music persisted as a national art, but the baroque preferences of the Court deprived the characteristic English elements of the patronage they needed.

The same was true of most of the forms of religious and cultural activity in the generation after the Restoration. The tastes of the Court were usually foreign tastes, and helped to separate the courtiers from the rest of the country. By 1700 the influence of the baroque had disappeared, but the division in culture between rich and poor lasted until the twentieth century.

## xi. Science, 1660–1700

It was in scientific discovery that Restoration England secured its greatest intellectual triumphs. These achievements owed little to foreign influences, for they derived directly from the English institutions of Gresham's College and the 'invisible College' of Boyle, Wilkins and their friends. The 'Philosophical Society' of Oxford followed Wilkins from Wadham College to London, and after a lecture in November 1660 the company resolved to found a 'Colledge for the promoting of Physico-Mathematicall Experimentall Learning'. Charles II's interest in whatever was curious or novel led him to join the society in 1661, and a year later he gave it a charter as the 'Royal Society of London for Improving Natural Knowledge'. The Society met weekly to hear lectures by its members, particularly on the conclusions they drew from their experiments.

Its success was immediate. The discussions and speculations of the previous decades gave it a good start, and members benefited from the discussions and criticisms which followed each lecture. It was an asset to have the patronage and interest of the King, and at first, at least, members were not troubled by the Licensing Laws censoring the press. In its insistence upon the need to experiment, without preconceived ideas based on ancient philosophers, the Society followed the principles advocated by Bacon – experiment first, theorize later. Its first volume of *Philosophical Transactions* was published in 1665; the next year it started a museum, by purchasing a private collection for £100; in 1667 Thomas Sprat wrote its first *History*. It attracted distinguished non-scientists – Evelyn and Pepys were both prominent members. It sponsored the publication of its members' researches, thereby giving them the seal of official approval; thus Newton's *Principia* appeared under the *Imprimatur* of Pepys. Louis XIV's minister Colbert complimented the Society by imitating it in 1666 with the foundation of the Paris *Académie des Sciences*.

In 1662 it appointed as its first curator of experiments Robert Hooke, on the strength of the skill he had shown in working with Boyle on atmospheric pressures. His varied responsibilities prevented him contributing major conclusions on anything except the elasticity of solid bodies (Hooke's Law), but he put forward important theories on gravity (anticipating Newton) and on the wave motion of light. His technical skill as a craftsman helped his fellows, particularly with improved microscopes, and he was elected Secretary of the Society from 1677 to 1683.

Robert Boyle, the most important chemist of the day, was the fourteenth child of the Earl of Cork who had been Strafford's antagonist. His work with Hooke led him to 'Boyle's Law', that the volume of a gas varies inversely with the pressure, and he later discovered the part played by air in carrying sound. His book *The Sceptical Chymist* (1661) published his speculations on the composition of matter and on the characteristics of chemical compounds. His critical mind forced him to consider all problems from first principles, rejecting traditional ideas. Nevertheless he spent a lot of time pursuing the old alchemists' dreams of changing base into precious metals, and in later years he learnt Hebrew and Syriac to help him in his theological studies.

Christopher Wren was an astronomer and mathematician before he was an architect; it was his lecture as Savilian professor of astronomy at Oxford which provoked the foundation of the Royal Society. In later years architecture absorbed most of his time, but in 1668 he published an important work which improved on Descartes's theories about colliding bodies, and helped to prepare for Newton's development of the Laws of Motion. Wren provides one of the best examples of the practical nature of the Royal Society in its early days, for science was expected to be useful. Thus the study of astronomy helped the navigator, and mathematics the architect and engineer.

The most distinguished and versatile scientist of the century was certainly Isaac Newton. Much of his best work was done in the years before his election to the Royal Society in 1672, at the age of twenty-nine. During the years when London was suffering from the Plague, the Fire and the Dutch fleet, Newton was working on the calculus,[1] quietly in his Lincolnshire home on the principles of motion, and on the properties of light. In 1668 he made the first successful reflecting telescope; his election to the Royal Society was the reward for presenting it with an early model. Experiments with glass prisms led him to the laws of refraction, on which he reported to the Royal Society in 1672, but his final conclusions were not published until 1704, in his *Opticks*. His great work on mechanics and dynamics, the 'Mathematical Principles of Natural Philosophy' or *Principia* was published in Latin in 1687. The *Principia*'s

[1] Also being developed (independently) at the same time by Leibniz.

three books defined the nature of mass and movement, deduced
the Laws of Motion, and applied their principles to the universe.
Here at last was proof of the theories of gravity, for Newton
showed that all bodies gravitated (or were attracted) towards
each other in proportion to their masses and in inverse proportion to the squares of their distances. The *Principia* – though
many of their theories were challenged by scientists as eminent
as Huygens and Leibniz – became the foundation on which
most subsequent mechanics, physics and astronomy had to be
based. Even Newton was not immune to the lures of alchemy,
however, and like Boyle was deeply interested in theology.
'Universal gravitation' was to him a proof of the existence of a
thinking Creator-God. Alexander Pope put things differently:

> Nature and Nature's Laws lay hid in Night.
> God said, Let Newton be! and all was Light.

Other distinguished scientists of the time included Wallis and
Halley, both mathematicians and astronomers; the botanists Ray
and Sherard, and Sydenham, a pioneer of medical research.
Nonetheless, scientific studies met increasing difficulties as time
went on. The Licensing Acts were imposed more strictly after
the Exclusion Struggle, Oxford and Cambridge expelled the
advocates of Bacon's experimental philosophy, and even the
Royal Society was diluted by the admission of noblemen with
little scientific knowledge. Newton and Boyle became preoccupied with theology, and the Society largely abandoned its
former concern for research in practical matters. It was left
to two humble men, Newcomen and Savery – a Baptist ironmonger and a retired mariner – to pioneer the first successful
industrial use of steam power. The Society was, after all, part
of the exclusive Court culture of the reign, cut off from the
country at large by the social as well as the intellectual super-
iority of its members.

Despite this falling-off, the Society's achievements were
remarkable enough, especially in the first generation after the
Restoration. Its members helped to give England a lead in
scientific research which was not lost until the nineteenth century.
Even English prose was influenced: the clear, cold, precise
language which the Society favoured for the recording of
experiments acted as an antidote to the florid pretentiousness

affected by many writers of the time. Similarly important was the effect upon theoretical and political philosophy, for philosophers like Locke[1] rejected the teachings of Aristotle and Plato and deliberately based their systems upon first principles. Here lay a danger for James II. Altogether, the scientific advances of the reign were probably the greatest achievement of the Restoration period – and the one which depended most upon the progress made in earlier years.

## EXTRACTS

1. RICHARD BAXTER AT THE SAVOY CONFERENCE, AND ITS SEQUEL (1661–2):

Dr. Gunning was their forwardest and greatest speaker; understanding well what belonged to a disputant; a man of greater study and industry than any of them, well read in Fathers and Councils, and of a ready tongue . . . but so vehement for his high imposing principles, and so over-zealous for Arminianism and church-pomp, and so very eager and fervent in his discourse, that I conceive his prejudice and passion much perverted his judgment. . . . For myself, the reason why I spake so much was the desire of my brethren, and I was loth to expose *them* to the hatred of the bishops. . . .

When Bartholomew Day came, about one thousand eight hundred or two thousand ministers were silenced and cast out. . . . And now came in the great inundation of calamities, which in many streams overwhelmed thousands of godly Christians, together with their pastors. . . . Hundreds of able ministers, with their wives and children, had neither house nor bread. . . . (Richard Baxter, *Autobiography*, pp. 169–75)

2. CHARLES II's LICENSING ACT MUZZLES THE PRESS (1662):

Whereas . . . by the general licentiousness of the late times many evil disposed persons have been encouraged to print and sell heretical schismatical blasphemous seditious and treasonable Bookes Pamphlets and Papers. . . . Be it enacted that . . . no private person or persons whatsoever shall att any time hereafter print . . . any Booke or Pamphlet whatsoever unlesse [it] be first entered in the Booke of the Register of the Company

---

[1] Himself a member of the Royal Society, from 1668 until his death in 1704.

of Stationers of London . . . and . . . shall be first lawfully
licensed and authorized to be printed by . . . the Lord Chancellor . . . the Principal Secretaries of State . . . the Earl Marshal
. . . and the Chancellors or Vice-Chancellors of [Oxford and
Cambridge]. (In Costin and Watson, *The Law & Working of
the Constitution*, pp. 29–30)

3. ANGRY WITH CLARENDON, THE MOB RIOTS OUTSIDE 'DUN-
KIRK' HOUSE (1667):

Mr. Hater tells me at noon that some rude people have been,
as he hears, at my Lord Chancellor's, where they have cut down
the trees before his house and broke his windows; and a gibbet
either set up before, or painted upon, his gate, and these three
words writ: 'Three sights to be seen: Dunkirk, Tangier, and a
barren Queen.' (Samuel Pepys, *Diary*, vol. ii, pp. 485–6)

4. THE STOP OF THE EXCHEQUER, AND THE DECLARATION OF
INDULGENCE, ALARM LONDON (1672):

The credit of this bank being thus broken, did exceedingly
discontent the people, and never did his Majesty's affairs
prosper to any purpose after it, for as it did not supply the
expense of the meditated war, so it melted away, I know not
how.

To this succeeded the King's Declaration for an universal
toleration; Papists, and swarms of Sectaries, now boldly showing
themselves in their public meetings. This was imputed to the
same council, Clifford warping to Rome as was believed, nor
was Lord Arlington clear of suspicion, to gratify that party, but
as since it has proved, and was then evidently foreseen, to the
extreme weakening of the Church of England. . . . (John
Evelyn, *Diary*, vol. ii, pp. 74–5)

5. THE DEATH OF SIR EDMUND BERRY GODFREY (1679):

Oates went to him the day before he appeared at the Council-
board, and declared upon oath the narrative he intended to
make, which Godfrey afterwards published. . . . On Saturday,
the 12th of October, he went abroad in the morning, was seen
about one o'clock near St. Clement's Church, but was seen no
more till his body was found, on the Thursday night following,
in a ditch about a mile out of town, near St. Pancras Church.
His sword was thrust through him, but no blood was on his
clothes or about him; his shoes were clean, his money was in his
pocket; a mark was all round his neck, which showed he was

strangled; his breast was bruised, his neck was broken, and there were many drops of white wax-lights on his breeches, which being used only by priests and persons of quality, made people imagine in whose hands he had been. (Gilbert Burnet, *History of My Own Times*, p. 154)

6. THE ARTICLES OF IMPEACHMENT PREPARED AGAINST DANBY (1679):
1. That he hath traitorously encroached to himself regal power, by treating of matters of Peace and War with foreign princes and ambassadors, and giving Instructions to his majesty's ambassadors abroad, without communicating the same to the secretaries of state, and the rest of his majesty's Council. . . .
3. That he . . . did propose and negotiate a Peace for the French king, upon terms disadvantageous to the interests of his majesty and his kingdoms. . . .
4. That he is popishly affected; and hath traitorously concealed . . . the late horrid and bloody Plot and Conspiracy contrived by the Papists against his majesty's person and government. . . .   (In Costin and Watson, *The Law & Working of the Constitution*, pp. 180–1)

7. ROYALIST ENTHUSIASM AT THE OXFORD PARLIAMENT (1681):
But that which is most to be noted is that all the way the king passed were such shoutings, acclamations, and ringing of bells, made by loyall hearts and smart lads of the layetie of Oxon, that the aire was so much pierced that the clouds seemed to divide.   The generall cry was 'Long live King Charles', and many drawing up to the very coach window cryed 'Let the king live, and the devill hang up all roundheads': at which his majestie smiled and seemed well pleased. . . .
March 28, Munday, the king having had notice how vigorously the parliament proceeded on Friday and Saturday (directly opposit to what he desired in his speech) did about ten of the clock in the morning send for his robes and crowne privatly, the former they say in a sedan, the other under a cloake – Half an hour after, sending for the Speaker and Commons dissolved . . . the parliament, to the amazement of all.   (Anthony à Wood, *Life and Times*, pp. 252–4)

8. THE PLAGUE RAGES IN LONDON (AUGUST 1665):
I went away, and walked to Greenwich, in my way seeing a

coffin with a dead body therein, dead of the plague, lying in an open close belonging to Combe farm, which was carried out last night, and the parish have not appointed anybody to bury it; but only set a watch there all day and night, that nobody should go thither or come thence: this disease making us more cruel to one another than . . . to dogs. . . .

Up: and, after putting several things in order to my removal, to Woolwich; the plague having a great increase this week, beyond all expectation, of almost 2000, making . . . the plague above 6000. . . . But it is feared that the true number of the dead this week is near 10,000: partly from the poor that cannot be taken notice of, through the greatness of the number, and partly from the Quakers and others that will not have any bell ring for them. (Samuel Pepys, *Diary*, vol. ii, pp. 156–7)

9. THE OUTBREAK OF THE FIRE (SEPTEMBER 1666):

Jane called us up about three in the morning, to tell us of a great fire they saw in the City. . . . So down, with my heart full of trouble, to the Lieutenant of the Tower, who tells me that it begun this morning in the King's baker's house in Pudding Lane, and that it hath burned St. Magnus's Church and most part of Fish Street already. . . . Everybody endeavouring to remove their goods, and flinging into the river or bringing them into lighters that lay off; poor people staying in their houses as long as till the very fire touched them, and then running into boats, or clambering from one pair of stairs by the waterside to another. And, among other things, the poor pigeons, I perceive, were loth to leave their houses, but hovered about the windows and balconies, till they . . . burned their wings, and fell down. (Samuel Pepys, *Diary*, vol. ii, pp. 314–15)

10. HOW THE FIRE AFFECTED THE NONCOMFORMISTS:

The loss in houses and goods is scarcely to be valued. And, among the rest, the loss of books was an exceeding great detriment to the interest of piety and learning. Almost all the booksellers in St. Paul's Churchyard brought their books under St. Paul's Church, where it was thought almost impossible that fire should come. But the church itself being on fire, the exceeding weight of the stones falling down did break into the vault and let in the fire, and they could not come near to save the books. The library also of Sion College was burnt, and most of the libraries of ministers, conformable and nonconformable, in the city, with the libraries of many Nonconformists

of the country, which had been lately brought up to the city.    I
saw the half-burnt leaves of books near my dwelling at Acton
six miles from London; but others found them near Windsor,
almost twenty miles distant.    (Richard Baxter, *Autobiography*,
pp. 198–9)

# 6

# PARLIAMENT DICTATES TERMS
## 1685–1702

☆

### i. James II

THE new King was in many ways a more suitable monarch than his brother. He was less extravagant, less debauched; he had the religious zeal of the sincere convert; in the Admiralty and in Scotland he had proved a conscientious and efficient administrator. But in twenty-five years as heir-apparent James had learned not a grain of political sense. The Exclusion Struggle had made him suspicious of parliaments, and he loathed the Whigs and Nonconformists who had nearly kept him from the throne. He never realized the strength of the Church of England. A hot temper made him intolerant of criticism, and of advice which did not accord with what he wanted to do. He was a poor judge of men: most of those he appointed betrayed him in the hour of need. His stubborn independence made him hesitate to bind England into a treaty with France – though he had no objection to asking Louis for money or military help. Not for the only time in Stuart history, the King's own character was his most serious handicap.

The disasters of 1688 need not have been. Few English Kings have come to the throne with powers such as James inherited. France, Holland and the Empire were anxious for his friendship. The Church was loyal, for he had never paraded his Catholicism too openly. The Crown's regular income of £1,500,000 was enough for normal purposes. The Tories were solidly behind him; the Whig party lay in ruins after Shaftesbury's downfall and the Rye House Plot. Parliament's independence had been undermined by Charles's tampering with the borough constitutions and by his success in managing for four years without this inconvenient institution.

Under Jeffreys, the judges were ruthless agents of the Crown. The King himself was popular – and this deceived him into thinking that his policies would be equally well received. Unfortunately, the glitter of his inheritance blinded James to its flaws – to the country's parliamentary experience, its social divisions, and its religious prejudices.

The honeymoon period at the start of the reign lasted barely nine months. He began well. He was crowned with Anglican rites (though he left before the Communion). He promised the Council to maintain the government of the country as established by law, to support the Church of England, and not to interfere with any man's property. These were empty promises, however. Over the next three years he repeatedly broke each of these principles. His expulsion in 1688 by an exasperated country was the direct consequence.

The King's power was, however, strengthened, not weakened, by two challenges in the spring of 1685, since they left him with a standing army and an increased income. Charles II had exiled his favourite bastard son, the Duke of Monmouth, after the Rye House Plot. The Duke went to Holland, where he joined up with the fugitive Argyle, and remained deaf to William of Orange's suggestions that he should remove himself to Hungary. Monmouth and Argyle found in the Netherlands a few hotheads prepared to join them in an invasion to arouse the more Protestant parts of Britain against the Catholic King. Monmouth was to land in the south-west of England, and Argyle to raise the Covenanting banner in the Campbell lands and the Borders; then both would march on London. Through bad timing and many indiscretions, their schemes fell to pieces. When Argyle landed in Kintyre in May, he found his lands already occupied by the loyal Marquis of Atholl, and his banner of 'No Prelacy – No Erastianism'[1] was slow to attract followers. He was captured on a forlorn march against Glasgow. On June 18th – the very day when Monmouth proclaimed himself King – Argyle was executed in accordance with the sentence passed in 1681.[2] The campaign in Scotland was particularly unfortunate for Monmouth. It had made Parliament vote money for a professional army, and James had time to borrow troops from the continent – even William of Orange sent help. Moreover, the Presbyterian connexions of

[1] State control of the Church.　　　[2] See above, p. 253.

Argyle helped the government to denounce Monmouth's followers as Nonconformists.

The enthusiasm he had aroused when visiting the west-country on Shaftesbury's orders four years earlier had led Monmouth to expect massive support from the western gentry and their dependants.  Early in June 1685 he landed at Lyme Regis.  There he issued a lengthy political Declaration, asserting among other things that James had started the Fire of London and had killed Charles by poisoning him.  Claiming the throne on the grounds of his (undoubted) Protestantism as well as his (very questionable) legitimacy, Monmouth marched inland, leaving most of his stores in Lyme Regis.  He collected a ragged army, largely of farm-labourers and cloth-workers, but very few gentry joined him.  The supplies he had brought from Holland were seized in Lyme Regis by a government ship; henceforth the rebels were too poorly equipped to risk open battle.  But confusion among the Somerset Militia enabled him to occupy Taunton, where he was proclaimed King. The rebels then marched towards Bristol, were halted at Keynsham, and then retreated to Bridgwater through Bath and Frome.  With barely 3000 men, mainly armed with scythes and pitchforks, Monmouth attempted a desperate night attack on the royal army, encamped east of the town among the marshes of Sedgemoor.  As Monmouth's cart-horse cavalry tried to cross in front of the foot-soldiers, the rebel forces were plunged into chaos.  The weakness of the royal commander led to some disorder in the other side, but his deputy, John Churchill, held the troops together.  The rebels were shot to pieces in the misty dawn of July 6th.  Monmouth fled, but was captured a few days later hiding in a ditch, by men of the Sussex Militia under Lord Lumley.  He was hurried to London, where Parliament had already passed an Act of Attainder against him.  On Tower Hill the executioner Jack Ketch[1] (with some difficulty – five blows were needed) cut his head off. The rebellion had never had a chance of success, for the plans had been too hasty and ill-concerted.  Monmouth's followers had quarrelled among themselves, and they had failed to get the support of more than a handful of important people.

[1] Ketch had previously written a pamphlet excusing himself for bungling the execution of Lord Russell in 1683, blaming the victim for holding his head awkwardly, and instructing others who might find themselves in similar circumstances how they should kneel to facilitate the operation.

The punishment of the other rebels was intended to teach England the peril of resisting an anointed King. Hundreds were cut down as they ran from Sedgemoor, or were caught and hanged by the roadside. The garrison returned from Tangiers, Colonel Kirke's 'Lambs', played a major part in the butchery. In the autumn, Chief Justice Jeffreys moved on a grisly progress through the western counties, continuing the work of retribution and terror. The Bloody Assizes moved from Winchester to Salisbury, Dorchester, Exeter, Taunton, Wells and Bristol. Hundreds were crammed into gaols, or into the churches pressed into service as makeshift prisons. They came out to suffer hurried trials and swift punishment. Witnesses were bullied, juries misdirected, prisoners cowed into silence. Rebels and those who had sheltered them faced transportation or the traitor's death of being hanged, drawn and quartered. After the formalities of law, about 300 were executed and hundreds more sentenced to transportation. Many of these unfortunates were given to the Queen and her maids of honour as slaves, human cattle to be sold off in the West Indies. Some of the wealthy, however, purchased their pardon; Prideaux alone paid £15,000. Jeffreys and the King shared the profits between them. The Bloody Assizes of 1685 showed how fully James was master of his Courts.

James's first and only Parliament seemed at first to be as loyal as the lawyers. Its composition was proof of Charles's success in tampering with the borough charters, for James was convinced that there were barely forty members on whom he could not rely. Only one of these, Sir Edward Seymour, dared criticize Parliament's generosity in voting James an additional £400,000 a year (bringing his income to nearly two millions) to crush the rebellions. During the summer adjournment, however, the attitude of many members altered. James was displaying his Catholicism more openly, and was relying greatly on Catholic advisers like Father Petre, Arundel and Talbot, and the crypto-Catholic Sunderland. In September Judge Jeffreys was appointed Lord Chancellor. In October Halifax, the moderate 'Trimmer', was dismissed from the presidency of the Council and his post later given to Sunderland, already a secretary of State. The official *London Gazette* deliberately concealed Louis XIV's persecutions of French Huguenots. By government order, that November no bonfires were lit to commemorate in the traditional way England's deliverance from the Gunpowder Plot of eighty years before. When Parliament reassembled on November 9th, James opened it by demanding that the standing army should continue, with ample money to pay and equip it, and that Catholics should be allowed to hold commissions despite the Test Acts. The Commons offered James £700,000, but asked for reassurances about religion. The Lords were more forthright. Led by Devonshire and Compton, the Bishop of London, they demanded positive guarantees. 'This was a great surprise in a parliament which people believed would have complied in all things' (Evelyn). This whiff of criticism turned the King sour. After less than a fortnight Parliament was adjourned. It never met again during the reign.

Parliament was no longer pliant, but the lawyers were, so James decided to use the law courts to remove the burden of the Test Acts from the Catholics. Sir Edward Hales had held a colonel's commission under Charles II without swearing the oaths prescribed by the Acts. Early in James's reign, Hales announced that he had become a Catholic. The King then gave him a royal dispensation, in letters patent under the great seal, to remain in his command without penalty. To secure judicial approval of such a dispensation, James encouraged Hales to arrange a collusive action, in which his coachman Godden sued him for accepting office in defiance of the Tests. Some unco-operative judges were hastily dismissed, with the consequence that eleven out of the twelve who tried the case agreed, in June 1686, in acquitting Hales. They declared that, as the laws of England were the King's laws, ' 'Tis an inseparable prerogative in the Kings of England to dispense with penal laws in particular cases, and upon particular necessary reasons' – and decided that the King himself should be sole judge of what was a 'necessary reason'. In other words, the case of *Godden* v. *Hales* decreed that the King had the right to give individuals leave to break the law. In doing so, it asserted in remarkable fashion a doctrine of absolute monarchy. Hales was quickly promoted to be governor of Dover Castle, and became a Privy Councillor.

In the following year James revived one of Charles's most controversial innovations. By now he had aroused the anger of the whole Church of England, and at last had come to realize that the Church would never agree to the repeal of the penal laws against the Catholics.   The process of individual dispensations approved by *Godden* v. *Hales* was a clumsy and inconvenient one.   Therefore in April 1687 James issued a Declaration of Indulgence modelled on that of 1672, a package deal of toleration and religious equality for Catholic and Nonconformist alike.   He accompanied it with professions of his belief in toleration, and a promise that Parliament should meet by November to consider the Declaration.   This was part of a hasty campaign to rally the Nonconformists to his side as allies against the Church, but it represented another serious challenge by the royal prerogative to Parliament and the laws it had made.   There was of course a wide difference in principle between the King's dispensing power – in effect a promise to pardon a particular man for breaking a particular law – and the claim to suspend the operation of a law throughout the whole country.   The Declaration was so strongly criticized that James knew that his existing Parliament would never accept the Declaration.   It had been repeatedly prorogued since its last meeting in November 1685; now, in July 1687, he dissolved it.

James redoubled his attempts to get the Nonconformists on to his side, and planned to use them to form an amenable Parliament.   The Council canvassed officials of the national and local administrations to get their support for the repeal of the penal laws.   Most of them returned evasive answers.   James then deprived of their offices those who would not commit themselves to repeal.   The King was replacing the Test Act with a private test of his own.

His reckless pursuit of privileges for the Catholics had taken James far along the road to arbitrary government.   He speeded up a desperate reorganization of local government, cancelling borough charters, sacking town corporations and J.P.s, and trying to place power in the hands of Nonconformists likely to support repeal.   While the King dared not hold an election, the country was soon demanding a free Parliament – and demanding it with a firmness not heard since 1640 and 1660.   James had forgotten his early promise to maintain the government as established by law.

James had also forgotten his promise to protect the Church of England.   For the first two years of his reign he tried to persuade the Anglicans to join him in removing the penal laws, on the grounds that the Church had more in common with Rome that with its own Nonconformists.   Dryden might consider the Catholic Church 'A milk white Hind, immortal and unchang'd' but to Anglicans she was still the Scarlet Woman of Rome, unrepentant in idolatry and still fomenting treason.   Moreover, it was difficult for James to plead convincingly for toleration for the Roman Church while thousands of Huguenot refugees were fleeing to England to escape Catholic persecutions in France.   Would James be content with religious and political equality for his Church?   It was more likely that the removal of the penal laws and the Tests would be followed by an attempt to enforce popery at pistol-point.   A few time-servers and professional turn-coats in the Church of England, now that popery was in fashion, absconded to Rome or professed their intention of doing so.   Such men James promoted.   But clergy who overstepped the bounds of caution in criticizing the Catholic church could expect no sympathy from the Supreme Governor of the Church of England.   Two leading Scottish bishops were dismissed for anti-catholic views.   In England, in barely three years, he drove the Church to abandon its supreme political principle – Non-Resistance to the King, the Lord's anointed.

The first threat to the Church was implied by the elevation of Catholics to high office, during the summer and autumn of 1685, but it was only in the November session of Parliament that the King showed his hand in demanding the repeal of the anti-Catholic laws.   A wiser man would have remembered how the Presbyterian attack on the Church had given his father a party of supporters in the Long Parliament.   The Catholic challenge to it now produced an opposition, from what had seemed a blindly loyal Parliament.

Throughout 1686 James headed hell-bent for Rome, encouraged by Sunderland as principal minister.   The Jesuit, Father Petre, as Clerk of the Royal Closet, was his confidential adviser; another Jesuit, Father Warner, guided the King as royal confessor.   Admiral Herbert was dismissed, and a Catholic, Strickland, given command of the fleet.   James sacked the Solicitor-General, and replaced him with a lawyer willing to declare that James could permit Catholics to hold Anglican benefices.   Catholics or Catholic sympathizers were installed as Bishops of Chester and Oxford, and as Dean of Christ Church, Oxford. Obadiah Walker, the Master of University College, Oxford, announced his conversion and began celebrating Mass in the college chapel. The opening of religious houses by the Benedictines, Dominicans, Franciscans and Jesuits inflamed passions still hot from the Titus Oates scare. Several Catholic bishops were appointed. The Catholic Earl of Tyrconnell was sent to Ireland as Deputy Governor, together with sixteen new Catholic judges and councillors. The King's printer was kept busy publishing Catholic tracts. Most ominous of all, James began to weed anti-papist officers out of the army, and to replace them with Catholics. In June 1686 James's army, 13,000 strong, took up station on Hounslow Heath, to the alarm of the citizens of nearby London. As was happening in France at that very time, a Catholic army might be used to crush Protestantism.

Another threat to the Church came in July. James appointed an Ecclesiastical Commission, with powers to inspect the bishoprics and the universities, and to alter college statutes. This aroused memories of the Court of High Commission and fearful comparisons with the Inquisition. Originally seven members were nominated to serve on the Commission, but Archbishop Sancroft refused to join it, and its constitution was such that Sunderland, Lord Chancellor Jeffreys and the pliant Chief Justice Herbert could act by themselves. The Commission immediately showed its teeth by suspending Henry Compton, the outspoken Bishop of London, for refusing to silence those of his clergy who preached against the Church of Rome. This was unwise, for Compton was a dangerous man to cross: his aristocratic lineage added to his importance as bishop of the capital city, and he had already played a prominent part in Parliament the previous autumn. The Commission itself was probably not unlawful, but its institution was ill-judged. With the army to enforce its authority, it could easily have become an instrument for rooting out Protestantism. As it was, with power great enough to humble a leading bishop, no churchman or scholar could feel safe from it.

The King's follies continued through 1687, partly because he had weakened his administration through further sackings of Anglican statesmen. Two of the ablest had incurred the Queen's wrath the previous year by bringing back to Court

James's former mistress, the Protestant Kate Sedley, in the hope of winning the King away from popery; Mary of Modena had sent her packing, and now James did the same to the ministers responsible. Rochester lost his post as a Treasury Commissioner, and his brother Clarendon was displaced as ruler of Ireland by the papist Tyrconnell. The King tried to Romanize the universities – essential parts of the Anglican system. The Ecclesiastical Commission deprived Vice-Chancellor Peachell of all his university appointments when Cambridge refused to give a degree to a Benedictine monk. James visited Magdalen College, Oxford, in person when the Fellows refused to elect his nominees, first Dr. Farmer and then Bishop Parker, as their President. The twenty-five recalcitrant Fellows were expelled. Parker soon died, and the King then appointed as President the Catholic Bishop Giffard; within a few months he turned Magdalen into a popish seminary.

So far, James had been clumsily trying to secure repeal by bending the Church to his will. During 1687, though, he veered away, and sailed off on a new tack. He now planned to win the Nonconformists to his side, by offering them toleration in return for helping him to win it for the Catholics as well. In April he issued his first Declaration of Indulgence and tried to woo to his side prominent Nonconformists like Richard Baxter and the Baptist merchant Kiffen. At the request of Penn (who maintained his curious friendship with the King) James released over a thousand Quakers from prison. But the Nonconformists did not react as the King had hoped. For twenty years they had been religious pariahs, and James had frequently denounced them as rebels and regicides. The Dissenting donkey was not fooled by the Catholic carrot. The Nonconformists distrusted the gift and feared its giver. The fate of the French Huguenots, lulled asleep by the Edict of Nantes, frightened them all. Halifax's *Letter to a Dissenter* warned the Nonconformist that he was being hugged now 'only that you may be better squeezed at another time'. The Declaration of Indulgence was an act of desperate folly. It gave few advantages to the Catholics that they did not already possess in practice; it added to the alarm of the Church of England (and made the more far-sighted Churchmen see the need to improve their relations with the Nonconformists); and it demonstrated that the King's determination to master the law did not end with the powers confirmed by *Godden* v. *Hales*. Only a reckless monarch, badly advised by his ministers, would have tried to overthrow the established Church by an unholy alliance of Catholic and Protestant Nonconformists.

Thus, by the summer of 1687, James had alienated the Church, but had not yet driven it into active opposition. He had already mastered the law courts and was defying parliamentary institutions; the universities had been humbled; the Crown had a standing army and the money to pay for it; the Catholics could worship freely and by dispensation hold office. Tyrconnell ruled Ireland in the interests of his co-religionists; Scotland was governed largely by Perth and Melfort, recent converts to Rome. Although he had broken the promises made at his accession, at this point he might have halted. Four things would have helped to preserve a balance. The standing army was stronger than any force which could be scraped together for an internal rebellion. Office-holders great and small throughout the country were unlikely to revolt against the 'establishment' which assisted them to honour, status and wealth. Above all, the Church of England was deeply committed to the doctrine of Non-Resistance, that the acts of God's anointed deputy must be suffered and obeyed, not resisted, and it thought that it would not have to maintain its patient submission indefinitely. There was no reason to expect James to survive by many years his elder brother. The heir to the throne – as James had no living children by his second marriage, to Mary of Modena – was the Protestant Mary, Anne Hyde's daughter, safely married to William of Orange. Provided the Protestant dawn was not too long delayed, the perils of the night might be endurable.

But the King was not prepared to leave things as they were. Louis XIV and the papal nuncio were perpetually urging him to swifter action in England, and offering him a military alliance against Protestant powers. Forced by heavy gambling debts into the pockets of Louis and the French ambassador Barillon, Sunderland joined in coaxing James along the primrose path to ruin. At the same time, and by no means alone, Sunderland was secretly ingratiating himself with William of Orange. James's principal minister had no confidence in his master, yet gave his encouragement to the policies which were to ruin him.

The first of these final follies was the King's determination to remodel local government so that a Parliament of M.P.s favourable to reform could be elected. Lord-lieutenants, deputies and sheriffs, J.P.s, mayors and aldermen were ejected from their offices if they failed to give satisfactory answers to James's referendum on the repeal of the Test Acts. They lost not just social prestige but also the profitable economic perquisites and privileges attached to those posts. The London Companies were similarly purged, and many of those in the Crown's service as tax collectors and army and navy officers also suffered. This was a flagrant interference with the rights of hundreds of important men. It was very rash. The King's actions now seemed a direct threat to property – not merely to men's estates and incomes, but to their privileges, their places in society. By these continued attacks on the Anglican gentry and town corporations James made his position precarious, for he made the propertied classes more afraid of absolute monarchy than they were of the perils of revolution. To the citizens of London, despotism seemed especially near. Not only was the Catholic-officered army encamped at Hounslow, but the Catholic Hales was promoted from Dover to command the Tower.

His next folly showed James's utter inability to learn from his mistakes. This time he drove the Church of England into a desperate rejection of its own ideal of Non-Resistance. In April 1688 he re-issued the Declaration of Indulgence. This time he ordered the Declaration to be read from the pulpit on two successive Sundays in every cathedral and parish church. By this, James was instructing the Church to pronounce its own doom. Throughout the country many – perhaps most – of the clergy defied the order. In London it was 'almost universally forborne' (Evelyn). Spontaneously, the clergy had abandoned the principle of Non-Resistance. In mid-May the Archbishop of Canterbury and six other bishops presented the King with a petition asking him not to force their clergy to read the Declaration, as it was based upon claims (to suspend the law) which seemed to them illegal. Angry and surprised, James sent them away with a command to obey him. The King's wrath increased when the terms of the petition 'leaked' out, were printed, and widely circulated.

A wiser, calmer, better-advised man would have done nothing

UBS

about it, but James swore to show the bishops that he was their Governor in fact as well as in title. Sure of the loyalty of the judges and certain of a conviction, he sent Archbishop Sancroft and the others to the Tower, to answer a charge of seditious libel. The subsequent trial of the Seven Bishops was a crisis which summed up most of the issues at stake. The privileges of the Anglican Church were in question; so were the powers and limitations of parliamentary statute and of royal prerogative; so was the independence or otherwise of the law courts, and the loyalty of the administration James had chosen. The cause of the Seven Bishops was the cause of the whole country. Anglican gentry and Nonconformist citizens all knew that if the bishops lost, arbitrary power threatened every man, his religion and his property.

The trial, in late June 1688, was an extraordinary affair. The prosecution was led by a turncoat Whig, the defence by a former Attorney-General. One of the prisoners, Bishop White of Peterborough, boldly asked Wright, the Lord Chief Justice, not to help the prosecution or intimidate the witnesses. The case turned, not on the King's dispensing power, but on whether the bishops had actually presented James with the petition attributed to them and, if so, whether its contents would 'disturb the government, or make a mischief and a stir among the people'. Of the four judges, Wright and Powell acted with fairness, while Holloway was actively on the side of the bishops in arguments with the Solicitor-General. Only one, the Catholic Allybone, advised the jury to convict the prisoners. The court was crowded with peers lending moral support to the bishops, and hisses greeted some of the Solicitor-General's remarks. After a nine-hour trial, the jury – which included the King's Brewer – acquitted the bishops. Long drugged with the opium of absolutism, the law courts had at last awakened.

There was a lane of people from the King's Bench to the waterside, on their knees, as the Bishops passed and repassed, to beg their blessing. Bonfires were made that night, and bells rung, which was taken very ill at Court. . . .[1]

James immediately sacked Powell and Holloway, but the sands of time were running out.

A new crisis speeded his downfall. Two days after the arrest

[1] J. Evelyn, *Diary*, vol. ii, p. 279.

of the bishops, Mary of Modena had given birth to a son who seemed likely to live. He would therefore succeed his father as a Catholic king. There could not now be a peaceful Protestant succession when James died. The prospect of a long line of popish kings, following the baby Prince James Edward, 'whose cradle is the tombe of heresy and schism', hastened the country towards revolution. Some men tried to discredit the child, by claiming that he was not the King's son, but had been smuggled into the Queen's bedroom in a warming-pan. The story was not convincing. More than the warming-pan fable would be required if the Protestant dawn was ever to come.

Only the standing army, the navy and the threat of French intervention kept James on the throne during the hysterical last months of the reign. Without foreign help the opposition could not act. All depended on Holland and William of Orange. For three years William had been expecting to come to England on James's death, as the husband of James's elder daughter, and he had naturally tried to win the friendship of important men in the country without losing that of his father-in-law. Moreover, he could not risk angering James while French troops were massing for attacks on the Netherlands. The birth of James Edward was a blow to William no less than to the Anglican Church, for the baby prince threatened to keep him off the English throne and to keep England from a military alliance with Holland. During 1687 William's envoys Dykveld and Zuylestein had been sounding many prominent men in England – Halifax, Danby, Clarendon, Rochester, Nottingham, and even Sunderland and General Churchill – and had been able to assure him of their support for the Dutch claim to the throne. Immediately the news of the birth reached the Hague, William sent Zuylestein to England to congratulate the parents – and collect the opinions of their opponents. Zuylestein, moreover, had to warn them that William would not intervene unless guaranteed adequate support in England.

A month later, only hours after the acquittal of the bishops, ex-Admiral Herbert set off from London, disguised as a common seaman, with a vital letter for William. In it, seven eminent men promised to join with William if he landed 'in a condition to give assistance this year sufficient for a relief', and assured him of the support of nineteen Englishmen out of every twenty. The invitation was vague, for those who signed it were so diverse a collection of statesmen that it would have been difficult to agree on a more precise letter. There was the old Cavalier Danby, a friend of Holland, and the man who had arranged the marriage of William and Mary. There was Henry Compton, the suspended Bishop of London. There were Whig survivors – Devonshire, Russell and Sidney, who had all lost relatives by blood and marriage after the Rye House fiasco. There were two converts *from* Rome – Shrewsbury and Lumley, who three years before had captured Monmouth. Others were known to be sympathetic, though too cautious to sign – Halifax the Trimmer, the loyal Anglican Nottingham, and Churchill, the Commander of James's army and the close friend of Princess Anne, James's younger daughter. William could be sure of the support he needed.

During the late summer and early autumn of 1688, James's government virtually collapsed. Sunderland was anxious to resign, and Lord Chancellor Jeffreys prudently obtained from the King a royal pardon for the injustices he had committed. In the army a group of officers under Colonel Langston formed a Protestant Association sworn to desert as soon as William landed – although James was now hanging all the deserters he caught. In August the King issued writs for a November election; in September he cancelled them. Finally, far too late, James saw his peril. Frantically he tried to unravel the follies of three crowded years. He tried to lean once more on the Church he had so much abused. On the advice of Archbishop Sancroft, he abolished the Ecclesiastical Commission, restored the evicted Fellows of Magdalen, reinstated Compton as Bishop of London, and cancelled all the new charters enforced upon the boroughs since the Exclusion Struggle. Even the command of the fleet was given to an Anglican, Dartmouth replacing Strickland. A year earlier these measures would have saved him. Now the wheels of revolution were already turning, and could not be stopped.

But could William do anything? France was threatening war, and her armies were poised on the Dutch frontier. With Louis waiting to pounce, the States-General would hardly risk sending troops to England. Moreover, Louis was still urging James to ally England with France; it seemed certain that any Dutch intervention in England would be the signal for Louis's troops to march against Holland. William, however, saw things differently. Given half a chance, he might by intervention be able to bring England firmly over on to Holland's side in the expected struggle with France. With England's help, Holland could survive; without it, she would probably fall. It was true that he coveted the English throne, but the English alliance was even more attractive to him. Intervention was a gamble, but William managed to persuade the Dutch States-General to share it with him, and to pay the troops Bentinck was recruiting for him in Germany.

James made it easy for William by refusing Louis's offers of alliance, although he begged the French King to keep his fleet on watch to check the Dutch. James rejected Louis partly out of stubborn independence, partly out of belated patriotism, and partly because he hesitated to repeat the catastrophic Treaty of Dover. By mid-September Louis's patience was exhausted. Jealous of the growing power of the Emperor and anxious to assert French authority in the Rhineland, Louis marched his troops away from the Dutch border and into the Palatinate. Now it was almost certain that there could be no French invasion of Holland before the winter made campaigning impossible.

This stupid act sealed James's fate. It was all that William needed to get the final consent of the States-General for his enterprise. At the end of October the Dutch troops embarked. The wind blew from the east, so the Dutch fleet headed westwards down Channel. The English navy, long neglected by its sovereign, sailed in half-hearted pursuit. Dartmouth was loyal to James, but his captains' hearts were with their old commander, Herbert, who was sailing with William. The French navy was even less able to intervene, for Louis had not moved it out of the Mediterranean. Without firing a shot the Dutch dropped anchor in Torbay.

William landed at Brixham on November 5th. The date was a happy omen. It was the anniversary of Gunpowder Plot. It was also exactly a hundred years since English and Dutch ships had driven away Philip of Spain's Armada. So far William's gamble was succeeding.

## ii. The Revolutionary Settlement

It was still very uncertain what William would do. He had not yet claimed the Crown, for either his wife or himself, though he had pointed out the interest which they both had in the English Succession, and had questioned the legitimacy of the 'pretended Prince of Wales'. In the same manifesto, published before he sailed from Holland, he had promised to contribute 'all that lies in us for the maintaining both of the Protestant Religion, and of the Laws and Liberties of those Kingdoms'. William was wise to be so vague, for anything more specific would have turned away many of those who now joined him. His Dutch supporters might also have wavered, for they feared the consequences to Holland if William involved himself too deeply in English affairs.

The troops he landed in Devon numbered barely half the total of the royal army around London. Remembering what had happened to Monmouth's followers, the westcountry gentry at first hesitated to join him, but by the end of November the King's indecisions had played into William's hands. In the middle of the month James marched his troops down to Salisbury Plain; then, like the Duke of York in the old song, he marched them back again. For General Churchill the decision to retreat was the signal to change sides. He was soon followed by the Duke of Grafton (one of Charles II's bastards) and many army officers. Langston's Protestant Association was proving its worth. Princess Anne fled from London, escorted by Bishop Compton, to join Devonshire in the midlands. In Cheshire Lord Delamere declared for William; in Yorkshire Danby, too, was busy collecting his friends and tenants to bring support. Certain now of the help he wanted, William left Exeter on November 21st and slowly marched towards the capital.

James might still have made a stand, for most of the bishops and some of the secular peers remained loyal. Halifax, Clarendon and Nottingham still hoped to keep James on the throne, but to use William's presence to extract suitable concessions and guarantees from him. The peers demanded that a free parliament should be summoned, the Catholic officers dismissed, and negotiations opened with William. But by now James was incoherently bewildered, perplexed and wounded by the disloyalty of his own family and household. Trying to gain time, he sent Halifax, Nottingham and Godolphin to meet William, at Hungerford in Berkshire. William's conditions were moderate and acceptable to the ambassadors – a free parliament, the removal of Catholics from office, the surrender of the Tower of London to the City authorities, and a grant of money for the Dutch army – but infuriated James when he learnt them.

Early on December 11th, he resolved to go abroad to escape this humiliation, and to shelter with Louis in France until his subjects should beg him to return on his own terms. The events of forty years before were not far from his thoughts. Already he had sent his Queen and the baby prince across the Channel for safety. Accompanied only by Hales, he slipped on board a small boat at Sheerness. A few hours later, the peers in Guildhall voted to assist William to obtain speedily 'a parliament . . . wherein our Laws, our Liberties and Properties may be secured, and the Church of England in particular, with a due liberty to Protestant Dissenters'. That night the London mob took its chance to burn down Catholic chapels and loot the houses of prominent Catholics. But London had not seen quite the last of James. His attempt to escape was foiled by fishermen who grabbed him off the coast of Kent, handled him roughly, and then surrendered him to loyal troops who escorted him back to London. Although the citizens seemed not hostile, the King's nerve failed him. A week after his return he again fled.[1] This time he was successful. A tiny boat took him to a fishing village near Calais, and the seamen carried him ashore in time to hear Mass. It was Christmas Day.

Many factors had helped William's venture: the universal dislike of James's policies, the poor morale of the English army and navy, long neglected by its royal admiral, the Protestant wind which speeded William down Channel while it kept Dartmouth bottled up in port, the fact that there was no fighting to provoke enmity between Dutch and English, Louis XIV's folly in attacking the Palatinate. William's own wisdom, in delaying intervention until assured of support, in issuing the political declarations and in the discussions, also played a major part. But by his flight James had greatly assisted him. Especially in a civil war, men would not fight for a king who ran away. The nature of his departure, moreover, made it easier for many Tories to smother their pangs of conscience. It was very convenient for them to pretend that James had abdicated and that the throne was vacant. Now they could join the Whigs in thinking about the future.

[1] William deliberately made it easy for him to escape.

The peers had asked William to summon a parliament; their request was repeated in informal meetings of the leading citizens of London and the available survivors of the last House of Commons. William accordingly approved election writs, for a Parliament to assemble on January 22nd. As in 1660, this broke the letter of the law, for the writs lacked the authority of the reigning sovereign. The Convention Parliament, however, had the support of every non-Catholic in the country; and in times of revolution popular approval is more important than the letter of the law. In the meantime, during the month before the Convention met, William agreed to direct public affairs, at the request of the peers, the ex-M.P.s and the citizens of London.

So far there were few who disapproved of the turn events had taken. On the checking of royal power by a parliament, all had agreed. But it was more difficult to decide what changes and reforms were necessary. The Tories were hopelessly split. A few wanted James back as King, under guarantees of good behaviour. Some wanted him acknowledged as King, but the powers of sovereignty given to his daughter Mary as regent; some wanted Mary as sole ruler in her own right, on the theory that James, by flight, had abdicated. The Whigs, however, were united. By his bad government, they claimed, James had broken the contract between ruler and subject, and must therefore be deposed. In his place they all wanted William and Mary to rule as joint sovereigns. The House of Commons in the Convention consisted overwhelmingly of opponents of James, and they were able to force on the more moderate Lords a compromise settlement which gave them, in fact if not in name, all they wanted. William speeded up the agreement by threatening to return to Holland with his troops if he were not given a share of the Crown; he was not willing to be his wife's 'gentleman usher'. Mary, for her part, insisted that he should reign jointly with her. As they feared an invasion by Tyrconnell's army from Ireland if William took his troops away, the peers submitted.

The members of the Commons were determined not to repeat the mistakes of 1660. At the Restoration, Charles II had come to the throne 'without conditions' other than the promises of Breda. This time Parliament carefully thrashed out the principles of the constitutional settlement before it acclaimed the new sovereign. Committees of the Lords and Commons prepared a joint Declaration of Rights, completed on February 12th; next day Halifax led a deputation from both Houses to offer the Crown to William and Mary jointly. They accepted. Ten days later the Convention declared itself a valid Parliament, and prescribed oaths of loyalty to be taken by its members to William and Mary. At the end of March, to deal with the problem of keeping discipline in the fast-deserting standing army, the Convention passed the Mutiny Act, giving parliamentary recognition to military law for the following six months. Then it turned to religion, and to rewarding the Nonconformists for refusing to be fooled by James's Declarations of Indulgence. Nottingham, who had been distinguished for his loyalty to James and the Church of England, now brought forward two Bills. One, the Comprehension Bill, was too radical, for it proposed to modify the Anglican ritual and doctrine to make the Church acceptable to most Nonconformists, and the Anglican Commons rejected it. The other was passed. This, the Toleration Act, simply ordered that the penal statutes should not be enforced on Protestant Nonconformists, provided they accepted the doctrine of the Trinity and held their religious meetings openly, having notified the Church authorities about them.[1] The purpose of this Act was expressed clearly in the preamble: it was to give 'some ease to scrupulous consciences in the exercise of religion . . . to unite their Majesties protestant subjects in interest and affection'. It was a matter of political convenience, not religious or philosophical principle.

In December 1689 the Convention tied together the main threads of the Revolutionary Settlement by passing the Bill of Rights. It began by repeating the February Declaration of Rights, which had recorded James's misdeeds and, in the spirit of Magna Carta, listed various things the King must not do. It was illegal to suspend or dispense with the laws. It was illegal to revive the Ecclesiastical Commission 'and courts of like nature'. It was illegal to collect taxes by prerogative or to maintain a standing army without consent of Parliament. It

---

[1] Nonconformist clergy were obliged in addition to swear their acceptance of all but three of the Thirty-nine Articles. They were not required to agree to the validity of Tradition, the value of the Homilies, or the ceremonies for consecrating bishops and ordaining priests.

was illegal to interfere with Parliamentary elections or with freedom of debate, and illegal to tamper in any way with juries. To these resolutions of the Declaration, the Bill of Rights added two more clauses, to make sure that England never again had a Catholic monarch.    One declared that no person could stand in line of succession to the English throne who was, or who married, a Catholic.    The other fixed the order of inheritance: after the deaths of both William and Mary, the throne would pass to Mary's children (at present she had none, and was already thirty seven), then to Princess Anne and her children (despite her frequent pregnancies, only the baby Duke of Gloucester was living) and then to William and his children (if he married again after Mary's death).

These were sweeping changes.    At a time when the King still decreed when Parliament should assemble, adjourn and dissolve, Parliament itself had declared who should be sovereign, where the succession lay, and – at least in a negative sense – what the monarch's religion should be.    For a century and a half the Bill of Rights remained the basis for nearly all constitutional disputes and changes, most of which were regarded merely as modifications of it.    It had flaws – some of which were corrected before William's death – but it amounted to a contract, established in law, between the King and the Country, represented by Parliament.    It paid lip-service to the Tory claim that James had abdicated and that the throne was therefore vacant, but in fact it was a full expression of the Whig views of 'social contract'.    In the very next year, the Whig philosopher John Locke expounded these views in his two Treatises on Civil Government – an exposition which became as much a part of English history as the Settlement itself.    The Revolution had been carried through by Tories – they were in a majority even in the Convention Parliament – but the Settlement could not be anything but a Whig one.    With the Seven Bishops' petition to James, and the magnates' invitation to William, the old principles of Non-Resistance had been thrown overboard.

The other parts of the Settlement were also of major importance.    The Mutiny Act was more significant than appeared at first sight.    The Crown's need to keep the standing army disciplined obliged the King to call and re-call Parliament frequently, for the courts-martial were authorized for only six or twelve months at a time. Even today the Mutiny Act is re-passed annually. The Toleration Act was the first step in the long process of removing the penalties and disabilities attached to Nonconformity.

There was, however, one unfortunate consequence of the oaths of loyalty prescribed by the Convention for its members. During 1689 these oaths were made compulsory for all in official posts, including those in the Church. Many of the clergy, having sworn fealty to James, were not prepared to swear loyalty to William, even though they were willing to accept him as *de facto* king. Eight bishops and about 400 other clergy refused the oath. The Non-Jurors included Archbishop Sancroft and four others who had stood in the dock with him a year before. In 1688 they had faced imprisonment; now they were unemployed. In the age of the Vicar of Bray, these Non-Jurors were men the Church could ill afford to lose. Not for the first time, the established Church was weakened by a purge administered by Parliament or its own supreme Governor. While the Non-Jurors devoted themselves to scholarship in their enforced idleness, their places were filled with conformist Whigs. By the end of 1692 fifteen new bishops had been consecrated, and the political colour of the episcopal bench had been changed from Tory Non-Resistance to the Whiggery of the Revolution Settlement.

The Settlement of 1689 was more revolutionary than the expulsion of James had been. The power of the monarchy was restricted within fairly narrow limits. The King had to be Protestant; could not interfere with justice either by suspending a law or by having his own special courts; could not levy taxes without Parliament's consent; could not keep an army without Parliament's approval, and was required not to intervene in elections or in debates in Parliament. Parliament gained the upper hand, since it alone could grant taxes and renew the Mutiny Acts. On the other hand, William kept control of foreign policy as a royal prerogative, and committed England to an anti-French alignment which lasted with only a few interruptions until 1815. The cost of foreign wars made the Crown even more dependent upon Parliament. Theories of Divine Right and principles of Non-Resistance faded rapidly: William and his successors were rulers by Act of Parliament, not act of God. The 'Glorious Revolution' split the Tory party, and made possible the revival of the Whigs.   The growth of toleration and the departure of the Non-Jurors led to a decline in the Church of England.

### iii. Scotland and the Revolution

In the Stuarts' ancestral kingdom the course of Revolution ran less smoothly, less gloriously, and towards a more radical destination than in England.   For this the policies of James VII must be blamed.   On his visit to Scotland in 1681 as High Commissioner, he had induced Parliament to declare that 'no difference in religion nor no law nor act of Parliament . . . can alter or divert the Right of Succession and lineal descent of the Crown'.   On the other hand, he agreed to a Test Act denouncing popery and the political aspects of the *Solemn League and Covenant*, so infuriating to his father and grand-father, and continued the traditional Stuart policy of building up the Episcopal Church to check Presbyterianism.   Although the 'Highland Host' of 1678 and the suppression of the Cameronians made the government's Church even more hated in the south-west of Scotland, in many other regions the episco-palians were slowly gaining in the century-long struggle.   The strength of the Crown's position in 1685 was shown by the speed with which James's first Scottish Parliament granted him Excise duties for the whole reign and made attendance at conventicles punishable with death.

In England James's greatest folly was to anger the Church of England; in Scotland it was to weaken its equivalent.   His accession was the signal for time-servers like Perth and his brother Melfort to announce their conversion to Rome; James used these and other converts to replace Protestants such as Queensberry (the High Commissioner and Treasurer) and 'the bluidy Mackenzie' (the Lord Advocate).   Command of Edin-burgh Castle went to another Catholic, the Duke of Gordon. As in England, James deliberately removed officials known to be hostile to Rome; among the victims were Archbishop Cairncross of Glasgow and Bishop Bruce of Dunkeld.   The penalty was death for taking part in anti-Catholic demon-strations, or even for expressing approval of them.   In April 1686 James offered to allow Scotland to trade freely with England if the anti-Catholic laws were repealed.   Next year, proclamations of toleration gave freedom to men of all religions to worship openly in 'private houses, chapels or places purposely hired or built for that use', though field conventicles were still outlawed. Thus, at the same time as encouraging the Catholics, James destroyed the privileged position of the Episcopal Church and permitted the revival of Presbyterianism.

Scotland took no direct part in the events of 1688, though many exiles crossed the Channel with William. James, however, had summoned to England the royal army commanded by Graham of Claverhouse, now Viscount Dundee; consequently, when news of William's landing reached Scotland, the Privy Council in Edinburgh had no army with which to enforce order. In the south-west the villagers 'rabbled' and expelled the hated Episcopalian ministers – nearly 300 of them – while in Edinburgh the mob sacked Holyrood Palace, chased away the Jesuits and broke up the Catholic printing press. Expecting sympathy from Calvinist William, especially as Cameronian and other Presbyterian fugitives in Holland had been cramming his ears with tales of Scotland's woes, over a hundred Scottish peers and gentry hastened to London and persuaded him to summon a Convention in Edinburgh. The Convention met in March under the Duke of Hamilton, and it was clear from the start that James's supporters were in the minority. Towering over the City, Edinburgh Castle remained loyal, but the Duke of Gordon did not dare to use its guns to cower the citizens back into allegiance. After a few days, Dundee led James's supporters away, planning to hold a rival Convention at Stirling. Henceforth the 'Whigs' and Presbyterians remaining at the Convention had things all their own way. By mid-April they had thrashed out a settlement in the Claim of Right, modelled on the English Declaration of Rights, but with two major differences.

James, the Claim declared, had 'invaded the fundamental constitution of the Kingdom', and altered it to 'an arbitrary despotick Power'; in consequence, 'he hath forefaulted the right to the Crown'. In England James had abdicated; in Scotland, less euphemistically, he was deposed. The Calvinist tradition of the *Vindiciae Contra Tyrannos*,[1] justifying the removal of an unjust king, had enabled backward Scotland to put into practice

---

[1] A famous Huguenot treatise, probably by Languet, written to justify the French Protestants' rebellions against their King in the later sixteenth century.

the theory of 'social contract' from which progressive England
had shied away.

The second difference between Scotland and England was
that the Claim condemned prelacy as an 'insupportable grievance and trouble to this Nation'.   By accepting the Claim of
Right as the price of his Crown, William committed himself to
the destruction of the Episcopal Church.   Misled by Scottish
exiles such as William Carstares, the King realized too late the
value of the Episcopal Church – 'the great body of the nobility
and gentry are for episcopacy, and 'tis the trading and inferior
sort that are for presbytery'.[1]   He could not save the bishops –
the Scottish Parliament would not vote him any taxes until he
consented in June 1690 to the enforced re-establishment of the
Presbyterian Church according to the recent Confession of
Faith – but he intervened repeatedly during the 1690s to restrain
the revengeful Kirk and to protect the moderate Episcopalian
clergy.

Two days after the Claim of Right the Convention passed
supplementary Articles of Grievances.   The most important of
these demanded the abolition of the Lords of the Articles, the
committee through which Stuart kings had controlled most of
their Scottish Parliaments.   When William finally agreed,
more than a year later, one of the most important ties between
England and Scotland was broken.   The way was open for the
two countries to drift into the crisis which could be resolved only
by the union of their Parliaments in 1707.

Viscount Dundee's plan to hold a Convention loyal to James
had been thwarted when the Edinburgh Convention sent troops
to occupy Stirling.   Thus forced into armed rebellion, 'Bonnie
Dundee' began to raise the Highlands for the Stuart cause, for
plunder and for the Roman and Episcopal Churches.   The
Scottish Estates sent General Mackay with a raw army after
him.   For a few weeks they chased each other around the
Cairngorms, while attempting to seize Blair Atholl.   This was
the seat of the large Murray clan, as yet undecided between
James and William.   It was also the base from which Montrose,
a greater member of the Graham clan than Dundee was, had
fought for his King some forty-five years earlier.   As Mackay
was marching his men through the narrow pass of Killiecrankie

[1] William's words quoted by Bishop Compton of London to Bishop Rose of
Edinburgh.   The remark is still partly true.

in July 1689, four miles south of Blair, Dundee led his barefoot warriors down the steep hillside in a wild dash on Mackay's terrified recruits. The highlanders swept all before them, plundering and looting in the traditional way. But they lacked a leader, for Dundee was killed in the fighting.

For a month the Camerons, Macleans and Macdonalds in the Jacobite[1] bands looted the villages of central Perthshire, while Mackay tried to scrape together a better army. The Cameronians formed the backbone of a new regiment, commanded by William Cleland, the victor of Drumclog ten years before. Appropriately, the decisive battle in the struggle for Scotland was fought between the ill-disciplined Catholic and Episcopalian highlanders and the bitter, persecuted, Psalm-singing Calvinists from the south. Besieged in Dunkeld by a much larger force, Cleland's men drove off the highlanders, humbled the clans, and dashed Stuart hopes in Scotland for a quarter of a century.

Had it not been for a foolish act of bureaucratic brutality, Jacobite fortunes might never have revived. The clansmen were generously treated after the battle of Dunkeld, for the government was too weak to do anything but allow the survivors to return to their glens. As a precaution, General Mackay built Fort William, on a strategic site overshadowed by Ben Nevis. At the western end of the Great Glen, and in the heart of Cameron, Maclean and Macdonald lands, it was well-chosen to guard against Jacobite risings in the Highlands or in the Western Isles, for the clans would not risk marching south while their crofts were exposed to punitive reprisals. As some clans still remained restless, in 1691 William ordered his agents to distribute £12,000 among them in return for oaths of loyalty to him as King. By the date fixed, January 1st, 1692, only Alexander Macdonald of Glencoe had failed to take the oath. Delayed – so he claimed – by bad weather, he did not walk the dozen miles to Fort William until the government sheriff appointed to receive the oaths had left. Macdonald now returned to Glencoe and trudged fifty-odd miles to the heart of the Campbell lands, where he swore the oath to the sheriff at Inveraray on January 6th.

Clan rivalries now wrecked William's attempt to pacify the Highlands. His London adviser on Scottish affairs was Sir

[1] So named after *Jacobus*, the Latin form of James.

John Dalrymple of Stair, aided in Edinburgh by the Campbell Earl of Breadalbane. Both families were inveterate enemies of the Macdonalds. As Alexander Macdonald was a known Jacobite who had fought at Killiecrankie, Dalrymple and Breadalbane took the chance to continue old feuds in the name of enforcing law and order. On January 11th Dalrymple got William's signature for an order authorising General Livingstone to march against the clan chieftains who had not sworn, though allowing him to give terms to those who had taken the oath after January 1st. A few days later, Dalrymple sent additional orders 'to extirpate that sect of thieves' in Glencoe. In Edinburgh the Privy Council's record that Macdonald had eventually taken the oath was destroyed – presumably Breadalbane's work – and orders were sent commanding his destruction. Captain Campbell of Glen Lyon with over a hundred soldiers (mostly Campbells) was quartered on the Glencoe Macdonalds early in February, and, with other government troops guarding the passes and tracks, Campbell was told on February 12th to put to the sword 'the old fox and his sones' the next morning. At five o'clock the signal echoed around the icy walls of the glen, and the soldiers rose up and murdered their unsuspecting hosts. But the job was botched. Although about forty men, women and children were slaughtered, others escaped into the mountains and fled to friendly clans. By Highland standards, the Massacre of Glencoe was only a minor skirmish in long years of clan feuds, but Jacobite propaganda from France seized upon it as an example of William's treachery. It was much more an example of poor administration. Preoccupied with the war against France, and forced to sign hundreds of documents each week without reading them, William's responsibility for causing the massacre was very slight. He aroused suspicion, however, by failing to punish adequately the guilty men. Breadalbane was imprisoned briefly in Edinburgh Castle, and Dalrymple allowed to escape justice after resigning his office. Both men were too influential for the King to punish them as they deserved. The unfortunate episode provided the Jacobites with much-needed ammunition – and to this day colours relations between Campbells and Macdonalds.

The effects of the Revolution in Scotland were therefore more extreme than in England, where the Glorious Revolution was moderate, and acceptable largely because it was bloodless throughout. Killiecrankie, Dunkeld, and Glencoe were the main recruiting agents for James VIII in the 1715 Rebellion and for his son thirty years later. Meanwhile, the Revolution had placed power in the hands of the Presbyterian and Whig families, so much that the Crown had to acknowledge the 'social contract' and that curious paradox whereby the sovereign has to worship as an Anglican in England and as a Presbyterian in Scotland. In some respects, therefore, the Glorious Revolution in Scotland had more in common with the experiments of the Civil War than with contemporary changes in England. Now out of step, Scotland was more free (through the disappearance of the Lords of the Articles) to drift towards greater independence, and towards the crisis in Anglo-Scottish relations which developed in the next two decades.

### iv. Ireland and the Revolution

Only by fighting a full-scale war could William enforce his authority on Ireland, in campaigns which merged into the general European conflict of the time. James's policies had of course been welcomed, not feared, in a land still largely loyal to Rome. At the start of his reign he had sent the Catholic Richard Talbot, first Earl of Tyrconnell, to Ireland as army commander and assistant to Clarendon, the brother-in-law on whose loyalty James thought he could depend. When Clarendon protested at the appointment of hundreds of Catholics to official posts throughout the country, James sacked him and made Tyrconnell Lord Deputy in his place. Before long most of the judges and sheriffs were Catholics, as were almost all army officers and the majority of the councillors on most town corporations. The Anglican minority which Clarendon had represented could only protest feebly, and the old Catholic families prepared to put the clock back two centuries by restoring papal power and removing that of the English parliament. The spectre of Strafford, and of Irish Catholic intervention in England on behalf of a despotic monarch, became more and more fearsome in the months when England was sliding towards Revolution. Tyrconnell, indeed, seriously considered intervening in England in the manner unjustly alleged against 'Black Tom Tyrant' fifty years before. In the end, the danger of an Irish invasion played into the hands of the Whigs in England, by forcing the Tories to accept William as King as the price for the protection given by the Dutch army.

Even before William's landing in England, the Presbyterians in Northern Ireland had taken up arms in self-defence, for in mid-September Londonderry fortified itself against the Catholic Earl of Antrim.   Soon Enniskillen joined Londonderry as a refuge for Protestants, though many thousands fled to England and Scotland as soon as the Irish Catholics began to arm to fight for James.   Tyrconnell himself was prepared to compromise, but the ambassador William sent to him betrayed his trust and joined the Catholic side.   An envoy Tyrconnell sent to France persuaded James that Ireland could be held for the Stuart and Catholic cause, and used as a base for the reconquest of England.   Having begged help from Louis – now at war with William – James landed at Kinsale in March 1689 with a number of French officers.   Thousands of ragged ruffians cheered as James and his party rode to Dublin; for once, the nobles and peasants could fight for their faith, their independence and their King at the same time.

James then moved north to supervise the sieges of Londonderry and Enniskillen.   Most of the garrison at Londonderry deserted to the Jacobite side, and joined the besiegers firing the new explosive shells into the city.   For a hundred days the citizens endured famine and disease, resisting bravely under Governor Walker, while all their children died and the English navy dithered incompetently outside.   It was not until the end of July that on Schomberg's direct orders the ships burst through the boom placed across the harbour mouth, and brought supplies to the starving survivors.   The siege was lifted.   On the same day Protestant volunteers under Colonel Wolseley relieved Enniskillen by routing a larger Catholic army at Newton Butler.   The double victory saved Northern Ireland for Protestantism.   Not until August 1689 could William send an army to Ireland; even then the force which sailed consisted largely of worthless recruits.   The expedition was deliberately sabotaged by the Commissary General, Henry Shales, who remained secretly loyal to James and made himself rich by keeping the money which should have equipped the army.   Even the Paymaster, Harbord, was drawing the pay for a regiment which did not exist. Dependent on such rogues, Schomberg had no chance: 7000 of his men perished from hunger and disease in the army's winter quarters at Dundalk. The English navy was in a comparable state of inefficiency, and Admiral Herbert was lucky to escape defeat when he attacked a French convoy in Bantry Bay as it was returning from landing supplies.

Meanwhile James had been ingratiating himself with the race he despised. In May 1689 he opened an Irish Parliament consisting almost entirely of Catholics. A rapid series of Acts declared that the Irish Parliament and law were independent of England, and that each man should pay tithes only to the Church to which he belonged.[1] The Parliament also repealed the 1662 Act of Settlement (thus dispossessing most Protestant landowners without compensation) and passed an Act of Attainder on some 2400 refugees who had fled from Ireland since the recent troubles began.

The English Whig Parliament of 1690 reacted violently to these measures. Things were going so badly that William had to appease public opinion by going to Ireland in person, despite the pressing needs of the campaigns on the continent. In mid-June 1690 he landed at Carrickfergus, at the head of a motley crew of mercenaries, half of them recruited from most of the states in northern Europe. The Ulster volunteers brought William's force to about 35,000 men. The crisis of the campaign came quickly. On July 1st William's army forced a crossing of the River Boyne, in the face of a Jacobite army almost equally strong, and in a good defensive position. Like W. S. Gilbert's Duke of Plaza-Toro, James led his regiment from behind, and was foremost in flight when the Catholics broke off the battle, and spurred back to Dublin and beyond. With the soldiers singing the words of Lord Wharton's scurrilous 'Lilliburlero', William marched his troops on to occupy Ireland's capital. The Battle of the Boyne was decisive only because James accepted it as being so. Depressed by the result of this skirmish – James lost only one man in twenty, William one man in sixty – James decided to return to the security of France and the comforts of his Court at St. Germain. Brilliantly led by Patrick Sarsfield, James's supporters fought on

---

[1] Hitherto (and subsequently until 1869) all Irishmen were obliged to pay tithes to the Anglican Church of Ireland.

and for the time being foiled William's plans to capture Limerick. As Schomberg was among the casualties at the Battle of the Boyne, William left the Dutch general Ginkel to continue the war while he returned to London and the centre of affairs. In September Churchill, now Earl of Marlborough, captured Cork and Kinsale in a brief campaign which demonstrated his military genius. During the autumn and winter hesitations by both William and Louis halted the war, though Louis unwisely insisted that a French general, St. Ruth, should take command over Sarsfield's Irishmen. Personal rivalries between the two generals handicapped the Jacobites in the major battle of 1691, which they might have won had not Sarsfield been told of St. Ruth's death too late to take effective command. In May Ginkel with 20,000 men attacked a stronger force of Jacobites on the slopes outside Aughrim Castle. Already certain of victory, St. Ruth was leading a final charge when a cannon-ball knocked his head off. Before Sarsfield could take control, Ginkel's cavalry counter-attacked and routed the Jacobite infantry. Eleven thousand men, a quarter of the combatants, remained on the field as casualties. The bloody battle of Aughrim made it impossible for the Irish to remain in the field without substantial French help, for by now only Limerick was holding out. Ginkel hurried to capture it before reinforcements arrived. As a precaution, he arrested – in the nick of time – Irish pilots waiting to guide the French ships up the Shannon to relieve Limerick. The beleaguered town had to surrender in early October, with the French ships waiting helplessly off shore.

The Articles of Limerick, negotiated between Ginkel and Sarsfield in October 1691, might have formed the basis of a moderate settlement in Ireland. The generosity of the original Articles reflected the weakness of William's position and his anxiety to be free to fight the continental war. Ginkel promised, on William's behalf, to allow all the soldiers under arms and *all such as were under their protection* to keep the lands and privileges they had possessed in the reign of Charles II (that is, before the confiscations made by the Irish after revoking the Act of Settlement) provided they swore allegiance to William and Mary. Moreover – a remarkable concession – all Irish soldiers who wished to go to France to fight in Louis's army might do so. About 11,000 took the opportunity, half of them sailing with the convoy which had arrived just too late to save Limerick.

Unfortunately the English Parliament, vindictive in a way William and Ginkel could not understand, refused to accept the Articles' moderate terms. The clause italicized above was left out of the draft given the King for signature; William then re-inserted it with his own hand. For years Parliament quarrelled over the 'omitted clause' and over William's promise to save from attainder all the Irish he could. The King's need for money was such that he had to give way. A Court of Claims in Dublin attainted some 4000 Catholic land-owners and seized from them over a million and a half acres of their property. The English Parliament amended the simple oath of allegiance originally required to one which no Catholic could accept, and made it obligatory for all office holders. Consequently when the Irish Parliament met in 1697 it was almost exclusively Protestant. The Anglican bishops, how-ever, were generally sympathetic to the Catholic natives, and almost managed to insist on the re-insertion of the 'omitted clause'. They intervened to save the Catholic schools and secular (parish) clergy from persecution, though the regular clergy (members of religious orders) had to leave. Despite these mitigations of the fervour of the English Whig M.P.s, the settlement imposed was a harsh and intolerant one, leaving the Catholics with barely an eighth of the land of their country. By rejecting the spirit of the original Articles of Limerick, the English Parliament added to the long roll of Irish grievances against their conquerors.

### v. The War of the League of Augsburg

The campaigns in Scotland and Ireland, though unavoidable if he wanted English support, distracted William's attention from Holland's latest struggle with France. Louis's attack on the Palatinate in 1688 once more scared the monarchs of Europe into war. Their alliance was based on the vague 1686 League of Augsburg. In it, the rulers of the Empire, Spain, Sweden and several German states had agreed to resist jointly any future French aggression. By the spring of 1689 the League of Augsburg had assembled 100,000 troops on the lower Rhine, ready to check a French attack on the Spanish Netherlands, the United Provinces or the Empire.

William now set himself to unite this loose alliance into a strong coalition. It was easy for him, as King of the one and Stadtholder in the other, to arrange in April 1689 a treaty between England and the United Provinces for naval co-operation between the two countries. Next month the States-General and Emperor Leopold signed an alliance, soon joined by William as King of England, Charles II of Spain, the Dukes of Lorraine and Savoy and the Electors of Brandenburg and Bavaria. The war-aims of these rulers varied widely. The States-General and Charles II hoped to preserve the United Provinces and the Spanish Netherlands from another French invasion. Lorraine and Savoy wanted to regain territory lost to France; Brandenburg and Bavaria to extend their frontiers at French expense. Leopold hoped to extract from a defeated France the acknowledgement that his son Charles should succeed to the whole Spanish empire when Charles II died – and as the price of the alliance forced William to promise secretly to support his claims. When England declared war in May 1689 she did so to defend the Revolutionary Settlement, and to keep James II off the throne. In England and Holland, popular enthusiasm for the war was increased by Louis's recent persecution of the Huguenots and massacre of the Palatinate Protestants. At the same time Leopold and Charles, both of them Catholics and Hapsburgs, were tormented by doubts about the propriety of allying with William, a Calvinist and a usurper. The diversity of their aims soon hampered the Allies' war effort, and it took all William's skill as a diplomat to keep the Alliance together.

On the other hand, William had no skill as a soldier, and showed no talent in the choice of his commanders. With consequences which were often disastrous, he usually depended on Dutchmen to lead English armies, even though Marlborough gave early proof of his genius by defeating Villars's French cavalry at Walcourt in 1689 and by capturing Cork and Kinsale in the Irish campaigns of the following year. He ignored even the House of Lords' petition in 1693 that only Englishmen should command English troops.

In fact, no Allied commander was a match for Luxemburg and Boufflers, particularly as both were so experienced in the art of warfare on the flat plains between the Scheldt and the Meuse, the scene of most of the fighting. They repeatedly outmanœuvred William and his generals in the set-piece battles, and were equally efficient in capturing fortresses by scientific sieges.    One by one they stormed the great barrier fortresses in the Spanish Netherlands, to give the French frontier defensive depth, and to make possible the spectacular triumphant entries Louis XIV loved to make into the towns his soldiers captured.    In 1690 the French won the battle of Fleurus and then took Mons.    Namur fell in 1692, and in that year Luxemburg slaughtered Mackay's British infantry at Steenkirk, after the Dutch general Solms had refused to move to help them.    Next year the Allies were again defeated, at the battle of Landen (or Neerwinden); most of the 16,000 casualties were British.    These reverses undermined William's popularity at home, for an army of over 100,000 men, raised at unprecedented expense by a nation which had never before competed with the the big battalions of the continental powers, had done little to justify its existence.    Not until 1695 – after Luxemburg's death – did the Allies achieve a land victory; after a fierce assault led by Lord Cutts, Boufflers surrendered Namur to William.    Though this brought William a short-lived popularity in England, the army's achievements still seemed ridiculously disproportionate to the expenditure in blood and treasure.    If the Whigs had not been so deeply committed to defending the 1688 Revolution, the English Parliament would have quickly abandoned this unprofitable struggle.

Even the war at sea went badly.    The French fleet was in good shape under Seignelai, son of the great Colbert who had founded it.    The English navy was in a poor state, despite the efforts of Pepys, and was badly directed, as the Secretaries of State often interfered with the Admiralty.    The navy was strained intolerably by the demands put upon it – the defence of trade, the convoying of reinforcements to the Low Countries, aiding Spain in the Mediterranean, arranging 'Commando' attacks to divert French troops from Flanders, and preventing supplies reaching the Jacobites in Ireland.    Admiral Herbert was lucky to escape lightly from an encounter with a superior fleet in Bantry Bay in 1689, for the French admiral did not bother to chase the fugitives.    Next year the government rashly ordered Herbert (now Lord Torrington) to fight a full-scale battle, despite the inferiority of his force.    At the end of June 1690 Tourville's French fleet routed the Allied navies in the battle of Beachy Head. Seventeen English and Dutch ships were lost, the French were masters of the Channel, and the Londoners in a panic unknown since De Ruyter's attack on the Medway. At the same time, French privateers under captains like Jean Bart were preying on English and Dutch merchant shipping, and forced William to use most of his ships to protect convoys.

Nonetheless the government's policy was not entirely passive, for it planned to invade France in the summer of 1692, with 1500 metal landing craft to transport the armies of Schomberg[1] and Ruvigny. At the same time Louis XIV and James II were preparing to invade England, and assembled near Cherbourg an army of 40,000 men. Instructed to convoy them across the Channel, Tourville ran into an Anglo-Dutch fleet twice the size of his own off Cape Barfleur. Admiral Russell (who had replaced Torrington) scattered the French fleet without doing serious damage, but Rooke subsequently burned thirteen of the fugitives in La Hogue bay. The battle of La Hogue, in May 1692, did no lasting harm to the French navy, but it helped to restore English prestige and avert the threat of invasion.

Next year, however, Tourville got his revenge. He drove off the escorts of the great Smyrna convoy, and destroyed about a hundred English and Dutch ships returning richly laden from the Eastern Mediterranean. This disaster angered the merchants, for it could have been averted if Nottingham had passed on to the convoy the news that the French fleet had put to sea. Further incompetence led to another disaster in 1694, when the government's plans for an attack on Brest became known to the enemy in time for Vauban to strengthen the city's defences. In consequence, the English troops landing in Camaret Bay were ambushed and routed.

These expensive failures, despite the success at Namur, gradually turned England against the war. The commercial classes suffered from the loss of merchant shipping, and the landowners especially groaned under war taxation averaging £5,000,000 a year. The economy was tottering, and the government widely criticized for corruption and incompetence. Neither on land nor sea was a decisive victory in sight for either side, even though France had defeated Savoy. Moreover,

---

[1] Son of the general killed in the battle of the Boyne.

Louis was growing tired of the war, bored with his royal sport. He lost interest finally when in 1696 his new invasion plan was foiled by Rooke, who beat Tourville in a race from the Mediterranean back to the Channel.

Peace negotiations began at Ryswick in May 1697. At first they were obstructed by the Emperor Leopold, hoping that Charles II would die soon enough for him to be able to keep Britain and Holland to their promise to support his son's claims to the Spanish inheritance. William then cut short the red tape in diplomacy by sending his friend Bentinck to negotiate directly with Boufflers as Louis's agent. In five months the discussions were complete. Louis promised to restore all his recent conquests except Strasbourg, recognized William as King of Great Britain 'par la grâce de Dieu', and promised not to help his enemies. France and Spain agreed that the Dutch should be allowed to occupy some of the barrier fortresses in the Netherlands, to give the United Provinces greater security. But of the great international issue, the Spanish Succession, there was no mention.

Because it ignored the question of who should succeed Charles II, the Treaty of Ryswick was more a truce than a lasting peace. Nevertheless, it showed that French aggression could be resisted successfully, it confirmed William as King (by Divine Grace, if not Divine Right) and thereby the fact of the Revolution, and it briefly lessened international tension. Many British and Austrian generals had gained much valuable experience in the war, and at home something had been done to increase the efficiency of the Admiralty and Army Office. Had it not been for the lessons of the War of the League of Augsburg, Britain and her allies would have fared far worse in the War of the Spanish Succession five years later.

## vi. Constitutional progress and party strife

The war led indirectly to the further development of the Revolutionary principles of 1688-9. William, an unpopular King, with few loyal friends in England, could not defend the surviving powers of monarchy while having to beg Parliament for unprecedented taxation. Had it not been for the King's urgent need for money, Parliament would have met far less frequently, and England might have remained indefinitely

balanced on the precarious experimental constitution hastily
concocted in 1689.   In fact, the constitutional nature of the
British monarchy derives almost as much from the war of
1689-97 as from the Revolution and Settlement.

England's new King was in some ways an unsatisfactory
sovereign.   He was shy and reserved, remote from his subjects.   Whereas the Stuarts had continued the old custom of
allowing the common people to enter Whitehall to watch them
dine in state, William insisted on eating privately.   His
preoccupation with the affairs of Holland and the war gave
him no time to tour England to show himself to the people.
It was not easy for him to forget that he owed his throne to the
nobles and other magnates, and inevitably he came to resent
their patronizing behaviour towards him.   It was natural for
him to prefer the company of his Dutch and German friends,
men whom he trusted – and whom he injudiciously rewarded
with English peerages, generous pensions and lavish grants of
land.   Physically he was not robust, but his intellectual powers,
strengthened by his Calvinist belief in predestination, made
him a dogged and tenacious adversary.   His co-sovereign,
Mary, was a more attractive and  popular person – though
many Tories thought it would have been more becoming for
her to show greater reluctance before accepting her father's
throne.   For help in managing the affairs of England, William
relied greatly upon his Queen, and her death at the end of 1694
was a grievous loss to him.

One development, resulting from William's long absences
from England, on campaign in Ireland or Flanders, was a
primitive form of the Cabinet system.   It had ancestors in the
Councils for Trade and Plantations after the Restoration, and
in an informal group of leading Privy Councillors at the end of
Charles II's reign.   William made a wider and less informal
use of such groups of Councillors.   When he sailed for Ulster
in 1690, for example, he left Mary with a small Cabinet of nine
(rather than the unwieldy sixty-strong Privy Council) to help
her govern in his absence.   Among the nine were Danby,
Devonshire, Shrewsbury and Nottingham.   This Cabinet had
full administrative authority, but its members had no common
policy and were not directly responsible to Parliament.   Even
so, Parliament was able to force William to dismiss Nottingham
from his post as Secretary after the Smyrna convoy disaster had

disgraced him.  The so-called 'Junto' of Whigs who led the government from 1695 to 1698 was more akin to the modern Cabinet: it relied on a Whig majority in the Commons, most of its members were heads of the great departments of State and all deliberated together on matters of policy and made collective recommendations to the King.  A further constitutional innovation, after Mary's death, was the appointment of lord justices to serve as regents during William's absences abroad.

These changes made government depend on the person of the sovereign rather less than hitherto.  At the same time William was having to call Parliament more often.  It was logical, therefore, for the King to try to build up in Parliament a body of loyal supporters, with bribes such as army commissions or lucrative sinecures in the administration.  To check this and to make the King keep his distance, Parliament forced William to accept the Triennial Act.  He had twice thwarted earlier Triennial Bills, but the need for money obliged him to give way in 1694.  The Act decreed that no Parliament should last for more than three years at the most, and that a new Parliament should be summoned by the Lord Chancellor if the King refused to do so.  The Triennial Act thereby made it less worth while for the King to buy a party of supporters, since a new election might soon disperse them; and it also made it lawful for a Parliament to meet in defiance of the King.  Another attempt by Parliament to limit the Crown's power was, however, frustrated: the Place Bill of 1694 – to ban from membership of the Commons anyone employed in the King's service – did not get through Parliament until the Tories forced it on William as part of the 1701 Act of Settlement.

By making elections more frequent, the Triennial Act increased the fervour of party activity.  This was heightened when the Licensing Act expired in 1695 and was not renewed. A feverish rash of pamphlets raised the political temperature – so much so that in 1701 there were on average six candidates for each seat in the Commons.  The parties were still embryonic and loosely-defined, and the labels of Whig and Tory still regarded as insolent nicknames.  M.P.s still voted as they thought fit, and it was never certain how many of the 'Court' party would support the Crown, and how far the 'Country' faction would go in opposing it.  It is, however, convenient (though rather inaccurate) to regard the 'Court' faction at this time as Whig and the 'Country' party as Tory.   In fact the parties were very much in transition.   The old High Tory party of Rochester and Clarendon disintegrated in the Whig triumph in the 1689 Convention, and it was not until a decade later that a recognizable new Tory party developed.   Many of the new Tories were former Whigs disgruntled at recurrent high taxation and hoping for a revival in the Church of England. Many of the statesmen of the 1690s – men such as Sunderland, Shrewsbury, Godolphin and even Danby – refused to be bound by party ties.   William, with no political aims greater than the efficient prosecution of the war, was forced to seek support from anyone prepared to offer it, even from men known to be in friendly contact with James II at St. Germain.   In the end, perhaps because he understood a crafty opportunist when he saw one, William trusted Sunderland more than any other Englishman.

Despite his lack of party prejudice, it was very difficult for William to find a stable government willing to press on with the war.   Only a year after his accession, the 1690 election produced a Commons less Whig than the 1689 Convention had been.   In such unsettled circumstances, it was natural for William to try to govern with the architects of the Revolution and their friends – Danby, Shrewsbury, Devonshire, Halifax, Nottingham, Godolphin and the like – but he found few of them satisfactory.   Halifax had to resign in 1690 as a scapegoat for the failures in Ireland, Nottingham was dismissed in 1693 after his incompetent interference in the Admiralty, and Danby fell from favour in 1694 after taking a bribe from the East India Company.   By 1695 it was clear that only the Whigs were loyal supporters of William and his war, and clear that the King could not depend on 'Trimmers' and Tories.

Many of the Tories still felt twinges of loyalty to James II, even though he was actively assisting Louis XIV.   James, for his part, tried assiduously to win the support of great men in England.   He found that many of them were prepared to insure themselves against a Stuart Counter-Revolution by discreet negotiations with the exiled court at St. Germain. The atmosphere of intrigue was such that even Marlborough was sent to the Tower, on the strength of a letter 'planted' by a professional informer in one of the Bishop of Rochester's flower-pots! By the beginning of 1695 most Tories were against the régime, for Queen Mary – James II's lawful successor – had died of smallpox at the end of 1694, and in their eyes William's claims to the throne were much weakened by her death. Moreover, the clergy disliked their Calvinist Supreme Governor, and the Tory squires were soured by the heavy Land Tax and the privileges granted to the (largely-Whig) Bank of England. Jacobite conspiracies such as the Fenwick plot of 1696 implicated many Tory leaders, as well as Shrewsbury and Godolphin. The Tories, moreover, were particularly bitter about William's distribution of lands and titles to his Dutch and Huguenot favourites – Bentinck (Earl of Portland), Ginkel (Earl of Athlone), Schomberg (Duke of Leinster), and Ruvigny (Earl of Galway). Already the Lords had petitioned against their commanding English troops, and Parliament was soon to force the King to cancel some of the grants. In the crisis of war, therefore, William could not trust the Tories.

As Sunderland warned him, there was nothing William could do but rely on those Whigs who had proved their zeal for the war. These included Lord Wharton; the financier Montagu; Somers, a lawyer and principal architect of the Bill of Rights; and Admiral Russell, flatteringly hailed as the victor of La Hogue. In the background, Shrewsbury and Sunderland gave cautious support. This Whig 'Junto' had the support of a largely Whig House of Commons after the 1695 election, and brought the war fairly smoothly to its end after surmounting a financial crisis. But the peace soon brought a Tory revival, when Robert Harley persuaded the Commons to demand the disbanding of all regiments raised since 1680 and to refuse to pass a new Mutiny Act. By the time that Parliament had to dissolve, according to the Triennial Act, in July 1698, the Whig 'Junto' had lost most of its influence in the Commons. In its short life, however, it managed to set a precedent for co-operation between King, Government and Parliament. Without such co-operation, the balanced constitution envisaged by the Revolution Settlement could not have been achieved.

When the Tories won a notable victory in the 1698 election, the 'Junto's' days were numbered. In May 1699 Shrewsbury, Montagu and Russell (now Lord Orford) resigned their offices, and even Danby (now Duke of Leeds) was ousted from the Presidency of the Council, to which he had clung tenaciously even after his disgrace in 1694. Within a year, Wharton and Somers also gave up their offices. The ministry of inexperienced nonentities (Lords Pembroke, Tankerville and Jersey) which replaced the 'Junto' could work neither with the King nor with Parliament. The Tory tail was soon wagging the ministerial dog. In December 1699 the Commons insisted on 'tacking' to a new Land Tax Bill a Bill ordering that the estates confiscated from Irish Jacobites should be sold for the Treasury's benefit, not given to William's favourites. Although the Lords disliked the principle of 'tacking', the King was compelled to accept this composite Bill. Next spring the Commons petitioned that no foreigner (except Princess Anne's husband George of Denmark) should be admitted to William's councils. In disgust the King prorogued Parliament and then dissolved it. In his anger he even threatened to abdicate and return to Holland. The unhappy experience of 1698–1700 emphasized the constitutional lessons to be learnt from the 'Junto'. Consequently in the autumn of 1700 William appointed a ministry more acceptable to the prejudices of the Parliaments of the time. Rochester, Clarendon and Godolphin, Charles II's loyal 'Chits' of the Exclusion Struggle, headed the new government.

In February 1701 a hotly-contested election again returned a Tory House of Commons. Within a few weeks the Commons were baying at the heels of ministers who had been party to recent negotiations with Louis XIV over the Spanish Succession – the Partition Treaties which Louis had just broken. They demanded the impeachment of Bentinck, Somers, Orford and Montagu (now Earl of Halifax[1]). When the magistrates and gentry of Kent sent a polite petition begging the M.P.s to vote money for the country's defence, the Commons ordered their arrest on the grounds that the petition was 'scandalous, insolent and seditious'. These rash acts led to a flaming row between Lords and Commons. In June 1701 the peers angrily dismissed the impeachments of the Whig leaders, and William soon adjourned and dissolved his fifth Parliament.

Before the irreparable split over the impeachments, however, Parliament had passed an Act of the utmost importance. It was an attempt by the Tories to carry further the principles of the Whig Bill of Rights, and to limit the Crown so narrowly that

[1] The 'Trimmer' Marquis of Halifax had died in 1695 without an heir to his title.

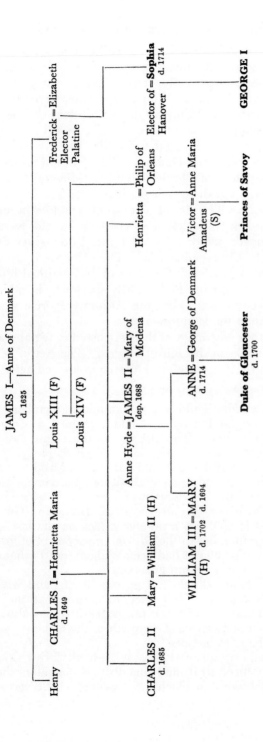

JAMES I—Anne of Denmark
d. 1625

Henry

Frederick = Elizabeth
Elector
Palatine

Elector of = Sophia
Hanover      d. 1714

GEORGE I

CHARLES I ■ Henrietta Maria
d. 1649

Louis XIII (F)

Louis XIV (F)

Henrietta = Philip of
Orleans

Victor = Anne Maria
Amadeus
(S)

Princes of Savoy

Anne Hyde = JAMES II = Mary of
dep. 1688    Modena

ANNE = George of Denmark
d. 1714

Duke of Gloucester
d. 1700

CHARLES II
d. 1685

Mary = William II (H)

WILLIAM III = MARY
(H)  d. 1702  d. 1694

Rulers of other countries indicated thus; (F) King of France; (H) Stadtholder of Holland; (S) Duke of Savoy.

*The English Succession, 1700–14*

it should not be able to help their political opponents.  Its immediate cause was the death in 1700 of the eleven-year-old Duke of Gloucester, the only one of Princess Anne's many children to survive infancy.  William and Mary were childless; Anne would succeed on William's death, but there was now no direct heir to follow her, and the spectre of a Stuart restoration appeared once more.  Two other families had claims to the throne, those of Savoy and Hanover.  The Duke of Savoy had married the daughter of Charles II's sister 'Minette', and had two sons by her.  But these were Catholic, and Savoy was now an ally of France.  The Act of Settlement therefore promised the crown – unless Anne left a direct heir – to old Electress Sophia of Hanover, the daughter of James I's daughter Elizabeth and the Elector Palatine.  The Hanoverians were Protestant, and Sophia's son George had distinguished himself in the recent war against France.  By specifying in advance where the succession was to lay, the Tories were already being more radical than the Whigs in 1689.

The Tories took advantage of their opportunity to paper over many of the cracks in the Bill of Rights.  The Act of Settlement also insisted, if Anne left no children to succeed her:

1. That the sovereign should be a Communicant member of the Church of England.  William had remained a Calvinist throughout his reign.  The insertion of this clause indicates the re-emergence of the Tories as the Anglican party.
2. That a foreign-born King should not take England to war in defence of his foreign possessions without Parliament's consent.  This was an obvious attempt to prevent England being committed to expensive wars assisting Hanover's German campaigns.  It was also a notable attack on the last great prerogative remaining to the Crown – the control of foreign policy.  Even in 1689, it had been William, not Parliament, who decided on war against France.
3. That future Kings should not go out of England without Parliament's consent.  This tried to ensure that the new rulers would make Britain their first concern; it may also have been an attempt to check the growth of the Cabinet system during the King's absences.
4. That the authority properly belonging to the Privy Council should be restored to it, and that Privy Councillors should sign the 'resolutions' to which they assented.  This was a bid

to prevent the Cabinet usurping the jurisdiction of the larger Council, and to prevent ministers pleading ignorance of a decision (as Halifax and Orford were currently claiming that they did not know the contents of the Partition Treaties they had approved).

5. That no foreigners should be Councillors or M.P.s, hold office under the Crown, or receive gifts of property from the Crown – a precaution in case the Hanoverians treated their German friends as lavishly as William had his Dutch favourites.

6. 'That no Person who has an Office or Place of Profit under the King or receives a Pention from the Crown shall be capable of serving as a Member of the House of Commons.' This was the substance of the Place Bill of 1694 – to make it more difficult for the King to buy supporters in Parliament.

7. That Judges should hold their offices 'Quam diu se bene gesserint' (so long as they shall behave themselves), and that they could be removed only by a petition from both Houses of Parliament. This was a safeguard against past Stuart practices, rather than against any arbitrary act of the present King. William had, however, vetoed a similar Bill in 1692 because it would have guaranteed each judge £1000 p.a. out of the King's purse.

8. 'That no Pardon under the Great Seal of England be pleadable to an Impeachment by the Commons in Parliament.' This increased the responsibility of ministers to Parliament by preventing the King pardoning them as Charles II had pardoned Danby in 1679. It may have been inserted in the Act to prevent William saving the Whig leaders now on trial.

Many of the clauses of the Act of Settlement were soon cancelled or modified, but even so it assembled a formidable collection of shackles ready for the Hanoverians if Anne died without a direct heir. The King's religion was prescribed – how different from the previous century when the sovereign had expected England to adapt itself to his current religious opinions! He could no longer declare war, go abroad, or give away Crown property at his pleasure; he must not bribe M.P.s, dismiss unco-operative judges or save ministers disliked by Parliament. In practice, the Act of Settlement proved too radical and had to be amended in the following reigns. Yet it did in a remarkable way commit the whole nation to the principles of the Glorious Revolution. In 1701, as in 1688, the

Tories' resentment against their monarch forced them to abandon their political principles. Even they could not reconcile the Divine Right of Kings, or Non-Resistance to the Lord's Anointed, with their decision to insist that the King must be an Anglican.

At the end of 1701 the imminence of war made a new election necessary. Voters, indignant at Louis's deceit and bad faith, demanded vigorous action. Like the Whigs, most Tory candidates supported war against France. They were even prepared to accept the taxation they had recently criticized so bitterly. Although losing several seats, the Tories had a narrow majority in the new House of Commons. The *volteface* of the Tory party was completed in May 1702, when the Tory leaders declared war on France. William, however, did not live to see this vindication of his policies. He had been thrown from his horse when it stumbled on a molehill, and died in March from his injuries. The mole, toasted by Jacobites as 'the little gentleman in black velvet', had succeeded where James II and Louis XIV had failed.

### vii. The War Economy

The cost of the war forced the government to devise or develop new means of raising money. The most important levy was the Land Tax, derived from the assessments of the Civil War period. A hasty survey early in the war estimated that landowners received altogether about £10,000,000 p.a. from their property. Consequently a Land Tax of 4s. in the £ would produce about £2,000,000. For most of the war years the Land Tax was collected at this high rate. Though the Tax itself was not new, it was a most unfamiliar and unwelcome experience for the country gentry to have to pay out regularly 20 per cent. of their income, even if they were able to pass on the burden by raising their tenants' rents. The belief that the prosperous commercial classes were being taxed more lightly helped to embitter the Tories against the Whigs. During William's reign, the Land Tax alone produced about £19,000,000.

The income from the customs, totalling £13,000,000 during the reign, was less reliable. The successes of French pirates made the yield least in the very years when William's need was greatest.

On the other hand, the direct collection of the customs (the Farm had ended in 1671) made it possible for the Crown to benefit immediately from the recovery of trade after 1697. A more flexible tax than the customs – since its imposition could not provoke hostility from foreign countries or well-organized London merchants – was the excise or purchase tax. This was also collected directly after the Farm expired in 1683, but the yield was more consistent – consumption of essentials like beer did not vary greatly! The excise was particularly useful in that 'new' impositions could always be used as guarantees for government borrowing. During William's reign the excise was extended to salt, spirits, malt and glass, and produced more than £13,000,000. The other taxes were less profitable: several Poll Taxes collected no more than £2,000,000 between them, even though they included a 5 per cent. income tax on officials' salaries. A clumsy Window Tax[1] was introduced in 1696, in place of the old Hearth Tax, but it produced more ill-feeling than money. Other new taxes, such as those on births, marriages and deaths, were soon abandoned: it was not easy to collect money from babies and corpses!

These taxes yielded very nearly enough to pay for the war, which cost on average £5,000,000 p.a., but they could not also cover the administration of the country, the payment of James II's debts, the interest on new loans, the King's household expenses and the pensions William gave his friends. Much of the revenue was embezzled by officials, many of them suspect of Jacobite sympathies, despite the efforts of the Commission for Public Accounts set up in 1690 to reduce corruption in the administration. The trouble partly resulted from the confusion between the cost of defending and administering the country and the King's own spending money. In 1697, however, Parliament voted William a Civil List of £700,000 p.a. for his personal expenses, and thus began to distinguish between public and private expenditure.

By the end of the war the Crown's debts exceeded £15,000,000, for William had had to borrow heavily in the previous years. It was not easy, however, for the Government to arrange new loans in wartime, when landowners were moaning about the Land Tax and merchants about the decay of

---

[1] It was steeply graded: houses with under 10 windows paid 2s.; those with 10–19 paid 6s.; those with over 19 paid 10s.

trade. All the financial skill of Montagu as Chancellor of the Exchequer had been needed to persuade men to lend money. One successful device was the Lottery Loan of 1693 – similar to the modern Premium Bonds in appealing to the gambler's instincts! Those who contributed to the loan received good interest (guaranteed by the excise duty on salt), and had a chance of winning up to £1000 in a special sweepstake. To other men Montagu sold life annuities – paying them £14 p.a. for every £100 they invested – as part of his 'tontine' system[1] of complicated gambles on the lenders' expectation of life.

But Montagu's main achievement was his development of a proposal made by the Scottish merchant William Paterson, for a Bank which would lend the government money in return for interest guaranteed by Parliament. The Bank of England was therefore established by the Tunnage Act of 1694, which imposed additional duties 'upon Tunnage of Shipps and Vessells and upon Beere, Ale and other Liquors' to provide £100,000 p.a. This was to be paid as interest at 8⅓ per cent. p.a. to those subscribing to a loan of £1,200,000, to be raised by the Bank as a joint-stock company. To allay the fears of those who thought that the Bank might finance a return to absolute monarchy, the Bank was forbidden to make additional loans without Parliament's consent. The scheme was a gamble, particularly as the government had to borrow from other people to pay the first interest due to the Bank, but the great Whig merchants, like Papillon and the Houblons, backed it loyally. Its position seemed very precarious when it issued bills of exchange worth nearly £2,000,000, with very little cash to back this paper money, but nonetheless it succeeded. Its loan helped William to capture Namur, and his increased popularity prepared the way for a Whig victory in the 1695 election. Moreover, it helped make the national debt a normal, accepted part of State finance, with investors more concerned with getting regular interest than with the swift repayment of their capital. It helped, too, to commit more men to working for the preservation of the Glorious Revolution, for fear that the Stuarts would cancel the debt if they returned.

The Tories, however, opposed the Bank hotly, for it gave valuable privileges to their opponents. In 1696 Montagu

[1] Explained in D. Ogg, *England in the Reigns of James II and William III*, p. 414.

cautiously accepted the proposals of the Tories Harley and
Chamberlayne for a rival Land Bank, to lend over £2,500,000
to the Crown at 7 per cent. interest guaranteed by new excise
duties on salt and glass. Although this Bank offered to issue
bills of exchange on the reliable security of landed property, it
was a ridiculous fiasco. Only £7000 was subscribed, for the
rate of interest was too low, and the scheme fell through.

The collapse of the Land Bank came at a time of financial
crisis, resulting partly from a decline in the currency. This was
caused largely from the illegal clipping of the edges of silver coins
and by the export of good coins for sale abroad. Inflation
caused by the Bank of England's reckless distribution of paper
money made things worse. In 1695 an Act forbade all except
members of the Goldsmiths' Company to export bullion, and
early the next year William accepted Montagu's Act for the re-
minting of the whole currency. With Sir Isaac Newton as
warden of the Mint, and ten furnaces in the Treasury garden
melting down the old coins as they came in, the currency was
re-coined at the rate of £100,000 a week. The new money had
milled edges, to defeat the coin-clippers. At first the new
coins were hoarded, and it was not until 1699 that they were in
common circulation. In the following year a legal decision improved the status of bills of exchange and made paper money
more respectable: Chief Justice Holt ruled that, as bills of exchange (unlike coins) were identifiable, their owner could bring
a law suit to recover those which had been stolen.

Like most wars, the struggle of 1689–98 provided a stimulus
to the development of English industries. More than a
quarter of the patents granted in the forty years after the
Restoration were issued in 1691–3. The number of joint-stock
companies increased ten-fold during the war; most of the new
companies were for home industries, not overseas commerce.
By 1697 the joint-stock companies had a total capital of over
£4,000,000, and the Stock Exchange had been incorporated to
handle their shares. Many new industries were introduced by
Huguenot refugees from France; by 1700 the *émigré* silk weavers
were employing 10,000 workers around Canterbury alone.
During William's reign many of the restrictions on the export
of corn, cloth and metals were removed. Various Acts of
Parliament encouraged landowners to exploit their mineral
resources, prevented price-fixing by coal merchants, and ended

the protectionist policies of the surviving cloth guilds and companies.

The most spectacular development, however, was in the navy, which became the country's largest centralized industry. During the war over £15,000,000 were spent on it – 29 per cent. of the Crown's total expenditure during those years. Although the number of men employed in the royal dockyard at Portsmouth quadrupled and a new yard was founded at Plymouth Dock, the Admiralty was forced to order many new ships from private yards – less than half the ships being built in 1693, for example, were in royal dockyards. At the same time the private yards were kept busy trying to replace the merchant ships sunk or captured by the French. Jean Bart and his fellow-pirates stimulated not only ship-building but also marine insurance, organized by the speculators who patronized Lloyd's coffee-house in London. Though they demanded high premiums – sometimes as much as 30 per cent. – Lloyd's insurers soon earned a reputation for honesty in meeting their commitments, and the lower premiums of peacetime allowed their business to increase rapidly after 1697.

William's parliaments removed many of the restrictions on commerce by ending the privileges of the old monopolistic companies. The Royal African Company had to open its trade to all in 1698, and from the same year the great East India Company had to share its trading rights with Papillon's rival Company. The Levant Company also lost its privileges, the Russia Company had to reduce its entry fee from £50 to £5, and the Merchant Adventurers had to admit newcomers without fee. On the other hand, the Navigation laws were made more strict, for a Navigation Act of 1696 insisted that inter-colonial goods should be carried only in English or colonial ships, and that colonial produce should not be landed in Ireland or Scotland.

The pattern of the changes brought about by the War of the League of Augsburg was remarkably consistent. The war led to a great increase in the activity of the State, while reducing the powers of the monarch. Parliament met more frequently, and the M.P.s and ministers had greater power independent of the Crown. The financial 'turnover' of the Treasury reached unprecedented heights, and Parliament started to separate the King's income from the needs of the country. The number of men employed in the army and navy, in the customs and excise offices and in the older departments of State rose to a total not far short of 200,000.

Yet these changes did not produce a bureaucratic or dictatorial Government such as that developed by Louis XIV. The limitations on monarchical power imposed by the Whigs in 1689 and extended by the Tories in 1701 prevented royal absolutism. The extension of bureaucracy was checked by the zeal of both Whig and Tory M.P.s in criticizing governmental inefficiency or excessive powers in the hands of private organizations like commercial companies. When Parliament removed the industrial and trading privileges dating from the days of Tudor and Stuart 'paternalism', it made the English economy much more competitive – even if mercantilist doctrines survived for another eighty years. In general, the war of 1689–97 did much to turn England into a more modern State.

### viii. Some toleration and more schisms

As the first section of this chapter described, James II managed in three years to turn against him the leaders of the Anglican Church, the very men who had helped to preserve his right of succession a few years before. Under the threat of popery, the bishops preferred to abandon their political ideals, of Divine Right and Non-Resistance, rather than sacrifice the privileges of their Church.

The change of monarch confronted the Church with several new problems. The first was that its Supreme Governor was a Calvinist – theologically as unwelcome as a papist (albeit less dangerous!). Mary, an Anglican, was more acceptable than her husband, but smallpox removed her in 1694. The Tories who framed the Act of Settlement were therefore careful to guard against another non-conforming sovereign by insisting that the Hanoverians should become communicating members of the Church of England.

The next problem was the assurance which several Church leaders had given to the Nonconformists to persuade them not to be fooled by James's Declarations of Indulgence – a promise that their burdens would be lightened once the crisis was over. To carry out this promise, the Earl of Nottingham (himself an

Anglican Tory) put two Bills before the Convention in 1689. One was a Comprehension Bill, to modify the Church's ritual and discipline to make them acceptable to Nonconformists. The Church party in the Commons frustrated this proposal by persuading the Convention to refer it to Convocation. The other Bill was passed: this Toleration Act[1] decreed that the statutes against Nonconformists should not be enforced, provided they swore loyalty to William and Mary. Dissenters could now worship freely, though they were still excluded from full political and educational privileges.

The third problem was the one which affected the Church most adversely. The bishops had sworn loyalty to James, and many of them could not be persuaded to take the new oaths of loyalty to William and Mary. The Bishop of Chester fled abroad to join James, and eight others refused to swear the new oaths. These included Archbishop Sancroft, Bishop Ken and three others of the Seven Bishops recently put on trial. By 1691 they had all died, resigned or been pushed out of their dioceses. About 400 parish clergy were also Non-Jurors, likewise putting their convictions before their self-interests.[2] The Non-Jurors survived as a separate Church for half a century, ordaining new bishops (under licence from James II), seeking union with the Eastern Orthodox Churches, and drawing up a new high-church liturgy based on that of 1549. In the nineteenth century the founders of the Oxford Movement tried to get back to the doctrine, liturgy, sincerity and zeal of the Non-Jurors of William's reign.

The bishops who filled the sees vacated by the Non-Jurors and by others who had died were of a very different type. Many of them were Cambridge Latitudinarians – Tenison, Stilling-fleet and Tillotson, who was Archbishop of Canterbury 1691–4 in succession to Sancroft. The newcomers were often distinguished scholars and preachers, but they were all Whigs. Their votes were often valuable to William in the House of Lords, and foreshadowed the bishops' part in maintaining the Whig supremacy of half the eighteenth century. Several of them were anxious for closer friendship between Anglicans and Nonconformists, but the squabbles between the different

---

[1] Dealt with more fully on p. 301.
[2] A contemporary estimated the income of an average bishop to be £1300 p.a. – worth perhaps ten times as much in modern money.

churches frustrated the bishops' wish for a more comprehensive church.

The parish clergy, on the whole, did not share the tolerant Whiggery of the bishops. A few were active Jacobites; many more of them regretted the oaths they had sworn to the Presbyterian King. Under Archbishop Tenison (1694–1715) there was as much ill-feeling between parish and diocesan clergy as there had been in Laud's time, but the rôles were strangely reversed, for now it was the lower clergy who were trying to force high-church ideals upon unenthusiastic superiors. The controversies came to a head in the Convocations of 1700, the Canterbury convention being little more than a boxing-ring in which a group of discontented clergy sparred with the bishops. These squabbles continued well into the eighteenth century, and weakened and discredited the Church.

Nonconformity continued to breed nonconformity. This was partly because the Toleration Act made it less necessary for the Dissenting congregations to retain their primitive unifying organizations. For a brief time there was a 'Happy Union' between Presbyterians and Independents, but doctrinal differences soon drove them apart. Many Presbyterians were influenced by Unitarianism, which stressed the One-ness of God and thus conflicted with the accepted doctrines of the Trinity. These Unitarians were excluded from the Toleration Act of 1689 because of the heretical boldness of their ideas.

A more insidious challenge came from the Deists, who believed in a simple natural religion, free from doctrines and superstitions, much as the Whigs believed in a simple, rational, Natural Law. Deism was in part a reaction against the theological hair-splitting of the previous century, and in part a development from the scientific thought of the time. The greatest influence on its early history was John Toland's *Christianity not Mysterious*, published in 1696. Some of the writings of Lord Herbert of Cherbury (brother of the parson-poet) early in the century, and of John Locke in Toland's time, also appeared to be Deistic in tone. The Deists claimed that religion must be reasonable, and that one should reject the things one could not understand – such as the divinity of Christ, or life after death. Even the Deists were divided by schism: as early as 1706 a critic listed four different sects among them. Their influence in England was less than it became abroad, particularly among French writers such as Voltaire and Rousseau.

The reign of William and Mary was therefore not a happy time for the Protestant Churches, and eight years of war against Louis XIV and James II made Catholicism once more synonymous with treason. The most hopeful development was the growth of religious societies. The first, formed in 1691 'for the Reformation of Manners', was a society of snoopers, committed to making sure that those guilty of moral lapses were brought to the judgement prescribed by the law. More commendable were the two societies formed by Thomas Bray, a Warwickshire parson whom Bishop Compton commissioned to reform the Church in Maryland. His preparations led him to see the need for missionary work at home as well. He founded the Society for Promoting Christian Knowledge in 1698 to open charity schools in Britain and to distribute Bibles and tracts at home and abroad. Three years later Bray started another, the 'Society for the Propagation of the Gospel in foreign parts'. This was authorized by Convocation, and tried to minister to Englishmen in the colonies as well as to preach Christianity to the natives. The S.P.C.K. and S.P.G. continue their work even in this present day. Bray also organized parish libraries of books on devotional subjects; these were among the earliest public libraries in Britain. The energies of this remarkable country parson affected the nation's life much more deeply than the activities of many of the great statesmen of his time.

### ix. The Whig philosophers

The century between Harrington and Burke produced only two major political theorists. Charles II's Licensing Act and the reaction against the radicalism of the previous generation largely stifled philosophical speculation. Not surprisingly, the two exceptions were intimately connected with the Revolutionary Settlement, one as architect, the other as apologist.

George Savile, first Marquis of Halifax, lived for a decade in the thick of political controversy. He helped Charles win the Exclusion crisis; then he resigned from James's government rather than yield up the Test Act. James sent him to negotiate with William while he himself took to flight; then Halifax helped draw up the 1689 Settlement, only to lose his office as the Lord Privy Seal as a scapegoat for the government's failures in Ireland. Throughout all these changes he remained a moderate Whig: party fanaticism was not for him. His *Letter to a Dissenter* helped frustrate James's first Declaration of Indulgence by warning the Nonconformists not to be fooled by honeyed promises. His main work, though, was *The Character of a Trimmer* – published in 1688 after being circulated privately for three years. It threw aside pompous, unrealistic political theories such as Filmer's *Patriarcha*, and in simple down-to-earth language showed that the faults of man's nature made laws necessary 'to tie up our unruly passions'. An absolute monarchy was a 'nuisance to mankind'. On the other hand, as Halifax commented in *Political Thoughts and Reflections*, 'The angry Buzz of a multitude is one of the bloodiest noises in the world.' He disliked the Catholic Church, failing to see how any rational man could follow Rome, but otherwise he wanted toleration and moderation. The essence of statecraft was to trim the boat, to balance it better. Halifax did not devise any comprehensive system of political philosophy, but by condemning fanaticism he prepared the way for the common-sense realism which suited England better than curious notions of the Divine Right of Kings.

For thirty years John Locke was closely attached to the Whig leaders, and his philosophy reflects these contacts. He served Shaftesbury as secretary of the Council of Trade and Plantations and drafted a constitution for the new colony of Carolina. During the Exclusion crisis he left Shaftesbury and returned to Oxford, but followed him into exile in Holland. He came back to England in 1689, re-joined the Whig leaders, and was one of the brains behind the 'Junto' of 1695–9. His *Letters on Toleration* argued that each man's conscience was his own, that the Church was a voluntary association, that Christian charity should be shown to the sects, and that a man's religion should not exclude him from civil liberties and rights. Nearly two centuries passed before England accepted these principles. His other main works were more immediately influential: these were the *Two Treatises of Civil Government*, published in 1690. The first of these demolished Filmer's *Patriarcha*. The second

developed the theory of contract between people and government – and took the theory to a point where it virtually ceased
to be a contract since only one party (the people) was to
benefit from it.

Locke's ideas provided a logical political philosophy. He
argued that men owned property before they formed governments, and that they formed governments chiefly to help protect
their property. When a government ceased to be beneficial to
those who created it, it had to be replaced. A government was
therefore the servant of the people – or at least of the property
owners. 'The reason why men enter into a society is the
preservation of their property; and the end why they choose
and authorize a legislature is that there may be laws made, and
rules set, as guards and fences to the properties of all the
members of the society, to limit the power and moderate the
dominion of every part and member of the society.' Writing
with the reasons for James's expulsion fresh in his mind, he
argued that the legislative or government forfeited its right to
continue if 'a single person or prince sets up his own arbitrary
will in place of the laws. . . . When the prince hinders the
legislative from assembling. . . . When by the arbitrary power
of the prince, the electors or ways of election are altered . . .'
and when the people are delivered 'into the subjection of a
foreign power'. When this happened the people had to appoint
a new legislative. These theories had a profound and long-
lasting influence on English politics, for Locke seemed to have
found the 'fundamental law' of the constitution, the law for
which the jurists and politicians had been searching earlier in
the century. Government by a landed aristocracy, in the
interests of the propertied classes, continued until gradually
whittled away by the parliamentary reforms of 1867, 1884,
1911 and 1918. Locke's logical explanation of the events of
1688–9 helped to persuade Britain to regard them as a Glorious
Revolution.

### x. Foreign Policy

James II came to the throne in a rare period of European
peace, when Louis XIV was enjoying intellectual and spiritual
conversations with his new wife, and was persecuting the
Huguenots of France rather than the Protestants in other

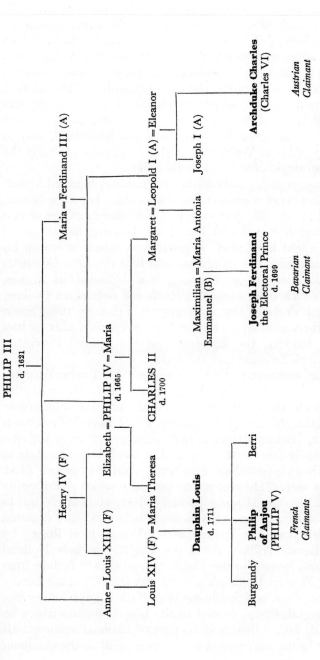

The Spanish Succession, *1699-1713*

Rulers of other countries indicated thus: (A) Emperor, and King of Austria; (B) Elector of Bavaria; (F) King of France.

countries.   Louis expected James to ally with him; after all, had not French subsidies saved James's inheritance during the Exclusion Struggle?   For various reasons James held back from a formal alliance, even when it became clear that William was planning to intervene in England.   At the same time, however, he begged Louis to police the Channel with the French fleet and keep his army poised on Holland's borders.   As was explained in the first section of this chapter, Louis became exasperated, marched his army into the Rhineland, and so made it possible to William to land in England – probably the greatest strategic blunder of Louis's reign.

The foreign policy of William's reign was dominated by two needs – to win one war and to avert another.   For a few months in the winter of 1688–9 the survival of Holland and the success of the English Revolution lay in the balance, for abnormal weather might have made it possible for Louis to march his troops back from the Palatinate and into the Low Countries before the League of Augsburg had collected its armies. William's luck held, and the French did not return in time. The Dutch declared war on France in February 1689; Spain entered the war in April; and in May, a few days after treaties between Bavaria, the Emperor and the United Provinces, William took England into the war.

William announced that the reasons for England's entry were Louis's invasion of the Empire, French attacks on English possessions in the Caribbean and North America, interference with English trade, and the persecution of English Protestants in France.   Some of these allegations were untrue or unjust – it was hardly fair for the England of the Navigation Acts to protest about interference with trade – but they served as an excuse for war.   The real reason for war – which could hardly be stated as James II was supposed to have abdicated – was to defend the Revolution.   Seven weeks before William declared war, James landed in Ireland with a French force loaned by Louis.   Before William could use England to save Holland from Louis, he had to use Dutch troops to save Britain from James.   Thus for William's new country the War of the League of Augsburg was principally the War of the English Succession. When English troops crossed to the Low Countries it was an incidental, rather than a vital, part of national strategy.   It was only in the next war that her army went to the continent deliberately to achieve the main purpose for which she entered the war. Consequently many hard-taxed Tories wanted William to concentrate on a naval war, since a strong fleet could keep James out, without the expense of maintaining a large British army.

William's need to keep the League of Augsburg intact greatly influenced his war strategy, for Spain and Savoy[1] would have been easy victims for France if the Allied fleet had not dominated the Mediterranean. Moreover, the dockyards' greedy consumption of Baltic timber forced him to keep on good terms with Sweden and Denmark, accepting unfavourable trading conditions even though unable to persuade either to enter the war. His alliance with Leopold committed William to supporting the Austrian claim to the Spanish empire – although the people of England and Holland did not know of the agreement. William certainly gave away or promised far more than he received in return from the Allies, but his policy was probably the correct one: in a struggle with Louis XIV's France, no price was too high to pay for support.

This attitude also explains why William was so eager to end the war without overwhelming victory – he could not be certain of winning a fight to the death. Nonetheless, France yielded ground, returning most of her recent conquests, allowing Holland a stronger frontier, and recognizing William as King of England. After this fairly satisfactory Treaty of Ryswick, William concentrated on trying to settle, by private negotiation with Louis, the outstanding problem of the Spanish Succession.

Charles II of Spain, 'the Sufferer', was a medical curiosity who spent most of his long reign hovering on the point of death. Since his accession in 1665 his relations by blood and marriage had been intriguing to get some share in the vast empire he was expected to leave behind at any minute. There were three main claimants. Louis XIV (Charles II's first cousin and the husband of Charles's half-sister Maria Theresa) claimed on behalf of his son the Dauphin Louis. His claim had already led Louis into the War of Devolution against the Spanish Netherlands. Another of Charles's cousins was the Emperor Leopold, who had married Charles's sister Margaret. Their only child married the Elector of Bavaria, and produced a son,

---

[1] France did eventually occupy Savoy.

Joseph Ferdinand, the Electoral Prince of Bavaria. However, Leopold remarried after his first wife's death, and was presented by his second wife with two sons. It was on behalf of the younger of these, the Archduke Charles, that Leopold demanded that the whole of the Spanish empire should go to Austria.

Should the inheritance go to the French son of Charles's half-sister, to the Bavarian grandson of his full (but younger) sister, or to the Austrian son of his cousin's second marriage? The laws of inheritance were too complicated for a simple answer. Powers like Britain, Holland and the North German states were vitally affected by the problem. If the whole of Charles's legacy – Spain herself, most of Italy, most of central and southern America, the Spanish Netherlands – were to pass into French hands, Louis XIV would be invincible. If it went to Austria the Emperor might be strong enough to impose despotic rule on the German states. Mercantilist England and Holland feared for their trade, the German princes for their independence, Protestants everywhere for their religion. In short, the Spanish Succession problem was one which William dared not leave to Spain to settle by herself.

Early in 1698 William began negotiating secretly with Louis, through Bentinck on one side and Tallard on the other. The cards were stacked heavily against him, for Parliament had forced him to cut the army and Louis believed that England would do anything to avoid war. Nevertheless, he persuaded Louis to agree that the bulk of Charles's legacy should go to the Electoral Prince, the neutral candidate who, unlike Louis and Leopold, commanded none of the big battalions. In October 1698, in the First Partition Treaty, William and Louis decided that the Bavarian claimant should inherit Spain, her American empire and the Netherlands; that the Archduke Charles should be compensated with Milan and Luxemburg; and that the French Dauphin should receive Naples and Sicily. This was a purely private arrangement between the two kings. Bavaria, Austria and Spain were not consulted. Only a handful of the Whig ministers in England were in the secret.

Louis had probably never intended to be bound by the Treaty, and in any case it was shattered when the Electoral Prince, rather ungratefully, died early in 1699. Only two candidates, neither of them 'neutral', were now left in the field. After new negotiations William again persuaded Louis to accept for the French claimant the less important part of the Spanish empire. The Second Partition Treaty, of March 1700, promised Spain, her 'Indies' and the Netherlands to the Archduke Charles; the Dauphin was to have Naples, Sicily and Lorraine, and the Duke of Lorraine was to be compensated with Milan. This treaty was not kept secret, and William tried hard to get the Emperor to agree to it. But Leopold refused. He knew that Spain wanted to keep her empire together, and he believed that she would bequeath it all to his son Charles.

He was wrong. Spain's reaction to the news of the Treaty was quite unexpected. D'Harcourt the French ambassador, and the Papal Nuncio together persuaded Charles and his advisers that the Spanish empire would be safer from attackers and heretics if it were all left to a Frenchman. The Spaniards insisted, however, that their possessions should never be absorbed into the French Crown. Therefore Charles chose as his sole heir not the Dauphin, but the youngest of the Dauphin's three sons – Philip of Anjou – on the condition that he gave up his rights of succession to the French Crown. In September 1700 his will declared his decision – and thus overthrew the diplomacy of several decades. Next month, Charles the Sufferer at long last died.

Louis hesitated and then took the plunge. He renounced the Partition Treaties, and accepted the whole Spanish empire on his grandson's behalf. He got the Paris Parlement to decree that Philip of Anjou still kept his rights of succession in France. Expecting Dutch hostility, and anxious to get his blow in first, he seized Antwerp, Mons and Namur, cities in the Spanish Netherlands which had been given to Holland to fortify. Then he ordered the Spaniards to exclude English and Dutch ships from all trade with the Indies – thus showing that he regarded the Spanish empire as a dependency of the French Crown, to be governed from Versailles, not from Madrid.

Attempting to appease the aggressor, both England and Holland recognized the Duke of Anjou as Philip V of Spain. Even Louis's later provocations[1] did not lead immediately to

[1] Louis maintained that William was the aggressor, for in 1700 the English fleet in the Baltic had assisted Sweden against France's ally Denmark. Moreover – with some justice – he accused England of having designs on Gibraltar.

war. But in England Defoe and other pamphleteers were whipping up public opinion against French treachery, and William began hastily to negotiate new alliances. In August 1701 England, Holland and the Emperor signed the Grand Alliance of the Hague, agreeing that Leopold must be given 'equitable satisfaction' in the shape of Italy and the Netherlands.

France's final provocation came when James II died at St. Germain in September 1701. Louis officially recognized his son as King James III. The Old Pretender's birth in 1688 had precipitated the Revolution; his 'accession' now committed England to the War of the Spanish Succession. A few days after William's sixth Parliament met, the Commons voted unanimously to support the King fully in his foreign policy, and in the following week resolved to raise an army of 40,000 and a navy of like size. It was not until William had been succeeded on the throne by his sister-in-law Anne that war was declared, but Louis's actions in the previous year had made it inevitable. Even most Tories were enthusiastic for it. The reasons for England's entry into the war were well summarized by the House of Lords early in January 1702: Englishmen, they voted, must resist the power of France for 'the security of their religion, liberty and property . . . their honour, their wealth and their trade'.

## EXTRACTS

1. POPERY COMES IN FASHION (1685):

To my grief, I saw the new pulpit set up in the Popish Oratory at Whitehall for the Lent preaching, mass being publicly said, and the Romanists swarming at Court with greater confidence than had ever been seen in England since the Reformation, so that everybody grew jealous as to what this would tend.

A Parliament was now summoned, and great industry used to obtain elections which might promote the Court-interest, most of the Corporations being now, by their new charters, empowered to make what returns of members they pleased. (John Evelyn, *Diary*, vol. ii, p. 216)

2. THE NONCONFORMIST MENAGERIE (1687):

> The bloudy *Bear* an *Independent* beast,
> Unlick'd to form, in groans her hate express'd.
> Among the timorous kind the *Quaking Hare*
> Profess'd neutrality, but would not swear. . . .

* * *

> The bristl'd *Baptist Boar*, impure as He,
> (But whitn'd with the foam of sanctity)
> With fat pollutions fill'd the sacred place,
> And mountains levell'd in his furious race. . . .

* * *

> More haughty than the rest the *wolfish* race,
> Appear with belly Gaunt, and famish'd face:
> Never was so deformed a beast of Grace. . . .
> The last of all the litter scap'd by chance,
> And from *Geneva* first infested *France*. . . .

(From John Dryden, The Hind and the Panther)

3. THE HOUSE OF LORDS ACCEPTS THE TOLERATION BILL (1689):

The Bill of Toleration passed easily. It excused Dissenters from all penalties for their not coming to church, and for going to their separate meetings. There was an exception of Socinians [Unitarians]; but a provision was put in it in favour of Quakers; and though the rest were required to take the oaths to the Government, they were excused upon making in lieu thereof a solemn declaration. (Gilbert Burnet, *History of My Own Times*, p. 304)

4. LETTERS TO SIR THOMAS LIVINGSTON, COMMANDING IN THE HIGHLANDS (1692):

Just now, my Lord Argile tells me that Glenco hath not taken the oathes, at which I rejoice, it's a great work of charity to be exact in rooting out that damnable sect, the worst in all the Highlands . . . (from Sir John Dalrymple).

You are hereby ordered and authorized to march our troops which are now posted at Inverlochy and Inverness, and to act against these Highland rebels who have not taken the benefite of our indemnity, by fire and sword, and all manner of hostility . . . (from the order signed by William III). (In Dickinson and Donaldson, *Source Book of Scottish History*, vol. iii, p. 222)

5. THE TRIENNIAL ACT LIMITS THE LIFETIME OF A PARLIAMENT (1694):

And be it further enacted. . . . That from henceforth noe Parliament whatsoever . . . shall have any continuance longer then for Three yeares onely att the farthest to bee accounted from the day on which by the Writts of Summons the said Parliament shall bee appointed to meet. (In Costin and Watson, *The Law & Working of the Constitution*, p. 80)

6. THE DECLARED PURPOSE OF THE GRAND ALLIANCE (1701):

Sa Sacrée Majesté Imperiale, Sa Sacrée Roiale Majesté de la Grande-Bretagne, & les Seigneurs Etats Generaux des Provinces-Unies, n'aiant rien tant à coeur que la Paix & la tranquillité de toute l'Europe, ont jugé qu'il ne pouvoit rien y avoir de plus efficace pour l'affermir, que de procurer à Sa Majeste Imperiale une satisfaction juste & raisonnable, touchant ses pretentions à la Succession d'Espagne, & que le Roi de la Grande-Bretagne, & les Seigneurs Etats Generaux obtiennent une sûreté particuliere et suffisante, pour leurs Roiaumes, Provinces, Terres, & Païs de leur obéïssance, & pour la Navigation & le Commerce de leurs Subjets. (In Trevelyan, *Documents for Queen Anne's Reign*, p. 6)

7. QUEEN MARY'S INTEREST IN CURIOSITIES (1693):

I saw the Queen's rare cabinets and collection of china; which was wonderfully rich and plentiful, but especially a large cabinet, looking-glass frame and stands, all of amber, much of it white, with historical bass-reliefs and statues, with medals carved in them, esteemed worth £4000, sent by the Duke of Brandenburgh . . . divers other China and Indian cabinets, screens, and hangings. . . . (John Evelyn, *Diary*, vol. ii, pp. 327–8)

8. THE FUNERAL SERMON ON A VERSATILE SCIENTIST (1692):

At the funeral of Mr. Boyle, at St. Martin's. Dr. Burnet, Bishop of Salisbury, preached. . . . He concluded with an eulogy due to the deceased, who made God and religion the scope of all his excellent talents in the knowledge of nature, and who had arrived to so high a degree in it, and accompanied with such zeal and extraordinary piety, which he showed in the whole course of his life, particularly in his exemplary charity on all occasions – that he gave £1000 yearly to the distressed refugees of France and Ireland; was at the charge of translating the Scriptures into the Irish and Indian tongues, and was now promoting a Turkish translation. . . . that he had settled a fund for preachers who should preach expressly against Atheists, Libertines, Socinians, and Jews. . . . He spake of his civility to strangers, the great good which he did by his experience in medicine and chemistry, and to what noble ends he applied himself to his darling [favourite] studies; the works both pious and useful which he published; the exact life he led, and the happy end he made. . . . And truly all this was but his due, without any grain of flattery. (John Evelyn, *Diary*, vol. ii, pp. 318–9)

# 7

# THE SWANSONG OF THE STUARTS
## 1702–14

☆

### i. Marlborough's War

THE Spanish Succession War dominated the whole of Anne's reign. The first shots were fired before her accession, and the last continental treaty was not signed until two months after her death. The war influenced the political and economic history of Britain even more than the previous struggle had done. Moreover, Britain's Allies were fewer in number than in the War of the League of Augsburg. Holland, the Empire and most of the North German princes came in, as before; but this time Savoy, Bavaria and the whole Spanish empire were fighting on Louis XIV's side, not against him. The struggle therefore promised to be even more arduous.

The Allies' greatest asset was Marlborough. William III had at last recognized his genius, forgiven him his flirtations with James II, and made him commander of the British forces. Marlborough's ability as a diplomat won two victories before Britain even went to war, for in 1701 he persuaded Charles XII of Sweden not to ally with France and next spring induced the Emperor to declare against 'the pretended Prince of Wales'. Had he failed in the former the Allies would have been desperately short of naval supplies (and have had to face a fierce little army as well); had he failed in the latter the Tories might have opposed the war from the start.[1] It was Marlborough who persuaded Anne to acknowledge Frederick I as King of Prussia, and who in 1706 hurried to Berlin to persuade him to use his army against France, not Sweden. At various times

---

[1] Some Tories, such as the old die-hard Seymour, had insisted that the Emperor should accept this as the price of assistance, as they were confident that he would refuse and thereby give Britain an excuse to keep out of the war.

during the war he hastened across Europe to confer with the Emperor, the King of Sweden, and the Elector of Hanover, to keep the Alliance intact and its enemies divided, to bolster up the ministry at home, or to use his great personal charm to calm the fearful, jealous Dutch. Most difficult of all, he had to allay the mutual suspicions of Holland and Austria on the future of the Spanish Netherlands, promised to the Emperor in the early treaties of alliance, but later demanded by the Dutch to increase their security from France. To placate the Dutch he had to turn down the Emperor's invitation, so attractive to a man of his ambitions, to rule the Netherlands as an Austrian viceroy. Moreover, Marlborough had a clear understanding of the overall strategy of the war, of the need to dominate the Mediterranean if the Archduke Charles was ever to be installed as King of Spain and Italy. Thus, unlike the generals in the 1914–18 war,[1] he did not try to concentrate all his troops in the Low Countries but urged the Government to send adequate forces to Spain, to capture Gibraltar, to seize Minorca with its valuable harbour of Port Mahon. Also unlike later commanders, he realized that France could be invaded by routes other than that through the Low Countries. Nonetheless, he knew that the main issue of the war would have to be settled in the Netherlands. The main objects of his campaigns were therefore to save Holland from the French, to keep the Alliance intact by aiding hard-pressed countries (as in the Blenheim campaign in 1704), to reconquer the Spanish Netherlands from the French, and to recapture the Barrier Fortresses which the Spaniards had allowed the French to garrison. Then the short route to Paris would be open.

For the first years of the reign he was the driving force in British as well as in continental politics. His power was based on a tight circle of friendship. For many years Anne, Marlborough, his wife Sarah, and Godolphin had lived informally as equals, as 'Mrs. Morley', 'Mr. and Mrs. Freeman' and 'Mr. Montgomery'. The first three had grown up together, for John Churchill had been a page in the Duke of York's household and Sarah Jennings had been one of Anne's childhood friends. Churchill's sister Arabella was one of James's mistresses, and

---

[1] Curiously, the strongest advocate of attacking Germany and her allies through the Mediterranean was Marlborough's descendant, Winston Churchill (then First Lord of the Admiralty).

bore him a son who became Duke of Berwick and one of Marlborough's ablest opponents in the War.    Later, Churchill was one of the many young courtiers who had shared Lady Castlemaine's favours with their royal master – once he had to leap out of the window as Charles came into her bedroom. Since his marriage, though, he had been devotedly loyal to Sarah.    By the time James came to the throne he had earned high military honours and helped to defeat Monmouth's rabble at Sedgemoor, but in 1688 he, Sarah and Princess Anne deserted to William's side.    Like Anne herself, Godolphin and the Marlboroughs had quarrelled with William ('Mr. Caliban') and all had been out of favour for most of his reign.    Their long friendship made it natural that Anne should govern with Godolphin as Treasurer (Prime Minister in all but name), Marlborough as commander-in-chief, and Sarah as royal favourite and the first lady and general busy-body of the Court.

Godolphin's ministry at first contained extremist Tories like Rochester and Seymour, and also the moderate Tory Harley to lead the Commons as Speaker.    The government with which Britain began the war was thus largely Tory, and its main strength lay in Marlborough's relations with the Queen and in her devotion to the great general.    For the first years, at least, Marlborough was a tower of strength to the ministry, for he was usually in London in the winters, when Parliament normally met, and in the summers when on campaign he would often spend hours on Cabinet business after a hard day in the field.

His true greatness was the single-mindedness of his objective – to defeat France – and the versatility of his methods.    As a diplomat and politician he was outstandingly able (and achieved more than William III, whose skill was mainly in such matters), but his fame rests mostly on his genius as a soldier. He was the only English general who never lost a pitched battle or failed to capture a fortress he was besieging.    Three things produced his success in battle.    First, he was a brilliant and courageous leader.    Then, his men were well-equipped (with flint-locks and bayonets which did not have to be plugged *into* the musket muzzles) and well-trained.    Marlborough's drill-manual remained in use until the nineteenth century, and he made his officers remain with their troops in winter quarters to continue their training.    Perhaps above all, Marlborough understood perfectly the use of all three sections of the army:

infantry, to maintain rapid, heavy fire before using the bayonet; cavalry, to break up the enemy by the shock of the moving mass (he issued the horsemen with only three rounds of ammunition, to force them to get to close quarters with the enemy); and artillery, which he usually sited himself to get the maximum cross-fire to break up enemy formations.    Many of his victories were won in spite of his allies, for the Dutch generals hated serving under him, and their Field-Deputies appointed by the States-General tried hard to prevent him from risking troops in uncertain battles, as at Peer in 1702.    Only Prince Eugène of Savoy, who became a close personal friend, was an ally worthy of him.    Apart from Eugène and the tiny circle at home, Marlborough had few friends.    The most reliable of the others was probably Heinsius, the Grand Pensionary of Holland, who tried hard to smooth Marlborough's relations with the querulous Dutch politicians.

His first triumph, at Blenheim in 1704, showed Marlborough's consummate abilities.    Louis XIV had decided to reinforce his Bavarian allies with a French army in preparation for a joint attack on Vienna to knock the Emperor out of the war.    By the end of May the Franco-Bavarian army at Ulm numbered 50,000, and Marlborough had set off from Holland in hot pursuit with an army of 19,000 British troops.    In mid-June he joined up with the Emperor's armies under Eugène of Savoy and Louis of Baden, and crossed the Danube to seize the town of Donauworth after a bloody battle for the Schellenberg heights.    For a month the Allies ravaged Bavaria while they tried to collect reinforcements.    In August, having formed a poor opinion of Prince Louis's ability, he allowed him to take 15,000 men away to besiege Ingolstadt.    Nevertheless, Marlborough and Eugène decided to attack the French at Blenheim, on the Danube a few miles upstream from Donauworth.    With about 56,000 Allied troops, Marlborough faced Tallard's 60,000 across the Nebel stream.    Resplendent in his Garter ribbon, he rode up and down in front of his troops to encourage them, at the same time siting his batteries and arranging the field hospitals.    When the battle started, the English cavalry under Palmes scattered the enemy horse, but the French counter-attacked and almost separated the forces of Marlborough and Eugène.    Eventually Marlborough concentrated a stronger force against the French centre, prevented the defenders in Blenheim from helping the others, and used his cavalry to break through. After fighting bravely the French fled, many being drowned as they tried to escape. That night Marlborough wrote to his wife:

Give my duty to the Queen, and let her know her army has had a glorious victory. Monsieur Tallard and two other Generals are in my coach . . .

Only a third of Tallard's army escaped; nearly 40,000 were dead or prisoners of the Allies. Marlborough's troops suffered about 13,000 casualties, one-third the total French loss. The consequences of the battle were enormous. The Empire was saved from French attack. Bavaria was beaten almost to her knees. The Dutch were placated, and the success silenced the Tories who had begun to criticize Britain's participation in the land war. In all, it was Britain's greatest victory since Agincourt.

Marlborough's other victories had less strategic importance than Blenheim, which was the only battle in which defeat would have cost the Allies the war. The cautious Dutch kept him idle in 1705, and most of his campaigning thereafter was confined to the Spanish Netherlands, giving the Dutch a stronger frontier and preparing for an invasion of France itself. In 1706 he shattered Villeroy's army at Ramillies, between Louvain and Namur, and swept on through Louvain to Brussels. The government in Brussels surrendered to him, renouncing Philip V and hailing the Archduke Charles as King of the Netherlands. In the following weeks the fortresses of Antwerp and Ostend yielded to him, and Louis XIV in desperation recalled armies from Italy and Germany to defend France. But the hesitations of the Dutch delayed the advance, which was hampered further by the Allies' lack of money and the jealousy among Marlborough's subordinates.

Two years later Marlborough had to fight again over the same battlefields. In July 1708 he marched his troops fifty miles in two days to intercept Vendôme's army at Oudenarde. With nearly 90,000 men on each side, Marlborough brilliantly encircled the French troops in the fierce battle which developed. Oudenarde was a great Allied victory, owing much to Natzmer's Prussian grenadiers and the Dutch cavalry

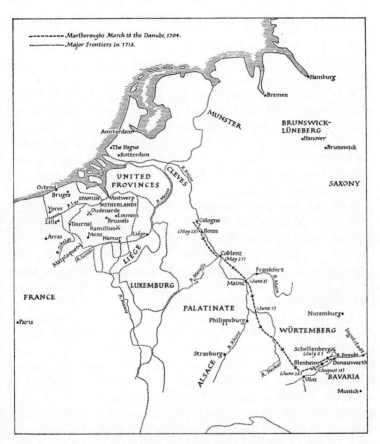

- - - - - - - - Marlborough's March to the Danube, 1704.
.................Major Frontiers in 1713.

Hamburg

Bremen

MUNSTER

BRUNSWICK-
LÜNEBERG
Hanover
Brunswick

Amsterdam

The Hague
Rotterdam

UNITED
PROVINCES

CLEVES

R. Rhine

SAXONY

Ostend
Bruges
SPANISH
Antwerp
NETHERLANDS
Oudenarde
Louvain
Brussels
Ramillies
Mons
Namur
Liége

R. Lys
R. Meuse

Ypres
Lille
Arras
Tournai

Cologne
(May 23) Bonn

Scheldt
R. Sambre
Malplaquet

LIÉGE

LUXEMBURG

R. Meuse

R. Moselle

Coblenz
(May 27)
Frankfort
Mainz
(June 3)
R. Main
(June 7)

FRANCE

Paris

PALATINATE

Philippsburg

Nuremburg

WÜRTEMBERG

Ingolstadt

ALSACE

R. Rhine

Strasburg

Schellenberg
(July 2)
R. Danube
Blenheim
Donauworth
(August 13)
BAVARIA

R. Neckar
(June 23)

Ulm

Munich

# Marlborough's Campaigns

daringly led by the nineteen-year-old Prince of Orange.[1] There were only 3000 Allied casualties, but the French lost more than 15,000 dead, wounded and captured.  The way to France was now open, for Vendôme's survivors lay scattered around Ghent in the north and Berwick's troops had not fully occupied the French frontier to the south.  Once again the fears of the Allies (this time including even Eugène) held him back.  The battle of Oudenarde made possible the siege and capture of Lille, but even this great Barrier Fortress was a poor dividend for such a victory.

Next year, while besieging the Barrier Fortress of Mons, Marlborough had to fight the most desperate battle of his career.  At Malplaquet, fighting ferociously under Villars to defend their own frontier, the French inflicted about 24,000 casualties on the Allies, at a cost to themselves of about 15,000. Nonetheless, the Allies broke through the French line, and were able to capture Mons.

With the four great battles of Blenheim, Ramillies, Oudenarde and Malplaquet behind him, Marlborough's power seemed unshakeable.  Prince Eugène worshipped him, even though he had displeased the Emperor by declining the viceroyalty of the Netherlands.  His friend Heinsius and other Dutch statesmen respected him deeply, even if there were jealous grumbles from their generals.

Outside the Low Countries the war had been less fortunate. In 1702 Rooke's fleet failed to capture Cadiz, though it was successful in attacking Spanish treasure fleets in Vigo Bay, thereby weakening Philip V's economy and persuading Portugal to join the Allies.  In 1704 marines from the fleet captured Gibraltar against light opposition, but Rooke was able to fight only an inconclusive battle when he met the French navy off Malaga.  After years of urging by Marlborough, the navy under Captain Leake at long last captured Minorca in 1708 and started to use Port Mahon as a base.  But by that time Allied power in the Mediterranean was on the wane. Between 1704 and 1706 Peterborough was able to conquer most of Spain and to crown the Archduke in Madrid, but 'Charles III's' reign was short-lived: in 1707 Galway's Anglo-Portuguese army was soundly beaten at Almanza, and in

[1] William III's cousin John William Friso, who died in 1711 without being accepted as Stadtholder of Holland. His posthumous son was Stadtholder 1747-51.

subsequent campaigns the Allies lost their conquests in Spain.

Strained by Marlborough's victories in the North and worried by Allied intervention in Spain, Louis XIV twice asked for peace. The Allies rejected his first proposals, after Ramillies, because he would not agree that Philip V should give up Spain. The Whigs in England insisted on 'No Peace without Spain'. Two years later, after Oudenarde and the fall of Lille, Louis again asked for peace. This time he was prepared to yield Spain, but could not agree to the outrageous English demand that he should use French troops to drive out Philip V if he refused to abdicate. The Allies' unreasonableness made Louis determined to fight to the end if he could not get better terms for France and his grandson.

By 1709, and especially after the carnage at Malplaquet, the Allies' enthusiasm was waning. The Dutch in particular doubted whether it was realistic to demand Spain for the Archduke. To get their support the Whigs in Britain had to offer a huge bribe. At the end of 1709 Townshend negotiated the Barrier Treaty with Heinsius. The Dutch agreed to go on fighting only if the Spanish Netherlands were given to them as a barrier, and not to the Archduke Charles as part of his inheritance. They insisted also that they should share equally with Britain in the trading privileges to be wrung from a defeated Spain, and, to deny Britain any advantage in the Mediterranean, made the Whigs promise that Minorca should be given up.

Despite Marlborough's victories, the Tories in England had turned violently against the war and, as the last of them had left the ministry by 1708, Marlborough and Godolphin had to rely entirely upon the Whigs – whom the Queen disliked – for support. Although the Whigs won the election of 1708, it was not long before the war-party was overthrown. The Duchess of Marlborough lost Anne's favour; the Queen abandoned Godolphin after he had permitted a foolish High Church parson to be impeached, and the Tories swept back into power, first in the government and then in the Commons. Although Marlborough in 1710 broke through the French *ne plus ultra* lines he was not allowed to dash on to Paris. By the autumn, in the utmost secrecy, a handful of leading Tories had begun to strike a private bargain with Louis XIV. Next year the British troops were withdrawn from the fighting line, and Britain soon ceased to take any part in the war. In the closing days of December Marlborough was unjustly accused of corruption by a partisan Tory Commons, and dismissed by the Queen in disgrace. At the same time the Tories pushed through Parliament a Peace Bill which approved the 'Preliminaries' for a final treaty with France.

The Peace Treaty followed in 1713. Called the Treaty of Utrecht, although most of it was negotiated privately between London and Versailles, it gave most of the spoils of war to Britain. Most of the French colonial empire went to her. She kept Gibraltar and Minorca (the latter in defiance of the Barrier Treaty). Also in contravention of the 1709 Treaty, Britain agreed that most of the Spanish Netherlands should go to Austria, and secured in the *Asiento* Louis's agreement that Britain alone should have the right to trade with the Spanish colonial empire. Louis agreed to recognize Anne as Queen, and the Hanoverian Succession after her, and to expel the Pretender James III; in return, the Allies accepted Philip V as King of Spain, on the condition that the thrones of France and Spain should never be occupied by the same person. Besides the Netherlands, Austria was compensated with Milan, Naples and Sardinia. Even this rich reward did not satisfy Charles, even though he had become Emperor in 1711 on the death of his elder brother. For another year his armies continued fighting, but after Villars had defeated Eugène he accepted the peace terms in the Treaty of Rastadt (1714). Holland had to be content with the right to garrison the Barrier Fortresses. Savoy, for no good reason, received Sicily.

The eventual result of the war and the Treaty was that the Bourbons kept Spain and Austria became ruler of Italy. France was exhausted, and her military power did not revive fully until the French Revolution. Holland, although strengthened by the Barrier Fortresses, was also gravely weakened, and never again became a great power. Britain gained a large empire and much trade, and established herself as ruler of the Channel, the Mediterranean and the Atlantic, and as the most powerful single nation in Europe. But by betraying her allies to drive the best bargain for herself she earned the contempt and hatred of the rest of Europe.

## ii. Godolphin's Ministries

The main reason for the unsatisfactory conclusion of the war was the bitterness of party politics in England. There were many reasons for this, the most important of them deriving from the war itself. The four-shilling Land Tax soon turned the Tories once more against continental campaigns. On the other hand, the thought of a major French victory revived fears of a Catholic Jacobite succession. Marlborough and his supporters grew very unpopular in England, for many men feared his ambition to be made Captain-General of the British forces for his lifetime. The Queen herself was the centre of party intrigues, particularly after the death in 1708 of her beloved, asthmatic, husband Prince George of Denmark. The ending of censorship in 1695 had set the political pamphleteers loose upon each other. By making elections more frequent, the Triennial Act of 1694 had inflamed political passions and made governments unstable. Matters became worse due to unscrupulous Tory attempts to use the Church of England to weaken the Whigs, and to the Whigs' foolish impeachment of Dr. Sacheverell in return. The personal rivalry between Tory leaders such as Harley and St. John, and the vindictiveness of the extreme Tories towards men like Walpole who had supported the war, produced violent intrigues which threatened the security of the Revolutionary Settlement. The lure of Jacobitism still had a fatal fascination for many Tories, and there were some who even hoped that peace with France would enable Louis XIV to help restore the Stuarts when Anne died.

In 1702 the Tories, to some extent caught in the net of their own plots, had supported the war, but they nonetheless tried to persuade the Cabinet to concentrate on a naval campaign to seize French and Spanish colonies. The General Election, which William's death made necessary in the summer of 1702, produced a Commons more Tory than that elected the previous December. Accordingly, in the following months the Tories moved against Whigs and Dissenters. They tried to get the Lords to accept a Bill to forbid 'Occasional Conformity', the practice whereby Dissenters had taken the Sacrament once a year to qualify for office according to the letter of the Clarendon Code. The Whig peers managed to out-manœuvre the

Bill in the House of Lords.   This increased Tory resentment against the Whigs – and against Marlborough and Godolphin, who had refused to support the Bill (although they were nominally Tories) because they deplored it for trying to split the country in time of war.   It was not long before the extreme Tories in the government became so opposed to the war that they had to go: Rochester in 1703, Nottingham, Jersey and Seymour in 1704.

Godolphin replaced them with Harley and his moderate Tory followers, with whom he formed a non-party ministry dependent on the Queen's favour and committed to supporting the war.   Success at Blenheim cheered the new ministry, and briefly silenced Tory moans about the Land Tax.   In the following winter, however, the High Church Tories again tried to pass a Bill against Occasional Conformity, by 'tacking' it to the Land Tax vote; again, the Whigs and wiser Tories obstructed it successfully.   By that time, both Houses of Parliament, the law courts and even the Queen herself had become deeply involved in the dispute of *Ashby* v. *White*.   Ashby was a Whig cobbler whom White, the Tory Mayor of Aylesbury, had unjustly deprived of his right to vote in the 1700 election.   Was this a case which should be settled by the law courts or by the Commons?   In the end the Lords upheld the law courts' verdict in favour of Ashby.   When other Aylesbury townsfolk sued White for the same offence, the Commons angrily sent them to Newgate gaol – where they lived royally at the expense of Whig peers.   The resulting constitutional *impasse* led Anne to dissolve Parliament early in 1705.

The 1705 election was a defeat for the extreme Tories, and Anne reluctantly had to strengthen the ministry by introducing some new Whigs – Walpole, Argyle and Cowper – while restoring others like Somers and Sunderland[1] to some of their former influence.   In the autumn of 1706 the Whigs demanded that one of the peers of the 'Junto' clique should enter the Cabinet.   For a while the Queen resisted this threat to the royal prerogative of choosing her own ministers, but eventually she gave way and accepted Sunderland as Secretary of State (partly because he was Marlborough's son-in-law).   This, and the successes at Ramillies and in Spain, put the Whigs in such good humour that they quickly voted the taxes needed for the War,

---

[1] Son of the turncoat statesman who had been adviser to both James and William.

and behaved as Anne hoped they would in the intricate matter of Union with Scotland.

Next year the Duchess of Marlborough, still reigning in Anne's favour despite her Whig sympathies, introduced to the Queen a poor relative she was trying to help, Abigail Hill. The Queen took an instant liking to her, married her off to the respectable Mr. Masham, and rapidly elevated her to the favoured position so long held by Sarah Churchill. By the end of 1707 Sarah was despondent. Marlborough and Godolphin were seriously alarmed, for Harley started to use Mrs. Masham to help him replace Godolphin as leader of the Government.

In February 1708 matters came to a crisis, for Anne tried to dismiss Godolphin and instate Harley as Treasurer in his place. Marlborough resigned his command in protest. Most of the Cabinet refused to serve without the two leaders, and the Queen soon had to climb down. Two days later Harley resigned, and the other Tories left the ministry in sympathy. Marlborough and Godolphin were reinstated, dependent now entirely on the Whigs. Frustrated, Anne and Mrs. Masham turned more and more away from the war-leaders and began to plot new ways to bring them down.

It was fortunate for Marlborough and Godolphin, but probably not for Britain, that the Whigs won the 1708 election, which produced what Sunderland called 'the most Wig Parliament since the Revolution'. In the following months they forced the Queen, prostrate by the death of her husband, to accept the 'Junto' peers Somers and Wharton into the Cabinet. Elated by the news of Oudenarde, the war-party came fully into power when Louis XIV was at his weakest and most willing to make a submissive peace. By demanding everything, the Whigs got nothing. The French Minister Torcy (one of Colbert's sons) was prepared to yield on most points, but even Marlborough realized how foolish it was to demand that Louis should be responsible for driving his grandson out of Spain. 'No Peace without Spain' meant no peace at all.

But the Whig triumph was soon cut short. The country's enthusiasm for the war evaporated in the fire of Tory attacks after Malplaquet, even though the British casualties were only one-tenth of the total Allied loss. Unfair pamphlets criticized the Allies' efforts in a war which, the Tories now claimed,

ZBS

Britain should have entered not as a principal but only as an auxiliary.  With more justice, the Tories attacked the Whigs for insisting that Spain must be secured for the Archduke.  It was, they thought, neither feasible nor strategically desirable to evict the Bourbon and install the Hapsburg claimant.  The Whig ministers finally turned the Queen against them when they arranged that the Rev. Dr. Sacheverell should be impeached, for attacking Godolphin in a rash sermon preached on the Protestant anniversary of November 5th.  When moderates like Shrewsbury joined Harley in criticizing the Cabinet, its downfall was certain.  With Mrs. Masham supreme in royal favour, the Duchess of Marlborough fled from Court, weeping hysterically.  Harley's triumph was soon complete.  In June 1710 Anne dismissed Sunderland. Two months later she sacked Godolphin; in disgust he broke his Treasurer's staff and threw the pieces in the chimney.  Next month Cowper resigned the Chancellorship.  Only Marlborough clung to office, still hoping to be able to invade France and take Paris, despite Anne's cruel sneers about his greed and ambition when he begged to be made Captain-General of the British forces for life.

Harley replaced Godolphin at the Treasury,[1] and persuaded Anne to dissolve Parliament a year before dissolution was due. The old grievances against the four-shilling Land Tax, especially harsh in the recent years of scarcity, made the Whigs' downfall almost certain.  Helped by the Crown's influence, by their superior party machine, and by Harley's vague promises of more toleration for the Nonconformists, the Tories triumphed overwhelmingly in the election in October 1710.  In the new Commons Tories outnumbered Whigs by more than two to one.  Godolphin's eight-year ministry, which had accomplished the Union of England and Scotland and almost won Britain's greatest war, had been rejected by the electors only two years after its sweeping victory in 1708.

### iii. Harley's Ministry

The new Treasurer had emerged from a Nonconformist and Whig background, and he had no liking for the revengeful

---

[1] Until March 1711 Harley ran the Treasury from the subordinate post of Chancellor of the Exchequer.

policies demanded by his followers. The ministry he formed was a coalition, containing at first Whigs like Newcastle and Walpole as well as Tories of widely-differing views. Following Godolphin's example, he did not sack the Treasury officials and other civil servants of the previous ministry to make room for his own toadies. He disliked the attempts made by the High Church Tories to weaken the political influence of the Dissenters. His quarrel with Henry St. John and the October Club extremists over the ministry's policies led to a violent personal rivalry between the two men for the leadership of the party. The split developed from the time in 1711 when St. John made use of Harley's illness to despatch to Quebec an expedition under Jack Hill, Mrs. Masham's worthless brother. Harley later accused St. John and his friends of pocketing three-quarters of the funds provided by the Treasury for the campaign. At least when sober, Harley was staid, respectable and a man of principle; St. John, a younger man, was more brilliant, more extreme, and thus able to seduce from Harley the support of the High Tories. Jealousy (in 1711 Harley received the Earldom of Oxford, but St. John had to wait until 1712 to become merely Viscount Bolingbroke)[1] and reckless lust for power made St. John drive the Tory coach so fast that within four years it fell to pieces.

When the Tory Parliament met at the end of 1710, Sir John Packington voiced the feelings of the majority by demanding that the war be ended 'to prevent the beggaring of the nation, and to prevent moneyed and military men becoming lords of us who have lands'. In the following months the Tories accordingly passed a number of Acts designed to harrass the Whigs. Early in 1711 Parliament enacted that county M.P.s must have an income of at least £600 p.a. and borough M.P.s one of at least £300 p.a. *from land alone*. The Landed Property Qualification Act tried to give the largely-Tory squires the exclusive right to govern, but the Whigs hastily bought estates and the lawyers devised ways to evade the letter of the law. To counter Nonconformist influence in London, Parliament voted new duties on coal imports to provide £350,000 to build fifty more Anglican churches in the capital. As the Bank of England was a strongly Whig institution, Harley encouraged the forming in 1711 of the South Sea Company to take over

[1] To avoid confusion, their titles are not used in this book.

£10,000,000 of the national debt, promising to pay investors 6 per cent. interest guaranteed out of the trading privileges which were to be extracted from France and Spain in the forthcoming peace settlement. The scheme delighted the Tories, cheated the Dutch (by infringing the Barrier Treaty), and led eventually to the South Sea Bubble crisis in 1720. The Tories tried to bribe Walpole, the ablest of the younger Whigs, to join them. When he refused, the Tory Commons sent him to the Tower on a charge of corruption.

For the only time between the Restoration and the present day, a bishop became a minister; Robinson of Bristol was made Lord Privy Seal and quickly packed off to the peace negotiations at Utrecht. Then the extreme October Club Tories revived their demand for the banning of Occasional Conformity. Their Bill easily passed the Commons, and to the amazement of those not in the plot, some Whig peers helped to get it through the Lords at the end of 1711. The reason for this remarkable betrayal of the Nonconformists was that the Whigs were desperate to prolong the war and to get allies to help them throw out the peace proposals which Parliament was discussing.

In October 1710, at the time of the Tory election victory, Jersey, Harley and Shrewsbury had opened secret negotiations with Torcy. The French minister was under orders to buy Britain off, for Louis realized that without Britain the Alliance would soon collapse. It was agreed verbally that Britain should receive great commercial privileges in return for accepting Philip V as King of Spain and Spanish America. The Barrier Treaty was to be ignored and the Dutch abandoned. St. John entered the negotiations in March 1711, when Harley was recovering from an attempt to assassinate him, and soon urged the discussions forward. In October 1711 St. John and Dartmouth (the Secretaries of State) signed the Preliminary Articles with Torcy's agent Mesnager, on the basis of the previous verbal agreement, even though it neglected the interests of Britain's allies. However, the Preliminary Articles did include Louis' recognition of Anne and the Protestant Succession after her, and his promise that the thrones of Spain should never be united.

These were proposals deliberately planned to 'dish the Whigs' by dishonouring their Treaties and by wooing the commercial classes previously so loyal to the Whigs. To make these terms acceptable to Britain the Tories set their pamphleteers to attack the war and the Allies, in works as vitriolic as Swift's *Conduct of the Allies*. Marlborough was disgraced on a bogus charge of embezzlement, and was dismissed by Anne with an insolent and ungrateful letter; Tory generals like Peterborough were fêted in his place. The Queen herself tried to win over doubtful peers. The Whigs tried frantically to obstruct the Peace Bill approving these Preliminaries. In the end they turned to Nottingham, the old Anglican Tory. They offered not to oppose the Occasional Conformity Bill if Nottingham persuaded the Lords to reject peace 'without Spain'. Nottingham agreed. In December his motion against the peace proposals was carried by eight votes, and in return the Whigs allowed the Tories to ban Occasional Conformity.

But Anne and Harley were not beaten. In January 1712 the Queen created twelve new Tory peers (including Mrs. Masham's husband) committed to supporting peace. In this way the Peace Act approving the Preliminary Articles was passed with a tiny majority. There were, however, serious constitutional consequences of the struggle. Neither Whigs nor extreme Tories gained credit from the devil's bargain over Occasional Conformity, and no politician liked the Crown's massive interference with Parliament by the creation of the twelve peers. Lord Wharton, sarcastically comparing them to a jury, asked in the Lords whether they voted by their foreman. A few years later the Whig John Toland called their elevation 'the deadliest blow which was ever struck at the vitals of Parliament' – and the Whigs then impeached Harley for having advised it.

By passing the Peace Act Parliament freed the hands of the British delegates assembling at Utrecht in January 1712. But Louis, now that Marlborough was disgraced and dismissed, suddenly put the cat among the pigeons by demanding that the Spanish Netherlands should be given to his ally the Elector of Bavaria. A series of deaths in the French royal family further complicated the negotiations by bringing Philip V closer to the French succession. The Dauphin Louis had died in 1711; his eldest son the Duke of Burgundy died in February 1712, and Burgundy's eldest son in March 1712. By then Louis had only three surviving descendants: Philip V of Spain, Philip's younger brother the Duke of Berri, and their nephew,

Burgundy's younger son Louis. With only the last, a sickly baby, standing between Philip and the legitimate French succession, it was more necessary than ever for the Allies to make sure that he renounced his rights to the throne of Louis XIV. While the ambassadors haggled ineffectively at Utrecht, the terms of the Peace were thrashed out in secret negotiations between Torcy and St. John, through their agents Gaultier and Matthew Prior.

The Tories had sent out the Duke of Ormonde to command the armies in place of Marlborough, but he was given orders to take no offensive action against the French. The other Allied generals, still loyal to Marlborough, cold-shouldered him and tried to get on with the war by themselves. So anxious were the Tories to ingratiate themselves with Louis that Harley and St. John even sent Torcy warning when they learnt that Prince Eugène was planning to attack Nieuport. In the summer of 1712, weeping in angry shame, the last British regiments marched away from the front and soon returned to England. Next spring the Treaty of Utrecht brought most of the fighting to an end, though Villars had to defeat Eugène before the Emperor accepted parallel terms in the Treaty of Rastadt in 1714. Through St. John's unscrupulous diplomacy, the Treaty of Utrecht[1] brought Britain much profit but little honour.

The peace brought even more bitter party rivalries, partly because many Tories hoped to set aside the Act of Settlement and hail James III as sovereign on Anne's death. They hoped that the new friendship with Louis would make this possible – and persuaded themselves that the Queen herself wanted to see 'justice' done to her half-brother. Only a duelling wound received from a Whig peer prevented the Jacobite Duke of Hamilton going to Versailles as ambassador. Both Harley and St. John were intriguing deeply with James III, the former as a policy of cautious insurance, the latter because he hoped to win for himself supreme power in Britain as a King-maker – though he probably did not care much whether it was the Stuart or the Hanoverian whom he was to crown.

With one Tory leader plotting to win power, and the other plotting not to lose it, the intrigues with James sowed the seeds of the party's collapse. In reaction to their leaders' follies, a

[1] The terms of the Treaty are outlined on p. 354.

number of moderate Tories collected around the eminently respectable Thomas Hanmer to defend the Protestant Succession. By the summer of 1713 these 'Hanover' Tories had begun to vote with the Whigs, as when they helped to throw out the commercial treaty which St. John proposed to make with France. Like the moderates, the extremists in the party became more clearly defined, for St. John was steadily consolidating his supporters. By this time he had won over the ungrateful Lady Masham (by bribing her with South Sea Company shares); and together they got Anne to accept the High Churchman Bromley as the other Secretary of State in place of Dartmouth, and to appoint the virulent Jacobite Dr. Atterbury as Bishop of Rochester.

Nonetheless, the Tory factions remained together long enough to win the election of 1713, though it was significant that the new Commons chose Hanmer as their Speaker. The election was even more corrupt than usual, and Anne's influence ensured that the Whig gains were few. But before Parliament met the Queen fell gravely ill. The Tories were not yet ready to proclaim James III, and had Anne died at that time the Hanoverian Succession would have been unchallenged. But to the Tories' joy – and the Whigs' unconcealed dismay – the Queen recovered.

The emergency made the Jacobites hasten their preparations. In February they asked James to forsake Rome and join the Church of England. To their alarm, he refused. He was not prepared to feign Anglicanism as Charles II had done in 1660. By sticking to his principles, the Pretender wrecked his supporters' plans. Only a handful of Tories were willing to see a Catholic inherit the throne. Men less cynical and less blind would not have rushed headlong into a dark lane leading only to Rome. By the spring of 1714 it was too late for them to turn back. In April old Electress Sophia of Hanover died, and her claims to the English throne were inherited by her soldier son George, who hated St. John and Harley for betraying the Alliance.

St. John's last chance to get power was to reunite the party behind him to help him bargain with Hanover. His only hope was another attack on the Nonconformists. He offered Parliament the bait of a Schism Act to prohibit the Nonconformists from teaching in schools, to try to cut off the supply of

new Dissenting ministers and to make it impossible for Nonconformists to get any professional education.   The Act insisted that,
with a few exceptions, all teachers should be Anglican communicants licensed by their bishop.   Harley disliked the Act, but
dared not oppose it for fear of offending the Queen.   St. John's
scheme was in part successful: it did not unite the Tory party,
but it emphasized his power as leader of the major part of it.

The stage was now set for the last scene in Anne's reign.
Harley's moderation (in all except drink) had become tedious to
her, and she doubted his loyalty to her own High Church
principles.   Distressed by the troubles of the time, the
Treasurer was now an alcoholic and frequently offended the
Queen by coming drunk into her presence.   The ascendancy of
St. John was almost complete.   When in early July the Lords
ventured to discuss charges of corruption made against him,
Anne went to the House and immediately prorogued Parlia-
ment to save her favourite.   On July 27th, she gave in to Lady
Masham's constant urging and dismissed Harley from his post
as Treasurer and unofficial Prime Minister.   St. John's hopes
ran high: the power he sought was almost within his grasp.   But
some last instinct of cautious good sense remained in the
Queen's sick mind, weakened as it was by her recent illness.
For four days she kept the Treasurer's post vacant.   Then,
on her death-bed, she gave the white staff to the veteran
Shrewsbury.   No prayers were said for her, even in her own
chapel, and her favourite physician Dr. Radcliffe was himself
too sick to attend her.   On the news of her death, so a friend
informed Dean Swift, 'stocks rose three per cent. in the city'.

Anne died on August 1st, the day when the Schism Act was
to come into force.   There was some danger that the leading
Jacobites – St. John, Bishop Atterbury and Harcourt the Lord
Chancellor – might proclaim James III, but their nerve failed
them.   They could not make up their minds to take so perilous
a step, and the crisis passed over.   At the last moment St.
John tried to win some of the Whigs to his side, but without
success.   In the end, his signature as Viscount Bolingbroke was
among those of the other Privy Councillors as they hastily
despatched messages to all parts of the kingdom – and to
Hanover.   The Whigs in fact were better prepared to raise
London in defence of the Protestant succession than the
Jacobite intriguers were to proclaim the Pretender.   By their

follies the Tory extremists sentenced their party to fifty years in the political desert, and made Britain willing to accept the safe Whig Supremacy.

## iv. Scotland, 1695–1714

Although at the time Marlborough's victories were more spectacular, the greatest achievement of Anne's reign was the long-delayed union with Scotland. In her first speech to Parliament in March 1702 Anne spoke hopefully of the prospects of union; in fact, the union then appeared more improbable than at any time since James VI had come to England ninety-nine years before.

A long history of disputes, jealousies and fears seemed bound to wreck the Queen's plans. Since the break-up of the Cromwellian union, which only Monck's army held together at all, Scotland had followed a path diverging from that of England. William III had speeded up this drift. After accepting the Scottish Estates' Claim of Right, in 1690 he agreed to establish Presbyterianism as the sole permitted Church in Scotland, and abolished the Lords of the Articles through whom previous kings had controlled the Scottish Parliament. Scottish law was still fundamentally different from English law, and the clan chieftains still kept their own ancient jurisdictions. The poverty of the people on the one hand and the relatively good education provided in burgh schools and the five universities (England had only two) on the other hand – as well as fierce clan traditions in the Highlands – produced a society totally unlike that of England. The Presbyterian Kirk, under the benevolent eye of Calvinist William III, had become the focus of national pride in Scotland; in 1702, with a High Church Tory on the throne, its future and its privileges became uncertain. Scottish money was worth only one-twelfth of the value of equivalent English coins. A union might impose on Scotland the high taxes to which the English were accustomed, and the Scots might have to help pay the interest on the English national debt. A customs barrier stretched from the Solway to the Tweed, and the Scots were jealously excluded from England's profitable colonial trade (especially after the 1696 Navigation Act). England's foreign policy, with three wars against Holland and two against France in the previous fifty years, interrupted Scotland's trade with her two main overseas customers. By 1700 Scotland was probably less prosperous than she had been a generation before. Jacobite propaganda had made much of the Massacre of Glencoe, to discredit England, and to demand that the exiled Stuarts should succeed Anne, on the throne of Scotland if not on that of England.

Above all, the Scots had been roused up against England by the failure of the recent 'Darien Scheme'. In 1695 the Scottish Parliament had set up the 'Company of Scotland trading to Africa and the Indies', largely through the initiative of William Paterson, other Scottish merchants in London, and some English friends eager to challenge the East India Company's monopoly. But the East India Company proved powerful enough to force the English subscribers to withdraw their capital, and the whole scheme was jeopardized. As a matter of national pride the Scots resolved to raise the necessary money entirely within Scotland: almost every man with money to invest subscribed to it. When the 1696 Navigation Act sternly warned the Scots to keep out of the English colonies, Paterson tried to get trading concessions in the Baltic. He failed, and then planned a crazy project which was a century out of date. This was to found at Darien on the isthmus of Panama – Spanish territory – a colony which would be able to muscle in on the trade of the Caribbean.

The Darien Scheme was bold but quite impracticable: with little capital and less experience the Scots were challenging most of the established commercial and colonial interests of the whole world. The first of three expeditions sailed to Panama in the autumn of 1698, when William III was concluding the first Partition Treaty with Louis XIV. To have allowed the Scots to seize part of the disputed Spanish empire would have wrecked the negotiations immediately. William's diplomatic discussions, no less than the pressure of London and Dutch merchants, forced him to order the English colonies in the West Indies to give no help to the Scots. In eighteen months the escapade was over, for in March 1700 the survivors surrendered to the Spanish. The Company of Scotland had lost some 2000 lives and £200,000. Its collapse, after several years of bad harvests at home, ruined people throughout the land. Rather unjustly, the Scots blamed England.

In these circumstances, war between England and Scotland seemed more likely than union. Those in the two countries who hoped for union had only a few things in their favour. The English wanted to get the Scots to acknowledge the Hanoverian Succession, thereby preventing the revival of French influence there, and thus close the 'back door' into England. On the other hand, the Scots wanted to be admitted to England's trading privileges; in no other way, her mercantilists argued, could Scotland be made more prosperous. These factors seemed too slight to break down centuries of prejudice, yet they were the only attractive concessions the two sides had to offer each other.

The reign started badly. Anne did not convene the Scottish Parliament as swiftly as she should have done, and she then angered the members by declaring war on their behalf only ten days before they assembled. Nonetheless, the 'Court' party passed an Act enabling Anne to appoint commissioners to discuss union – after the Duke of Hamilton (leader of both the Jacobites and the opposition 'Country' Whigs) had stalked out of the chamber with his followers behind him. As the English Parliament passed a similar Act, the commissioners on both sides were able to begin their discussions at the end of 1702.

Then Anne very unwisely dissolved the Scottish Parliament,[1] and the election of 1703 returned an assembly hostile to union. The Tory Commons elected in England in 1702 was also reluctant to proceed with the discussions, for the High Churchmen objected to confirming the Scottish Presbyterian Church in unchallenged power, and the merchants still feared the effects of Scots competing for their trade. When the moderate Scots proposed a Toleration Act to help Episcopalians (and placate the English Tories), the Edinburgh mob rioted so violently that the Act had to be dropped. In 1703 and 1704 the Scottish Parliament passed four insolent Acts, which inflamed English passions and took the two countries to the brink of war. The Act Anent Peace and War declared that, after Anne's reign, the right of beginning and ending wars should belong to the Scottish Parliament, not to the sovereign. The Wine Act and the Act allowing the Exportation of Wool encouraged Scots to trade

---

[1] As there was no Triennial Act in Scotland, there was no duration to the lifetime of a Parliament. There was thus no need for Anne to dissolve the Parliament – even though it had existed since 1689.

with France, despite England's attempt to blockade Louis. Worst of all, the Act of Security declared that the Scottish Parliament should, when Anne died, 'nominate and declare the successor to the Imperial Crown of this Realm' – and arranged for the immediate arming and training of a militia. The Queen resisted the Act of Security for nearly a year, but, with the ablest men in Scotland – Queensberry, Hamilton and Atholl – opposing her over it, she had to give way.

When the English Parliament met again at the end of 1704 it loudly attacked Anne for accepting the Act of Security and thus signing away the Hanoverian succession. The Whigs were as critical as the Tories. To give Godolphin practical support in the crisis, the Queen attended many of the debates in the Lords. Eventually Wharton and the other peers of the Whig 'Junto' saved the day by persuading Parliament to take action which was both stern and friendly. Their proposal, the Alien Act, was passed in March 1705. It offered the Scots three choices – to accept full union, to remain politically independent but recognize the Hanoverian succession, or to lose their legal rights as English citizens (under the 1608 *Post-Nati* decision) and to have their export of cattle and linen across the border prohibited. The Act gave the Scots until the end of the year to make up their minds.

The threat of economic sanctions infuriated and horrified them. The Duke of Roxburgh lamented 'If that's done, we are ruined'. The Edinburgh mob, at times the strongest force in Scotland, insisted on the execution of Captain Green and the crew of the *Worcester*, an English ship which had rashly sheltered in the Forth on its way back from India. Chancellor Seafield knew that they were innocent of the charge of piracy trumped up against them, but he also knew that to refuse the mob their blood might well wreck the cause of union by implying that he was just a tool of the English. Green and two of his men were therefore hanged while a crowd of 80,000 'huzza'd in triumph'. When the Scottish Parliament met at the end of August 1705 to debate its answer to the Alien Act, Hamilton (himself expecting to be chosen king if the succession went neither to the House of Hanover nor to James III) failed by only two votes to get a defiant answer sent to London.

But the next day Hamilton changed sides, now hoping to be able to help dictate terms to England. He proposed that

Parliament should invite the Queen herself to choose Scottish commissioners to negotiate with English commissioners to arrange the political union of the two countries. After this *volte-face* the opposition temporarily collapsed. Anne chose from each Parliament about thirty men believed to be favourable to union. Accordingly in December 1705 the English Parliament cancelled the Alien Act, and in April 1706 the two sets of Commissioners met in London. From Scotland Queensberry brought a party which (except for the Jacobite Lockhart included by mistake) was largely won over by the sweet reasonableness of Godolphin, Harley, Somers and Archbishop Tenison.

The Treaty of Union, in effect a treaty between the two Parliaments, was prepared after only nine weeks' work. It proposed that:

1. The Scottish Parliament should cease to exist; Scotland should send forty-five M.P.s and sixteen peers (chosen as their representatives by the other Scottish peers) to the British Parliament at Westminster. Not wanting to be swamped by hard-up backwoods nobles from 'North Britain', the English peers had insisted on limiting the number of recruits to the House of Lords.
2. Scotland should keep her own laws and law courts, including the private 'feudal' courts of the chieftains.
3. English currency and English weights and measures should be used throughout Britain.
4. Scotland should pay about one-fortieth of the English Land Tax.
5. As compensation for contributing taxes to pay the interest on the English national debt, England should pay Scotland nearly £400,000 as an 'Equivalent', plus an 'Arising Equivalent' amounting to the extra sums Scotland would pay in the next seven years through being subject to the higher English customs and excise duties. It was intended that much of the 'Equivalents' should be used to compensate the Darien scheme shareholders for their losses.
6. There was to be free trade between England and Scotland, and Scottish merchants should be admitted to all the trading privileges enjoyed by English merchants.

All that now remained was for the two Parliaments to ratify the Treaty, and for the religious question to be settled. It took over three months for Queensberry and Argyle to force the Treaty through the Scottish Parliament, in the teeth of opposition raked up by Hamilton and Atholl from elements so diverse as the Edinburgh mob, the Episcopalian gentry, the Jacobites of the north-west, and the Cameronian Presbyterians of the south-west. Much of the opposition faded, however, after Parliament had appeased the General Assembly of the Kirk with an Act 'for securing the Protestant Religion and Presbyterian Church Government'. Bribes, out of the £20,000 sent by Godolphin to Queensberry, helped to convince some of the waverers, and in January 1707 the Scottish Parliament finally approved the Treaty. The English Parliament swiftly did the same.

The United Kingdom of Great Britain formally came into being on May 1st 1707. On that day Anne drove to St. Paul's to give thanks, in a procession of 400 coaches. The Scots were more cautious: thirty-one whales had just been washed up on the coast of Fife opposite Edinburgh – surely a fearful omen!

The years immediately after the Union seemed to justify its critics rather than its supporters. Only a few extreme nationalists opposed the abolition of the Scottish Privy Council in 1708, but the English system of J.P.s was then extended in Scotland to weaken the power of local chieftains. The English customs official soon became a familiar sight, representing southern tyranny, and there was a consequent boom in smuggling. The Jacobites tried to exploit this unrest. In March 1708 a fleet of French privateers slipped out of Dunkirk harbour with 5000 French troops and 'James VIII' on board. Admiral Byng and Protestant gales like those of 1588 chased them up the east coast, prevented a landing in Scotland, and forced them to return to France by the stormy seas around Ireland. The Whig peers, together with some Tories anxious to limit Scottish privileges, made Anne agree in 1711 that no Scottish peer, unless chosen as one of the sixteen representatives, could sit in the House of Lords by virtue of receiving a title of nobility in 'the peerage of Great Britain'. In 1712, after the Presbytery of Edinburgh had rashly prosecuted an Episcopalian minister called Greenshields for using the Anglican Book of Common Prayer, the High Church Tories alarmed the Kirk by passing a Toleration Act designed to help the Episcopalians.

They also passed an Act to restore to former patrons the right of 'presenting' – in effect nominating – the parish ministers. New duties on linen in 1711 and on malt in 1713 added fresh grievances to the fears of the Kirk and anger of the nobles.

Many Scots claimed that these measures invalidated the Treaty of Union. Consequently, in June 1713 the Scottish members at Westminster demanded its repeal. When the resolution was debated in the Lords, many of the Whigs now supported the Scots, and it was the Tories who saved the Union they had criticized a few years before. Within two years the peaceful Hanoverian succession, and the Catholic Jacobite attempt to upset it in the 1715 Rebellion, together convinced the Kirk and the burghs that they were safer in the Union than outside it. In the following decades Scotland's economy boomed, and their new prosperity reconciled all but a few fanatics to the continuance of the United Kingdom.

The most appropriate contemporary comment on the Union is that by Gilbert Burnet, the Scottish Whig whom William III made Bishop of Salisbury in 1689, and a life-long worker for the Union:

The Union of the two kingdoms was a work of which many had quite despaired, in which number I was one; and those who had entertained better hopes, thought it must have run out into a long negotiation for several years; but, beyond all men's expectation, it was begun and finished within the compass of one.[1]

## v. Ireland, 1695–1714

It may be wondered why Anne, so set on union with Scotland, did not try also to bring Ireland into the United Kingdom. The main reason was that such a union would not have benefited England. For two centuries the Parliament in Dublin had been subordinate to that at Westminster, unable to pass any law unless the English Parliament also approved it. At times, the English Parliament legislated by itself on Irish matters, without reference to Dublin. One such law was the

---

[1] G. Burnet, *History of My Own Times*, p. 402. By 'one year' Burnet is of course referring to the period between the 1706 meeting of the commissioners and the inauguration of the Union.

1701 Act of Settlement. As it promised the Crown of Ireland, as well as that of England, to the Hanoverians, the few Irishmen who hoped for union did not possess the one vital bargaining counter which the Scots held. Thus the English Parliament could gain nothing from a treaty of equality with a body it already controlled. There were also several other factors obstructing any move towards union. In 1707 English merchants assented only very grudgingly to Scottish merchants sharing their commerce, and would certainly have tried hard to prevent similar privileges going to the more numerous Irish – especially as the latter's geographical position would have given them many advantages in trading with the American colonies. In Scotland the majority accepted union only when the powers of the Presbyterian Kirk were guaranteed; it would have been unthinkable for Parliament to have offered even a tolerated equality to the Church to which most Irishmen belonged. The English attitude to Ireland remained one of victor towards vanquished. The political, religious and economic grievances of the past centuries made it too late for conciliation. There was therefore no point in trying to close England's western back-door with a political treaty like that which sealed her northern frontier. Even if there had been a political union, England would still have been so afraid of France helping the natives to revolt that she would have had to preserve indefinitely a large standing army in Ireland.

So the English Government and its puppet in Dublin continued to try to crush the natives' religion and traditions and to seize their remaining land. To his credit, William III did not wish to persecute the Irish, but was spurred on by greedy English nobles and their cronies in Ireland. Even before they made the King, in 1697, break his promise and accept the Treaty of Limerick without the 'omitted clause',[1] they had forced him to give way on several matters. The English Parliament insisted that the Test Acts be applied in Ireland, to exclude Roman Catholics totally from the Dublin Parliament. When Lord Deputy Capel's Parliament met in 1695, without Catholic members, it forbade Catholics to teach, to go abroad for education, and to own arms. Another Act converted most Irish land tenures into tenancies 'at will': the peasant could then be turned off his land, or made to pay higher rent,

[1] See above, pp. 312-3.

at a moment's notice.    Rather than give any concession to the Presbyterians of Ulster, the Irish Parliament refused William's request to pass a Bill similar to the 1689 Toleration Act.    In 1697 the Parliament ordered all monks, friars and higher clergy to leave Ireland, banned from public office all Protestants who married Catholic girls, and decreed that all such Catholic wives should forfeit half their property – a vicious attempt to stop mixed marriages.    Despite the pleas of Emperor Leopold, William had also to accept the Security Act; this ordered life imprisonment and confiscation of property for all who refused to take the oath of supremacy.    As the oath acclaimed William as head of the Church, it was obviously intolerable for Roman Catholics – but fortunately a shortage of gaols made it impossible to enforce.    The King also quarrelled with the English and Irish Parliaments about the sale of land recently confiscated from Tyrconnell and other Jacobites; only a little was sold or given back to former owners, most of it eventually being traded to colonists for under £1 an acre.

The mercantilist lobby in England was also active.    It persuaded the English Parliament in 1696 to forbid Ireland to trade directly with the overseas colonies, in 1698 to impose prohibitive duties on the export of almost all Irish draperies, and in 1699 to prevent Ireland exporting woollens except to England.    Only in linen (as there was no linen industry in England) were the Irish permitted to export freely.

These repressions continued in Anne's reign under both Whigs and Tories.    In 1703 an Act repeated the ban on the Catholic bishops (partly because it was known that the exiled Stuarts were nominating them), and threatened with the penalties of treason any Catholic priests who refused to take a purely secular oath of allegiance to Anne.    Next year Parliament ordered that Protestants should not sell land to Catholics. Very cruelly, it also ordered that Catholic landowners must bequeath their property in *gavelkind*, dividing it up equally among all their sons; however, if the eldest son became a Protestant, he could inherit the whole estate.    Squeezed in this vice, many landowners became Protestants – in name, at least. Another law in 1709 forbade Catholics to sit on grand juries, and threatened heavy punishments for any who tried to practise law.    The attacks on the Ulster Nonconformists also continued: in 1704 Parliament insisted that all 'office holders' should take the Anglican Sacrament, and in 1710 Harley's Tory government stopped paying the *regium donum*, a small subsidy for Nonconformist ministers.    At the same time Harley was listening seriously to the appeals of one of his own literary hacks, Jonathan Swift, the non-resident Canon of St. Patrick's Cathedral in Dublin, urging that the Queen should increase the incomes of the Anglican clergy in Ireland by giving up her right to 'first-fruits and tenths'.

It was clear that the government of Ireland was conducted solely in the interests of the small minority of Anglican settlers – so much so that Swift could speak of these alone as 'the nation'. For the rest of Ireland's inhabitants, it did not greatly matter whether laws were passed by a Parliament in London or a Parliament in Ireland.    It was from a few members of the Anglican minority – who alone were represented in Parliament – that the only proposals for union came.    In 1698 one of these, William Molyneux, wrote *The Case of Ireland's being Bound by Acts of Parliament in England stated*.    Owing more to Locke than its clumsy title suggests, Molyneux argued that Irishmen should share in the government by sending M.P.s to Westminster. Then, in 1703 and 1707, influenced by Molyneux as well as by England's negotiations with the Scots, the Irish House of Commons asked Anne to consider taking Ireland into a full political union with England.    The requests went unheeded.

As the policy of repression continued, even under 'old Irish' viceroys like Ormonde (1703–7 and 1710–13), so the Catholics became more and more a servile population.    Deprived of their land, persecuted for their faith, their native language partly suppressed, with education and the professions barred to them, a once proud people was reduced to a helot class.    Their old leaders were dead, or had deserted to the enemy, and it was not until the Protestant settlers themselves came to resent English overlordship that new leaders emerged. In the meantime, the conquerors continued to hold down their wretched victims.

### vi. War and the economy

Marlborough's war affected the English economy very much as William III's had done.    Although there was no naval battle except the inconclusive scrap off Malaga in 1704, the pirates from Dunkirk and Brest kept the English dockyards busy. Even to maintain 'the fleet in being', as a rather static strategic threat, cost Godolphin's ministries on average nearly £2,000,000 a year. The unprecedented demand for metals encouraged ironmasters like the Foleys and their associates to develop their industrial empire stretching from Cheshire to the Forest of Dean, from Derbyshire to Sussex. The dockyards' greedy appetite for timber led to technical improvements in the metal industries. A new 'reverberatory' furnace made it possible to use coal instead of wood for smelting copper and lead, and it was during the war that Abraham Darby devised his process for smelting iron with coke – one of the great scientific 'break-throughs' which made the Industrial Revolution possible. By the end of the war many mines were being drained by the steam pumping engines invented by Newcomen and Savery. The days of King Coal and the Industrial Revolution were close at hand. It was not surprising, therefore, that Harley's Government tried in 1710 to prevent price-fixing agreements among the Newcastle 'hostmen' and colliers, in an unsuccessful attempt to reduce the price of this vital fuel.

The war did little harm to Britain's home economy, despite the grievances of the Tories about the crushing Land Tax and their claims that Whig manufacturers were profiting unjustly. Except in 1710, following a bad harvest, prices remained steady, and were actually lower in the last years of the war than in the first. The enormous army and navy, exceeding a quarter of a million men, was recruited without great disturbance to industry or agriculture. Marlborough's superb troops were enlisted largely from convicts, debtors and Scots, while the navy got its men by the time-honoured way of press-ganging the unemployed and the layabouts in the coastal towns.

One consequence of the presence of large British armies on the Continent was a growth in the use of bills of exchange. Chief Justice Holt's decision in 1700 had made bank notes respectable and safe, and in 1705 Parliament declared that promissory notes were freely negotiable.[1] Godolphin subsequently built up a comprehensive network of exchanges in many cities in western Europe, with the help of two merchants –

---

[1] i.e., if A gave B a promissory note admitting a debt to him of £100, B could then use this note to purchase £100-worth of cloth from C. C would then claim payment from A.

Henry Furnese and the Huguenot *émigré* Theodore Janssen. In 1709 alone, the government sent over £3,000,000 to the Continent, almost all of it in bills of exchange negotiated by Godolphin's agents. The perils of shipping gold and silver overseas in wartime made merchants deal as far as possible through these bills. The amount of bullion exported consequently fell: in 1710 silver exports to the East Indies were barely a quarter of those of 1699. Only the soundness of English government finance made it possible for the economy to rely so much on paper money. By contrast, when Louis XIV increased the circulation of paper money in France it drove coins almost entirely out of circulation.

Nonetheless many economists worried about the increase in the national debt, which rose to £36,000,000 by the end of the war. Many more men challenged the political power gained by the companies which loaned money to the Crown. For its loyalty to William III, the Bank of England received new privileges in 1697 and 1708 which gave it a near-monopoly of joint-stock banking in England. The Bank responded willingly to the Whigs' war-demands, its Governor, Sir Gilbert Heathcote, protesting to Godolphin in 1709 'I call anything a rotten peace unless we have Spain'. For this and other, earlier, reasons the Tory government in 1710 resolved to weaken the Bank. Therefore Harley established the South Sea Company, to take over £10,000,000 of the national debt. Investors were promised 6 per cent. interest, to be earned by the Company after Spain gave it permission (the *Asiento*) to trade with South America. To Holland's indignant disgust, St. John secured the *Asiento* in the peace negotiations with Louis.

Party politics and commercial jealousy also shook the East India Company. Papillon and his Whig friends persuaded Parliament in 1696 to investigate the affairs of this strongly Tory company; in 1698 the Whig 'Junto' allowed Papillon's group (after it promised to raise a loan of £2,000,000 for the government) to found a new concern in competition with the old Company. For ten years the two Companies waged almost open war in the Far East. As neither could prosper in such conditions, Godolphin in 1708 persuaded them to amalgamate. With more capital, initiative and experience than its predecessors, the new 'United' Company prospered. Its dividend rose from only 5 per cent. in 1708 to 10 per cent. in 1711, and it remained at 10 per cent. for a whole decade.

It was inevitable that the controversies of the war should inspire the pens of the political pamphleteers. One early quarrel resulted from the Methuen Treaty of 1703, in which England allied with Portugal and promised to expand Anglo-Portuguese commerce. Claret-loving Tories attacked the Treaty, with its promise that England would buy Portuguese wines. As the war interrupted shipments of claret to England, port became a symbol of Whiggery and the war-party, claret of those who wanted peace with France. A more serious dispute, threatening to break up the Alliance, was whether the Dutch should continue to trade with France. Many Tories hoped that if they were faced with an ultimatum, the Dutch would end the war rather than lose profitable trade. Unrestricted commerce, they thought, helped 'induce ye United Provinces to protract the war'. In the *Review*, Defoe demanded 'Let us make them stop the Trade, or send over no more Forces to help them; a Parcel of Dutch Sons of Whores, and the like...' In the circumstances[1] Godolphin sent his economic expert, Charles Davenant, to Holland in 1705 to find out whether Franco-Dutch trade enriched Louis or impoverished him. Davenant, knowing his patron's wishes, returned an official report that the trade benefited the Allies more than France. Five years later the Tories came to power. Anxious to keep his post (as Inspector-General of the customs and excise, his salary alone was worth £1000 p.a.), Davenant then changed his tune, and condemned the trade he had previously approved. He kept the post. Many of the economic arguments advanced during the war derived, like Davenant's, from blatant self-interest – whether the arguments were for the continuation of the war, for the reduction of the Land Tax, for 'No Peace without Spain', or for a naval campaign to grab colonies. In the end, the Tory victories of 1710 made it possible for St. John to arrange a peace treaty almost entirely in Britain's self-interest, building up a great empire at the expense of Spain, France and Holland, and thus securing a peace which benefited all in Britain except Whig industrialists and victualling contractors. With Holland exhausted and the French fleets ashamed to leave port, the

---

[1] Which may be compared with the U.S.A.'s opposition to her allies trading with Communist countries.

Peace of Utrecht gave a great share of the world's commerce to the only country with a navy large enough to defend it.

## vii. The Churches under Anne

The differences between 'High Church' and 'Latitudinarian' or 'Broad' Church can be explained in political terms more easily than in theological ones. The High Churchmen were the descendants in a direct line (slightly twisted in 1688) of the Restoration Church, and still supported the Anglican-Cavalier alliance which had begotten the Clarendon Code. The Revolution, the Bill of Rights and the Act of Settlement had weakened their political philosophy of the Divine Right of the King, to whom all subjects owed at least the passive duty of Non-Resistance, but there were still among the High Churchmen many zealots continuing to preach those theories. A few were active Jacobites; many admired the Non-Jurors; most of them felt guilty about abandoning James II, and all had been unhappy serving William III. On the whole they believed that the Church should be something more than just the servant of the State, and they expected the Crown to be on their side. In Anne's reign they were still hostile to the Nonconformists, resentful of Calvinist Holland, suspicious of Presbyterian Scotland, and usually sympathetic towards James III (though not to his religion). In contrast the Latitudinarians were more tolerant, believing that controversial matters such as church organization and the actual form of worship were relatively unimportant. Many of them would have welcomed a Church broad enough to include the Presbyterians, and some even approved of Dissenters practising Occasional Conformity. They accepted the common-sense of the Revolutionary Settlement and the promised Hanoverian Succession, and they followed Locke in upholding the authority of the 'contractual' State through a representative government. While most High Churchmen were Tories, virtually all the Broad Churchmen were Whigs.

For the first time since Charles I's reign, the Church of England had in Anne a sovereign who was genuinely devoted to it. The Queen had all her grandfather's piety. Even if she was wise enough not to lay claim to Divine Right, she believed in the spiritual nature of a monarch's powers. She continued the practice of 'touching' persons with scrofula, the 'King's Evil'. In later years the great Dr. Johnson remembered how in his childhood he had been touched by the Queen, magnificent in diamonds and a black hood. Some of her theological sympathies lay with the Non-Jurors, as she respected their principles of loyalty to her father, but the surviving Non-Jurors had become too tainted with Jacobitism for her to help them. So it was the High Church party which basked in the sun of royal favour. Accordingly the High Churchmen were able to enlist her support in their attacks on Occasional Conformity, and almost all her appointments as bishops were Tory High Churchmen.

As William had filled most vacant dioceses with Whig Latitudinarians, few of whom died during Anne's reign, there were not many bishops whom she liked. From 1693 to 1714 Thomas Tenison was Archbishop of Canterbury, a good preacher and a man of 'learning, piety and prudence' (Evelyn). Swift, however, thought him a dull dog, as he disapproved of the clergy playing whist. Tenison was a loyal Whig and a Latitudinarian, and Anne much preferred John Sharp, the High Churchman whom William strangely had made Archbishop of York. Sharp and Bishop Burnet persuaded the Queen to turn to better use the income from 'first-fruits and tenths' which the Crown had gained at the Reformation. Currently the money was providing pensions for Charles II's mistresses and bastards and for various other royal favourites. In 1704 therefore, Parliament instituted 'Queen Anne's Bounty', giving the income (£16,000 p.a.) from first-fruits and tenths to supplement the incomes of the poorer clergy. Seven years later, largely for political reasons, Harley's government set about building fifty new churches in London to challenge the Nonconformists in the capital.

In religion as well as in politics, the pamphleteers were very active, whipping up antagonism between different groups. The ablest of the High Church writers was Jonathan Swift. His first satire, A Tale of a Tub, was published in 1704 (though written several years earlier). It tells the story of three brothers, Peter (the Catholic Church), Martin (the Anglican) and Jack (the Nonconformists) squabbling over their inheritance, and ends by making all three look silly. Swift became a follower of Godolphin; and as a Canon of Dublin Cathedral he tried to persuade him to get Queen Anne's Bounty extended to the Anglican Church in Ireland. In 1708 Swift annoyed the Whigs by attacking those who wished to give Irish Presbyterians the toleration permitted to English Dissenters, and in 1710 he made a timely transfer of allegiance to the Tory party. He joined the Brothers' Club, became the friend of both Harley and St. John, and tried hard to reconcile them after they had quarrelled. As well as political pamphlets about *The Conduct of the Allies* and *The Barrier Treaty*, Swift published attacks on Bishop Burnet and on Deism, and various reflections on Church and State. But he ended his life a disappointed man; by the violence of some of his works he turned Queen Anne as well as the Whigs against him, and all that St. John could get for him was the Deanery of Dublin Cathedral. His best-known book appeared in 1726, twelve years after the Hanoverian succession finally dashed his hopes of a bishopric. Reflecting in *Gulliver's Travels* on his own career, Swift satirized those who quarrelled over petty things – how high heels should be and whether eggs should be opened at the big or little end. It was a curious Dean who in retrospect saw in terms of the 'Big-enders' and 'Little-enders' dispute the issues which had confronted his Church in Anne's reign!

The two most outspoken extreme High Churchmen were Francis Atterbury and Henry Sacheverell. The former had pleaded successfully for the revival of Convocation, and had helped in 1700 to lead the Lower House in its attack on the bishops; in later years he became a friend of St. John, a Jacobite and, despite the Queen's misgivings about him, Bishop of Rochester. In August 1714 he was the most ardent Jacobite of them all, offering to proclaim James III himself, and cursing St. John for a pusillanimous fool when the latter feared that all their throats would be cut if he did so. Another narrow-minded bigot, Dr. Sacheverell earned at Oxford a reputation for preaching fiery sermons against Whigs, Broad Churchmen and Dissenters. In a sermon in St. Paul's on November 5th, 1709, Sacheverell criticized Godolphin as 'Volpone' (the deceitful foxy merchant in Ben Jonson's play), damned the Whigs and some of the bishops, and claimed that the Church was in danger under a government too tolerant towards Noncon-formists. Not for the first time, he tried to revive the old Anglican doctrines of Divine Right and Non-Resistance. The

Whigs impeached him for preaching in this way on the hallowed anniversary of Gunpowder Plot and William's landing in Torbay. Sacheverell's trial in March 1710 was the scene of frenzied excitement. Christopher Wren hastily installed scaffolding and gallery seats in Westminster Hall to accommodate those clamouring for admission. For a month the theatres were empty. The City mob – showing opposition to the war rather than support for Sacheverell's theology – took the chance to burn down Nonconformist chapels, and would have sacked the Whig Bank of England if the Queen had not sent the Horse Guards to stop them. The Queen herself attended the debates on his impeachment as a critic of the administration and 'a public incendiary', to show her support for him. Despite this, Sacheverell was found guilty. The sentence, however, was a trivial one: he must not preach again for three years. This was virtually an acquittal, and the crowd and the Queen treated it as such. After this, Anne soon plucked up courage to dismiss Godolphin and the Whigs who supported him.

Sacheverell's impeachment was not the only attempt to stop those who were apparently preaching High Church doctrines. There appeared in 1702 a pamphlet entitled *The Shortest Way with the Dissenters*, calling for the total suppression of Nonconformity:

This is the time to pull up this heretical weed of sedition, that has too long disturbed the peace of our church, and poisoned the good corn. . . . The poison of their nature makes it a charity to our neighbours to destroy those creatures, not for any personal injury received, but for prevention; not for the evil they have done, but for the evil they may do. . . .

In fact, the pamphlet was an attempt to ridicule with heavy satire those intolerant Churchmen who wished to persecute the Nonconformists. Its author, Daniel Defoe, was himself a Nonconformist. Unfortunately, the pamphlet was too persuasive – people thought that Defoe was genuinely calling for a massacre of the Dissenters. He quickly wrote another pamphlet, to explain the first, but was put in the pillory and imprisoned for his rashness.

Whatever the wisdom of pillorying Defoe and impeaching Sacheverell, Godolphin's ministries were undoubtedly more tolerant than the Tory government which followed. As they knew the danger of splitting the country more deeply, Godolphin and Marlborough risked Anne's anger more than once in using the Whig peers to obstruct that darling of the Tory M.P.s, the Occasional Conformity Bill. Inevitably, in 1710 and 1711 the Tories again pressed for the Bill. The last time the Whig peers, so anxious to get help for rejecting the Peace Bill, let the Bill become law. Three years later St. John followed it with the Schism Act, to suppress Nonconformist education. These Acts were significant in the political history of the reign more than in the religious, and both were repealed by the Whigs in 1718. But if it had been possible to enforce them, they might well have helped to remove 'this heretical weed of sedition'. The Occasional Conformity Act imposed heavy fines (which the informers would receive) on all holders of civil and military office who attended Nonconformist services in England and Wales, and deprived them of their offices; no longer could Dissenters qualify for public office by taking the Anglican Sacrament in accordance with the letter of the Clarendon Code. The Schism Act forbade Nonconformists to run schools, or to teach as assistant masters any subjects except English, mathematics and science. The Act also ordered bishops (who might otherwise be too tolerant) to issue licences to teach other subjects only to men certified by their own parish clergy to be regular worshippers.

The Nonconformists in England and Wales were a disorganized minority, but this was not true of the Presbyterians in Scotland. They had formed for a generation the established Church, they were in an overwhelming majority, and they had in the presbyteries and General Assembly an efficient and proud organization. It was therefore extremely rash for St. John to upset the Kirk and endanger the Union by two Acts of 1712. One, the Toleration Act, tried to give a guarantee of fair treatment for the Scottish Episcopal Church. The other was an attempt to restore to the lairds their rights of patronage over the parish churches. The Scots regarded both Acts as infringements of the Treaty of Union, and complained so strongly that they tried in 1713 to end the Union. Nonetheless, neither Act was repealed under the Hanoverians. It was clearly equitable that Episcopalians should enjoy in Scotland the privileges allowed in England to Nonconformists; patrons on the whole made good use of the rights restored to them, by choosing ministers more enlightened than the narrow bigots many congregations would have preferred.

To be so deeply involved in party politics did not help the churches. Christianity had become a shuttlecock between Whig and Tory, Hanoverian and Jacobite, Dissenter, Latitudinarian and High Churchman. When the Hanoverians came to Britain, party passions gradually cooled – and religious animosities with them. It seemed irrational in the Age of Reason to persecute a man for his religious beliefs, or lack of them. More than a century and a half passed after Anne's death before the Clarendon Code was finally lifted from the backs of the Nonconformists, but it was not long before the Whigs made it possible for them to ignore most of the Code. Although it took so long for Britain to become genuinely tolerant,[1] the country had made notable advances by the end of the Stuart period. In the middle of the seventeenth century there were few men who thought of toleration as more than a matter of temporary convenience, but among them were Anglican divines like Jeremy Taylor and the Cambridge Platonists, and there were many Independents preaching toleration[2] – for all except popery and prelacy. By the end of the period Locke's *Letters Concerning Toleration* were commending the concessions granted to Nonconformists in the 1689 Act. The successors of the Cambridge Platonists held – like the Laudians before them – 'all the best sees'. The Dissenting academies were providing much of the best education in England; Marlborough had shown that Britain need no longer fear French soldiers bringing Roman missals on their bayonet points, and the sovereign was learning how to be an Anglican for English purposes and a Presbyterian for Scottish. Such was the progress towards toleration.

The more tolerant attitude also reflected a decline in religious enthusiasm; no longer struggling for the right to exist, many of the churches lost their earlier fire. Disappointed in their belief that Christ was about to come in Person to rule the world,

---

[1] Anti-Jewish prejudices, in many parts of Britain, and occasional damage to Catholic chapels in the remoter parts of Scotland, make it arguable that Britain is not yet fully tolerant.

[2] Christopher Hill has suggested that some Independents preached toleration, without believing in it, to make their doctrines more attractive to the Army (*The Century of Revolutions*, p. 166).

the Nonconformists did not share the urgent hopefulness of
Puritanism in the 1640s, when the God of battles was humbling
the proud and His saints were ruling the land.   No Church
could be satisfied with its position at the end of Anne's reign.
Despite the efforts of Bentley (soon to be helped by the philosopher bishops Butler and Berkeley) Deism remained attractive
to the intellectuals, seduced by a religion based on Reason.
The Non-Jurors were split over their liturgy, tainted with
Jacobitism, and gradually dying out despite their consecration
of three new bishops at the end of Anne's reign.   The Tory-
High Church alliance was soon to crack under the strain of
fifty years of Whig supremacy.   The great expansion of towns
like Birmingham, Liverpool and above all London loosened the
churches' hold on the people.   In the capital, even the new
church buildings voted by Parliament could not cope with the
increased population, and in most other cities no attempts
at all were made to provide enough churches to hold the
newcomers.   Although there were many Dissenting chapels
in the cities, religion scarcely touched most eighteenth-century
townsfolk.

Even the Nonconformists were in decline, until the Wesleys
sparked off a revival.   Like the Presbyterians, the Baptists
were weakened by the influence of the Unitarians, and only
the Independents (or Congregationalists) remained true to
their Calvinist origins.   The Quakers grew richer and quieter,
more like Dryden's 'timorous . . . Quaking hare'.   The 30,000
Catholics in England lived quietly, disturbed only occasionally
by Jacobite intrigues or the passions of the London mob.   The
Church of England itself was torn by the rivalry between the
bishops and the lower clergy, weakened by the virtual suspen-
sion of Convocation after the rows between the House, and was
still expected to be the partner of the dominant political party.
For another generation or two the parish clergy continued to
live in poverty and the Church had to be content with many
priests of poor education.   The eighteenth-century Church
may not have been as disreputable as some of its critics have
made out, but it is significant that when Keble and Newman
tried to revive the Church's spiritual life in the nineteenth
century, it was to the Non-Jurors that they turned for their
example.

## viii. The Colonies during the French Wars, 1689–1714

Not all Frenchmen were as blind as Louis XIV was to the wealth to be won overseas. As soon as Frontenac, the French governor of Canada, heard of the outbreak of War in 1689 he loosed his Red Indian allies in raids against the outlying English settlements in New England. Many a tiny homestead along the Mohawk and Hudson rivers was surprised in a dawn attack, and the settlers scalped by the Indians or dragged back to Montreal as prisoners of the French. These French and Indian raids forced the New England colonies to counter-attack against the centre of French power. Their small fleet under Phipps seized Port Royal, on the east coast of Acadia (Nova Scotia), but failed to weaken the French hold on the St. Lawrence further north. Meanwhile, a splendid French ruffian called d'Iberville was driving the English out of their settlements on the shores of Hudson's Bay, capturing the blockhouses and throwing the garrisons out into the winter snows. As the French also recaptured Port Royal, almost all the fighting was in Louis's favour. Nonetheless France did not bother to secure any concessions at Ryswick; as in Europe, Louis lightly threw away the conquests of his soldiers.

The New England alliance broke up soon afterwards, despite the pleas of William Penn that the colonies should send delegates to an annual congress and have a common currency and code of laws. With the colonists disunited and the English Government neglectful of their interests, New England was unprepared for the Indian attacks when they began again in 1703. With the exception of the 'Five Nations' of the Iroquois, most of the eastern tribes were on the side of the French, serving them in return for alcohol, firearms and the exhortation of Jesuit missionaries. In 1704 a force of French and Indians captured the village of Deerfield, less than a hundred miles from Boston; many of the defenders were scalped or boiled alive to amuse the Indians, the survivors being marched to Canada to receive spiritual instruction from the Jesuits. The Deerfield atrocities coloured many of the subsequent campaigns.

It was not until 1709 that the British government agreed to send help to the New England colonists – and even then the five regiments promised never arrived. Two years later, mainly for political reasons, St. John sent out a good force of seven veteran regiments, to join with a colonial expedition in an attack on Quebec.  St. John's main motives were to vindicate the familiar Tory cry for a naval campaign, to challenge Marlborough's reputation with a spectacular victory elsewhere, and to please Mrs. Masham, whose brother Jack Hill was placed in command of the troops.  Nevertheless, St. John had a genuine belief in Britain's destiny overseas, and saw the strategic importance of the St. Lawrence as clearly as Pitt did fifty years later.  But not even under Buckingham had an expedition been so mismanaged.  In command of the fleet was Admiral Walker, an incompetent fool who was a worse bungler than even Hill.  They collected a large force of colonists and persuaded the Iroquois to join them, but Walker did not bother to find pilots to take his fleet up the St. Lawrence. Eight of his ships ran on to the rocks, with a loss of 700 men, and Walker immediately lost heart and returned home.  Although the colonists captured Port Royal and Acadia in 1710 (after unsuccessful attempts in 1704 and 1707), the balance of the fighting again probably favoured France, for the French also made three successful raids on Newfoundland.  It was therefore not as a result of the fighting in the New World that Britain gained such substantial concessions from Louis at Utrecht.  Fifty years later Pitt managed to 'win Canada on the banks of the Elbe'; equally it was Marlborough who secured the other colonies by his victories on the Meuse and Scheldt.

In the peace, Louis surrendered Newfoundland and Acadia to Britain (although the French kept Cape Breton Island and the right to dry fishing-nets on the Newfoundland coast). From Carolina in the south to Nova Scotia in the north the English colonies formed an unbroken line; then, beyond the French settlements around the St. Lawrence, there was the island of Newfoundland, with the richest fisheries in the world. Valued by many merchants even more highly, Britain gained the *Asiento*, the right to send one ship a year to trade with Spanish America and to export 5000 slaves a year from Africa to the Spanish territories.  The South Sea Company grossly over-estimated the profits which the *Asiento* would bring, but even so St. John had managed to get for Britain a fitting reward for sixty years of mercantilist wars.

The Treaty of Utrecht also brought Britain the French part

of the island of St. Kitt's, in the West Indies.   In the Caribbean
the Anglo-French wars were little more than incidents in the
usual life of piracy, smuggling and robbery.   The disturbance
to trade, particularly when the French and Spanish colonies
could not get their produce home, made these illegal activities
even more important than usual.   The Whigs in England were
very embarrassed when, having sent out Captain Kidd in the
*Adventure Galley* to attack the pirates, the gallant captain found
it more profitable to join them than to fight them!   In the first
war the English tried to capture Martinique, but failed, and
the French were likewise unsuccessful in attacking Jamaica.
In the second war the cowardice of some of his captains prevented Admiral Benbow crushing the small French fleet, but in
1708 Admiral Wager managed to sink many of the Spanish
treasure ships as their convoy returned to Europe.   Apart
from these naval skirmishes there was surprisingly little fighting
in the West Indies.   The war did not spread to the Far East,
and the East India Company continued to fear the French less
than its English and Dutch rivals.

The last forty years of the Stuart period saw many developments in the economic relationship between Britain and her
colonies.   The investors who had financed the foundation of
the colonies seldom visited them, and the joint-stock companies
naturally relied more and more upon their factors resident at
Boston, or New York, or Charlestown.   The planters in turn
began to use agents in London to negotiate for them.   The
initiative gradually passed to the planters, and it was not long
before many of the London and Bristol merchants engaged in
colonial trade were reduced to shipping contractors.   Britain
was a market for colonial produce, not the colonies for British
manufactures.   Few vessels had their holds full when they
sailed for America; but the majority came back heavily laden.
As a country, Britain profited from the colonies mainly because
her merchants and her ships distributed their produce to the
rest of Europe.   In contrast, the value of colonial markets for
British goods was bound to be limited, for even by 1714 the total
white population of all the colonies was only 8 or 9 per cent. of
that at home.   Most of the colonies had come to specialize in
one or two exports, usually either sugar or tobacco.   In 1714
neither trade was as prosperous as it had been thirty or forty
years before, for profit margins narrowed even though the

volume of trade increased.    The high price of Negro slaves and
the exhaustion of the soil made sugar more expensive to grow.
Tobacco plants so poisoned the soil that the estates had to move
to new land every twenty years or so.    Nonetheless, there were
huge fortunes to be made, especially by sugar planters: the
Beckfords and Codringtons of Jamaica were able to live in great
luxury, usually in England, while their slaves toiled and died
like animals.

Some of these changes sowed the seeds of future revolution.
The British navy was now strong enough to enforce the
Navigation Acts, still a burden even though after 1707 Scottish
merchants were able to compete with the English in offering
favourable shipping rates.    The time was not far distant when
the tactless application of the Acts, and duties which threatened
an economy based narrowly on a single product, would drive
the colonies to unite more effectively against Britain than they
ever did against Louis XIV.

The history of British expansion in the Far East was very
different from that in the New World.    The distances and the
delays were far greater, and the merchants far fewer.    By the
time of Charles II's death, the East India Company's factories
seemed no more than a few tiny spiders spaced around the
edges of a vast ceiling.    A few men, like Richard Keigwin in
the 1680s, tried to make the Company realize that the 'spiders'
were very insecure, but they won more sympathy from
Charles and James than from the Company's directors.    Then
a new charter from James II encouraged a more aggressive
policy, and in 1687 the directors told the governor of Surat to
prepare 'the foundation of a large well-grounded sure English
dominion in India for all time to come'.

The first attempt at expansion was disastrous.    A campaign
against Chittagong aroused the fury of the Mogul emperor
Aurungzebe, who captured the factories at Surat on the west
coast, Vizagapatam and Masulipatam on the east, and Patna
and Casimbazar in Bengal.    It was only by stopping Moslem
pilgrims crossing the seas to Mecca that the Company could
force Aurungzebe to make peace, and it had to pay him £17,000
in 1690 to have its trading rights restored.    During the
campaign, however, a site had been seized near the mouth of
the Hugli River by Job Charnock, the Company's energetic
agent in Bengal.    Despite an appalling toll from fever, the

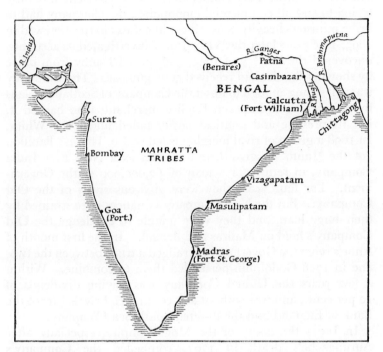

The East India Company's Factories

Company built Fort William there in 1697, acquired authority over the neighbouring land, and gradually built up the great city of Calcutta around it.

Under Charles II and James II, the Company had become increasingly loyal to the Court. After the Revolution it suffered for these Tory connexions. As Parliament was busy trying to end all commercial monopolies, the Company had to bribe ministers heavily before it could get its charter renewed in 1693. Two years later the Whig 'Junto' investigated its accounts, uncovered the bribery of 1693, and ousted Danby from office by showing that he had received 5000 guineas. The Company was still strong enough to upset the Company of Scotland's plans by threatening to impeach English merchants who backed it, but its prestige and political power faded under the Whigs. In 1698 a group of rival merchants led by Sir Thomas Papillon got the 'Junto' to give them a charter as a New East India Company, in return for a loan of £2,000,000 to the Government. For four years they were vigorous rivals of the Old Company. But the New Company's finances were strained by their huge loan, and they were unable to challenge the Old Company's hold on Madras and Bengal. In the first month of Anne's reign the Government arranged a truce between the two, and in 1708 Godolphin persuaded them to combine. Within a few years the United Company was paying dividends of 10 per cent., and was without any commercial rivals except the Bank of England and the ill-fated South Sea Company.

In India the decay of the Mogul empire, especially after Aurungzebe's death in 1707, compelled the Company's governors to protect themselves more effectively. Thomas Pitt, a 'roughling immoral man', had turned from being a near-piratical interloper into a ferocious President of Madras; like the governors of Bombay and Calcutta he found that he had to defend the neighbouring natives as well as the Company's own traders. Only by expanding inland could the traders secure themselves.

The spiders on the ceiling were beginning to spin their webs. For half a century Mogul power continued to crumble. Then the grandson of Governor Pitt, and a young genius called Clive, somehow managed to make those spiders' webs hold up the whole ceiling.

## *ix. Literature and the Arts, 1685–1714*

At the end of the seventeenth century most English writers were suffering from a prolonged Restoration hangover, still fawning upon royal absolutism and still preoccupied with the conventions of elegant sex.   Dryden showed the former weakness when he hailed the birth of Prince James Edward in 1688 with *Britannia Rediviva,* an unfortunate and rather bad poem

> See on his future Subjects how He smiles
> Nor meanly flatters, nor with craft beguiles;
> But with an open face, as on his Throne,
> Assures our Birthrights, and assumes his own.
>     Born in broad Day-light, that th'ungrateful Rout
> May find no room for a remaining doubt. . . .

So much for the warming-pan story!   In the following years he wrote several more dramas, including words for an opera about King Arthur, but eventually he turned aside from plays and satirical poetry.   He spent the last years before his death in 1700 in translating Homer, Virgil and Ovid into English verse, and in modernizing some of the stories in the Canterbury Tales – the Knight's, the Nun's Priest's, and the Wife of Bath's.

His ablest successor as a playwright was young William Congreve, who won fame with *The Old Bachelor, The Double Dealer* and *Love for Love* before he was twenty-five.   His last play, *The Way of the World* (1700), was among the finest achievements of Restoration comedy, with brilliantly witty conversation between the lovers Mirabel and Millamount.   It was deeper and more contemplative than the plays of the early Restoration period, and was not a success at the time.   Dryden was greatly impressed by *The Double Dealer* (1694), and congratulated Congreve as a man who combined the power of Shakespeare and Jonson with the grace of the Restoration wits:

> But what we gained in skill we lost in strength. . . .
>
>                    *   *   *
>
> Till you, the best Vitruvius, came at length;
> Our beauties equal, but excel our strength.

Congreve's contemporary John Vanbrugh was a versatile man more celebrated as an architect than as a dramatist.   His plays – *The Relapse* (1696) and *The Provok'd Wife* (1697) – lacked the imagination, style and wit of Congreve, but were nevertheless popular enough to provoke the wrath of the moralists. In 1698 Jeremy Collier, a Non-Juror clergyman, published a *Short View of the Immorality and Profaneness of the English Stage*, directing his attacks largely at Congreve and Vanbrugh. Later the Society for the Reformation of Manners condemned Vanbrugh as 'a man who has debauched the stage beyond the looseness of all former times'. This revival of a quasi-puritanical challenge had some effect, particularly when Queen Anne tried to raise the standard of morality at Court. After 1700 Congreve wrote no play and Vanbrugh finished only one.

A young Irishman, George Farquhar, finally broke from the characteristics of Restoration drama. Farquhar's plays were gay and good-humoured, and free from the artificiality of their predecessors. *The Constant Couple* (1700), *The Recruiting Officer* (1706) and *The Beaux' Stratagem* (1707) provided splendid models of witty social comedy, models imitated later in the century by two other Irish writers – Goldsmith and Sheridan.

It was Goldsmith who called Queen Anne's reign the 'Augustan Age' of English literature, comparing it with the time when Virgil, Ovid and Horace were working in the peaceful prosperity of the Roman Empire under Augustus. This is a curious comparison, for Anne's reign was above all an age of desperate wars abroad and violent party feuds at home, an age when many writers were hacks hired by parties or individual statesmen to act as publicity agents for their factions. As a Roman Catholic, Alexander Pope kept apart from the main controversies, though even he complimented the Tories on the Treaty of Utrecht in *Windsor Forest*:

> Hail, sacred peace! hail, long-expected days,
> That Thames's glory to the stars shall raise!

> \* \* \*

> No more my sons shall dye with British blood
> Red Iber's sands, or Ister's foaming flood. . . .

This poem won Pope admission to the Scriblerus Club of Tory writers, but of his major works only the *Rape of the Lock* and the

*Essay on Criticism* were published in Anne's reign.   The former poem defied Restoration conventions, for fair Belinda lost her hair, not her virtue.   The latter was written in 1711, when Pope was only twenty-one.   Its tripping couplets advise poets to 'follow nature' and write 'works without show, and without pomp', following the examples of classical authors.   Pope's verses were polished and easy, like the manners of the Court, and their sentiments were usually just as trivial.

The form of literary activity most characteristic of Anne's reign was political pamphleteering.   Something has been said previously on Defoe's misdirected satire on Anglican intolerance,[1] and on Swift's attack on the Whigs' foreign policy.[2] Both sold themselves to Harley and the Tories, Defoe for money and Swift in the hope of a bishopric.   Both edited periodicals.   Defoe founded and edited the *Review* (1704-13) and the *Mercator* (1713-14) to represent 'the commercial interest', while Swift for nine months ran St. John's *Examiner*, a paper largely devoted to attacking Whig periodicals.   Both left their major literary achievements until George I's reign.   Defoe's *Robinson Crusoe* (1719), *Moll Flanders* (1722) and *Journal of the Plague Year* (1722) were among the most important early novel , and despite its allegorical nature Swift's *Gulliver's Travels* (1726) deserves to be numbered among them.

The most important Whig pamphleteers were the two Charterhouse friends, Richard Steele and Joseph Addison. After a military career had led him to the household of Prince George of Denmark, Steel started the *Tatler* in 1709, and later helped to edit and write the *Spectator* (1711-12), the *Guardian* and the *Englishman*.   In 1713 he was one of the Whigs elected to Parliament, but the Tory majority expelled him from the Commons for publishing a pamphlet supporting the Hanoverian succession.   Like Steele, Addison was a leading member of the Whig Kit-Kat Club, and co-operated with him in producing the above-mentioned periodicals.   This was an exacting task, for the *Tatler* came out three times a week and the *Spectator* six times.   Together they raised the tone of political journalism, for their articles were often of high literary merit and were much less violent and vitriolic than those of the Tory hacks.   In the *Spectator* Addison devised the character of Sir Roger de Coverley – a narrow-minded, sincere, lovable old Tory squire, a man to

---

[1] See above, p. 381.       [2] See above, p. 361 and pp. 379-80.

attract sympathy rather than arouse indignation.   A few years later, though, Addison described in the *Freeholder* a less pleasant sort of Tory, a Jacobite who thought that 'The Church of England will always be in danger, till it has a Popish King for its Defender', that there had been no good weather since Charles II died, and that 'there had not been one good law passed since King William's accession to the Throne, except the act for preserving the Game'.   But this was still basically a humorous portrait, much less savage than the writings of some of the Tories.   Here is Swift:

> I write this paper for the sake of the Dissenters, whom I take to be the most spreading branch of the Whig party, that professeth Christianity. . . .   By the Dissenters . . . I mean the Presbyterians, as they include the sects of the Anabaptists Independents and others, which have been melted into them since the Restoration.   This sect, in order to make itself national, having gone so far as to raise a Rebellion, murder their King, destroy monarchy and the Church, was afterwards broken into pieces by its own divisions. . . .[1]

Such words could only infuriate, and never convert or persuade.

An interest in history was characteristic of the whole Stuart period, from the time when Coke and the other lawyers started to rummage for precedents to hurl at James I.   Gilbert Burnet's *History of the Reformation* won praise from the Exclusion Parliaments, and for thirty-five years afterwards its author remained in the centre of political affairs.   Burnet was a Scottish Episcopalian, and a famous preacher outspoken enough to rebuke Charles II for his profligate life.   He left England to become chaplain to Princess Mary in Holland, sailed with William's fleet in 1688, and served with distinction as Bishop of Salisbury from 1689 until his death in 1715.   As a Whig, his sermons and political writing annoyed the Tories, and the intemperate Dr. Sacheverell singled him out for a special attack in his celebrated sermon.   His most important work, published posthumously, was the *History of My Own Times*, mainly on the period 1660–1702.   For most of that time Burnet had been in a position for him to be able to write with as much authority as Clarendon[2] on the Great Rebellion.   The

[1] In Trevelyan, *Documents for Queen Anne's Reign*, pp. 63–4.
[2] It was not until Anne's reign that Clarendon's *History* was published.

tone of Burnet's *History* was clearly Whig, and Swift tried to dismiss it as based on 'coffee-house scandals'.

The age was also interested in manuscripts and documents, essential for scientific and unbiased history. Harley was himself a great collector of manuscripts, and built up a library of them which was to become the Harleian Collection in the British Museum. William III engaged Thomas Rymer as an official historiographer, and encouraged the researches which led to the heavy volumes of *Foedera*. These were published between 1704 and 1735, and contain a most important collection of official documents from early mediaeval times onwards. Another work still useful to the historian is Thomas Madox's *History of the Exchequer*, published in 1711.

The universities had not yet sunk into the Hanoverian torpor awaiting them, and scholars were particularly active in linguistic studies. For over forty years the Master of Trinity College, Cambridge, was Richard Bentley, the enemy of the Deists and one of the greatest classical scholars of the century. In textual criticism he had no equal – as his *Dissertation on the Epistles of Phalaris* showed in 1699. George Hickes organized a vast amount of research on the Teutonic languages while he lived around Oxford, in seclusion and often in hiding as a leading Non-Juror. He published an Anglo-Saxon grammar in 1689, and the massive *Treasury of the Northern Languages* in 1703–5, in addition to other works appropriate for one who was ordained by the Non-Jurors as a bishop and accepted by them eventually as their leader. The major works of Laud's protégé Edward Pococke appeared much earlier, but the old man remained at Oxford until he died there at the age of eighty-seven, having made the university a centre of Hebrew and Arabic scholarship.

\*          \*          \*

Huguenot fugitives and Dutch soldiers carried to England a wave of foreign influence as strong as that which the Cavaliers brought back in 1660. This was especially noticable in architecture. In spite of the expensive wars, the subjects of William and Anne were great builders. In the towns the prosperous bourgeois looked for a house more comfortable and spacious than the top-heavy, narrow little houses crammed together on either side of streets serving also as open sewers. Dutch craftsmen, the high price of timber, and the fire hazard in wooden houses, helped to make brick buildings more popular.    Mompesson House in Salisbury is a good example of the comfortable new houses which were larger, often with sash windows (a Dutch invention), built alongside wider streets, and usually with better sanitation.    The exteriors often carried decorative ironwork, or pipes and cisterns of lead; in working both iron and lead Dutch and French craftsmen were the most expert.    Some houses, as at Topsham in Devon, even imitated the step-gabled roofs popular in Holland.    By the end of Anne's reign, many of the scenes painted by de Hooch and Vermeer might have been found in England as well as in Holland.

Outside the towns many squires built houses in the styles now known as 'William and Mary' and 'Queen Anne', often with high chimneys standing proudly above the prominent roofs in the way made fashionable by Pratt at Coleshill.    The façades of these houses kept the balance and good proportions which the Palladian style had brought to English architecture, and were generally free from the fussy ornamentation popular on the continent.    However, Dutch designs gradually came to hide the chimneys and even the roof, as at Chicheley House in Buckinghamshire.

The best-known country-houses built around this time reflected French rather than Dutch influence.    The massiveness of Louis XIV's buildings fascinated Englishmen, and they commissioned architects to try to rival the glories of Versailles. Sir John Vanbrugh, in particular, was obsessed by size and weight, and had a chance to build on an enormous scale when Queen Anne commissioned him to put up Blenheim Palace at her expense as a reward for Marlborough.    His design for Castle Howard in Yorkshire was almost equally massive. Blenheim perhaps was rather coarse and clumsy in details, effective chiefly because it filled so much of the skyline.    Only Vanbrugh's smaller works, such as his own Haymarket Theatre and some of the buildings at Stowe in Buckinghamshire, showed delicacy and refinement.    Another architect in the grand manner was Nicholas Hawksmoor, who collaborated with Vanbrugh in designing the Clarendon Building in Oxford, and with Wren in rebuilding many of the City churches.    Although some of Hawksmoor's finest works, such as Easton Neston in Northamptonshire, were built in Anne's reign, most of his greater achievements were a generation later, when he was a contemporary and rival of Gibbs, Kent and Adam in the supreme period of British architecture.

The English painters of the reigns of William and Anne also achieved less than their successors. In both reigns the Court portrait painters were dominated by the German Godfrey Kneller. Like Van Dyck and Lely, Kneller was rewarded with a knighthood. The Englishman James Thornhill was equally fortunate, for he specialized in historical paintings of battles and great events, and the victories of Anne's reign excited such a demand for them that Thornhill was knighted and died a rich man. But it was Kneller who became president of the first English academy of painting, in 1711, which helped to found a national tradition and style.

Foreign influences continued in the other decorative arts. Traders brought back cabinets, screens and wall-papers from the Far East, and lacquering or 'Japanning' often formed part of a young lady's education. As the Dutch had a more extensive trade with China and Japan than the English merchants had, they helped to distribute oriental goods such as the Chinese porcelain which Princess Mary brought to England in 1688. Even after her arrival in England, Mary continued to commission glazed earthenware from the factory of Kocks at Delft, and it was not long before the Delft potters were imitating oriental designs. Evelyn admired the Queen's collection, and in 1700 noticed that his friend Pepys's home at Clapham was a 'wonderfully well-furnished house, especially with Indian and Chinese curiosities'. In the middle of the century the Dutch had invented the mechanism of the 'grandfather' clock; after the Revolution the English clock-makers followed Dutch designs also in the clock cases. Again under foreign influence, furniture designs became as elegant as their purposes would allow – for chairs had to have strong legs and wide seats to hold the plump figures of those who ate over-well – and Anne's reign saw chair backs becoming higher and the graceful curve of the cabriole chair leg coming into fashion. With thousands of officers campaigning on the continent, and hundreds of young nobles and squires making the 'Grand Tour' with their tutors, British culture gradually became more cosmopolitan. Moreover, as Britain moved towards political and military preeminence in Europe, so in turn other countries began to copy and admire the achievements of British culture.

It was therefore particularly unfortunate that his tragically-early death prevented Henry Purcell from establishing a reputation which might have challenged that of the great eighteenth-century Germans. Purcell's early musical education was as a chorister in the Chapel Royal under Cooke and Humphrey, and it was there, inevitably, that he came under the influence of Lully, the composer whose music was sweeping the French Court. In 1682, when he was only twenty-three, Purcell became organist of the Chapel Royal, where music was considered as little more than a discreet entertainment for the fashionable men and women of the Court. There, it was no disadvantage to him that he was a Roman Catholic. In the following years he composed a large number of anthems (usually taken from psalms), as well as music for royal occasions. His work was characterized by a skilful 'ground bass' and above all by music which expressed precisely the emotions and rhythms of the words he was setting.

Purcell co-operated with many of the playwrights, providing incidental music and setting songs for Dryden's *King Arthur* and *The Faery Queen* (which was based on *A Midsummer Night's Dream*), and for Congreve's *Double Dealer*. His finest work was the opera *Dido and Aeneas*, written in 1689 to be performed by a girls' school. It stands by itself in isolated grandeur as the only great English opera for two centuries or more. Much of his music had the popular touch. When William III's Protestant troops bawled 'Lilliburlero' as they chased James II out of Ireland, they were singing words by an atheist peer, to a tune by the Catholic organist of the Chapel Royal!

After his death in 1695 the only distinguished English musician left was John Blow, who had once been Purcell's tutor in composition. Blow died in 1708, and English music – like the English Crown – soon passed into German hands. Even before Anne's death Handel had established himself in London. Georgian England had nothing to set against the German domination except the light-weight works of Boyce and Arne, and the hymns of the Wesleys.

## x. British Society, 1685–1714

The pulse and throb of social changes provided a noisy background to the other disputes of Anne's reign. Since the

Civil Wars, the smaller landowners, the petty squires and yeomen, had been squeezed by fines, assessments and Land Taxes so much that many of them had had to sell out to richer men. The new landlord usually had no sense of responsibility to tenant or peasant, and did not scruple to rack-rent or to enclose the common-land of his manors. Many of the wealthiest landowners were former merchants, rich from the India trade or from Jamaican sugar. Such men were envied sourly by those they forced off the land. Another change was the increased respect paid to military men after 1689, especially during the winter when the ladies lionized officers home on leave for the season. An army career was something few yeomen's sons could afford, for commissions and promotion were usually bought, and a young officer's progress depended largely on how extravagant he could be. It was for these reasons that John Packington of Worcestershire demanded in 1710 that the war be ended 'to prevent moneyed and military men becoming lords of us who have lands'. Despite such protests, successful merchants went on buying land, not so much as a financial investment, but to get the social prestige and political power associated with it. When the Tories in 1711 made it compulsory for M.P.s to own large estates, they did not drive the merchants out of politics; instead, they drove them into the countryside.

Even if the gentry were in trouble, a great gulf still separated them from the labourers. The peasant was still largely *adscriptus glebae*, in the sense that if found wandering he had to be sent back to his parish of origin. This tie held most Englishmen firmly to their birth-places, for the great majority lived by and on the land. Unlike those in France and Germany, most peasant families in England were able to eat meat regularly, and in times of distress could get help from the parish. In the towns the poor were usually less fortunate, and a lot of them had to live by their wits. In London, for example, there was a large network of thieves, receivers and confidence tricksters, controlled by Jonathan Wild, king of the City's underworld – and a magistrate!

London dominated, but did not monopolize, the social life of Britain. Edinburgh and Dublin had their own societies, and by Anne's death the prosperity of towns like Bristol, Liverpool and Portsmouth was helping to make them more attractive to ladies exiled to the provinces.    Even in Roman days, Bath had been famous for its waters.    In 1678 Anthony à Wood went there from Oxford for a month's cure, at a cost of £8, 'but received no benefit'.    In 1705, however, Beau Nash opened the Assembly Rooms and quickly made them famous – even though he had to drill etiquette and good manners into the clodhopping squires when they first came.    Elsewhere, the purgative waters of Tunbridge Wells, Harrogate and Buxton also provided expensive laxatives for the idle and fashionable.

The popular coffee-houses were found in most towns, but nowhere were they as important as in London.    They served the Englishman as his club, and sometimes as his office too – a large part of the country's business was negotiated in popular places like Lloyd's Coffee House in Lombard Street.    The political parties had their own favourites – the Whigs went to the St. James, the Tories to the Cocoa Tree Chocolate House. They were centres of gossip and news, sometimes offering their patrons the most recent copies of foreign journals.    Many businessmen got into set routines, visiting the same coffee-houses at the same times each day, so that their friends would know where to find them.    Although White's was patronized almost entirely by fashionable gamblers, many coffee-houses saw nobles and gentlemen, merchants and tradesmen, often with their wives, sitting on the same benches while they sipped coffee or 'tay' or 'the best chocolate at twelve pence the quart'. They were a levelling influence on society.    As they did not serve alcoholic drinks, they were also a sobering influence.

The different social classes might also meet at church (though segregated into pews for which families paid varying rents), and the males at least might also meet in the course of education. The sons of the very wealthy usually had their Homer and Virgil whipped into them at Eton or Winchester or Westminster.    Most squires, though, were content to send their sons to the village schools.    This was better for them socially than educationally, for the quality of most grammar schools and village schools had declined since the days when Cromwell was trembling before the formidable Dr. Beard and the village school at Malmesbury was teaching Hobbes his Latin and Greek.

It was, however, becoming quite common for the well-to-do to engage tutors for their sons.    Many Anglican parsons taught in this way under the Commonwealth.    So did many

Nonconformist ministers after the Clarendon Code drove them from their pulpits. Despite the wars, many young gentlemen completed their education by going on the 'Grand Tour', spending a year or two visiting the sights of Florence and Rome and other European cities. During the reigns of William and Anne, the best basic education was probably that provided by the Dissenting academies, particularly in mathematical and scientific studies. Founded in secret, they came into the open at the Revolution. They were so effective as nurseries for Nonconformists that St. John tried to outlaw them in 1714. He knew very well how successful they were; like Harley, he had been educated at one!

The Dissenting academies survived. Their work was supplemented by a large number of charity schools founded by the Society for Promoting Christian Knowledge. These charity schools often taught girls as well as boys. They were careful not to train their pupils above their expected positions in life, and often arranged for them to be put into suitable apprenticeships. Although the schools spread rapidly – there were over a thousand by Anne's death – most girls received no formal education. Reading, embroidery and singing could usually be learnt at home. Only a small number of girls went away to boarding schools, or walked with their brothers to the village schools.

Nonconformists who wanted higher education had to go to Scotland or Holland to get it. Oxford and Cambridge were exclusively for Anglicans, and the Inns of Court had virtually stopped all teaching. At Oxford and Cambridge the wealthy student, entered as a 'gentleman commoner', dined with the dons; the poor student, working his way through college as a sizar or servitor, would have to wait on him at table. For the gentleman commoner, the university provided a chance to meet his social equals, to hunt and gamble with them, and to try to drink them under the table with either port or claret (depending on whether they were Whig or Tory). To the scholar or sizar it offered a narrow training in Latin and Greek literature, and a degree entitling him to apply for ordination. The wealthy man might despise the other, but he would remember his university acquaintances when it came to appointing a tutor for his son, finding a parson for a church of which he was patron, or possibly recommending a clergyman for ecclesiastical promotion.

No matter how able or industrious he was, an ambitious man had to win the patronage of some important or wealthy man. This was usually achieved largely by an extravagant display of hypocritical flattery.    Writers and composers were poorly rewarded for their talents.    Farquhar died in poverty while his plays were the rage in London.    *Gulliver's Travels* was the only one of Swift's many works to bring him any money at all – £200.    In Anne's reign the politicians expected to reward their followers at the Crown's expense, by placing them in profitable Treasury or customs sinecures (or, as Swift hoped, with promotion in the Church).    Godolphin and Harley both lost many supporters because they refused to turn experienced officials out of office to make room for the hangers-on of Whig or Tory M.P.s.    Before the eighteenth century was much advanced, it became difficult to publish a book or stage a play without the help of some patron or sponsor.    Many M.P.s were themselves the dependents of members of the House of Lords, or of the Crown itself.    Before long, 231 out of Walpole's 241 supporters in the Commons were sharing between them about £200,000 of Crown pensions every year.

A more creditable aspect of early eighteenth-century Britain was its attitude towards charity, both voluntary and enforced.    During Anne's reign the amount contributed by parish rates to help the poor rose above a million pounds a year.    Greenwich Hospital for crippled sailors was built by public subscription, partly in commemoration of Queen Mary. John Evelyn, who gave £10 a year, was among the thousands contributing to the S.P.G. and S.P.C.K.    Both run energetically by Dr. Thomas Bray until his death in 1730, they sent large numbers of Bibles and devotional works to Marlborough's troops on the Continent and to the colonists in the New World.

The pastimes of most Englishmen were still coarse and brutal, appealing most to gamblers and to those who enjoyed watching men and animals in pain.    The most popular national sport was cock-fighting.    There was less deer-hunting as enclosures were eating away at the common land; the squires began fox-hunting instead.    Many a moaning Tory squire spent far more on his foxhounds than on his Land Tax.    Even the Jacobite squire in Addison's *Freeholder* admitted that William III's Game Laws (for preserving pheasants) were an advantage! Many courtiers had come to share Charles II's enthusiasm for horse-racing, and Godolphin and others imported Arab and Barbary stallions to improve the breed. Men and women gambled heavily on both horse-racing and cock-fighting: in 1699 the Duke of Devonshire lost £1900 on a single horse-race at Newmarket. The townsfolk had their entertainment provided at the Crown's expense, for hangings were public and frequent, and carried out in an atmosphere of 'Cup-Final' excitement. The grotesque, leering faces of the mobs Hogarth sketched mocked hundreds of people along the grisly road to Tyburn.

But at least in England no one was executed for his religious beliefs – or lack of them. As late as 1697 a Scottish youth was hanged for questioning the authority of the Bible. The Scots burned a witch in Perthshire as late as 1727. In England after 1688 the law courts were fair (so far as harsh laws allowed them to be) and independent of the Crown and of the mob; the fate of the *Worcester*'s crew showed that in Scotland justice could still be swayed by the mob and by political factors. 'North Britain', as the Treaty of Union called it, was still more violent and turbulent than its southern partner. The Highlands remained untamed until the S.P.C.K.'s missionaries took Bibles and education into the glens, and until the Whig clans were policing the roads General Wade was soon to build across the hills and moors. At the time of Union, the most prosperous part of Scotland – along the coasts of the Forth estuary – was poorer than the more backward parts of England. Except around the capital, there were almost no parks and almost no country houses designed for comfort rather than defence. Even Edinburgh was a poor apology for a capital city, with crowded streets stinking of human excrement thrown out of the dwellings. Sundays were particularly unpleasant, for the city guard, putting cleanlinesss a poor second to godliness, piously did not clean the streets on the Sabbath.

The main reason for Scotland's backwardness was the poverty of her agriculture. Even areas which should have been fertile normally grew no grain except oats for porridge and barley for brewing. In the Highlands the custom of run-rig[1] was almost universal, and handicapped farming so much that the peasant was always close to starvation. His scrawny black cattle never

---

[1] In the run-rig system, the peasants farmed together, each year the land was re-distributed among them by lot, and the peasant harvested and kept the grain on the 'ridge' falling to him.

fetched more than a pound or two in the great annual market at
Crieff. There was almost no way in which the peasant could
escape from the control of his laird. Even if they and their
clans held huge stretches of land, not many Scottish nobles
could boast of money incomes greater than those of middling
English squires.

The 1696 Navigation Act and the collapse of the Darien
scheme impoverished Scotland so much that the wiser heads
realized her only hope was to get a share of the English commercial empire. Perhaps because of the thrift they had learnt
in adversity, the Scottish merchants were soon very successful.
Within two generations they built up an extensive trade with
the New World, particularly in sugar and tobacco, and by
developing their earlier linen and cattle exports to England the
Scots steadily raised their country out of economic stagnation.
Edinburgh and Glasgow (the centre for the American trade)
grew in size and wealth – and in cleanliness. The Presbyterian Kirk became less severe and bigoted, and it worked
nobly to send charity-school education into the Highlands. In
David Hume and Adam Smith the Scottish universities produced two of the best minds of the eighteenth century, and
hundreds of English Nonconformists crossed the Border to be
educated at them. Such were the results for Scotland of the
Union, the greatest political achievement of Anne's reign.

The social structure of Ireland was even more complicated
than that of Highland and Lowland Scotland, for in Ireland
there were three distinct groups – almost distinct castes, in fact.
Virtually all power was in the hands of the English settlers.
Almost all of them were 'new' colonists who had arrived during
and after the Elizabethan plantations. Almost all of them were
members of the Anglican Church of Ireland, to which many of
the 'old' English also conformed to save their estates. For
these a comfortable, civilized and even cultured life was soon
to be possible; it was Dublin which heard the first performance
of Handel's *Messiah*. Trinity College, Dublin – though less
eminent than it became in later years – reared Jonathan Swift
and Bishop Berkeley, probably the greatest British philosopher
of the eighteenth century. Like the government itself, Trinity
College was the exclusive monopoly of the English element in
Ireland. For the vast majority of Ireland's inhabitants there
were no opportunities for education, for entry to the professions,

or for careers in government service.  The Presbyterians in the north, mainly of Scottish descent, had no Toleration Act to soften the harshness of Anglican prejudice; and although the government did not normally interfere with Catholic priests it tried to keep their bishops out of the country.  Both Non-conformists and Catholics had to pay tithes to the Anglican Church, as well as maintaining their own clergy – a heavy burden for a desperately poor people.  Even overseas trade, which proved so beneficial to the Scots, was barred to the Irish by jealous Parliaments in London; the Irish were not allowed even to send their cattle for sale in England.  Ireland's only wealth was in her land, at least nine-tenths of which was in the hands of the Anglo-Irish.

In spite of their justified grievances the Irish were peaceful for most of the eighteenth century, even though the Jacobite risings in Scotland might have tempted some of the hotheads to join in revolt.  Many of the Irish were *too* poor, *too* dispirited to think of rebellion.  By Anne's reign, the most active and vigorous of the Irish were already going abroad, to join the 'Wild Geese' fighting for France and the Jacobite cause under Patrick Sarsfield and the Duke of Berwick.  Probably over half a million Irishmen left their homeland to serve as mercenaries in the armies of France and Spain and Naples – and even Austria and Russia – in the years between the Treaty of Limerick and the end of the Austrian Succession war in 1748.  Under foreign flags, at least, the Irish could still fight against the oppressors of their country.

## xi. The Constitutional Legacy

The economic and cultural achievements of the Stuart period cannot disguise the fact that it was above all an age of great political instability.  In 1642, in 1649, in 1653, in 1660 and in 1688 the course of English history was changed by violent acts against the existing constitution.  Similar revolutions might also have happened in 1681 and 1714, if the Whigs had managed to exclude James from the throne and the Jacobites to restore his son to it.  In contrast, the constitutional settlement of the years immediately after George I's accession was a firm and lasting one, and it remained unaltered in essentials for over a century.  The changes made by Stanhope's ministry were not great – mainly the Septennial Act of 1716 prolonging the maximum lifetime of a parliament from three to seven years, and the repeal in 1718 of the Occasional Conformity and Schism Acts.

It could therefore be argued that the political structure of Anne's reign was very close to that which proved satisfactory under her successors. But this was not so. In 1714 much depended on the monarch, and upon the monarch's interest in political and religious affairs. The last of the Stuarts was as careful as the last of the Tudors to guard the remaining powers of monarchy, particularly in matters of religion. On the other hand, George I and George II bothered little about these things. They were both the heirs of William III rather than of Anne: preoccupied with continental affairs, indifferent to the Church of England, they were uninterested in domestic squabbles provided the government gave them the money they wanted. Neither George I nor George II spoke much English, and both were content to rely upon politicians like Walpole and Newcastle to run Britain for them. This contrasted sharply with the attitude of Anne. Her reign checked and even reversed the drift of Parliament away from the Crown's control. Although the Act of Settlement did not handicap her – it was not to come into force at all if she left a direct heir – nonetheless her reign saw it amended substantially. The Regency Acts of 1706 and 1707 repealed those parts of the Act of Settlement designed to prevent the growth of the Cabinet, and also largely repealed the 'Place' clause. Consequently in the first Hanoverian House of Commons almost exactly half the M.P.s were 'Placemen'. Queen Anne frequently interfered in political matters: her interventions on behalf of Dr. Sacheverell, the Occasional Conformity Bills and the Peace Bill (by creating twelve new peers) were noted earlier in this chapter. The clause in the Act of Settlement which forbade the Crown to pardon ministers impeached by Parliament remained; but the events of 1710 and 1714 showed that the government was still the Queen's government, even if pressure from Parliament occasionally forced her to include men (such as the Whig 'Junto' peers) she did not want.[1] Although the Triennial Act

[1] Even in the twentieth century the sovereign has sometimes intervened, as when George V agreed to create enough new peers to get the 1911 Parliament Act through the Lords, and when he invited Mr. Baldwin and not Lord Curzon to become Prime Minister in 1922.

fixed the maximum lifetime of a Parliament, there was no restriction on the Crown's power to prorogue or dissolve it within that period – as the 1707 Regency Bill specifically confirmed. The Crown still had the power to refuse royal assent to Bills which Parliament had passed, even though Anne's veto of a minor Bill in 1708 was the last time this right was used. The monarch was richer than for many years, as the Civil List of £700,000 gave the Crown an income independent of what was needed for governing the country.

So the sovereign still possessed substantial power and influence, even though Parliament had been nibbling away at the Crown's prerogatives from 1624 (the Statute of Monopolies) down to the Act of Settlement. Some of the remaining power was indirect, but positive (the sovereign's right to create new peers, and to reward loyal supporters in Parliament). Some of it (the right to dissolve Parliament or veto a Bill) was direct but negative. It would not have been impossible for a monarch to recover a great deal of the lost prerogatives, particularly if supported by an ambitious and unscrupulous political leader. Godolphin and Harley, both moderate men, had supported Anne's power just because she in turn supported them; in such circumstances it helped them to keep the Crown's authority as great as possible. If a rogue like St. John had come to power under Anne or 'James III', he might well have restored the lost prerogatives so that his own power should be greater. In the *Patriot King*, which he wrote in 1738, St. John strongly urged that the monarch should govern, as well as reign.

Thus by 1714 it was still not wholly certain that Parliament would be the dominant power in the constitution. Within a few decades, however, the characters of the first two Hanoverians, and their indifference to British affairs made a royal revival much less likely. As Britain was prosperous, stable and fairly peaceful during the Whig Supremacy it was unthinkable that any serious politicians would try to engineer a second Restoration of royal power.

Many of the constitutional disputes of Anne's reign developed from rivalry between the two Houses of Parliament. One result of William's elevation of Whig politicians and churchmen was that the House of Lords was predominantly Whig during Anne's reign, when the Queen herself was Tory and normally used her influence to get Tory majorities in the Commons.

This made it much more difficult for the Tories to use impeachment and attainder as weapons to dispose of their political
enemies. Attainder was never used again after 1697, when
Parliament hurried Fenwick to the scaffold after his plot against
William. The process of attainder was employed on this
occasion partly because the evidence against him was not
enough for a law court to have convicted him of treason – and
partly because many politicians feared that in a law court he
might speak too freely about their own Jacobite intrigues.

Where the parties were most unscrupulous was in using a
majority in the Commons to decide election disputes in the
interests of their own party. After each general election the
Committee of Privileges and Elections considered petitions
from fifty or more disappointed candidates, and almost always
judged the cases purely on a party basis. The cases of *Ashby*
v. *White* and the other Aylesbury electors were notorious
examples. With the successful petitioners to reinforce their
numbers, the majority party could be sure of keeping power.

This jerrymandering was partly a consequence of the almost-
universal corruption at elections. Most voters had their
price – and it was a steadily rising price. Even before the
Landed Property Qualification Act, only a wealthy man, or a
careerist prepared to represent in the Commons the 'interest' of
a peer, could afford to stand for election. Nonetheless,
membership of Parliament was often a profitable investment,
bringing social prestige and the opportunity of winning some
Government sinecure. The rewards went usually to those most
consistent in attending Parliament: the careerist had to be
prepared to spend the winter and spring months in London,
from November or December through to May or even June.

The men who filled the benches of the Commons in the early
eighteenth century do not compare favourably with those who
were there a century earlier. There were fewer lawyers, and
fewer men of genuine piety. Many of the Tories who
clamoured for the Occasional Conformity and Schism Bills were
Deists, or debauched rakes (or both, like St. John). The
Whigs opposing them included Lord Wharton, an atheist
renowned even in those days for his profligate life. In the
time of Coke and Eliot it was the Commons who led the country
against the corruption of the Court and the administration. The
examples set by Wharton and St. John were rather less edifying.

In some respects an irresponsible Parliament was a greater threat to the laws than was an irresponsible King. One wonders how Coke would have reacted to the case of the Aylesbury electors, when the Commons and the law courts were at each other's throats!

If Coke had returned in Anne's reign to survey the structure of Parliament, he would have found that many things had changed, even though the outward appearances had not. The Speaker was as important as ever in controlling debates; but he was chosen by the majority interest in the Commons, and not nominated by the Crown's supporters. His function was that of Leader of the House, not the Commons' spokesman with the Lords and the sovereign. The monarch opened and closed Parliament, but if he kept a Parliament longer than three years the officers of State would arrange new elections in spite of him. Parliament had at last shouldered the responsibility for the nation's finances. As it thereby made itself indispensable, it seldom had to fear a premature dissolution.[1] In Anne's reign it became accepted that the *maximum* lifetime of a Parliament was its *normal* lifetime as well, for the party in power did not want to risk the costly gamble of a new election any earlier than was necessary under the Triennial Act. The life of a Parliament did not end automatically with that of the monarch: an Act of 1697 allowed Parliament to sit for up to six months after the monarch's death, to discourage assassination attempts such as the Fenwick Plot.

In Coke's day, the principle of 'redress before supply' was applied by Parliament against the King, and not, as in Anne's reign, by a Tory Commons 'tacking' Bills for Church reform on to Land Tax Bills to try to get them through the Lords together. Even in Coke's time, government supporters expected to be rewarded with peerages, and a career wholly in the Lower House was therefore usually an unsuccessful career. What Coke would not expect was the speed with which an election could reverse the balance of parties and turn government opponents into government supporters. In Anne's reign, therefore, a critic of the current government might have to wait longer for his reward than one who supported it, but the next election would give him the chance to return to royal favour.

---

[1] William's sudden dissolution in 1701 was exceptional – and therefore hotly opposed.

Most M.P.s were ambitious; a few years after Anne's death it was only the opposition of 'backswoods' members, hoping for peerages, which threw out Stanhope's Bill to prevent any new nobles being created.

The change which would have surprised Coke most was the new structure of government.   In Anne's reign the government was perched uncomfortably, in some ways independent of both Parliament and Crown, and in some ways responsible to both of them.   The enormous rise in government expenditure naturally made the Treasury the hub of the administration. Anne's Parliaments resolved, in Standing Order No. 66, that only ministers of the Crown might propose parliamentary Bills for spending public money; the individual M.P. lost some of his power as a result.   From 1679 until 1702 a board of commissioners ran the Treasury, but for most of Anne's reign a single man presided over it as Lord Treasurer – Godolphin from 1702 to 1710, Harley from 1711 to 1714.   After Shrewsbury's few months of office in the summer of 1714, however, there was never again a single Lord Treasurer.   Godolphin and Harley both based their ministries on their control of the Treasury.   It gave them almost unlimited patronage in the Treasury office itself, and in the customs and excise departments.   In practice, though, both Treasurers recruited officials for their competence, not their political connexions.   These developments – the single Treasurer, Standing Order No. 66, and the refusal of political patronage – might have taken the Treasury further out of the direct control of Parliament if the M.P.s had not insisted on strict accounting.   During William's reign Parliament had saddled the Treasury with Committees of Public Accounts, to protect the principle of 'appropriation of supply', that money should be spent only on the purposes for which it was voted.   This made the government work out its probable expenditure as accurately as possible.   By the end of Anne's reign the Treasurer each year presented Parliament with an accurate and detailed Budget showing how much it would have to spend in the coming year.

Such was the importance of the Treasurer that both Godolphin and Harley were often referred to as 'Prime Ministers'. At first the nickname was used insultingly, accusing the Treasurers of making themselves more powerful than the other ministers.   The Cabinet system was also strongly criticized.

Nevertheless, the practical advantages of a small or inner council were such that it gradually became accepted. In the Act of Settlement the Tories had shown their dislike for the small, responsible council which William used to appoint to help Mary or his 'regents' run the country when he went abroad, but the 1706 Regency Act largely reversed the Act of Settlement on this point. The one successful Cabinet in William's reign, that of the Whig 'Junto,' had been based on a Whig Commons, a Whig Lords, and a King whom the Tories had driven into the hands of the Whigs. At other times party differences made this combination and co-operation almost impossible. As Anne's governments normally had to work with a Tory House of Commons and a Whig Upper House, she tried to prevent Godolphin ruling with a Cabinet chosen on the basis of 'party'. At first Godolphin and Marlborough agreed. It was only the war which drove 'Mrs. Morley, Mr. Montgomery and Mr. Freeman' to rely entirely on the Whigs in 1708. Only opposition to the war made Anne abandon her old friends two years later and turn to the Tories. At the close of her life she again showed her dislike for party extremism when she gave the Treasurer's staff to Shrewsbury, not St. John.

When her pregnancies and illnesses allowed, Anne normally attended the Cabinet meetings in person. They were usually held once a week, but met more frequently when Parliament was sitting, or if important despatches arrived from Marlborough during the campaigning season. In the winter Marlborough himself was often present. The Cabinet was still essentially an informal, advisory body of ministers. Its members had no obligation to agree with the Treasurer or with each other. It was not until 1916 that it began to keep minutes of its discussions. However, the Whig 'Junto' had shown some signs of collective responsibility in William's reign, and this characteristic gradually developed during the long years of one-party government after 1714.

The changes at Westminster probably mattered less to most people than what happened in their own Town Halls. Until the nineteenth-century reforms, local government was administered in a bewildering variety of different ways, but on the whole it was largely in the same hands as national government, and protected the interests of the same classes of people. In the major towns, the mayor and aldermen had great influence over elections, and so played a large part in choosing M.P.s and making laws. As the principal officials of the towns were also J.P.s, by virtue of their posts, they then administered the laws which they had helped to make. In many towns – for example Bristol – all power was in the hands of a closed oligarchy; its members chose all the officials from among themselves, and elected new members to the 'court' when old ones died. Often a neighbouring magnate dominated the town and its officials, particularly if he owned substantial property within it, or if the electors were few. In such circumstances it was easy (though sometimes expensive) for a peer to get his son or a family dependent into the House of Commons as one of the town's M.P.s. Even in Anne's reign there were several successful collectors of pocket boroughs, although no man controlled as many as the Duke of Newcastle did under George II. In this way the towns formed part of an administrative network dominated by wealthy landowners.

This was even more true of the administration of the counties. In the counties the source of power was the Lord-Lieutenant, usually a peer and a member of the Privy Council, and normally a landowner in the county. He commanded the militia – recruited solely from the squirearchy – nominated the Deputy-Lieutenants, and recommended the J.P.s. Almost as important as in Tudor times, the J.P.s presided over the Quarter Sessions and Petty Sessions, and through these courts supervised most of the local administration: repairing roads and bridges, maintaining prisons and workhouses, fixing prices and wages, issuing licences to sell or to beg. To be a magistrate was a clear sign of social and political status in the area. In protecting the property of the landowners, the J.P.s did not abuse their powers unlawfully: the laws were already so biased in favour of the landowner that the magistrate found it easy to deal brutally with the sheep-stealer, the poacher who broke the Game Laws, or the stallkeeper guilty of sharp practices at market.

The Tudors had overloaded the parish, as well as the J.P., with heavy administrative responsibilities. Each parish had a number of officers, and a representative body – the parish 'vestry'. The senior officials were unpaid, and if need be the J.P.s could compel men to serve in the posts of churchwarden, surveyor of the highways, overseer of the poor, and parish constable. Usually, though, men accepted these offices for the prestige which they brought. Of the lesser officials, the beadle was usually employed full-time by the parish, and others such as the hayward and the ale-taster were appointed and paid as the need arose. Even if there were thousands of petty tyrants like Mr. Bumble, the beadle in Dickens's *Oliver Twist*, the system worked fairly well within the parish.

At first sight it seems surprising that the ecclesiastical unit of the parish should have become so vital to the country's administration, and that the parson should have only a minor part in the parish's secular work. It would have been more logical for the parish system to be so important if Nonconformity and heresy had still been crimes against the state, and if the parson himself had possessed powers to punish malefactors. In fact, the parish organization got its authority from the State rather than from the Church. It reflected the same social and economic interests as the magistrate and M.P. – the squire or other lay patron chose the parson, the parson and the vestry of important parishioners chose the churchwardens, and the J.P.s chose the overseer of the poor and the surveyor of the highways.

There was therefore a remarkable uniformity in the different parts of the administration. At every level power was in the hands of the men of property, and ultimately largely in the hands of a few wealthy families. Most of the leaders of this oligarchy were in the House of Lords, with sons or dependents representing them in the Lower House as M.P.s for the pocket boroughs they controlled. Their slightly less prosperous neighbours were the J.P.s; their nominees the bishops and parish clergy; their tenants the churchwardens and vestry members. Merchants newly rich from the India trade or from sugar plantations could buy and marry their families into the charmed circle of great landowners. Before Britain had spent many years under the Hanoverians, Walpole was working to reduce and abolish the Land Tax – partly to pacify the Tories, partly because the Whigs were now landowners no less than the Tories.

Teaching that the first purpose of government was to protect property, John Locke appeared to be the prophet of this long-lasting oligarchy of landowners. Locke, however, was merely commenting on the changes which had already taken place in the thirty years before 1688, and providing a logical excuse for the Glorious Revolution. Apart from the menace of Revolutionary France and the shouts of Tom Paine about *The Rights of Man*, there was no serious challenge to Locke's theory until the nineteenth century. Then the Chartists took up the old claims of the Levellers, after nearly two centuries of silence. After a further century Britain bowed to their demands.

Under the Hanoverians and their successors, most of Britain was remarkably free from revolution and disorder. In England, Wales and Scotland the same classes of people held firmly to almost all the power – political, economic, social, religious, judicial, military, administrative. This was only partly true of Ireland, and it was not true at all of countries like France, Austria and Italy. In France one hereditary class almost monopolized political and military power, but allowed administrative and judicial authority to slip into the hands of the despised *tiers état*. Much the same happened in Austria, and in Italy where the papacy was also disputing for a share in the power. Whatever the injustices of the British system, it did provide stability.

Let 'Trimmer' Halifax have the last word on the revolutions of seventeenth-century Britain. 'When the people contend for their liberty they seldom get anything by their victory but new masters.'

## EXTRACTS

1. QUEEN ANNE TELLS GODOLPHIN HER OBJECTION TO PARTY GOVERNMENT (1706):

All I desire is, my liberty in encouraging and employing all those that concur faithfully in my service, whether they are called whigs or tories not to be tied to one, nor the other; for if I should be so unfortunate as to fall into the hands of either, I shall not imagine myself, though I have the name of queen, to be in reality but their slave, which as it will be my personal ruin, so it will be the destroying all government; for instead of putting an end to faction, it will lay a lasting foundation for it. (In Costin and Watson, *The Law & Working of the Constitution*, pp. 359–60)

2. ST. JOHN EXPOSES HIS PARTY'S POLICY IN A LETTER TO A FRIEND:

I am afraid that we came to court in the same dispositions as all parties have done; that the principal spring of our actions was to have the government of the state in our hands; that our

principal views were the conservation of this power, great
employments to ourselves, and great opportunities of rewarding
those who had helped to raise us, and of hurting those who stood
in opposition to us. . . . The view therefore of those amongst
us who thought in this manner, was to improve the Queen's
favour, to break the body of the Whigs, to render their supports
useless to them, to fill the employments of the Kingdom down
to the meanest with Tories. We imagined that such measures,
joined to the advantages of our numbers and property, would
secure us against all attempts during her reign; and that we
should soon become too considerable not to make our terms in
all events which might happen afterwards; concerning which, to
speak truly, I believe few or none of us had any very settled resolution. (In Trevelyan, *England Under Queen Anne*, vol. iii, p. 96)

3. THE FIRST ARTICLE OF THE TREATY OF UNION (1707):
That the Two Kingdoms of England and Scotland shall upon
the First day of May which shall be in the year One thousand
seven hundred and seven, and for ever after, be united into one
Kingdom by the name of Great Britain; and that the Ensigns
Armorial of the said United Kingdom be such as Her Majesty
shall appoint, and the Crosses of St. George and St. Andrew be
conjoined in such manner as Her Majesty shall think fit, and
used in all Flags, Banners, Standards and Ensigns, both at Sea
and Land. (In Dickinson and Donaldson, *Source Book of
Scottish History*, vol. iii, p. 480)

4. A SCOTTISH PRESBYTERIAN, CAPTAIN BLACKADDER, RECORDS
THE BATTLE OF BLENHEIM (1704):
Many deliverances I have met with, but this day I have had
the greatest ever I experienced. We fought a bloody battle,
and, by the mercy of God, have obtained one of the greatest and
completest victories the age can boast of. . . . During all the
little intervals of action, I kept looking to God for strength and
courage. . . . My faith was so lively during the action, that I
sometimes said within myself, Lord, it were easy for thee to cause
thy angels to lay all these men dead on the place where they stand,
or bring them in all prisoners to us. . . . Twenty-six regiments
(some say thirty) surrendered themselves prisoners. . . . (In
Trevelyan, *Documents for Queen Anne's Reign*, pp. 143–4)

5. JONATHAN SWIFT ATTACKS THE WAR (1711):
To have a Prince of the Austrian Family on the Throne of
Spain, is undoubtedly more desirable than one of the House of

Bourbon; but to have the Empire and Spanish Monarchy united in the same Person, is a dreadful Consideration. . . . We who bore the Burthen of the War, ought, in reason, to have the greatest share in making the Peace. If we do not hearken to a Peace, others centainly will; and get the Advantage of us there, as they have done in the War. . . . We have been Fighting for the Ruin of the Publick Interest, and the Advancement of a Private. We have been fighting to raise the Wealth and Grandeur of a particular Family; to enrich Usurers and Stock-jobbers; and to cultivate the pernicious Designs of a Faction, by destroying the Landed-Interest. (Swift, *The Conduct of the Allies*, pp. 59–68)

6. ADDISON MEETS A TORY INN-KEEPER (1715):

The landlord had swelled his body to a prodigious size, and worked up his complexion to a standing crimson by his zeal for the prosperity of the Church, which he expressed every hour, as his customers dropped in, by repeated bumpers. He had not time to go to church himself, but, as my friend told me in my ear, had headed a mob at the pulling down of two or three meeting houses. While supper was preparing, he enlarged upon the happiness of the neighbouring shire; 'for,' says he, 'there is scarce a Presbyterian in the whole county, except the Bishop'. In short, I found by his discourse that he had learned a great deal of politicks, but not one word of religion, from the Parson of his parish; and indeed, that he had scarce any other notion of religion, but that it consisted in hating Presbyterians.' (From *The Freeholder*. In Trevelyan, *Documents for Queen Anne's Reign*, p. 72)

# SUGGESTIONS FOR FURTHER READING

*Books marked with an asterisk are available in cheap editions*

### I. GENERAL BOOKS

C. Hill, *The Century of Revolution*. An excellent survey of the whole period, particularly good on economics and 'the movement of ideas'.

C. Hill, *Puritanism and Revolution*. A collection of essays on many important seventeenth-century subjects.

G. M. Trevelyan, *England under the Stuarts*. An old book, but still valuable despite the strength of the author's opposition to most of the kings!

G. M. Trevelyan, *England under Queen Anne*.(3 vols.)

D. Ogg, *England in the Reign of Charles II* (2 vols.).

D. Ogg, *England in the Reigns of James II and William III*. These three works by Trevelyan and Ogg are brilliant surveys of government and society in the second half of the Stuart period.

G. Davies, *The Early Stuarts*, and

G. N. Clark, *The Later Stuarts* are the two relevant volumes in the *Oxford History of England*. They are admirable as works of reference, although neither has a particularly good index.

C. V. Wedgwood, *The King's Peace*,

C. V. Wedgwood, *The King's War*, and

C. V. Wedgwood, *The Trial of Charles I* are the first volumes of this superb writer's history of the Civil War period.

M. Ashley, *England in the Seventeenth Century*, in the *Pelican History* series, provides a good short introduction to the period.

W. L. McElwee, *England's Precedence*. A very readable narrative, with useful introductions to the minor characters, and a lot on Court intrigue.

### 2. BIOGRAPHIES – ALSO OF GENERAL INTEREST

D. H. Willson, *James VI and I* is the best recent study of this complex character.

C. V. Wedgwood, *Strafford – a Reappraisal* is excellent on the administration of Ireland and the political manœuvres of 1640 and 1641.

H. R. Trevor-Roper, *Archbishop Laud*, and

J. R. Hexter, *The Reign of King Pym* are two very effective studies of different kinds of tyranny.

C. V. Wedgwood, *Montrose*. A delightful portrait, with much useful information on Scotland during the 1640s.

R. S. Paul, *The Lord Protector* is the best full-length recent biography, but

C. H. Firth, *Oliver Cromwell* is still useful.

A. Bryant, *Samuel Pepys* (3 vols.) is a history of Restoration England, centred around Pepys's career.

H. C. Foxcroft, *A Character of the Trimmer*, and

W. S. Churchill, *Marlborough* (4 vols.) deal with two of the most important men in late seventeenth-century England.

### 3. POLITICAL AND CONSTITUTIONAL

J. R. Tanner, *English Constitutional Conflicts of the Seventeenth Century* is a masterpiece of lucid explanation of the constitutional issues.

D. L. Keir, *The Constitutional History of Modern Britain.* Solid and reliable.

W. Notestein, *The Winning of the Initiative by the House of Commons.* This is a brilliant little pamphlet, still valuable on the Stuart period although J. E. Neale's *Elizabeth and her Parliaments* disproves some of his ideas on the earlier period.

G. E. Aylmer, *The King's Servants* is a recent study of the administration under Charles I.

K. G. Feiling, *A History of the Tory Party, 1640–1714.* From Cavalier to Jacobite.

H. N. Brailsford, *The Levellers* and

B. Kemp, *King and Commons, 1660–1830* are both useful recent studies.

W. Holdsworth, *A History of the English Law* (especially vols. iv and vi) is an old classic, massive and irreplacable.

### 4. ECONOMIC AND SOCIAL

E. Lipson, *The Economic History of England* (vols. ii and iii) is awkwardly arranged, but a mine of information for those who use the index!

J. U. Nef, *\*Industry and Government in France and England, 1540–1640* and

J. U. Nef, *The Rise of the British Coal Industry* are both established authorities.

R. H. Tawney, *Business and Politics under James I* deals mainly with the career of Cranfield.

R. H. Tawney, *\*Religion and the Rise of Capitalism* is a famous book which is a 'must' for the serious student.

P. J. Bowden, *The Wool Trade in Tudor and Stuart England.* The most recent study of England's principal manufacture.

F. J. Fisher (ed.), *Essays in the Economic and Social History of Tudor and Stuart England.* Most of the essays are on the seventeenth century, and all are very useful.

G. N. Clark, *\* The Wealth of England* is an excellent brief economic history.

C. Wilson, *Profit and Power* deals with the mercantilist policies of the three Dutch Wars.

H. R. Trevor-Roper, *The Gentry, 1540–1640.* A pamphlet which aroused a long controversy among historians.

G. M. Trevelyan, *\*English Social History.* A superb survey; the illustrated edition is particularly useful.

W. Notestein, *\* The English People on the Eve of Colonisation, 1603–30* sketches English institutions and social groups at the beginning of the century.

W. K. Jordan, *Philanthropy in England, 1480–1660,* is complicated, but disproves the old charge that Puritans were misers.

The *Economic History Review* frequently contains articles of outstanding importance, and should be taken by every good school Library.

### 5. RELIGION AND PHILOSOPHY

J. R. H. Moorman, *A History of the Church in England* is a comprehensive study of the country's religious history.

C. Hill, *Intellectual Origins of the English Revolution,*

C. Hill, *Society and Puritanism in Pre-Revolutionary England,* and

C. Hill, *The Economic Problems of the Church, 1583–1640* are three of the most important books on seventeenth-century history published in the last decade.

W. Haller, *\*The Rise of Puritanism*. Traces the development of the sects under Elizabeth and the early Stuarts.

R. H. Tawney, *\*Religion and the Rise of Capitalism*. See previous section.

G. R. Cragg, *\*The Church in the Age of Reason*. A useful recent survey of religious developments in England and abroad from 1648 to 1789.

D. C. Douglas, *English Scholars, 1660–1730* contains a number of interesting biographies.

W. Schenk, *The Concern for Social Justice in the Puritan Revolution* suggests that the political reformers had little interest in social equality.

G. P. Gooch, *\*Political Thought from Bacon to Halifax*, and

H. J. Laski, *\*Political Thought from Locke to Bentham* are both excellent brief studies.

G. P. Gooch and H. J. Laski, *History of Democratic Ideas in the Seventeenth Century*. A standard work.

The *Oxford Dictionary of the Christian Church* provides admirable short notes on most of the important churchmen, doctrines and sects.

### 6. BEYOND THE BORDERS

P. Hume Brown, *History of Scotland*. An old, discursive work, largely replaced by

G. S. Pryde, *A New History of Scotland*, and

J. D. Mackie, *\*A History of Scotland*.

E. Curtis, *\*A History of Ireland*. Rather Celtic in flavour, but the best available single volume.

J. A. Williamson, *A Short History of British Expansion* (vol. i), and

Lord Elton, *Imperial Commonwealth* are both standard works.

A. P. Newton, *The Colonising Activities of the Early Puritans*. Useful, though rather old.

C. M. Andrewes, *\*Our Earliest Colonial Settlements* describes the constitutions of the plantations, but is 'thin' on economic matters.

R. Pares, *Merchants and Planters*. An excellent pamphlet, describing how Britain lost the initiative in trade.

### 7. SCIENCE AND THE ARTS

H. Butterfield, *The Origins of Modern Science, 1300–1700* gives an historian's view, and

A. R. Hall, *The Making of Modern Science* that of a scientist; both books are comprehensible to non-scientists.

R. J. Forbes and E. J. Dijksterhuis, *\*A History of Science and Technology* (2 vols.), is useful and cheap, but some scientific knowledge is needed to understand it fully.

D. L. Hurd and J. J. Kipling, *\*The Origins and Growth of Physical Science* (vol. i) is cheap and straightforward.

B. Farrington, *Francis Bacon*. A good biography of one of the most profound and versatile men of the seventeenth century.

R. Anthony, *Isaac Newton*. The style is rambling, but the book is easy to understand.

\*      \*      \*

C. V. Wedgwood, *Seventeenth Century English Literature*. An excellent short introduction.

D. Daiches, *A Critical History of English Literature* (2 vols.), is a stimulating work, for the author doesn't 'pull his punches'!

B. Willey, *The Seventeenth Century Background* shows how literature and society reflect each other. A minor classic.

A. Nicholl, *A History of Restoration Drama* is the standard work.

P. Harvey (ed.), *The Oxford Companion to English Literature*. This is a most important reference book, despite occasional inaccuracies.

*     *     *

Grove's *Dictionary of Music and Musicians*. In the absence of any wholly satisfactory recent work on seventeenth-century music, it is probably best to dip into this enormous reference work.

*     *     *

E. Mercer, *English Art, 1553–1625*, and

M. Whinney and O. Millar, *English Art, 1625–1714* are excellent companion volumes on the graphic arts of the Stuart period.

*     *     *

J. Summerson, *Architecture in Britain, 1530-1830*, is a standard work, while

B. Fletcher, *A History of Architecture*, and

N. Lloyd, *A History of the English House* both contain a lot on the development in the seventeenth-century, and are superbly illustrated.

*     *     *

R. Fastnedge, *English Furniture Styles, 1500–1830* is a useful little 'Pelican' book. Remember that furniture provides a lot of evidence about social history!

## 8. ORIGINAL SOURCES

### (The most important section of this Bibliography)

#### (a) Collections of Documents

J. R. Tanner (ed.), *Constitutional Documents of the Reign of James I*.

S. R. Gardiner (ed.), *Constitutional Documents of the Puritan Revolution*.

W. C. Costin and J. Steven Watson (ed.), *The Law & Working of the Constitution* (vol. i).

W. C. Dickinson and G. Donaldson, *A Source Book of Scottish History*, (vol. iii).

K. Muir (ed.), *Elizabethan and Jacobean Prose*.

P. Ure (ed.), *Seventeenth-Century Prose*.

H. Grierson and G. Bullough (ed.), *The Oxford Book of Seventeenth-Century Verse*.

#### (b) Diaries and contemporary histories

R. Baxter, *Autobiography*.

J. Evelyn, *Diary*.

S. Pepys, *Diary*.

G. Burnet, *History of My Own Times*.

(In addition to other editions, the above are published in the *Everyman series. In this, the volumes of Pepys and Burnet are abridged.)

A. à Wood, *The Life and Times of Anthony à Wood*.

E. Ludlow, *Memoirs* – of a parliamentary commander written by himself.

L. Hutchinson, *Memoirs of the Life of Col. Hutchinson* – of a parliamentary commander written by his wife.

J. Aubrey, *Brief Lives*. Potted biographies of prominent people.

Clarendon, *History of the Great Rebellion* (6 vols., ed. Macray). The most important source for the Civil War period. A volume of *\*Selections* is published in the World's Classics series.
T. Mun, *England's Treasure by Fforraign Trade*. Not very easy to obtain, but important as the basic English treatise on mercantilism.

### (c) Literary works of major historical importance

F. Bacon, *\*Essays*; *\*New Atlantis*; *\*Advancement of Learning*.
J. Milton, *\*Selected Prose* (World's Classics); *\*Sonnets*; *\*Paradise Lost*; *\*Samson Agonistes*.
J. Dryden, *Absalom and Achitophel*; *The Hind and the Panther*.
S. Butler, *Hudibras*.
J. Locke, *Second Essay of Civil Government*.
Lord Halifax, *The Character of a Trimmer*.
J. Bunyan, *\*Pilgrim's Progress*.

### 9. RECENT PUBLICATIONS

(The works listed here were published after the Bibliography was prepared for the first printing of this book)

C. Wilson, *England's Apprenticeship, 1603–1763*, describes the economic and technological developments which made it possible for England to lead the world in the first Industrial Revolution.
M. Ashley, *The Glorious Revolution of 1688*, shows how the Revolution originated in the Exclusion struggle of 1678–81.
D. T. Witcombe, *Charles II and the Cavalier House of Commons, 1663–74*, argues that the Cavaliers were more loyal to the Church of England than to their King, that 'pensions' did not greatly influence the M.P.s in this period, and that Charles lacked supporters able to control or guide the Commons.
A. M. Everitt, *The Community of Kent and the Great Rebellion, 1640–60*, demonstrates how the gentry of this influential county resented and opposed interference from any government, in Church or State.

# INDEX

The more important page references are printed in heavy type. Except where additional details are necessary to avoid confusion, names and titles are not given in full; in particular, knighthoods are not recorded here.